Miscellanies by the Honourable Daines Barrington.

Daines Barrington

Miscellanies by the Honourable Daines Barrington.
Barrington, Daines
ESTCID: T039448
Reproduction from British Library
Includes: 'Journal of a voyage in 1775. to explore the coast of America, .. By Don Francisco Antonio Maurelle, .. ', a reimpression of the setting of [1780?]; 'Tracts on the possibility of reaching the North Pole', and other essays. Pp.541-546 omitted fr
London : printed by J. Nichols. Sold by B. White, and J. Nichols, 1781.
iv,viii,342,[3],344-468,[2],*471-*477,[1],471-540,547-557,[1]p.,plates ,t ,tables : ill.,map,music ; 4°

Gale ECCO Print Editions

Relive history with *Eighteenth Century Collections Online*, now available in print for the independent historian and collector. This series includes the most significant English-language and foreign-language works printed in Great Britain during the eighteenth century, and is organized in seven different subject areas including literature and language; medicine, science, and technology; and religion and philosophy. The collection also includes thousands of important works from the Americas.

The eighteenth century has been called "The Age of Enlightenment." It was a period of rapid advance in print culture and publishing, in world exploration, and in the rapid growth of science and technology – all of which had a profound impact on the political and cultural landscape. At the end of the century the American Revolution, French Revolution and Industrial Revolution, perhaps three of the most significant events in modern history, set in motion developments that eventually dominated world political, economic, and social life.

In a groundbreaking effort, Gale initiated a revolution of its own: digitization of epic proportions to preserve these invaluable works in the largest online archive of its kind. Contributions from major world libraries constitute over 175,000 original printed works. Scanned images of the actual pages, rather than transcriptions, recreate the works ***as they first appeared.***

Now for the first time, these high-quality digital scans of original works are available via print-on-demand, making them readily accessible to libraries, students, independent scholars, and readers of all ages.

For our initial release we have created seven robust collections to form one the world's most comprehensive catalogs of 18th century works.

Initial Gale ECCO Print Editions collections include:

History and Geography
Rich in titles on English life and social history, this collection spans the world as it was known to eighteenth-century historians and explorers. Titles include a wealth of travel accounts and diaries, histories of nations from throughout the world, and maps and charts of a world that was still being discovered. Students of the War of American Independence will find fascinating accounts from the British side of conflict.

Social Science

Delve into what it was like to live during the eighteenth century by reading the first-hand accounts of everyday people, including city dwellers and farmers, businessmen and bankers, artisans and merchants, artists and their patrons, politicians and their constituents. Original texts make the American, French, and Industrial revolutions vividly contemporary.

Medicine, Science and Technology

Medical theory and practice of the 1700s developed rapidly, as is evidenced by the extensive collection, which includes descriptions of diseases, their conditions, and treatments. Books on science and technology, agriculture, military technology, natural philosophy, even cookbooks, are all contained here.

Literature and Language

Western literary study flows out of eighteenth-century works by Alexander Pope, Daniel Defoe, Henry Fielding, Frances Burney, Denis Diderot, Johann Gottfried Herder, Johann Wolfgang von Goethe, and others. Experience the birth of the modern novel, or compare the development of language using dictionaries and grammar discourses.

Religion and Philosophy

The Age of Enlightenment profoundly enriched religious and philosophical understanding and continues to influence present-day thinking. Works collected here include masterpieces by David Hume, Immanuel Kant, and Jean-Jacques Rousseau, as well as religious sermons and moral debates on the issues of the day, such as the slave trade. The Age of Reason saw conflict between Protestantism and Catholicism transformed into one between faith and logic -- a debate that continues in the twenty-first century.

Law and Reference

This collection reveals the history of English common law and Empire law in a vastly changing world of British expansion. Dominating the legal field is the *Commentaries of the Law of England* by Sir William Blackstone, which first appeared in 1765. Reference works such as almanacs and catalogues continue to educate us by revealing the day-to-day workings of society.

Fine Arts

The eighteenth-century fascination with Greek and Roman antiquity followed the systematic excavation of the ruins at Pompeii and Herculaneum in southern Italy; and after 1750 a neoclassical style dominated all artistic fields. The titles here trace developments in mostly English-language works on painting, sculpture, architecture, music, theater, and other disciplines. Instructional works on musical instruments, catalogs of art objects, comic operas, and more are also included.

biblio life
old books. new life.

THE

POSSIBILITY

OF APPROACHING THE

NORTH POLE

DISCUSSED.

Ρεια δε τοι και τηδε καταγραψαιμι θαλασσαν,
Ου μεν ιδων απανευθε πορους, ου νηι περησας,

Αλλα με [γαιογραφων] φορεει νοος, οι τε δυνανται
Νοσφιν αλημοσυνης πολλην αλα μετρησασθαι.

Dionysii, Orbis Descrip.

PREFACE

TO THE

POLAR TRACTS.

THE following tracts relative to the poſſibility of near approaches to the Pole of our own hemiſphere, as likewiſe of a communication between the Atlantick and Pacifick oceans in any Northern direction, were firſt publiſhed in 1775 and 1776.

I now think it right to print them a ſecond time, becauſe they contain many well-atteſted facts with regard to reaching high Northern Latitudes, which are not to be found elſewhere, and have a tendency to promote geographical diſcoveries. I am very ready to admit indeed, that the purpoſes of commerce can never be anſwered by the great uncertainty of a conſtant paſſage (even when ſuch communication is diſcovered) in ſeas which are ſo frequently obſtructed by the ice packing in vaſt fields. I find likewiſe that ſince the *Reſolution* and *Endeavour* returned from their laſt voyage, many conceive a N. E. or N. W. paſſage to be impracticable, becauſe our ſhips in two ſucceſſive years were not able to penetrate beyond 71, by impediments of ice. Beſides, however, that the ice packing in particular ſituations varies often in different

 years;

years; both these attempts were made in the month of August, which I flatter myself to have proved, is the very season of the year when the ice breaking up on the coast, is floating in every direction, and consequently often packs in masses of an immense extent.

These vast fields of ice, indeed, often are dispersed; but who hath, or indeed should have, the fortitude of waiting for this accident, whilst he is already in a high Northern Latitude, and the winter is fast approaching? If the ice, however, should thus pack in April or May (which I conceive it would not, as little must be left to float from the preceding summer), yet as the warm weather is then increasing from day to day, the navigator would wait with some degree of patience till his ship may be released from this temporary obstruction. The situation of the discoverer under these circumstances, may be compared to a traveller passing over a large tract of sea-sand, when the tide is flowing or ebbing. In the first instance he spurs his horse because the sea may be expected at his heels; in the latter he proceeds with great composure, as every instant he loses in point of time the sea is further removed.

Others again have despaired of a N. W. passage, from Captain Pickersgill not having succeeded in his attempt for this purpose, during the year 1776[a].

This voyage was intended for two purposes (at least as I have been informed), the first to protect some of our whale fishers on the coast of W. Groenland from the Americans then in rebellion; and the second (if the time after this service permitted) to join Captain Cook, should he have been so fortunate as to have ac-

[a] In the *Lion armed Brig*.

complished

complished his passage from the Pacifick Ocean, when he would probably have returned to England by Davis's straits.

This plan seems to have been very well laid, but that persevering navigator was delayed at the Cape by Captain Clark's ship not arriving till a considerable time after his own reaching that place of rendezvous, and in the further progress of his voyage by adverse winds, which drove him to the Friendly Islands instead of Otaheitee, so that he did not make his attempt of a passage till 1777.

Captain Pickersgill did not leave Scilly till the 10th of June, 1766, and consequently whatever obstructions he met with from floating or packing ice, might be reasonably expected when he reached the coast of West Groenland. It appears, however, by what I shall copy from the conclusion of his journal on the 31st of August, that he did not find these to be considerable, and that after the trial his hopes of a passage were very sanguine.

"I shall conclude with a few observations on this part of the "world (sc. Greenland) and so terribly represented by people, "who, in order to raise their own merit, make dangers and dif- "ficulties of common occurrences, merely because the places are "unknown, and there is little or no probability of their being "ever contradicted. I do not mean this as a personal reflexion; "but having discoursed with many of the masters of Greenland "vessels as well as their employers, and heard such dreadful "stories of those countries, I cannot help remarking it as tending "to mislead those who from a laudable principle, would be "benefactors to their country, but are deterred from it by these "misrepresentations. I shall communicate observations on the "ice, the atmosphere, the land of Forbisher, *and the probability* "*of a N. W. passage, in a short time*[b]."

[b] Ph. Transf. for 1778, Part II. p. 1063.

This,

This, however, hath unfortunately been prevented by Captain Pickerſgill's death; but the Aſtronomer Royal, who communicated Captain Pickerſgill's Journal to the Royal Society, hath informed me by letter, "That he had often heard this Navigator "expreſs himſelf as well aſſured of a N. W. paſſage; adding, "that he received accounts of it from the inhabitants on the "ſide of Davis's Straits, and that it was directly N. W. very different from Baffin's track.

"Captain Pickerſgill likewiſe thought that *the beſt method to "find the paſſage, was to get out early before the ice broke away in "the upper part of Davis's Straits.*"

It thus appears that the laſt attempts of a N. W. paſſage ended with the officer's employed thereon, being thoroughly perſuaded that it was not only practicable, but highly probable.

As the late geographical diſcoveries have given ſuch general ſatisfaction, I have little doubt but that they will be further proſecuted when a peace takes place, and ſhall therefore here venture to throw out my poor thoughts with regard to the yet remaining deſiderata for the more perfect knowledge of the planet which we inhabit. When we are informed by proper trials, that the attempt in any particular direction cannot ſucceed, we ſhall then be as much at reſt as with regard to Lunar oceans or continents, if ſuch there be.

I have mentioned in the following Tracts, that the Parliamentary rewards given for approaching within one degree of the North Pole are not likely to produce the effects intended, becauſe the Greenland whale ſhips are all enſured; if they were therefore to go beyond the common fiſhing latitudes, it would be ſuch

ſuch a departure from the voyage enſued, that they would not be able to recover, if accidents happened in ſuch a deviation.

I am informed, however, that there are ſome veſſels employed in time of peace by government, to prevent ſmuggling on the Northern coaſt of Scotland. Theſe ſhips might be inſtructed, when a promiſing wind blows from the Southward, to proceed as far North as the ice will permit. The crew of ſuch a ſhip would be encouraged by expectations of the Parliamentary reward; and though one attempt might fail, another might ſucceed. The expence to the publick would be trifling, whilſt the ſmugglers would not know how ſoon the ſhip might return to its ſtation.

Our Commodore upon the Newfoundland ſtation might alſo ſend a veſſel, at a ſmall expence, to explore all the Northern part of Hudſon's Bay, with which we are ſo imperfectly acquainted at preſent.

Such attempts during peace might take place almoſt every ſummer; and I ſhould ſuppoſe that this ſcientific and opulent nation would never heſitate (whilſt there is the leaſt dawning of hopes) to ſend proper veſſels occaſionally to make further trials both of a N. W. paſſage by Baffin's Bay, and a N. E. beyond Nova Zembla.

The coaſt of Corea, the Northern part of Japan, and the Lequieux Iſlands, ſhould alſo be explored; the cheapeſt, and perhaps beſt method of doing this would be to employ a veſſel in the India Company's ſervice, which might be victualled at Canton.

Thus much with regard to diſcoveries, or better knowledge of the more unfrequented parts of the Northern hemiſphere.

The deſiderata in that of the South ſeem to be the following:

To make the compleat circumnavigation of New Holland, ſo as at leaſt to be better acquainted with ſome parts of the coaſt of this immenſe iſland, a veſſel for this purpoſe might be victualled at the Cape of Good Hope, or Canton; nor is the voyage a diſtant one, when compared with thoſe of Captain Cook. New Guinea alſo ſhould be better explored.

We ſcarcely know more of the iſlands of Triſtan da Cunha than their Longitude and Latitude; but their interior parts ſhould be examined. Not vaſtly diſtant is *Sandwich Land*, which many on board Captain Cook ſuppoſed to be a vaſt continent. It may be objected indeed that if it is ſo, it will turn out to be a continent of ice and ſnow; I am not here, however, recommending diſcoveries for the purpoſe of commerce, but for the improvement of geography.

I ſhould conceive that a voyage either from the Cape or Braſil would eaſily give opportunity of effectuating both theſe purpoſes.

Perhaps whilſt diſcoveries by ſea are thus dwelt upon, encouragement ſhould be given to travellers by land, for procuring better information with regard to the central parts of Aſia, Africa, and America. In ſhort, let us endeavour to know as much as we may of our globe; nor ſhould this be conſidered as a vain and trifling curioſity, though no benefits to commerce may reſult from theſe inquiries.

INSTANCES OF NAVIGATORS WHO HAVE REACHED HIGH NORTHERN LATITUDES.

Read at a Meeting of the Royal Society, May 19, 1774.

AS I was the unworthy propoſer of the voyage towards the North Pole, which the Council of the Royal Society recommended to the Board of Admiralty, I think it my duty to lay before the Society ſuch intelligence as I have happened to procure with regard to navigators having reached high Northern latitudes[a]; becauſe ſome of theſe accounts ſeem to promiſe, that we may proceed further towards the Pole than the very able Officers who were ſent on this deſtination laſt year were permitted to penetrate, notwithſtanding their repeated efforts to paſs beyond eighty degrees and an half.

I ſhall begin, however, by making an obſervation or two with regard to the Greenland fiſhery, which will in a great meaſure account for our not being able to procure many inſtances of nearer approaches to the Pole than the Northern parts of Spitzbergen.

Fifty years ago ſuch apprehenſions were entertained of navigating even in the looſe, or what is called *ſailing ice*, that the

[a] It is well known that there are many ſuch accounts in print, but to theſe I need not refer the Society.

crews commonly continued on ſhore [b], from whence they only purſued the whales in boats.

The demand, however, for oil increaſing, whilſt the number of fiſh rather decreaſed, they were obliged to proceed to ſea in queſt of them, and now by experience and adroitneſs ſeldom ſuffer from the obſtructions of ice [c].

The maſters of ſhips, who are employed in this trade, have no other object but the catching whales, which, as long as as they can procure in more Southern latitudes, they certainly will not go in ſearch of at a greater diſtance from the port to which they are to return : they therefore ſeldom proceed much beyond N. lat. 80, unleſs driven by a ſtrong Southerly wind or other accident.

Whenever this happens alſo, it is only by very diligent inquiries that any information can be procured ; for the maſters, not being commonly men of ſcience, or troubling their heads about the improvement of geographical knowledge, never mention theſe circumſtances on their return, becauſe they conceive that no one is more intereſted about theſe matters than they are themſelves. Many of the Greenland maſters are likewiſe directed to return after the early fiſhery is over, provided they have tolerable ſucceſs ; ſo that they have no opportunity of making diſcoveries to the Northward.

To theſe reaſons it may be added, that no ſhips were perhaps ever ſent before laſt ſummer with expreſs inſtructions to reach the Pole, if poſſible, as moſt other attempts have been to diſcover

[b] There were houſes ſtill ſtanding on Spitſbergen, where the Dutch uſed to boil their train oil. Martin's Voyage, p. 24. See alſo Callander, Vol. III. p. 723.

[c] Theſe particulars I received from Captain Robinſon, whom I ſhall have hereafter occaſion to mention.

a N. E. or N. W. paſſage, which were ſoon defeated by falling in with land, or other accident.

Having thus endeavoured to ſhew that the inſtances of ſhips reaching high Northern latitudes muſt neceſſarily be rare, I ſhall now proceed to lay before the Society ſuch as I have been able to hear of ſince the voyage towards the N. Pole was undertaken during laſt ſummer.

When this was determined upon, and mentioned in the News Papers, it became matter of converſation amongſt the crews of the guardſhips; and Andrew Leekie, an intelligent ſeaman on board the Albion (then ſtationed at Plymouth), informed ſome of the officers that he had been as far North as 84½.

When he was aſked further on this head, he ſaid that he was on board the Reading, Captain Thomas Robinſon, in 1766, and that, whilſt he was ſhaving the captain, Mr. Robinſon told him that he had probably never been ſo far to the Northward before, as they had now reached the above-mentioned degree of latitude.

Having happened to hear this account of Leekie's, on my return to London this winter, I found out Captain Robinſon, who remembered his having had this converſation with Leekie, but ſaid that he was miſtaken in ſuppoſing that they had reached 84½ N. lat. as they were only in 82½.

Captain Robinſon then explained himſelf, that he had at this time computed his latitude by the run back to Hakluyt's Headland in 24 hours; from which, and other circumſtances mentioned in my preſence before two ſea officers, they told me afterwards that they had little or no doubt of the accuracy of his reckoning. Mr. Robinſon likewiſe remembers that the ſea was then open, ſo that he hath no doubt of being able to reach 83, but how much further he will not pretend to ſay.

 This

This ſame captain, in the ſhip St. George, was, on the 15th of June 1773, in N. lat. 81° 16′, by a very accurate obſervation with an approved Hadley's quadrant, in which he alſo made the proper allowance for the refraction in high Northern latitudes, at which time ſeeing ſome whales ſpouting to the Northward, he purſued them for five hours, ſo that he muſt have reached 81½, when the ſea was open to the Weſtward and E.N.E. as far as he could diſtinguiſh from the maſt-head. His longitude was then 8 degrees E. from the meridian of London.

Captain Robinſon is a very intelligent ſeaman, and hath navigated the Greenland ſeas theſe twenty years, except during the interval that he was employed by the Hudſon's Bay Company[d].

I could add ſome other, perhaps intereſting, particulars, which I have received from Captain Robinſon, with regard to Spitzbergen and the Polar Seas; I will only mention, however, that he thinks he could ſpend a winter not uncomfortably in the moſt Northern parts we are acquainted with[e], as there are three or four ſmall ſettlements of Ruſſians in this country, for the ſake of the ſkins of quadrupeds, which are then more valuable than if the animal is taken in ſummer.

[d] He lived during this winter in Queen-ſtreet, near Greenland-dock, Rotherhithe. he hath ſailed, probably, by this time on the Greenland fiſhery. With regard to his having been in N. lat. 81° 30′, in June 1773, he can prove it by his journal, if that evidence ſhould be required.

[e] See the Narrative of eight ſailors who wintered in Greenland A. D. 1630, and who all returned in health to England the enſuing ſummer. Churchill's Voyage, vol. IV. p. 811.

They did not ſee the ſun from the 14th of October till the 3d of February. By the laſt day of January however they had day-light of 8 hours. They wintered in N. Lat. 77—4°. Ibid.

The

The next inſtance I ſhall mention of a navigator who hath proceeded far Northward is that of Captain Cheyne, who gave anſwers to certain queries drawn up by Mr. Dalrymple, F. R. S. in relation to the Polar ſeas, and which were communicated laſt year to the Society.

Captain Cheyne ſtates in this paper, that he hath been as far as N. lat. 82, but does not ſpecify whether by *obſervation* or his *reckoning*, though from many other anſwers to the interrogatories propoſed, it ſhould ſeem that he ſpeaks of the latitude by *obſervation*. Unfortunately Captain Cheyne is at preſent on the Coaſt of Africa, ſo that further information on this head cannot be now procured from him.

Whilſt the ſhips deſtined for the N. Pole were preparing, a moſt ingenious and able ſea officer, Lieutenant John Cartwright, told me, that twelve years ago he had been informed of a very remarkable voyage made by Captain Mac-Callam as far nearly as 84 N. lat.

This account Mr. Cartwright had received from a brother officer, Mr. James Watt, now a maſter and commander in the royal navy, who was on board captain Mac-Callam's ſhip.

I thought it my duty to acquaint the Admiralty with this intelligence, who would have ſent for Mr. Watt, but he was then employed on the coaſt of America.

On his return from thence within the laſt month, Mr. Cartwright introduced a converſation with regard to Captain Mac-Callam's voyage, when Mr. Watt repeated all the circumſtances which he had mentioned to him twelve years ago; after which Mr. Cartwright, thinking that I ſhould be glad to hear the particulars from Mr. Watt himſelf, was ſo good as to bring him to my chambers, when I received from him the following information.

In the year 1751 Mr. Watt, then not quite ſeventeen years of age, went on board the Campbeltown of Campbeltown, Captain Mac-Callam, which ſhip was at that time employed in the Greenland fiſhery.

It ſeems that during the time the whales are ſuppoſed to copulate, the crews of the Greenland veſſels commonly amuſe themſelves on ſhore.

Captain Mac-Callam however (who was a very able and ſcientific ſeaman) thought that a voyage to the N. Pole would be more intereſting, and that, the ſeaſon being a fine one, he had a chance of penetrating far to the Northward, as well as returning before the later fiſhery took place. He accordingly proceeded without the leaſt obſtruction to 83½, when the ſea was not only open to the Northward, but they had not ſeen a ſpeck of ice for the laſt three degrees, and the weather at the ſame time was temperate; in ſhort, Mr. Watt hath never experienced a more pleaſant navigation.

It need be ſcarcely obſerved, that the latitude of 83½ was determined by obſervation, as the great object of the voyage was to reach the Pole; the Captain therefore, the mate, and young Mr. Watt, determined the latitude from time to time, both by Davis and Hadley's quadrants: to this I may add, that their departure and return were from and to Hakluyt's Headland.

When they were advancing into theſe high Northern latitudes, the mate complained that the compaſs was not ſteady, on which Captain Mac-Callam deſiſted from his attempt, though with reluctance; knowing that if any accident happened, he ſhould be blamed by his owners, who would be reminded certainly by the mate of the proteſts he had made againſt the ſhip's proceeding further Northward.

Several

Several of the crew however were for proſecuting their diſcoveries, and Mr. Watt particularly remembers the chagrin which was expreſſed by a very intelligent ſeaman, whoſe name was John Kelly; Captain Mac-Callam alſo, after his return from that voyage, hath frequently ſaid, in the preſence of Mr. Watt and others, that, if the mate had not been faint-hearted, the ſhip poſſibly might have reached the pole.

Both Captain Mac-Callam and the mate are now dead, and it is rather doubtful whether the ſhip's journal can be procured.

It remains therefore to be conſidered what may be objected to the credibility of this very intereſting account.

I have ſtated that Mr. Watt was not at the time this voyage took place quite ſeveenteen years of age; but I have alſo ſtated that he obſerved himſelf (as well as the maſter and mate) from time to time. Is it therefore more extraordinary he ſhould remember with accuracy that, two and twenty years ago, he had been in N. lat. 83½, than that, at the ſame diſtance of time, he might recollect that he had been at a friend's houſe, which was ſituated 83 miles and an half from London? Or rather indeed is not his memory, with regard to this high latitude, much more to be depended upon, as the circumſtance is ſo much more intereſting, eſpecially as Mr. Watt was even then of a ſcientific turn?

To this I may add, that it being his firſt voyage, and ſo remarkable a one, Mr. Watt now declares that he remembers more particulars relative to it, than perhaps in any other ſince that time: other ſea officers have likewiſe told me, that the circumſtances of their firſt voyages are moſt freſh in their memory, the reaſon for which is too obvious to be dwelt upon.

If Mr. Watt's recollection however is diſtruſted, this objection extends equally to Captain Mac-Callam's frequent declarations, that, if the apprehenſions of the mate had not prevented, he might poſſibly have reached the N. Pole; and how could he have conceived this, unleſs he had imagined himſelf to have been in a very high Northern latitude?

But it may be poſſibly ſaid, that this voyage took place above twenty years ſince, and that therefore at ſuch a diſtance of time no one's memory can be relied upon.

It is true indeed that Mac Callam made this attempt in 1751; but Mr. Watt continued his ſervices the following year in a Greenland ſhip, and therefore, traverſing nearly the ſame ſeas, muſt have renewed the recollection of what he had experienced in the preceding voyage, though he did not then proceed further than N. lat. 80.

This however brings it only to 1752; but I have already ſtated, that within theſe twelve years he mentioned all the particulars above related to his brother officer, Lieutenant Cartwright.

Mr. Watt alſo frequently converſed with Captain Mac-Callam about this voyage after both of them had quitted the Greenland ſhips; Mr. Watt riſing regularly to be a Maſter and Commander in His Majeſty's ſervice, and Captain Mac-Callam becoming Purſer of the Tweed man of war.

It ſo happened, that in the year of the expedition againſt Belliſle, Mr. Watt, Captain Mac-Callam, and Mr. Walker (commonly called Commodore Walker, from his having commanded the Royal Family privateers in the late war), met together at Portſmouth, when they talked over the circumſtances of this Greenland voyage, which Mr. Walker was intereſted in, by having been the principal owner of the Campbeltown.

Mr. Watt and Captain Mac-Callam met alſo eleven years ago in London, when they as uſual converſed about the having reached ſo high a Northern latitude.

 I now

I now come to my laſt proof, which I received from the late Dr. Campbell, the able continuator and reviſer of Harris's Collection of Voyages.

In that very valuable compilation, Commodore Roggewein's circumnavigation makes a moſt material addition, ſome of the moſt intereſting particulars of which were communicated by Dr. Dallie, who was a native of Holland [f], and lived in Racquet-court, Fleet-ſtreet, about the year 1745, where he practiſed phyſick.

Dr. Campbell went to thank Dallie for the having furniſhed him with Roggewein's voyage, when Dallie ſaid that he had been further both to the Southward and to the Northward than perhaps any other perſon who ever exiſted.

He then explained himſelf as to the having been in high Southern latitudes, by ſailing in Roggewein's fleet [g]; and as to his having been far to the Northward, he gave the following account:

Between fifty and ſixty years ago it was uſual to ſend a Dutch ſhip of war to ſuperintend the Greenland fiſhery, though it is not known whether this continues to be a regulation at preſent.

Dr. Dallie (then young) was on board the Dutch veſſel employed on this ſervice [h]; and during the interval between the two fiſheries, the Captain determined, like Mr. Mac-Callam, to try whether he could not reach the Pole, and accordingly penetrated (to the beſt of Dr. Campbell's recollection) as far as N. lat. 88, when the weather was warm, the ſea perfectly free from ice, and

[f] He was a grandſon of Dallie, who was author of a book, much eſteemed by the Divines, intitled "*De Uſu Patrum.*"

[g] Roggewein reached S. lat. 62° 30′. See Harris.

[h] Dr. Campbell does not recollect in what capacity he ſerved; but, as he afterwards practiſed phyſick, he might probably have been the ſurgeon.

rolling like the bay of Biſcay. Dallie now preſſed the Captain to proceed; but he anſwered that he had already gone too far by having neglected his ſtation, for which he ſhould be blamed in Holland, on which account alſo he would ſuffer no journal to be made, but returned as ſpeedily as he could to Spitzbergen.

There are undoubtedly two objections which may be made to this account of Dr. Dallie's, which are, that it depends not only upon his own memory, but that of Dr. Campbell, as no journal can be produced, for the reaſon which I have before ſtated.

The converſation, however, between Dr. Campbell and Dallie aroſe from the accidental mention of Roggewein's voyage to the Southward; and can it be ſuppoſed that Dallie invented this circumſtantial narrative on the ſpot, without having actually been in a high Northern latitude?

If this be admitted to have been improbable, was he not likely to have remembered with accuracy what he was ſo much intereſted about, as to have preſſed the Dutch Captain to have proceeded to the Pole?

But it may be ſaid alſo, that we have not this account from Dallie himſelf, but at ſecond-hand from Dr. Campbell, at the diſtance of thirty years from the converſation.

To this it may be anſwered, that Dr. Campbell's memory was moſt remarkably tenacious, as is well known to all thoſe who had the pleaſure of his acquaintance; and, as he hath written ſo ably for the promotion of geographical diſcoveries in all parts of the globe, ſuch an account could not but make a ſtrong impreſſion upon him, eſpecially as he received it juſt after the firſt edition of his compilation of voyages.

No one eaſily forgets what is highly intereſting to him; and, though I do not pretend to have ſo good a memory as Dr. Campbell, I have ſcarcely a doubt, but that if I ſhould live thirty years longer, and retain my faculties, I ſhall recollect with precision every latitude which I have already ſtated in this paper.

What credit, however, is to be given to all theſe narratives is entirely ſubmitted to the Society, as I have ſtated them moſt fully with every circumſtance which may invalidate, as well as ſupport them; and if I have endeavoured to corroborate them by the obſervations which I have made, it is only becauſe I believe them.

It ſhould ſeem upon the whole of the inquiries on this point, that it is very uncertain when ſhips may proceed far to the Northward of Spitzbergen, and that it depends not only upon the ſeaſon, but other accidents, when the Polar ſeas may be ſo free from ice as to permit attempts to make diſcoveries[1].

Poſſibly, therefore, if a king's officer was ſent from year to year on board one of the Greenland ſhips, the lucky opportunity might be ſeized, and the Navy Board might pay for the uſe of the veſſel, if it was taken from the whale fiſhery, in order to proceed as far as may be towards the North Pole.

[1] Captain Robinſon hath informed me, that at the latter end of laſt April a Whitby ſhip was in N. lat. 80, without having been materially obſtructed by the ice. Capt. Marſhall was alſo off Hakluyt's Headland ſo early as the 25th of April, without obſerving much ice.

DAINES BARRINGTON, F. R. S.

ADDITIONAL

PROOFS, &c.

Read at a Meeting of the Royal Society, Dec. 22, 1774.

AS I happen to have collected many additional facts since my paper, containing Instances of Navigators who had reached high Northern Latitudes, was read before the Society in May last, I shall take the liberty to state them according to chronological order; together with some general reasons why it may be presumed, that the Polar seas are, at least sometimes, navigable.

I think it my duty to do this, not only because I was the unworthy proposer of the Polar voyage in 1773, which was recommended by the Council of the Royal Society to the Board of Admiralty; but because it would not redound much to the credit of the Society, if they planned a voyage to reach the N. Pole, if possible, when a perpetual barrier of ice prevented any discoveries in the Spitzbergen seas to the Northward of 80½, which is not a degree beyond the most common station of the Greenland fishers.

I must here, however, repeat, that no one is more entirely satisfied than myself of the great abilities, perseverance, and intrepidity, with which the officers who were sent on this destination, attempted to prosecute their discoveries; but I conceive, from the arguments and facts which will follow, that they were

stopped

ſtopped by a moſt unfortunate barrier of ice (of great extent indeed), but which was only temporary, and not perpetual.

If ſuch a wall of ice hath been conſtantly fixed in this latitude, and muſt continue to be ſo, there is an end to all diſcoveries to be made to the Northward of Spitzbergen; but if it is only occaſional, the attempt may be reſumed in ſome more fortunate year [k].

The point therefore being of ſo much importance to geography, I hope the Society will pardon me, if I more fully enter into the ſubject than I did in my former paper.

The Engliſh have long taken the lead in geographical diſcoveries. One of our ſhips of war is lately returned, after having penetrated into the Antarctic circle; and is it not rather a reflection upon a ſcientific nation, that more is not known with regard to the circumpolar regions of our own hemiſphere, than can be collected from maps made in the time of Charles I. eſpecially when the run from the mouth of the Thames to the N. Pole is not a longer one than from Falmouth to the Cape de Verde iſlands?

Though I have the honour to be a Fellow of a Society inſtituted for the promotion of Natural Knowledge, the prejudices of an Engliſhman are ſo ſtrong with me, that I cannot but wiſh the diſcoveries to be made in the Polar ſeas may be atchieved by my countrymen; but if we are determined to abandon the enterprize, ſcience is to be honoured from whatever quarter it may come, and it hath therefore given me great ſatisfaction to hear,

[k] Upon the firſt return of the King's Ships from the Polar Voyage, this notion of a perpetual barrier of ice at N Lat. $80\frac{1}{2}$ had prevailed ſo much, that ſome very diſtinguiſhed Philoſophers of this country had ſhewn thoughts of proceeding to the Pole over the ice, in ſuch a wind boat as the Dutch have ſometimes made uſe of.

that

that Monſ. de Bougainville is ſoon to be ſent on diſcoveries to the Northward[l].

In the outſet of my former paper, I ſaid I ſhould not trouble the Society with any inſtances of navigators having reached high Northern latitudes, which had appeared in print. During the courſe of this ſummer, however, I have happened to find three ſuch accounts which were never before alluded to, and which are extracted from books that are not commonly looked into, or at leaſt often conſulted upon points of geography.

When the Royal Society was firſt inſtituted, it was uſual to ſend queries to any traveller who happened to reſide in England, after having been in parts of the world which are not commonly frequented[m],

In the year 166⅔, Mr. Oldenburg, then ſecretary of the Society, was ordered to regiſter a paper, entitled, "Several Inquiries "concerning Greenland, anſwered by Mr. Grey, who had "viſited thoſe parts."

The 19th of theſe queries is the following:

"How near any one hath been known to approach the Pole?"

Anſwer. "I once met, upon the Coaſt of Greenland, a Hol"lander, that ſwore he had been but half a degree from the "Pole, ſhewing me his journal, which was alſo atteſted by his "mate; where they had ſeen no ice or land, but all water[n]."

[l] I have ſince been informed, that this intended voyage was dropt, by the French miniſter for the marine department being changed.

[m] Richard Hakluyt rode 200 miles to hear the narrative of Mr. Thomas Butt's voyage, temp. Hen. VIII. from England to Newfoundland. Hakluyt, P. III. p. 131.

[n] Mr. Boyle mentions a ſimilar account, which he received from an old Greenland maſter on the 5th of April, 1675. See Boyle's Works, vol. II. p. 397 to 399. folio. The whole of this narrative is very circumſtantial, and deſerves to be ſtated at length. The title is, Experiments and Obſervations made in December and January 1662.

After

After which Mr. Oldenburgh adds, as from himſelf, "This is "incredible [o]."

It may not be improper, therefore, after mentioning this firſt inſtance of a navigator's having approached ſo near to the Pole, to diſcuſs upon what reaſons Mr. Oldenburgh might found this his very peremptory incredulity.

Was it becauſe the fact is impoſſible upon the very ſtating it?

This puts me in mind of the diſbelief which is generally ſhewn to a paſſage in Pliny, even after the actual fact hath ſhewn not only the poſſibility, but eaſy practicability, of what is alluded to. Pliny informs us [p], that Eudoxus flying the vengeance of king Lathyrus ſailed from Arabia, and reached the Straits of Gibraltar: yet no one ſcarcely will believe this account of Eudoxus's navigation, notwithſtanding this courſe is ſo often followed.

Was it becauſe no Engliſhman had then been ſo far to the Northward?

It is very eaſy, however, to account why ſuch attempts ſhould rather be made by the Dutch than the Engliſh in the infancy of the Greenland fiſhery.

[o] See Dr. Birch's Hiſtory of the Royal Society, vol. I. p. 202. Theſe queries are nineteen in number, to which the anſwers are very circumſtantial. I had an opportunity of reading them over to three very intelligent maſters of Greenland ſhips, who confirmed every particular. One circumſtance I think it right to take notice of, though it does not immediately relate to the point in diſcuſſion, which is, that there are coals in Spitzbergen, by which ſeven of Mr. Grey's crew were enabled to bear the ſeverity of the winter, having been left behind by an accident. One of the Greenland maſters, to whom I read Mr. Grey's anſwers, confirmed this particular; ſaying, that he had burnt himſelf Spitzbergen coals, and that they were very good.

[p] L. II. ch. 67.

The

The Southern parts of this country were discovered by Sir Hugh Willoughby, A. D. 1553; after which, no English ships were sent on that coast for nearly fifty years. In the beginning of the last century, however, a competition arose between the English and Dutch, with regard to the whale fishery, and the English drove the Dutch from most of the harbours, under the right of first discoverers[r], in which they were supported by royal instructions; so that the Dutch were obliged to seek for new stations, whereas the English were commonly in possession of the Greenland ports, which they considered as their own[s].

Did Mr. Oldenburgh disbelieve the Dutchman's relation, because ice is frequently met with to the Southward of N. lat. 80?

Ice is commonly seen upon the great bank of Newfoundland, and the harbour of Louisburgh is often covered with it, which is only in N. lat. 46; yet Davis and Baffin have penetrated, under nearly the same meridians, beyond 70.

I will now suppose the tables changed between the two hemispheres of our globe, and that a Southern discoverer, meeting with ice upon the banks of Newfoundland, returns to his own hemisphere fully impressed with the impossibility of proceeding much to the Northward of N. lat. 46; would not his countrymen be

[r] It is also assigned in the Supplement to Wood and Martens' Voyages, p. 179, 8vo. 1694. as a reason why the English never proceeded further than 78 on the E. coast of Spitzbergen, because the Dutch were commonly superior on that side of the island.

Robert Bacon of Crowmers in Norfolk was the first discoverer also of Iceland. See the Itinerary of William of Worcester, p. 311. Cambridge, 1778, octavo.

[s] See Purchas, *passim*. Whilst these disputes continued, the Dutch often sent ships of war to protect their Greenland traders, which accounts for Dr. Dallie's sailing in such a vessel to 88, as I have stated in my former paper.

deceived

deceived by the inferences which were drawn from what had been observed in the feas of the Northern hemifphere ?

Bouvet, in 1738, failed to 53 S. lat. and in a meridian 5 degrees to the W. of the Cape of Good Hope, in which fituation he fell in with floating ice ; after which he did not proceed any further. Our two fhips of war, lately fent upon difcoveries to the Southward, however, have been fome minutes within the Antarctic circle, upon a no very diftant meridian from that in which Bouvet failed.

Muft the fact be difbelieved becaufe all the ice in the Polar feas comes from the Northward ? But this is not fo, as Mr. Grey informs us [t], that the S. E. wind brings the greateft quantity of ice to the coafts of Spitzbergen ; which indeed is highly probable, as this wind blows from thofe parts of the *Icy Sea* into which the great rivers of Siberia and Tartary empty themfelves [u]. My own poor conception, with regard to the floating ice in the Spitzbergen feas, is, that thefe maffes come almoft entirely from the fame quarter, as it is fo difficult to freeze any large quantity of falt water. Thefe pieces of ice, therefore, being once launched into the *Icy Sea*, are difperfed by winds, tides, and currents, in every direction, fome of them being perhaps carried to very high Northern latitudes, from which they are again wafted to the Southward.

But allowing, for an inftant, that all the ice may come from the Northward, muft not then an open fea be left in the higher

[t] Dr. Birch's Hift. R. Soc.

[u] The ice is faid to be never troublefome in the harbour of Newport (Rhode Ifland, N. America); becaufe no frefh water rivers empty themfelves by this port, whereas the harbour of N. York (though much to the Southward) is often obftructed by the ice, which floats down from Hudfon's River.

Northern

Northern latitudes, from which theſe maſſes of ice are ſuppoſed to have floated?

Was it becauſe the more one advances towards the Pole, vegetation invariably is diminiſhed?—But this is not the fact.

Nova Zembla, ſituated only in N. lat. 76, produces not even any ſorts of graſs [w]; ſo that the only quadrupeds which frequent it are foxes and bears, both of which are carnivorous. In the Northern parts of Spitzbergen, on the other hand, they have reyn-deer, which are often exceſſively fat; and Mr. Grey mentions three or four plants, which flower there during the ſummer [x].

Was it becauſe no one had ever conceived it poſſible to proceed ſo far as the Pole [y]?

Thorne, however, a merchant of Briſtol, had made ſuch a propoſal in the reign of Henry VIII. and I ſhall now alſo ſhew, that not only Mr. Oldenburgh's contemporaries continued to believe ſuch a voyage to be feaſible, but many great names in ſcience who lived after him.

Wood ſailed on the diſcovery of a N. E. paſſage to Japan in 1676; and, in the publication of his voyage, he hath ſtated the grounds upon which he conceived ſuch a voyage to be practicable; the ſtrongeſt of all which, perhaps, is the relation of Captain Goulden, with regard to a Dutch ſhip having reached N. lat. 89. Though this account hath often been referred to, I do not recollect to have ſeen it ſtated with all the circumſtances which

[w] Purchas, vol. I. p. 479.

[x] Dr. Birch's Hiſt. R. Soc. vol. I. p. 202. *et ſeq.*

[y] A Map of the Northern Hemiſphere, publiſhed at Berlin (under the direction of the Academy of Sciences and Belles Lettres), places a ſhip at the Pole, as having arrived there according to the Dutch accounts.

ſeem to eſtabliſh its veracity beyond contradiction: I ſhall therefore copy the very words of Wood [z].

" Captain Goulden, who had made above thirty voyages to " Greenland, did relate to his majeſty, that, being at Greenland " ſome twenty years before, he was in company with two Hol- " landers to the eaſtward of Edge's iſland [a]; and that the whales " not appearing on the ſhore, the two Hollanders were deter- " mined to go further Northward, and in a fortnight's time re- " turned, and gave it out that they had ſailed into the lat. 89, " and that they did not meet with any ice, but a free and open " ſea; and that there run a very hollow *grown* [b] ſea, like that of " the Bay of Biſcay. Mr. Goulden being not ſatisfied with the " bare relation, they produced him four journals out of the two " ſhips, which teſtified the ſame, and that they all agreed within " four minutes [b].

[z] Moxon's account of a Dutch ſhip having been two degrees beyond the Pole, was alſo much relied upon by Wood, which hath never been printed at large, but in a now very ſcarce tract of Moxon's, and in the ſecond volume of Harris's Voyages, p. 396. In confirmation of this very circumſtantial and intereſting narrative, I have only to add, that Moxon was hydrographer to Charles II. and hath publiſhed ſeveral ſcientific treatiſes. See the Catalogue of the Bodleian Library.

[a] Edge's iſland was diſcovered, A. D. 1616, by Captain Thomas Edge, who had made ten voyages to thoſe ſeas. See the Supplement to the N. E. Voyages, London, 1694, 8vo. Wyche's Iſland, ſo called from a Gentleman of that name, was diſcovered in the following year. Ibid.

[b] Wood's Voyage, p. 145. *Grown Sea*, is the expreſſion in the original. " Which is not practicable in theſe tempeſtuous high *grown* ſeas." Dr. Halley, in his Journal, p. 45. Wood's Voyage was publiſhed by Smith and Walford, Printers to the Royal Society in 1694, together with Sir John Narborough's, Marten's, and other Navigators. The book is dedicated to Pepys, Secretary to the Admiralty; and he is complimented therein for having furniſhed the materials.

Having thus ſtated Wood's own words, it ſhould ſeem, that they who deny the authenticity of the relation muſt contend that the crews of both theſe Dutch ſhips entered into a deliberate ſcheme of impoſing upon their brother whale fiſhers, and had drawn up four fictitious journals accordingly, becauſe ſo many are ſtated to have been produced out of the two ſhips to Captain Goulden, whilſt each of them varied a few minutes in the latitude; whereas, if they had determined to deceive Captain Goulden and his crew, the journals would probably have tallied exactly. I muſt beg leave alſo to make an additional obſervation on the account as ſtated by Wood, which is, that the Dutch ſhips only went to the Northward, in ſearch of whales, but did not give it out that they intended to make for the Pole, which if they had done, it might poſſibly have been an inducement to carry on the deception by forgeries and miſrepreſentations. To this it may likewiſe be added, that the Dutch are not commonly jokers.

I have already remarked, that Wood makes this account one of the principal reaſons for his undertaking the N. E. paſſage to Japan. Wood therefore (Mr. Oldenburgh's contemporary) was not a diſbeliever before his voyage of the poſſibility of reaching ſo high a Northern latitude, nor of any of the circumſtances ſtated in this narrative.

But Captain Wood is not a ſingle inſtance of ſuch credulity, as, the very year before he ſailed on his voyage, we find in the Philoſophical Tranſactions for 1675 [c] the following paſſage: "For it "is well known to all that ſail Northward, that moſt of the "Northern coaſts are frozen up many leagues, though in the "open ſea it is not ſo, *No nor under the Pole itſelf*, unleſs by ac-

[c] N° 118.

"cident."

"cident." In which paſſage, the having reached the Pole is alluded to as a known fact, and ſtated as ſuch to the Royal Society.

Wood indeed, after not being able to proceed further than N. lat. 76, diſcredits in the lump all the former inſtances of having reached high Northern latitudes, in the following words:

"So here the opinion of William Barentz was confuted, and "all the Dutch relations [d], which certainly are all forged and "abuſive pamphlets, as alſo the relations of our country-"men [e]."

In juſtice, however, to the memoirs of both Engliſh and Dutch navigators, I cannot but take notice of theſe very peremptory and ill-founded reflections, made by Wood; and which ſeem to be dictated merely by his diſappointment, in not being able to effect his diſcovery.

Wood attempted to ſail in a N. E. direction between Spitzbergen and Nova Zembla, but was obſtructed by ice, ſo that he could not proceed further than the W. coaſt of Nova Zembla in N. lat. 76. Thinking it, therefore, prudent to return, he at once treats as fabulous, not only the ideas of that moſt perſevering ſeaman William Barentz, but likewiſe all other accounts of ſhips having reached high Northern latitudes. Now that the ice which obſtructed Wood in N. lat. 76. was not a perpetual, but only occaſional barrier, appears by the Ruſſians having not only diſcovered, but lived ſeveral years in the iſland of Maloy Brun,

[d] The Dutch made three voyages for the diſcovery of the N. E. paſſage in three ſucceſſive years, the third being in 1596, which laſt was by the encouragement of a private ſubſcription only. See Gerard de Veer, p. 13. Amſterdam, 1609. folio.

[e] Wood's Voyage, p. 181.

which

which lies between Spitzbergen and Nova Zembla, and extends from N. lat. 77° 25′ to 78° 45′ [f]. The Dutch alſo ſailed round the Northern coaſt of Nova Zembla, and wintered on the Eaſtern ſide in 1596 [g].

As for Wood's treating all diſcoveries towards the Pole, from the Northern parts of Spitzbergen, as fabulous, he had not the leaſt foundation, from what he had obſerved on his own voyage, for this unmerited aſperſion upon their veracity; becauſe, if Wood's barrier between Spitzbergen and Nova Zembla, in N. lat. 76, had been perpetual, what hath this to do with the courſe of a ſhip ſailing from the Northern parts of Spitzbergen upon a meridian towards the Pole?

I cannot, however, diſmiſs Wood's voyage without making ſome further remarks on his concluding that the obſtructions which he met with in N. lat. 76 were perpetual.

Almoſt every voyage to ſeas, in which floating ice is commonly to be found, proves the great difference between the quantities, as well as ſize, of theſe impediments, to navigation, though in the ſame latitude and time of the year.

[f] See the Engliſh Tranſlation of profeſſor Le Roy's account of this iſland, p. 85. London, 1774, 8vo, printed for C. Heydinger. As alſo the Sieur de Vaugondy's *Eſſai d'une Carte Polaire Arctique*, publiſhed in 1774, who repreſents this iſland as extending from N. lat. 77° 20′ to 78° 30′, its longitude being 60 degrees E. from Fero.

[g] See the map of the circumpolar regions which accompanies Wood's voyage. The Northern point of Nova Zembla, in this map, is in 77 nearly. There were factions in Holland, with regard to the method of diſcovering the N E. paſſage. Barentz, inſtigated by Plancius the Geographer, was for making the trial to the N. of Nova Zembla; the other two ſhips which failed on that expedition of diſcovery were to attempt paſſing the Weygatz. Recueil des Voyages au Nord, tom. IV. Linſchoten's Preface.

Davis-

Davis, in his two first voyages to discover the N. W. passage, could not penetrate beyond 66; but in his third voyage, in 1587, he reached 72° 12′ [h].

In the year 1576, Sir Martin Frobisher passed the Straits (since called from their first discoverer) without any obstructions from ice: in his two following voyages, however, he found them in the same month, to use his own expression, "in a manner shut "up with a long mure of ice [i]."

In the year 1614, Baffin proceeded to 81, and thought he saw land as far as 82 [k] to the N. E. of Spitzbergen, which is accordingly marked in one of Purchas's maps. During this voyage he met, near Cherry island, situated only in 74 N. lat. two banks of ice; the one, 40 leagues in length, the other 120; which last would extend to 25 degrees of longitude in N. lat. 76, where Wood fixes his barrier.

It need therefore scarcely be observed, that such a floating wall of ice, 120 leagues long, by being jammed in between land, or other banks of ice, might afford an appearance indeed of forming a perpetual barrier, when perhaps, within the next 24 hours, the wall of ice might entirely vanish.

Of the sudden assemblage of such an accumulation of ice, I shall now mention two, rather recent, instances.

I have been very accurately informed, that the late Colonel Murray happened to go, in the month of May, from one of our Southern colonies to Louisburgh, when the harbour was entirely open; but on rising in the morning, it was completely filled

[h] See Hakluyt and Purchas, vol. I. p. 84.

[i] Purchas, ibid.

[k] See also the Supplement to Wood and Marten's Voyages, in the 8vo publication of 1694, in which point Purchas is stated to be in N. Lat. 82.

with

with ice, ſo that a waggon might have paſſed over it in any direction [l].

I have alſo received the following account from an officer in the royal Navy, who was not many years ago on the Newfoundland ſtation.

In the middle of June, the whole ſtraits of Belliſle were covered in the ſame manner with the harbour of Lewiſburgh, and for three weeks together a carriage might have paſſed from one ſhore to the other; but during a ſingle night the ice had almoſt entirely diſappeared. Such is the ſudden accumulation of ice, in latitudes 24 and 30 degrees to the Southward of Wood's ſituation.

Linſchoten aſſerts, that, being in the ſtraits of Weygate the laſt day of July, he was told by the Samoieds on that coaſt, that in ten or twelve days afterwards the ice in the ſtraits would be all góne, though they were then quite blocked up with it. When he repaſſed theſe ſtraits afterwards on the 13th of Auguſt, he found not the leaſt veſtige of it, ſo quickly do theſe huge maſſes diſſolve after they once begin to thaw [m].

On the other hand, Callander admits, that by accumulation of floating ice places are now inacceſſible which were not formerly ſo, and inſtances the eaſtern coaſt of Greenland, as alſo Frobiſher's ſtraits [n]. Kergulen, in his account of Iceland, likewiſe mentions, that the ſea between Iceland and Greenland was entirely cloſed during the whole Summer of 1766.

[l] On the 19th of December, 1759, the Potowmack, in a part where it was two miles broad, and nearly in N. lat. of only 38, was frozen entirely over in one night, when the preceding day had been very mild and temperate.—Burnaby's Travels through N. America, p. 59.

Camden, in his Annals of Elizabeth, aſſerts, that Davis reached 83, where the ſtraits, called after him, were narrowed to 40 leagues—See Camden, Anno 1585. We have not ſince been able to proceed ſo far to the Northward.

[m] Callander's Pref. p. 38.

[n] Ibid.

I ſhall now endeavour to ſhew, that Dr. Halley was no more incredulous with regard to the poſſibility of reaching high Northern latitudes, than Captain Wood was before the ill ſucceſs of his voyage on diſcovery.

Mr. Miller, in his Gardener's Dictionary, hath the following paſſage, under the article, THERMOMETER:

" Mr. Patrick has fixed his thermometer to a ſcale of ninety " degrees, which are numbered from the top downwards, and " alſo a moveable index to it. The deſign of this is to ſhew, how " the heat and cold is changed from the time it was laſt looked " upon, according to the different degrees of heat and cold in all " latitudes. As by the trial of two thermometers, which have " *been regulated abroad*; the one by Dr. Halley, in his late " Southern voyage; and the *other by Captain* Johnſon, *in his* " *voyage to Greenland*; the firſt hath a heat under the equinoctial " line, and the other *a degree of cold in* 88 *degrees of N. latitude.*"

I have taken ſome pains to find out a more full account of this voyage of Captain Johnſon's; but have only met with the following confirmation of it perhaps, in the 1ſt vol. of Monſ. de Buffon's Natural Hiſtory [c].

" I have been aſſured, *by perſons of credit*, that an Engliſh captain, whoſe name was Monſon, inſtead of ſeeking a paſſage to " China between the Northern countries, had directed his courſe " to the Pole, and had approached it within two degrees, where " there was an open ſea, without any ice."

As the Captain *Monſon* mentioned in this paſſage, reached exactly the ſame degree of latitude with Captain *Johnſon*, I ſhould rather think, that this is the ſame voyage; eſpecially, as it is well known, that the French writers ſeldom trouble themſelves about the orthography of foreign names.

[c] Vol. I. p. 215, quarto.

If

If this, however, ſhould not be the caſe, it muſt be admitted to be an additional inſtance of a ſhip's having reached N. lat. 88, as well as Monſ. de Buffon's giving credit to ſuch relation [p].

Having therefore not been able to pick up any other circumſtances in relation to Captain Johnſon's voyage, I ſhall now ſtate what ſeems to be fairly deducible from the paſſage which I have copied from Miller's Gardener's Dictionary.

Dr. Halley made his voyage to the Southward in 1700; on the return from which, he probably employed Patrick, as the moſt eminent maker of weather glaſſes [q], to graduate a thermometer according to the heat he had experienced under the equator. It was very natural therefore, when ſuch a point of heat was to be marked upon the inſtrument, to make the ſcale either for high Southern or Northern latitudes.

It ſhould ſeem, then, that Dr. Halley had procured Captain Johnſon (who was maſter of a Greenland ſhip) to carry a thermometer on his voyage to Spitzbergen, and that he fortunately was able to reach ſo high a degree of latitude as 88.

If the thermometer had been calculated only for imaginary degrees of heat and cold, it would have been marked for the Equator and the Pole; whereas it was only regulated for 88 degrees of N. latitude, which Captain Johnſon therefore had as clearly reached, as Dr. Halley had the Equator.

[p] To this liſt of credulous perſons (as perhaps they may be conſidered by ſome) I ſhall beg leave to add the names of Maclaurin and Dr. Campbell. The former of theſe was ſo perſuaded of the ſeas being open quite to the Pole, that he hath not only adviſed this method of proſecuting diſcoveries, but, as I have been told, was deſirous of going the voyage himſelf.

[q] I have been informed, that his ſhop was in the Old Bailey, and that he died about fifty years ago. Patrick was a great ringer, and ſome of the moſt celebrated peals were invented by him more than fifty years ago.—He ſtyled himſelf, in his advertiſements, Terricellian Operator.—Sir John Hawkins's Hiſtory of Muſic, vol. IV. p. 154.

At all events, Patrick's thermometer muſt have been made under Dr. Halley's inſpection; and would he have permitted it to be marked for 88 degrees of N. latitude, according to Captain Johnſon's voyage, if he had diſbelieved his narrative?

My third and laſt inſtance, from any printed authority, but in a book which is not commonly to be met with, is that of Captain Alexander Cluny, as by a map, engraved under his direction, the very ſpot is marked to the Weſtward of Spitzbergen, and in ſomewhat more than 82 degrees of N. latitude, where he ſaw neither land nor ice[r].

Before I proceed, however, to ſtate ſeveral other inſtances of reaching high Northern latitudes, which have never appeared in print, and which I have collected ſince my laſt paper on this head, I muſt beg the indulgence of the Society, whilſt I lay before them ſome additional reaſons why the Polar ſeas may be conceived to be navigable[s].

Speculative geographers have ſuppoſed, that there ſhould be nearly the ſame quantity of land and ſea in both hemiſpheres, in order to preſerve the equilibrium of the globe.

[r] See the American Traveller, London, 1769, quarto; as alſo, the Sieur de Vaugondy's *Eſſai d'une Carte Polaire Arctique*, publiſhed in 1774; in which, however, he lays down this ſpot from Cluny's map in little more than 81, whereas it is fully in 82. The longitude of this ſpot is 30 degrees E. from Fero.

[s] I have received a letter from the Rev. Mr. Tooke, Chaplain to the Factory at St. Peterſburg, dated December 30, 1774, which he concludes in the following manner: "I have a fact or two to communi-"cate, which ſeem to indicate, if not to a certainty, yet at leaſt to a "degree of probability, that the ſea is open to the Pole the year through-"out; but my paper will not hold them." From the accuracy with which ſeveral other intereſting particulars are ſtated in this letter, I have great reaſon to regret, that I have not an opportunity of laying the facts alluded to before the Public, with all their circumſtances, as I ſuppoſe that Mr. Tooke's information came from Archangel ſeamen.

It

It is possible, indeed, that this may be accounted for by the Antarctic seas being more shallow than those near the North Pole; as we do not know this, however, by the actual soundings, but are informed by Captain Furneaux, that there is no land even as far as the Antarctic circle, upon the meridian in which he sailed, as also that no land was observed during the course of his circumnavigation in 55 S. lat. at a medium, it seems necessary, as the quantity of land so greatly preponderates in the Northern hemisphere, that from N. lat. 80½ to the Pole itself must be chiefly, if not entirely, sea[t].

Let us now consider, whether such a sea is probably at all times in a state of congelation.

I do not know, whether it hath been settled by thermometrical observations, that there is any material difference between the heat under the Equator, and that which is experienced within the Tropics; most travellers complain indefinitely of its excess in such latitudes.

As this point, therefore, seems not to have been settled by the thermometer, let us have recourse to what is found to be the freezing point upon mountains, situated almost under the Equator, and compare it with the same height on the Pic of Teneriff, which being in N. lat. 28, is five degrees to the Northward of the tropical limits.

The French Academicians suppose, that the freezing point, at which all vegetation ceases, and ice takes place, commences on Cotopaxi, at 1411 toises above the level of the sea; or, by our measure, at the height of about a mile and three quarters[u].

Mr.

[t] It is now known that Captain Cook also found very little land during his persevering attempts to the southward.

[u] Cotopaxi is the highest mountain of the Andes, at least in the neighbourhood of Quito. The plain of Carabuca, from which it rises, is 1023

Mr. Edens, on the other hand, hath given us a very particular account of what he obſerved in going to the top of Teneriff[w]; and ſo far from ſeeing ſnow or ice (except in a cave) his coat was covered, during the night, with dew, at the very ſummit, which, according to Dr. Heberden's computation, is 15,396 feet high, or wants but 148 yards of three miles[x].

Now as it is thus ſettled, that the Pic of Teneriff is nearly three miles high, which exceeds by more than a mile the height of the freezing point on Cotopaxi, ſituated under the Equator, it ſhould ſeem that there is no material difference between the heat under the Equator and within the Tropics; for if it is urged, that Teneriff is more ſurrounded with ſea than Cotopaxi, it muſt on the other hand be recollected, that this mountain is ſituated 5 degrees to the Northward of the Tropic, at the ſame time that the ſummit exceeds the freezing point on Cotopaxi by more than a mile; both which circumſtances ſhould render it colder than the freezing point on Cotopaxi.

The inference to be drawn from this compariſon ſeems to be, that, as the heat varies ſo little between the Equator and the tropical limits, it may differ as little between the Arctic circle and the Pole.

Nothing hath been ſuppoſed to ſhew more ſtrongly the wiſdom of a beneficent Creator, than that every part of this globe ſhould (taking the year throughout) have an equal proportion of the Sun's light.

1023 toiſes above the level of the ſea, and the height of the mountain above this plain is 1268 toiſes, making together 2291 toiſes. If 880 toiſes therefore are deducted from 2291, 1411 toiſes become the height of the freezing point upon this mountain. See Ulloa's Account of S. America.

w Phil. Tranſ. Abr. vol. V. p. 147. Sprat's Hiſt. R. Soc.

x See Hawkeſworth's Voyages, vol. II. p. 12. Goats alſo reach the very ſummit, which muſt be in ſearch of food, as they do not bear cold well.

It

It is admitted, that the equatorial parts have rather too much heat for the comforts of the inhabitants, and thoſe within the Polar circles too little; but, as we know that the tropical limits are peopled, it ſhould ſeem that the two Polar circles are equally deſtined for the ſame purpoſe; or if not for the benefit of man, at leaſt for the ſuſtenance of certain animals.

The largeſt of theſe, in the whole ſcale of Creation, is the whale; which, though a fiſh, cannot live long under water, without occaſionally raiſing its head into another element, for the purpoſe of reſpiration[y]: moſt other fiſh alſo occaſionally approach the ſurface of the water.

If the ice therefore extends from N. lat. 80½ to the Pole, all the intermediate ſpace is denied to the Spitzbergen whales, as well perhaps as to other fiſh; and is that glorious luminary, the Sun, to ſhine in vain for half the year upon ten degrees of latitude round each of the Poles, without contributing either to animal life or vegetation? for neither can take place upon this dreary expanſe of ice.

If this tract of ſea alſo is thus rendered improper for the ſupport of whales, theſe enormous fiſh, which require ſo much room, will be confined to two or three degrees of latitude in the neighbourhood of Spitzbergen; for all the Greenland maſters agree, that the beſt fiſhing ſtations are from 79 to 80, and that they do not often catch them to the Southward.

I will now aſk, if the ſea is congealed from N. lat. 80½ quite to the Pole, when did it thus begin to freeze, as it is well known, that a large quantity of ſea water is not eaſily forced to aſſume

[y] "Sometimes the ice is *fixed*, when there are but few whales ſeen, for "underneath the ice they cannot breathe" Martens's Voyage to Spitzbergen.

The whales likewiſe are ſuppoſed to come from the North; but how can this be, if there is an incruſted ſea over them?

the

the form of ice[z]? Can it be contended, that ten degrees of the globe round each pole were covered with frozen ſea at the original creation[a]? And if this is not inſiſted upon, can it be ſuppoſed, that, when the ſurface of the Polar ocean firſt ceaſed to be liquid, it could have afterwards reſiſted the effects of winds, currents, and tides?

I beg leave alſo to rely much upon the neceſſity of the ice's yielding to the conſtant reciprocation of the latter; becauſe no ſea was ever known to be frozen but the Black Sea, and ſome ſmall parts of the Baltic[b], neither of which have any tides, at the ſame time that the waters of both contain much leſs ſalt than thoſe of other ſeas, from the great influx of many freſh water rivers. For this laſt reaſon, it may likewiſe

[z] "There are three kinds of ice in the Northern ſeas. The firſt is "like melted ſnow which is become partly hardened, is more eaſily "broken into pieces, leſs tranſparent, is ſeldom more than ſix inches "thick, and when diſſolved, is found to be intermixed with ſalt. This "firſt ſort of ice is the only one which is ever formed from ſea water.

"If a certain quantity of water, which contains as much ſalt as ſea "water, is expoſed to the greateſt degree of cold, it never becomes firm "and pure ice, but reſembles tallow, or ſuet, whilſt it preſerves the "taſte of ſalt, ſo that the *ſweet* tranſparent ice can never be formed in "the ſea. If the ice of the ſea itſelf, therefore, confined in a ſmall "veſſel without any motion, cannot thus become true ice, much leſs can "it do ſo in a deep and agitated ocean." The author hence infers, that all the floating ice in the Polar ſeas comes from the Tartarian rivers and Greenland, as I have before contended. See a Diſſertation of Michel Lomonoſof, tranſlated from the Swediſh Tranſactions of 1752. *Collection Académique*, Tom. XI. p. 5. & *ſeq*. Paris, 1772, quarto. The Diſſertation is entitled, "*De l'Origine des Monts de Glace, dans la Mer du Nord.*"

[a] If there had been a fixed barrier of ice from the time of the creation, extending from 80½ to the North Pole, the height of ſuch ice muſt have been exceſſive, by the accumulation of frozen ſnow from winter to winter. Martens therefore obſerves, that the ice mountains in Spitzbergen are conſtantly encreaſing by the ſnow and rain which falls freezing, and which ſeldom melts at the top, p. 43.

[b] To theſe perhaps may be added the White Sea.

be

be preſumed, that the circumpolar ſeas are very ſalt, becauſe there is probably no ſuch influx beyond N. lat. 80, Spitzbergen itſelf having no rivers.

Having thus given ſome general reaſons, why the ſea ſhould not be ſuppoſed to be frozen in the ten higheſt degrees of latitude, I ſhall now proceed to lay before the Society, ſeveral inſtances, which I have lately collected, and which prove that it is not ſo covered with ice conſiderably to the N. of $80\frac{1}{2}$.

I ſhall, however, previouſly make two obſervations; the firſt of which is, that every inſtance of exceeding N. lat. $80\frac{1}{2}$, as much proves that there is no perpetual barrier of ice in that latitude, as if the navigator hath reached the Pole. The ſecond is, that as four experienced Greenland maſters have concurred in informing me, that they can ſee what is called the *blink of the ice*[c], for a degree before them, they never can be off Hakluyt's Headland, which is ſituated in 79° 50′, without obſerving this effect of the ice upon the ſky, if there was a perpetual barrier at $80\frac{1}{2}$, which is not much more than half a degree from them, when in that ſituation. Now Hakluyt's Headland is what they ſo perpetually take their departures from, that it hath obtained the name of *The Headland* by way of preeminence.

This mountain alſo is ſo high, that it can be diſtinguiſhed at the diſtance of a degree: in ſuch inſtances, therefore, which I ſhall produce, that do not ſettle the latitude by obſervation, whenever the reckoning depends upon the approach or departure from this Headland, the account receives the additional check of

[c] This is deſcribed to be an arch formed upon the clouds by reflection from the *packed ice*. Where the ice is *fixed* upon the ſea, you ſee a ſnow-white brightneſs in the ſkies, as if the ſun ſhined, for the ſnow is reflected by the air juſt as a fire by night is, but at a diſtance you ſee the air blue or blackiſh. Where there are many ſmall ice fields, which are as meadows for the ſeales, you ſee no luſtre or brightneſs of the ſkies.—Martens's Voyage to Spitzbergen.

the

the mountain's being increaſed or diminiſhed gradually to the eye of the obſerver.

My ſecond previous remark ſhall be, with regard to all inſtances of reaching high Northern latitudes; for which the authority of the ſhip's journal may be required, that it is almoſt impoſſible to procure this ſort of evidence, except the voyages have been recent; not only for the reaſons I have given in my former paper, but becauſe I find, that if the ſhip's journal is not wanted by the owners in a year or two (which ſeldom happens) it is afterwards conſidered as waſte paper.

Without the leaſt impeachment alſo of the knowledge in navigation of the Greenland maſters, when they are in the actual purſuit of fiſh, they do not trouble themſelves about their longitude or latitude; they are not bound by their inſtructions to ſail to any particular point, and their only object is to catch as many whales as poſſible; the ſhip's ſituation therefore, at ſuch time, becomes a matter of perfect indifference. It will appear, however, that they not only keep their reckonings, but obſerve, when they are not thus employed in fiſhing.

Having made theſe previous remarks, I ſhall now proceed to lay before the Society, ſuch inſtances of navigators having penetrated beyond 80½, as I have happened to procure ſince the reading of my former paper on this ſubject, in May laſt.

James Hutton (then belonging to the ſhip London, Captain Guy) was, thirty years ago, in N. lat. 81½, as both the captain and mate informed him; but did not obſerve himſelf. A very intelligent ſea officer was ſo good as to take from him this account, together with the following particulars, which perhaps may be intereſting to Greenland navigators.

Hutton hath been employed in the whale fiſhery nearly theſe forty years, during which he hath been ſeveral times at the Seven Iſlands, and the Waygat Straits. In ſome of theſe voyages the ſea hath been perfectly clear from ice, and at other times it

hath

hath ſet in ſo rapidly towards the Waygat[d], as to oblige the veſſels which happened to be thereabouts, to force all ſail poſſible, to eſcape being incloſed.

This hardy old tar likewiſe ſuppoſes, that he hath been further up the Waygat than perhaps any perſon now living; for he was once in a ſhip which attempted to paſs through it, nor did the maſter deſiſt, till they ſhoaled the water to three fathoms, when the ſea was ſo clear, that they could diſtinguiſh the bottom from the deck.

Mr. John Phillips, now maſter of the Exeter, but then mate of the Loyal Club, in the year 1752, reached N. lat. 81 and ſeveral minutes by obſervation, which circumſtance was confirmed by another perſon on board the Exeter laſt ſummer, on her return from the Greenland fiſhery. Captain Phillips added, that it was *very common* to fiſh in ſuch latitudes.

Mr. George Ware, now living at Erith in Kent, ſerved as chief mate in the year 1754, on board the Sea Nymph, Captain James Wilſon, when, at the latter end of June, they ſailed through floating ice from 74 to 81; but having then proceeded beyond the ice, they purſued the whales to 82° 15′, which latitude was determined by Mr. Ware's own obſervation.

As the ſea was now perfectly clear, as far as he could diſtinguiſh with his beſt glaſſes, both Mr. Ware and Captain Wilſon had a ſtrong inclination to puſh further towards the Pole; but the common ſailors hearing of ſuch their intention, remonſtrated, that if they ſhould be able to proceed ſo far, the ſhip would fall into pieces, as the Pole would draw all the iron work out of her.

[d] The Weighgatt is ſo called from the wind which blows through this ſtrait, [*waiben*, to blow] becauſe a ſtrong S. W. wind blows out of it. Another name for it is *Hindelopen*.—See Martens's Voyage, p 27.

On this Captain Wilſon and Mr. Ware deſiſted, as the crew had theſe very ſingular apprehenſions; eſpecially as they had no whales in ſight to the Northward, which alone would juſtify the attempt to their owners[e]. It need ſcarcely be obſerved, however, that the notion which prevailed among the crew ſhews, that the common ſeamen on board the Greenland ſhips conceive, that the ſea is open to the Pole; they would otherwiſe have objected on account of the ice being ſuppoſed to increaſe. It ſhould ſeem alſo, that the practicability of reaching the Pole is a point which they often diſcuſs amongſt themſelves.

In *this ſame year and month*, Mr. John Adams (who now is maſter of a flouriſhing academy at Waltham Abbey, in Eſſex) was on board the Unicorn, Captain Guy, when they anchored in Magdalena Bay[f], on the Weſtern coaſt of Spitzbergen and N. lat. 79° 35′.

They continued in this bay for three or four days, and then ſtood to the Southward, when the wind freſhning from that quarter, but the weather foggy, they proceeded with an eaſy ſail for four days, expecting to meet with fields of ice, to which they might make faſt; but they did not encounter ſo much as a piece that floated. On the fifth day the wind veered to the Weſtward, the weather cleared up, and Mr. Adams had a good obſervation (the Sun above the Pole [g]) by which he found himſelf three degrees to the Northward of Hakluyt's Headland, or in N. lat. 83.

Captain Guy now declared, that he had never been ſo far to the Northward before, and crawled up to the main-top maſt head,

[e] This circumſtance of not ſeeing any whales in that direction accounts for Captain Guy's deſiſting, in the following inſtance, from ſailing to the Northward, as alſo in many others which I ſhall have occaſion to ſtate.

[f] The Greenland maſters moſt commonly call this bay Mac-Helena.

[g] The old navigators to theſe parts call this a *South Sun*.

accompanied

accompanied by the chief mate, whilſt the ſecond mate together with Mr. Adams went to the fore-top maſt head, from whence they ſaw a ſea as free from ice as any part of the Atlantic ocean, and it was the joint opinion of them all, that they might have reached the N. Pole.

The ſhip then ſtood to the Southward, and twelve hours afterwards Mr. Adams had a ſecond good obſervation (the Sun beneath the Pole) when their latitude was 82° 3′. In both theſe obſervations, Mr. Adams made an allowance of 5′ for the refraction, which, he ſays, was his captain's rule, who was now on his 59th or 60th voyage to the Greenland ſeas.

In the year 1756, Mr. James Montgomery, now a merchant in Preſcot-ſtreet, Goodman's-fields, but then maſter of the Providence, followed the whales during the month of June till he reached N. lat. 83, by obſervation. Another Greenland maſter informs me, that he remembers well the ice packed much to the Weſtward, but that the ſea was open to the Northward during that ſummer.

In 1762, David Boyd, then mate of the brig Betſy, was driven by a gale of wind from 79 to 82, odd minutes, by obſervation; during all which time he was beſet in ice. A Greenland maſter has likewiſe told me, that he recollects many other ſhips were driven to the N. E. from their fiſhing ſtations during that ſeaſon.

Mr. Jonathan Wheatley, now maſter of a Greenland ſhip, was in 1766 off Hakluyt's Headland[h], whence, not meeting with ſucceſs, he ſailed N. W. to 81½, in which latitude he could ſee no ice in any direction whatſoever from the maſt head, though there was a very heavy ſea from the N. E.

Mr. Wheatley alſo informs me, that whilſt he was off the Coaſt of Greenland, three Dutch Captains told him, that a ſhip

[h] He was then on board a ſhip called the Grampus.

of

of their nation had been in 89, and they all ſuppoſed, that the ſea in ſuch a latitude might be as free from ice as where they were fiſhing This account probably alludes to the Dutch man of war, on board of which Dr. Dallie happened to be, the circumſtances of which voyage I have ſtated in my former paper.

This ſame captain is ſo thoroughly perſuaded of being able to approach the Pole, that he will attempt it whenever an opportunity offers of doing it, without prejudice to his owners. On ſuch a voyage of diſcovery, he would not wiſh a larger veſſel than one of 90 tons[1], nor more than ten hands. I find, indeed, that this is the ſize of the ſhip, in which moſt of the early navigators attempted to proceed far to the Northward.

In 1769, Mr. John Thew, now maſter of a Greenland ſhip called the Riſing Sun, was in N. lat 82, and 100 leagues to the W. of Hakluyt's Headland. The circumſtances by which he ſuppoſed himſelf to have been in this ſituation, were ſtated to me in the preſence of a very able ſea officer, who told me afterwards, that he was perfectly ſatisfied with the accuracy of his account.

Captain John Clarke, of the Sea Horſe, at the latter end of June 1773, ſailed from the Headland N. N. E. to 81½, which he computed by his run from the Headland in 18 hours, having loſt ſight of it. At this time there was an open ſea to the Northward, and ſuch a ſwell from the N. E. that the ſhip would not ſtay, being under her double reef'd topſails, whilſt the wind blew freſh.

During this run from the Headland, Mr. Clarke fell in with Captain Robinſon in 81° 20′, whom I mentioned in my former paper as having reached 81½ in the ſame month and year, by a very accurate obſervation.

[1] Clipperton reached China in a bark not much exceeding ten tons, as did alſo Funnell, in another ſuch veſſel. Callander, vol. III. 223

This

This ſame Captain Robinſon, on the 28th of June laſt, paſſed by Hakluyt's Headland, lying off and on for ſeveral days, during which he was ſometimes a degree to the Northward of it, and till the 20th of July following, there was no obſtruction to his proceeding Northward; to which, however, he had no inducement, as he caught two large whales in this latitude[k].

Captain John Reed, of the Rockingham, alſo in July laſt, purſued ſome whales 15 leagues to the Northward of the Headland, and confirms Captain Robinſon's laſt account, by ſaying, he could then ſee no ice from his maſt head.

Captain Reed was brought up in the Greenland fiſhery, and remembers well, that whilſt on board his father's ſhip, the Thiſtle, the mate told him, that they had reached 81° 42′, when there was indeed a good deal of ice, but full room to ſail in any direction.

Mr. Reed likewiſe hath informed me, that about 15 years ago, a Dutch Captain (whoſe name was Hans Derrick) told him, whilſt they were together in the Greenland ſeas, that he had been in N. lat. 86, when there were only ſome ſmall pieces of floating ice to be ſeen. Hans Derrick moreover added, that there were then five other ſhips in company, which took one with another eighteen ſmall whales.

I have great reaſon to expect ſeveral other inſtances of the ſame kind, in a ſhort time, from the different ports of this kingdom where there is any conſiderable Greenland trade: I ſhall not, however, trouble the Society with them, till I know whether they would wiſh any further information on this head.

I ſhall now recapitulate the different latitudes which have been reached by the ſeveral navigators whoſe names I have mentioned

[k] The ſecond part of Marten's's voyage (who received certain queries from the Royal Society) begins almoſt by ſaying, "We failed to the "81ſt degree, and no ſhip ventured further that year," viz. 1671.

in

in this and my former paper. I ſhall alſo take credit for nearly a degree to the Northward of their ſeveral ſituations, becauſe the *blink. or glare* of the *packed ice* is to be diſtinguiſhed at this diſtance, when the weather is tolerably fair.

80°. 45′. Captain John Reed.
81°. For three weeks together, Captain Thomas Robinſon.
81°. odd minutes, Captain John Phillips.
81°. 30′. Four inſtances; *viz.* James Hutton, Jonathan Wheatley, Thomas Robinſon, John Clarke.
82°. Two inſtances; *viz.* Captains Cheyne and Thew.
82°. odd minutes. Two inſtances; *viz.* Cluny and David Boyd.
82°. 15′. Mr. George Ware.
83°. Two inſtances; Mr. John Adams and Mr. James Montgomery.
83°. 30′. Mr. James Watt, lieutenant in the royal navy.
86°. Five ſhips in company with Hans Derrick.
88°. Two inſtances; Captain Johnſon and Dr. Dallie; to which, perhaps, may be added Captain Monſon, as a third.
89°. Relation of the two Dutch maſters to Captain Goulden[g].
89°. 30′. Dutch relation to Mr. Grey.

DAINES BARRINGTON, F. R. S.

[g] This inſtance, however, hath before been relied upon, though never, perhaps, circumſtantially ſtated, but by Captain Wood.

POST-

POSTSCRIPT.

January 8, 1775.

HAVING procured the three following inſtances before the reading of my paper was finiſhed, it may not be improper to add them in a poſtſcript.

In Harris's Voyages [h] is the following paſſage, "By the Dutch Journals they get into N. lat. 88° 56′, and the ſea open."

I have within theſe few days aſked Dr. Campbell, the very able compiler of theſe voyages, upon what authority he inſerted this account? Who informs me, that he received it from Holland about 30 years ago, as being an extract from the journals, produced to the States General in 1665, on the application for a diſcovery of the N. E. paſſage to Japan, which was fruſtrated by the Dutch Eaſt-India Company.

In the *Journal des Sçavans*, for the month of October 1774 [i], is likewiſe the following paragraph:

"To theſe inſtances produced by Mr. Barrington" [of navigators having reached high Northern latitudes], "our countrymen "(*viz.* the Dutch) could add many others. An able officer in "the Engliſh ſervice hath in his cuſtody the journals of a "Greenland ſhip, wherein he hath remarked, that in the month "of May he had penetrated as far as 82° 20′, when the ſea was "open."

My third and laſt inſtance is that of Captain Bateſon, who ſailed in 1773, from Liverpool, in a ſhip called the Whale, on the Greenland fiſhery, and who, on June 14, reached N. lat.

[h] Vol. II. p. 453.

[i] Part II. p. 503.

82°

82° 15′, computed by his runback to Hakluyt's Headland [k]. As this happened so recently, Captain Bateson (as well as many of the other masters, whose accounts I have before mentioned) hath his journal to produce, if it should be required.

This seems to be the strongest confirmation of both Captain Robinson and Captain Clark's having been, during this same year and month, in 81½; as also of their having met each other in 81° 20′, according to what I have already stated.

I must not lose this same opportunity of laying before the Society the information which I have just now received from M. de Buffon, in relation to what I have cited from his Natural History of Captain Monson's having reached N. lat. 88°, "*as he was* "*told by persons of credit.*"

Upon my taking the liberty to inquire, *who those persons of credit were?* Monf. de Buffon refers me to Dr. Nathan Hickman, who in 1730 travelled as one of Dr. Ratcliff's fellows [l]; and who supposed, that Captain Monson's journal might have been at that time procured in England. Monf. de Buffon also recollects, that a Dutchman was then present, and confirmed the account.

[k] His inducement to proceed so far North, was the pursuit of whales. I have shewn the extracts from Captain Bateson's journal to a very able sea officer, who is perfectly satisfied with the accuracy of it.

[l] He was also a fellow of the Royal Society in 1730.

ADDI-

ADDITIONAL PAPERS

FROM

H U L L.

WHILST I was waiting in expectation of several additional instances of Dutch ships, which had been in high Northern latitudes, I received the following answers to certain queries relative to the Greenland seas from a very eminent merchant of Hull, and which he is so obliging as to permit me to lay before the public. March 31, 1775. *D. B.*

I. From Captain John Hall of the *King of Prussia*.

Answer to 1st Query, *viz.* How near hath any ship approached the Pole?

I have known ships go into the latitude of 84° North, and did not hear of any difficulty they met with; but it is not often that the ice will permit them to go so far North.

N B. On enquiring of Captain Hall what ships he had known proceed so far? He replied, they were some Dutch ships he heard had done so, but knew no particulars.

2d Query. When are the Polar seas most free from ice?

The seas are most incumbered with ice from about the 1st of September to the 1st of June following; and in consequence, between the 1st of June and September, the ice lieth furthest from Spitzbergen. And I know no other precaution to be taken,

 respecting

respecting the Pole, than that they must watch the opportunity when the ice lieth furthest from the land.

3d Query. How far to the Southward have you first seen ice?

In the space of twenty years, I have twice known that we met with the ice in the latitude of 74° 30′ North, and could not find a passage to the Northward till the month of July, and then got into the latitude of 78° with much difficulty, in running through the openings of great bodies of ice; and some years we find a passage to the latitudes 79 and 80° North, without much difficulty from the ice. Some years I have known ships go round the North part of Spitzbergen, and so come out between Nova Zembla and the South part of Spitzbergen; but this passage is seldom to be found free from ice.

4th Query. From what quarter is the wind coldest whilst off Spitzbergen?

Northerly and E. N. E. winds are most frosty; but snow and frost we have very common with all winds, except during part of June, July, and August. If the winds be Southerly the weather is milder, but subject to snow, sleet, and thick weather. The winds, currents, and the ice are very variable.

The opinion of the old seamen is, that we may proceed further North than ever has been yet attempted; but this must be done with caution. An opportunity is to be watched for in those seas. The most likely time for such discoveries to be made is in the months of July and August, when the ice is most commonly furthest from the land; but some years not to be found open at all from the land. And when it is open, they must observe the ice to lay a long way from the North part of Spitzbergen; for I have known ships that made attempts to go to the Northward,

Northward, and before they returned back, the ice ſet in with the land, ſo that they have been obliged to leave the ſhips to the Eaſt of Spitzbergen.

N. B. The ice always ſets in with the land the back of the year.

II. From Captain HUMPHRY FORD of the *Mancheſter*.

1ſt. I was once as high as the latitude 81° 30′ North, in the ſhip Dolphin of Newcaſtle, in the year 1759 or 60, and have been ſeveral times ſince as high as the latitude 81° in the ſhips Annabella and Mancheſter, in which latitude I never met with any uncommon circumſtances, but ſuch as I have met with in the latitudes 75, 76, 77, 78, and 79°; if to the weſtward, I was commonly incumbered with large quantities of ice.

2d. I ſuppoſe that the Greenland ſeas are moſt incumbered with ice in the months of December, January, February, and March; for in the latter part of April, and the firſt of May, the ice generally begins to ſeparate and open; and in the months of June and July, we generally find the Greenland ſeas moſt clear of ice.

3d. The only precaution to be taken, in order to proceed towards the Pole, is to fit out two ſtrong ſhips that are handy and ſail faſt, well equipped, and ſecured in the manner of thoſe that are generally ſent to Greenland on the whale fiſhery. Such ſhips ſhould be manned with about forty able ſeamen in each, and victualled for eighteen months or two years, and be entirely under the command of ſome expert, able, and experienced ſeaman, who has frequented thoſe ſeas for ſome time paſt. They ſhould ſail from England about the middle of April, in order to be be in with the edge of the ice about the 10th of May, when it begins to ſeparate and open.

4th. There is not the leaſt reaſon to ſuppoſe, that the ſeas to the Weſt, North-weſt, and North of Spitzbergen are covered with permanent and perpetual ice, ſo as never to be opened by the operation of the winds; for daily experience ſhews us, that a Northerly wind, when of any long duration, opens and ſeparates the ice, ſo as to admit of ſhips going amongſt it in ſundry places to a very high latitude, if attempted.

N. B. I never was to the Eaſtward of Spitzbergen; but am of opinion, that the ice is much the ſame there as to the North and North-weſt of Spitzbergen.

I generally find that Northerly winds bring froſt and ſnow; on the contrary, Southerly winds bring mild weather and rain; but none of thoſe winds appear to be periodical, except cloſe in with the land, called Fair Foreland, where I generally find the winds in the months of June and July to blow moſtly from the S. S. W. and very often exceſſive ſtrong.

It is my opinion, by obſerving the above, that in ſome years ſhips might ſail very nigh the Pole; if not, the impracticability muſt ariſe from the large quantity of ice that lies in thoſe ſeas.

III. From Captain Ralph Dale of the *Ann and Elizabeth.*

I am willing to give you my opinion, in regard to the queries received of you, ſo far as my obſervations will juſtify.

1ſt. In the year 1773, I ſailed North 81°, when I was much incommoded with large fields of ice, but the air was not ſen-

 ſibly

ſibly different there from what I found it a few more degrees Southerly.

2d. I have for many years uſed the Greenland fiſhery ; and have, by experience, found thoſe ſeas the leaſt incumbered with ice betwixt the forepart of May till July.

3d. The ſame year I ſailed to the latitude above-mentioned, I found in May, to the Weſt of Spitzbergen, a fine open ſea, the wind then blowing South-weſt, and the ſea (as far as I could obſerve from the maſt-head) was little incumbered with ice, which fully convinced me that there was a probability of proceeding to a very high latitude.

4th. I have obſerved, that let the wind blow from what quarter it will, it is at times impregnated with froſt, ſnow, &c. ; but when moſt ſo I am not able to determine. As for rain, I do not recollect ever ſeeing any there. The weather I have generally found mildeſt when the wind blows Southerly. As for periodical winds, I do not ſuppoſe there are any in Greenland.

IV. From Captain JOHN GREENSHAW.

In regard to the Queries ſent to me, all I have to ſay is, that if a paſſage to the North Pole is ever to be accompliſhed, my opinion is, it muſt be obtained by going betwixt Greenland and Nova Zembla, as I myſelf have been to the Weſtward of Greenland, and reached ſo far to the Northward as 82° of North latitude, and to the North and North-weſt of that found nothing but a ſolid body of ice : my opinion, therefore, is, that it is impoſſible ever to obtain a paſſage that way. Captain John Cracroft, in the South Sea Company's time[1], was once ſo far as 83°

[1] The South Sea Company ſent a ſmall number of ſhips, for about nine years, on the Greenland fiſhery.

North

North latitude, and to the Northward of Greenland, and met with nothing but a ſolid field of ice. And in regard to the winds and weather, it freezes continually; but the wind from the Southward doth commonly bring rain and thick foggy weather, which is chiefly in the latter end of June and July. If you are to the Northward and Weſtward of Greenland, the wind from the N. W. and N. N. W. doth always open the ice; but at the ſame time, if it come to blow any time from that quarter, packs it cloſe in with the land; and the winds from the Southward have the contiary effect.

V.

The Queries anſwered by ANDREW FISHER, maſter of a Greenland ſhip at Hull, who has been twenty-four voyages from England to the Greenland ſeas.

1ſt. Said Andrew Fiſher ſays, that in the year 1746, being on board the ſhip Ann and Elizabeth from London, on a voyage to the Greenland ſeas, he ſteered from Hakluyt's Headland in Spitzbergen North and N. N. W. in clear water till they were in latitude 82° 34′, where they met with a looſe pack of ice, and made their fiſhery, or otherwiſe they might have got through that looſe ice, and doubt not, but that they might have gone conſiderably further Noith; they returned, however, in clear water to Spitzbergen.

2d. Beſt ſeaſons of the year are, to be at or near Spitzbergen from the 15th of May to the 1ſt of June, though the years differ, and the laying of the ice exceedingly; ſome years it is not poſſible to get North of 80°; at other times you may meet with very little ice, which is chiefly owing to the weather in winter, and the winds in April and May.

3d. There

3d. There is not any reaſon to ſuppoſe, that there is any permanent ice, either North or Weſt of Spitzbergen, ſo far as 90°; and it hath been always found, by able and experienced navigators, that there is not near the quantity of ice, nor ſo liable to ſet faſt to the North of Spitzbergen, as there is to the South of 80° as far as 74°, owing to the continent of America (called Gallampus land by the ſailors) and Spitzbergen, which makes a narrow paſſage in proportion to what it is to the North of Spitzbergen. The land of America is ſometimes ſeen by our Greenland traders from latitude 74° to 76°; and as it is not ſeen any further North, is ſuppoſed to round away to the North-weſt, which makes it imagined by many, that there is not any land near the Pole.

4. South winds bring moſt ſnow; North winds bring froſt; but that is in the month of April and two-thirds of May; after that time, to the 1ſt or 10th of July, it is in general mild, fine, clear, ſun-ſhine weather, and winds variable; after that again, often thick fogs and high winds.

5. It is very poſſible, by ſteering North or N. N. E. by the ſhip's compaſs, (if it can be ſo contrived as to have the card on the needle ſteady, and the winds prove favourable,) with a little perſeverance, a ſhip may get near the Pole, if they do not meet with rocks.

VI.

SIR,

IN the year 1766, trade being dull, I fitted a ſhip at my ſole expence to the Greenland ſeas; and the ſaid ſhip returned with one fiſh, eleven feet bone. Finding the trade could be conducted better in private hands than a company's, I was induced to ſend a ſecond ſhip in 1767, and as I had other concerns in ſhipping, thought it moſt prudent (being brought up to the ſea, and having made an eaſy fortune from it) to go a voyage to the Greenland ſeas, to ſee with my own eyes what chance there might be of making or loſing a fortune. So ſailed from Hull the 14th day of April, in my ſhip the British Queen, with an old experienced maſter, and on the 24th and 25th of April was in the latitude of 72°, catching ſeals amongſt great quantities of looſe ice. As we did not chooſe to ſtay in that latitude, we made the beſt of our way North; and after ſailing through looſe ice, which is commonly the caſe, about the 6th of May we were as far North as latitude 80°, (which is near what the maſters call *a fiſhing latitude*) and about 15 leagues Weſt of Hakluyt's Headland. I found the further North the leſs quantity of ice; and from the enquiry I made, both from the Engliſh and Dutch, which was very conſiderable, there is a great probability of ſhips going to the Pole, if not ſtopped by meeting land or rocks. It appeared to me, that the narroweſt place in thoſe ſeas was betwixt Spitzbergen and the American ſhore, where the current is obſerved to come always from the North, which fills this narrow place with ice, but in general looſe and floating in the ſummer, though I believe congealed and permanent in winter. Thoſe from whom I enquired informed me, that the ſea was abundantly clearer to the North of Spitzbergen, and the further North the clearer. This ſeems to prove a wide ocean and a great opening to the North, as the current comes from thence that fills this paſſage as aforeſaid. The beſt method of reaching the higheſt latitude in my opinion is, to hire two veſſels of about 250 tons burthen each, and if done on a frugal ſcheme, the ſame ſhips might be fitted for the whale fiſhery, and premiums given both for the uſe of the ſhip and crew, in proportion to their approach to the Pole, which,

from

from many circumſtances that may intervene, might be two or three years before they could complete their wiſhes. And it is more likely they might make their fiſhery ſooner than to the Southward; as, if they met with ice, the fiſh would be undiſturbed; if clear water and a good wind, they very ſoon might reach the Pole. What I mean by two veſſels is, one to foreſail the other at the diſtance of three or four leagues, as the latter may avoid the dangers the firſt might run into; and to be always ready, on ſeeing and hearing proper ſignals, to aid and aſſiſt, and by that means ſecure a retreat. I am alſo of opinion, that ſuch ſhips being ſent on diſcoveries are much more likely to ſucceed than his majeſty's ſhips and officers. The above hints I have pointed out for your conſideration; and if I can be of any further ſervice, may command, Sir,

Your moſt humble ſervant,

Hull,
March 4, 1774.

SAM. STANDIDGE.

I TAKE this opportunity of laying before the Public the following letter from Captain MARSHALL, maſter of a Greenland ſhip, to Captain HEATH, of the 41ſt Regiment, who formerly made two voyages to Spitzbergen.

SIR,

IN compliance with your requeſt of Wedneſday laſt, I acquaint you, that ſix years ago I was as high as eighty-two degrees, thirty minutes, North latitude, by obſervation, which is the higheſt I have ever been in; at that time I was mate of the Royal Exchange Greenlandman, of Newcaſtle. I do not know of any one who has been in a higher degree; but it has been reported at Newcaſtle (with what truth I cannot ſay) that Captain Greenſhaw, of London, had told his friends, that he had been as high North as eighty-four degrees.

The Dutch, I have been informed, have proceeded to eighty-three degrees, thirty minutes; but I have it only by hear-ſay.

In reſpect to your ſecond query, I remember, that about five years ſince, when I was maſter of the above-mentioned ſhip, I was in eighty-one degrees, North latitude, by obſervation, when there was a clear ſea to the Northward, as far as the eye could reach from the maſt-head; and I could not help obſerving to my people, that if it had happened that we were then upon diſcovery, we might have had a fine run to the North, as the wind blew freſh at South. The like clear ſea I have obſerved ſeveral times during the time I have been in the Greenland ſervice, which is now about twenty-one years. I have no doubt but that a navigator might reach a higher latitude than I have been in, provided he was well acquainted with the currents and the ice, for much depends thereon; and took the advantage of a favourable ſeaſon. I have remarked, that when the froſt has been ſevere in England, and to the ſouthward [m], there has been a great deal leſs ice to the northward, the enſuing ſummer than uſual; and the weather has been remarkably fine in Greenland: I have, for this reaſon, great expectations that the approaching ſeaſon will produce a ſucceſsful fiſhery, and that it will alſo afford an opportunity for a trial to reach the pole [n].

[m] I conceive that this ariſes from the ice becoming of a greater thickneſs during ſuch ſevere winters, and conſequently cannot be ſo ſoon broken up, or obſerved by the Greenland ſhips which return to the Southward, before the ice can have floated to them in the Spitzbergen ſeas.

[n] I am ſorry to have been informed, ſince the Bill for promoting diſcoveries paſſed, that the attempts to penetrate to the Northward will not be ſo frequent as I had flattered myſelf; becauſe, moſt of the Greenland veſſels being inſured, if any accident ſhould happen to a ſhip which is not proſecuting the whale fiſhery, the owners will not be entitled to recover.

But

But the greateſt difficulty attending a navigator in very high latitudes is how to get back again, for, ſhould he be beſet there in the ice, his ſituation would be very dangerous; for he might be detained a long time, if not for the whole winter. I ſpeak this from experience, for I was once beſet for three months, and was given up for loſt, and with difficulty got out.

Any further information in reſpect to the land, the currents, ice, or other particulars, you may wiſh to have, I ſhall very readily communicate it, and am,

SIR,

Your very humble Servant,

JAMES MARSHALL.

N° 5, Spring-ſtreet, Shadwell, Feb 25 1776

Captain Heath, to whom I am indebted for this communication, alſo informs me, that on the 15th of December, 1777, he minuted the following particulars from a perſon employed in the whale fiſhery.

" That being on board the Prince Frederick of Liverpool in " 1765, commanded by James Biſbrown, he reached the lati- " tude of 83° 40′, where he was beſet in ice for three weeks to " the Southward, but that he ſaw, during this time, an open " ſea to the North."

The Aſtronomer Royal having been ſo good as to furniſh me with the following memorandum, which he made at the time it bears date, I here ſubjoin it, as a well authenticated inſtance of a Navigator's having reached 84 degrees and a half of Northern latitude.

Mr.

Mr. Stephens, who went many voyages to the East-Indies, and made much use of the Lunar method of finding the Longitude, in which he is very expert, tells me this 16th of March, 1773, that he was formerly two voyages on the Greenland fishery; that in the 2d, in the year 1754, he was driven off Spitzbergen, together with a Dutch ship, by a S. S. E. wind, N. N. Westerly by compass into latitude 84 degrees and a half, or within 5 degrees and a half of the Pole, in which latitude he was near the end of the month of May. They saw no land after leaving Hackluits Headland, (or the Northern-most part of Spitzbergen,) and were back in the month of June. Did not find the cold excessive, and used little more than common clothing; met with but little ice, and the less the further they went to the Northward: met with no drift-wood. It is always clear weather with a North wind, and thick weather with a Southerly wind; nevertheless they could take the Sun's altitude for the latitude most days. The sea is quite smooth among the ice, as in the river Thames, and so they also found it to the North of Spitzbergen. Met with no ice higher than the ship's gunnel. Imagines it would hardly have been colder under the Pole, than they experienced it; although he thinks the cold rather increased on going Northward. Thinks the currents are very variable, and have no certain or constant direction. Says he has often tasted the ice, when the sea water has been let to run or dry off it, and always found it fresh. That the sea-water will freeze against the ship's bows and rigging, but he never saw it freeze in the ship. That it never freezes in the pumps. A little piece of ice detained under a large piece of ice, when it gets loose from it and comes up to the surface of the water, is very dangerous, it emerging with a force which will sometimes knock a hole in the bottom of the ship. The Dutch ship which was driven with them from

 Spitzbergen

Spitzbergen ran againſt a large piece of ice, and was loſt, the ſhips being then ſeparated to a conſiderable diſtance. The winds in theſe ſeas are generally Northerly; the Southerly winds are commonly damp and cold.

Having thus ſtated the memorandum as I received it from Dr. Maſkelyne, I ſhall now make ſome obſervations on the contents.

It appears by the preceding pages, that in this ſame year, *viz.* 1754, both Mr. Ware and Mr. Adams [o] ſailed to 82° and an half, and 83 degrees during the month of June, and both of them conceived that they might have reached the North Pole.

Mr. Maſter, by letter from Hull, dated February 24, 1777, hath procured me the following information from a friend of his, who, at my deſire, inquired at Whitby with regard to any ſhips having reached high Northern latitudes.

"Captain Brown of the Freelove ſays, that in the year 1770, "he was certainly in 82° North latitude, when the water was "clear. Captain Cole alſo of the Henrietta ſays, that in 1776, "he was near the latitude of 81° North, and after he was certain "of being in that latitude, he was, with ſtrong South Eaſt gales, "drove for three days to the Northward, but as he had thick "weather, the diſtance was uncertain. In the courſe of this "drift he met with nothing but looſe ice."

It appears alſo by the above account that Mr. Stephens had proceeded as far as 84° and an half, the ſea being open to the Northward a month earlier in this ſame year.

From this and other facts of the ſame kind, I cannot but infer that the attempt ſhould be made early in the ſeaſon; if I am right alſo in what I have before ſuppoſed, that the ice which often packs near the coaſts of Spitzbergen comes chiefly from the rivers, which empty themſelves into the Tartarian

[o] See the Probability of reaching the North Pole, p. 42, &c.

ſea,

ſea, it ſeems highly probable that this is the proper time of puſhing to the Northward, as the ice in ſuch rivers cannot be then completely broken up. What other ice therefore may be ſeen at this time is probably the remains of what was diſembogued during the preceding ſummer.

Another proof of this ariſes from what happened in 1773, for the Carcaſe and Race Horſe were obſtructed, at 80° and an half, by an immenſe bank of ice, during part of the months of July and Auguſt; but four Greenland maſters were a degree further to the Northward, during the [p] months of May and June, in the ſame year.

No one winters in Spitzbergen, but ſome few Ruſſians, from whom however we have not been informed what happens during that ſeaſon, though it ſhould ſeem from the obſervations of Barentz, thoſe of the Ruſſians in Maloy Brun, and a ſhip having puſhed into the Atlantic, from Hudſon's Bay, during the midſt of December [q], that the Northern Seas are then navigable.

For the ſame reaſon probably Clipperton [r], who paſſed the Straits of Magellan in the midſt of winter, ſaw no ice, which is ſo frequently met with at Midſummer by thoſe who ſail to the Southward of Cape Horn.

I take this opportunity of recapitulating the years ſince 1746 [s], during which it appears from the inſtances I have ſtated, that the ſea to the North of Spitzbergen hath been open, ſo as to permit

[p] See the Probability of reaching the North Pole, p. 4, 45, 46, and 57.

[q] See ibid. p. 83.

[r] See Callander's Collection of Voyages, vol. III. p. 461. Frezier was as far South as 58° in the middle of May, and ſaw no ice, though he ſpeaks of a S. E. wind as cold.

[s] Viz. 1746, 1751, 1752, 1754, 1756, 1759, 1763, 1765, 1766, 1769, 1771, and 1773.

attempts of approaching the Pole, which will ſhew that ſuch opportunities are not uncommon, and it is hoped that they will be more frequently embraced, from a parliamentary reward of 5000l. being given to ſuch of his Majeſty's ſubjects as ſhall firſt penetrate beyond the 89th degree of Northern latitude; the Bill for which purpoſe hath already paſſed both Houſes of Parliament [t].

AS it appears, by the two firſt collections of inſtances, that I have had much converſation with the officers of the royal navy, as well as maſters of Greenland ſhips, about a Polar voyage, I ſhall now ſtate ſeveral hints which have occaſionally dropped from them, with regard to proſecuting diſcoveries to the Northward.

The ſhip ſhould be ſuch as is commonly uſed in the Greenland fiſhery, or rather of a ſmaller ſize, as it works the more readily when the ice begins to pack round it.

There ſhould, on no account, be a larger complement of men than can be conveniently ſtowed in the boats, as it ſometimes happens, that the Greenland veſſels are loſt in the ice; but the crews generally eſcape by means of their boats. The crew alſo ſhould conſiſt of a larger proportion of ſmiths and carpenters than are uſually put on board common ſhips.

As it may happen, that the crews in boats may be kept a conſiderable time before they can reach either ſhip or ſhore,

[t] By the ſame Bill, a reward of 20,000l. is given to ſuch of his Majeſty's ſubjects as ſhall firſt diſcover a communication between the Atlantic and Pacific Oceans, in any direction whatſoever of the Northern Hemiſphere.

there ſhould be a ſort of awning, to be uſed occaſionally, if the weather ſhould prove very inclement.

As it is not wanted that the boats ſhould laſt many years, it is adviſed, that they ſhould be built of the lighteſt materials, becauſe on this account they are more eaſily dragged over the packed ice [u].

As it is poſſible alſo, that the crew may be obliged to winter within the Arctic circle, it is recommended, that the ſhip ſhould be balaſted with coals.

That there ſhould be a framed houſe of wood on board, to be made as long as poſſible, for the opportunity of exerciſe within doors [w].

That there ſhould be alſo a Ruſſian ſtove, as a fire in a common chimney does not warm the room equably.

It appears, by the accounts of the Dutch who wintered in Nova Zembla [x], as well as the Ruſſians who continued ſix years in Maloy Brun, that during this ſeaſon there are ſometimes days of a tolerable temperature; ſnow ſhoes, therefore, ſhould be provided, as alſo ſnow eyes, not to loſe the benefit of air and exerciſe during ſuch an interval [y]. The beard likewiſe ſhould be ſuf-

[u] General Oglethorpe informs me, that the Dutch veſſels on the Greenland fiſhery have three boats faſtened on each ſide of the ſhip, which may be ſufficient to contain the whole crew in caſe of accidents; and that the early diſcoverers had always what was called *a ſhip in quarters* on board, which might be put together when a creek, &c. was to be explored. He alſo adviſes, that the ſailing of the two ſhips, to be ſent in concert on diſcoveries, ſhould be previouſly tried, as there ſhould not be too great a diſparity in that circumſtance.

[w] On the Labradore Coaſt the furriers raiſe a wall of earth all round their huts, as high as the roof, which is found to contribute much to warmth within doors, ſo as to want little more heat than ariſes from the ſteam of lamps. Such wall is commonly three feet thick.

[x] The Ruſſian Hereticks, *of the old faith*, as they are ſtiled, ſometimes winter in Nova Zembla.—Account of Maloy Brun.

[y] A barrelled organ, which plays a few country dances, might amuſe during the dark months, as alſo be of uſe in the firſt intercourſe with the ſavages, muſick being a ſort of univerſal language; and Sir Francis Drake for that reaſon carried out muſicians with him.

fered to grow on the approach of winter, from which the Ruſſian couriers are enabled to ſupport the ſeverity of the open air.

Ruſſian boots, and the winter cap of the furriers of North America, are alſo recommended; but recourſe ſhould not be had to this warmeſt cloathing upon the firſt approach of winter, for by theſe means the Ruſſians do not commonly endure cold ſo well as the Engliſh; becauſe when the weather becomes exceſſively ſevere, they cannot well add to their warmth.

When the weather is very inclement, leads for the hands, dumb bells, and other ſuch exerciſes, ſhould be contrived for within-doors.

In order to prevent the ſcurvy likewiſe, frequent uſe of the fleſh-bruſh is recommended, as alſo occaſionally a warm bath, from which James's crew received great benefit, when they wintered on Charlton Iſland.

With regard to the proviſions, I ſhall here inſert a method of curing meat, communicated to me by Admiral Sir Charles Knowles, the good effects of which both himſelf and others have frequently experienced [z].

The

[z] So ſoon as the ox is killed, let it be ſkinned and cut up into pieces, fit for uſe, as quick as poſſible, and ſalted whilſt the meat is hot; for which purpoſe, have a ſufficient quantity of ſalt-petre and bay-ſalt pounded together, and made hot in an oven, of each equal parts; with this ſprinkle the meat, at the rate of about two ounces to the pound. Then lay the pieces on ſhelving boards to drain for 24 hours; which done, turn them and repeat the ſame operation, and let them lay for 24 hours longer, by which time the ſalt will be all melted, and have penetrated the meat, and the juices be drained off. Each piece muſt then be wiped dry with clean coarſe cloths, and a ſufficient quantity of common ſalt, made hot likewiſe in an oven, and mixed (when taken out) with about one-third brown ſugar. The caſks being ready, rub each piece well with this mixture, and pack them well down, allowing half a pound of the ſalt and ſugar to each pound of meat, and it will keep good ſeveral years.

The flour ſhould be kiln-dried, and put into tight barrels which are capable of holding liquids[a]. Flour thus preſerved and packed hath been perfectly good for more than three years, without the leaſt appearance of the weevils.

To make the beſt uſe of flour thus preſerved, there ſhould be both a biſcuit-maker and an oven on board.

With regard to liquors, a large quantity of ſhrub from the beſt ſpirits and fruits is recommended, which ſhould alſo be made juſt before the voyage takes place; the ſtronger the ſpirit, the leſs ſtowage. Dampier preferred Vidonia to other wines, on account of its acidity; and perhaps Old Hock might ſtill anſwer better.

I ſhould ſtand in need of many apologies, for having ſuggeſted theſe hints to Northern diſcoverers, had I not received them from officers of the royal navy, as well as Greenland maſters, and eminent phyſicians; if any one of theſe particulars, however, would not have been otherwiſe thought of upon fitting out the ſhip for ſuch a voyage, and ſhould be attended with any good effects, it will become my beſt excuſe.

In order alſo to promote ſuch a voyage of diſcovery, I ſhould conceive, that extending the parliamentary reward of twenty thouſand pounds by 18 G. II. c. 17. for the paſſage to the Pacific Ocean through Hudſon's Bay, to a Northern communication

N. B. It is beſt to proportion the caſks or barrels to the quantity conſumed at a time, as the ſeldomer the meat is expoſed to the air the better. The ſame proceſs does for pork, only a larger quantity of ſalt, and leſs ſugar; but the preſervation of both equally depends on the meat's being hot when firſt ſalted. Sir John Narborough ſalted young ſeals, and Sir Richard Hawkins many barrels of Pengwyns, both of which are ſaid to have been wholeſome and palatable: fiſh likewiſe caught at the approach of winter might be ſo cured, or indeed preſerved, by the froſt without any ſalt. Captain Cook's precautions need not be here alluded to.

[a] Woodes Rogers obſerves in his voyage, that the water which he had brought with him from England on his arrival at Juan Fernandez, was all ſpoiled by the caſks being bad. Callander 3. p. 259.

between

between the Atlantic and Pacific Oceans in any direction whatsoever, might greatly contribute to the attempting such an enterprize.

To this, another incitement might be perhaps added, by giving one thousand pounds for every degree of Northern latitude which might be reached by the adventurer from 85° to the Pole, as some so very peremptorily deny all former instances of having penetrated to such high latitudes. An Act hath accordingly passed for the first of these purposes; and for the second, with this variation, that a reward of 5000l is given only for approaching within a degree of the Pole.

I shall conclude, however, in answer to their incredulity, by the following citation from Hakluyt:

"Now, lest you should make small account of ancient writers, or of their experience, which travelled before our times, reckoning their authority amongst fables of no importance, I have, for the better assurance of those proofs, set down part of a discourse written in the Saxon tongue, and translated into English by Mr. Nowel, servant to master secretary Cecil, wherein is described a navigation, which one Ochter made in the time of king Alfred, king of West Saxe, anno 871; the words of which discourse are these: 'He sailed right North, having always the desert land on the starboard, and on the larboard the main sea, continuing his course till he perceived the coast bowed directly towards the east, &c.' Whereby it appeareth, that he went the same way that we do now yearly trade by St. Nicholas into Muscovia, which no man in our age knew for certainty to be sea, till it was again discovered by the English in the time of Edward VI.

"Nevertheless, if any man should have taken this voyage in hand, by the encouragement of this only author [b], he should "have

[b] Perhaps the same sea is alluded to in the following line of Dionysius:

Πόντον μὲν καλέουσι, πεπηγότα, κρόνιόν, τε.

As the name of *Frozen* can scarcely be applied to that of the Baltic.

As

" have been thought but simple, considering that this navigation
" was written so many years past, in so barbarous a tongue, by
" one only obscure author; and yet, in these our days, we find
" by our own experience, his reports to be true."

As for the Thule of the ancients, about which so many conjectures have been made, it seems to have most clearly been Ireland, from the manner in which Statius addresses a poem to Crispinus, whose father had carried the Emperor's commands to Thule:

——tu duce patrem, quantusque nigrantem
Fluctibus *occiduis*, *fessoq Hyperione* Thulen
Intravit *mandata* gerens.

It should also seem, from other parts of the same poem, that this General had crossed from Scotland to the North of Ireland, or Thule.

Quod si te magno tellus *frænata* parenti
Accipiat, quantum ferus exultabit Araxes?
Quanta *Caledonios* attollet gloria campos?
Cum tibi longævus referet trucis incola terræ,
Hic suetus dare jura parens, hoc cespite turmas
Affari; nitidas speculas, castellaque longé.
Aspicis? ille dedit cinxitque hæc mœnia fossâ.

Statius, v. 14.

Crispinus's father, therefore, must have resided some time in Scotland, from whence he went to Thule or Ireland, for the Hebrides (the only land to the *West* except Ireland) could not have been of sufficient consequence for the Emperor's commission, or the fortifications alluded to, besides, that the expression of *fessoque Hyperione* implies, that the land lay considerably to the Westward.

THOUGHTS

THOUGHTS

ON

The PROBABILITY, EXPEDIENCY, and UTILITY, of discovering a PASSAGE by the NORTH POLE[c].

THE possibility of making discoveries in this way (that is, by steering directly North) though now treated as paradoxical by many, was not, as will hereafter appear, formerly looked upon in that light, even by such as ought to be reputed the properest judges. There have been a variety of causes that at different times have retarded undertakings of the utmost importance to the human species. Among these we may justly consider the conduct of some great philosophers, who, as our judicious Verulam wisely observes, quitting the luminous path of experience to investigate the operations of nature, by their own speculations, imposed upon the bulk of mankind specious opinions for incontestable truths; which being propagated by their disciples, through a long series of years, captivated the minds of men, and thereby deprived them of that great instrument of science, the spirit of enquiry[d]. In succeeding ages a new impediment arose from the setting up profit as the ultimate object of discovery; and then, as might well

[c] I have lately received these reflections from a learned friend, who is now deceased, and who permitted me to print them, though not to inform the public to whom they are indebted for this very valuable communication. D. B.

[d] Baconi Opera, tom. IV. p. 100. *et alibi passim*. But these passages may be found collected in Shaw's Abridgement of Bacon's Works, vol. II. p. 52.

be

be expected, the preferring the private and particular gain of certain individuals to the general interests of the community, as well as to the interest of the whole world, in the extension of science. This it was that induced the States General, at the instance of their East India Company, to discourage all attempts for finding a North East passage, and to stifle such accounts as tended to shew that it was practicable. We may add to these, the sourness of disappointed navigators who endeavoured to render their own miscarriages proofs of the impracticability of any like attempts. This was the case of Captain Wood, who was shipwrecked upon Nova Zembla, and who declared, that all endeavours on that side were, and would be, found vain; though Barentz, who died there in a like expedition, affirmed, with his last breath, that, in his own opinion, such a passage might be found.

That the earth was spherical in its form, was an opinion very early entertained, and amongst the learned generally admitted. It seemed to be a plain deduction from thence, that a right line, passing through the globe, would terminate in two points diametrically opposite. Plato is thought to be the first who spoke of the inhabitants (if such there were) dwelling at or near those points, by the name of Antipodes. This doctrine occasioned disputes amongst philosophers for many ages; some maintained, some denied, and some treated it as absurd, ridiculous, and impossible [e]. Whoever will examine impartially the sentiments of these great men, weigh the contrariety of their opinions, and consider the singularity of their reasonings, will see and be convinced how unsatisfactory their notions were, and discover from thence,

[e] Lucr. de Natura Rerum, lib. I. ver. 1063. Cicer. Acad. Quæst. lib. V. Plin. Hist. Natural. lib. II. cap. 65. Plutarch. de Facie in Orbe Lunæ. Macrob. de Somn. Scip. lib. II.

thence, how inſufficient the ſubtle ſpeculations of the human underſtanding are towards ſettling points like theſe, when totally unaſſiſted by the lights of obſervation, and actual experience.

The diviſion of the globe by zones being agreeable to nature, the ancients diſtinguiſhed them very properly and accurately into two frigid, the Arctic and Antarctic circles; two temperate, lying between thoſe circles and the tropics; and the torrid zone within the tropics, equally divided by the equinoctial. But judging from their experience of the nature of the climates at the extremities of the zone which they inhabited, they concluded, that the frigid zones were utterly uninhabitable from cold, and the torrid from intolerable heat of the Sun. Pliny laments very pathetically upon this ſuppoſition, that the race of mankind were pent up in ſo ſmall a part of the earth. The poets, who were alſo no deſpicable philoſophers, heightened the horrors of theſe inhoſpitable regions by all the colouring of a warm and heated imagination [f]; but we now know, with the utmoſt certainty, that they were entirely miſtaken as to both. For within the Arctic circle there are countries inhabited as high nearly as we have diſcovered; and, if we may confide in the relations of thoſe who have been neareſt the Pole [g], the heat there is

[f] Cicero in Somnium Scipionis. Virgil. Georg. lib. I. Ovidii Met. lib. I. Tibullus Panegyr. ad Meſſalam, lib. IV. Plin. Hiſt. Natural. lib. II. cap. 68. Pomp. Mela de Situ Orbis, lib. I. cap. 1 Claudian. de Raptu Proſerpinæ, lib. I.

[g] That the earth had inhabitants even under the Poles, ſeems to have been believed by many at the latter end of the 16th Century, from the following lines.

“ Fond men! if we believe that men do live
 “ Under the zenith of both frozen poles,
“ Though none come thence advertiſements to give,
 “ Why bear we not the like faith of our ſouls.

Sir John Davis's *Noſce te ipſum*, probably written in 1596, from a compliment to Lord Keeper Egerton on his firſt receiving the Great Seal. D. B.

K very

very confiderable, in refpect to which our own navigators and the Dutch perfectly agree. In regard to the torrid zone, we have now not the leaft doubt of its being thoroughly inhabited; and, which is more wonderful, that the climates are very different there, according to the circumftances of their fituation. In Ethiopia, Arabia, and the Moluccas, exceedingly hot; but in the plains of Peru (and particularly at Quito) perfectly temperate, fo that the inhabitants never change their cloaths in any feafon of the year. The fentiments of the ancients therefore in this refpect are a proof how inadequate the faculties of the human mind are to difcuffions of this nature, when unaffifted by facts.

The Pythagorean fyftem of the univerfe revifed, and reftored near two hundred and fifty years ago by the celebrated Copernicus, met with a very difficult and flow reception, not only from the bulk of mankind, for that might have been well expected, but even from the learned; and fome very able aftronomers attempted to overturn and refute it[h]. Galileo Galilei wrote an admirable treatife in its fupport, in which he very fully removed moft of the popular objections[i]. This, however, expofed him to the rigour of the inquifition, and he was obliged to abjure the doctrine of the earth's motion. Our noble philofopher, the deep and acute Lord Verulam, could not abfolutely confide in the truth and certainty of the Copernican fyftem; but feems to think, that its facilitating aftronomical calculations was its principal recommendation, as if this had not been alfo a

[h] Amongft the moft confiderable of thefe was John Baptift Riccioli, who publifhed his *Almageftum Novum* with this view. Yet afterwards, in his *Aftronomia Reformata*, he found himfelf obliged to have recourfe to the doctrine of the earth's motion, that he might be able to give his calculations with a proper degree of exactnefs.

[i] This celebrated work of his was entitled, *Dialoghi de Siftemi di Tolomeo, e di Copernico.* This is much better known to the learned world by a Latin tranflation, which fo clearly proved the fuperiority of the Copernican fyftem, that the only means of refuting it was by the cenfures of the church.

very ſtrong preſumption at leaſt, if not a proof, of its veracity [k]. It was from this conſideration that the church of Rome at length thought fit ſo far to relax in her deciſions, as to permit the maintaining the earth's motion in phyſical and philoſophical diſquiſitions. But Sir Iſaac Newton, who built upon this baſis his experimental philoſophy, hath diſperſed all doubts on this ſubject, and ſhewn how the moſt ſublime diſcoveries may be made by the reciprocal aids of ſagacity and obſervation. On theſe grounds, therefore, all enquiries of this nature ought to proceed, without paying an implicit ſubmiſſion to the mere ſpeculative notions even of the greateſt men; but purſuing ſteadily the path of truth, under the direction of the light of experience.

It may be urged, in excuſe of the ancients, and even of our anceſtors in former times, that, as they were unaſſiſted by facts, they could only employ gueſs and conjecture, and that conſequently their concluſions were from thence erroneous. But to waive the viſible impropriety of deciding in points (where obſervation was ſo obviouſly neceſſary) without its direction; let us ſee whether this plea of alleviation may not be controverted in both caſes. Cornelius Nepos reports, that ſome Indians being caſt on ſhore in Germany were ſent by a prince of the Suevi to Quintus Metellus Celer, then the Roman proconſul in Gaul [l]. A very learned writer in diſcuſſing this point hath ſhewn, that it was poſſible for theſe Indians to have come by two different routs into the Baltic. He thinks, however, that it is very improbable they came by either, and ſuppoſes that they were either Norwegians, or ſome other wild people to whom, from their ſavage appearance, they gave the name of Indians [m]. But though this

[k] Shaw's Abridgment of Bacon's Works, vol. II. p. 21. where the doctor endeavours to defend this opinion.

[l] Plin. Hiſt. Nat. lib. II. cap. 67.

[m] Huet Hiſtoire de Commerce, et de la Navigation des Anciens, p. 531.

obſervation may well enough apply to the Romans, who at that time had no knowledge of theſe Northern people, yet it is not eaſy to conceive, that the Suevi could fall into this miſtake; or, if they did not, that they ſhould attempt to impoſe upon the Romans. It appears inconteſtably, that, in the time of king Alfred, the Northern ſeas were conſtantly navigated upon the ſame motives they are now; that is, for the ſake of catching whales and ſea-horſes [n]. Nicholas of Lynn, a Carmelite friar, ſailed to the moſt diſtant iſlands in the North, and even as high as the Pole. He dedicated an account of his diſcoveries to King Edward the Third, and was certainly a perſon of great learning and an able aſtronomer [o], if we may believe the celebrated Chaucer, who, in his Treatiſe on the Aſtrolabe, mentions him with great reſpect.

After Columbus diſcovered America under the auſpices of Ferdinand and Iſabella, the ſovereigns of Europe, and eſpecially Henry the Seventh, turned their thoughts towards, and gave great encouragement to diſcoveries. Mr. Robert Thorne, who reſided many years as a merchant in Spain, and who was afterwards mayor of Briſtol, wrote a letter to Henry the Eighth, in which he ſtrongly recommended a voyage to the North Pole. He gave his reaſons more at large in a long memorial to our ambaſſador in Spain, which ſhew him to have been a very judicious man, and for thoſe times a very able coſmographer; and accompanied this memorial with a map of the world, to prove

[n] See Barrington's Tranſlation of Oroſius from the Anglo-Saxon of king Alfred, part II. p. 9.

[o] Leland. Comment. de Script. Britan. cap. 370. Bale, vi. 25. Pits, p. 505. His deſcription was intituled, *Invent o Fortunata*; beſides which, he wrote, amongſt other things, a book, *De Mundi Revolutione*, which poſſibly may ſtill remain in the Bodleian Library. This friar, as Dr. Dee aſſerts, made five voyages into theſe Northern parts, and left an account of his diſcoveries from the latitude of 54° to the Pole.

the practicability of his proposal [p]. Though this project of his was not attended to, yet a variety of expeditions were made for discovering a passage by the North-west, and others by the North-east, into the South Seas on the one side, and into the Tartarian Ocean on the other, until at length both were declared impracticable by Captain James, and Captain Wood; soured by their own miscarriages, and being strongly persuaded, that, as they did not succeed, none else could. But even these unsuccessful voyages were not unprofitable to the nation upon the whole, as they opened a passage to many lucrative fisheries, such as those in Davis's Straits, Baffin's Bay, and on the Coast of Spitzbergen. Besides this, they laid open Hudson's Straits and Bay with the Coast on both sides, which have been already productive of many advantages, and which, in process of time, cannot fail of producing more, in consequence of our being in possession of Canada, and being thereby sole master of those seas and coasts.

It is, however, very remarkable, that notwithstanding the views, both of our traders and of such great men as were distinguished encouragers of discoveries, the ablest seamen (who without doubt are the best judges) were still inclined to this passage by the North, such as Captain Poole, Sir William Monson [q], and others; and this was still the more remarkable, as they were entirely guided therein by the lights of their own experience, having no knowledge of Mr. Thorne's proposal, or of the sentiments of each other. From the reason of the thing, however, they uniformly concurred in the motives they suggested for such an undertaking. They asserted, that this passage would be

[p] Hakluyt's Voyages, vol. I. p. 212—220. The letter to Dr. Lee who was the king's ambassador in Spain, is dated *A. D.* 1527. This Mr. Thorne's father was engaged, with others, in the discovery of Newfoundland.

[q] Naval Tracts, p. 435.

much

much ſhorter and eaſier than any of thoſe by the North-weſt or North-eaſt; that it would be more healthy for the ſeamen, and attended with fewer inconveniences; that it would probably open a paſſage to new countries; and, finally, that the experiment might be made with very little hazard, at a ſmall expence, and would redound highly to our national honour, if attended with ſucceſs. It may be then demanded, why it has not hitherto been attempted, and what objections have retarded a ſcheme ſo viſibly advantageous? Theſe objections, as far as they can be collected, are the fear of periſhing by exceſſive cold, the danger of being blocked up in ice, and the apprehenſion that there could be no certainty of preſerving the uſe of the compaſs under or near the Pole.

In reſpect to the firſt, we have already mentioned that the ancients had taken up an opinion, that the ſeas in the frigid zone were impaſſable, and the lands, if there were any, uninhabitable. The philoſophers of later ages fell into the ſame opinion, and maintained that the Poles were the ſources and principles of cold, which of courſe increaſed and grew exceſſive in approaching them [r]. But when the lights of experience were admitted to guide in ſuch reſearches, the truth of this notion came to be queſtioned, becauſe from facts it became probable, that there might be a diverſity of climates in the frigid as well as in the torrid zone. Charlton Iſland, in which Captain James wintered, lies in the bottom; that is, in the moſt Southern part of Hudſon's Bay, and in the ſame latitude with Cambridge, and the cold there was intolerable. The ſervants of the Hudſon's Bay Company trade annually in places ten degrees nearer the

[r] In the language of thoſe times, the Pole was ſtiled *Primum Frigidum*; and it was by ſuch groundleſs phraſes that men pretended to account for the operations of nature, without giving themſelves the trouble of experimental enquiries.

Pole,

Pole, without feeling any ſuch inconvenience. The city of Moſcow is in the ſame latitude with that of Edinburgh, and yet in winter the weather is almoſt as ſevere there as in Charlton Iſland. Nova Zembla hath no ſoil, herbage, or animals; and yet in Spitzbergen, in ſix degrees higher latitude, there are all three; and, on the top of the mountains in the moſt Northern part, men ſtrip themſelves of their ſhirts that they may cool their bodies[s]. The celebrated Mr. Boyle, from theſe and many other inſtances, rejected the long received notion that the Pole was the principle of cold. Captain Jonas Poole, who in 1610 ſailed in a veſſel of ſeventy tons to make diſcoveries towards the North, found the weather warm in near ſeventy-nine degrees of latitude, whilſt the ponds and lakes were unfrozen, which put him in hopes of finding a mild ſummer, and led him to believe, that a paſſage might be as ſoon found by the Pole as any other way whatever; and for this reaſon, that the Sun gave a great heat there, and that the ice was not near ſo thick as what he had met with in the latitude of ſeventy-three[t]. Indeed, the Dutchmen, who pretend to have advanced within a degree of the Pole, ſaid it was as hot there as in the ſummer at Amſterdam.

In theſe Northern voyages we hear very much of ice, and there is no doubt that veſſels are very much hindered and incommoded thereby. But after all, it is, in the opinion of able and experienced ſeamen, more formidable in appearance than fatal in its effects. When our earlieſt diſcoveries were made, and they reached farther North than we commonly ſail at preſent, it was performed in barks of ſeventy tons, with ſome trouble, no doubt, but with very little hazard. At this day it is known, that in no part of the world there are greater quantities of ice ſeen than in Hudſon's Bay, and yet there is no navigation ſafer,

[s] See Marten's Account of Spitzbergen, p. 105.

[t] Purchas's Pilgrims, vol. III. p. 702.

the

the company not loſing a ſhip in twenty years, and the ſeamen who are uſed to it are not troubled with any apprehenſions about it. It is no objection to this, that we hear almoſt every ſeaſon of ſhips loſt in the ice on the whale fiſhery; for theſe veſſels, inſtead of avoiding, induſtriouſly ſeek the ice, as amongſt it the whales are more commonly found, than in the open ſea. Being thus continually amongſt the ice, it is no wonder that they are ſometimes ſurrounded by it; and yet the men, when the ſhips are loſt, generally ſpeaking, eſcape. But in the ſeas near the Pole, it is very probable, there is little or no ice, for that is commonly formed in bays and rivers during winter, and does not break up and get into the ſea till the latter end of March or the beginning of April, when it begins to thaw upon the ſhores. It is alſo, when formed, very uncertain as to its continuance, being broken and driven about by the vehemence of the winds. As a proof of this we have an inſtance of a veſſel frozen in one of the harbours of Hudſon's Bay, which, by the breaking of the ice, drove to ſea, and, though it was Chriſtmas, found the Straits quite free from ice[u], which are frequently choaked with it in May and June, and made a ſafe and ſpeedy paſſage home. All our accounts agree that in very high latitudes there is leſs ice. Barentz, when his ſhip was frozen in Nova Zembla, heard the ice broken with a moſt horrible noiſe by an impetuous ſea from the North, a full proof that it was open. It is the invariable tradition of the Samoides and Tartars, who live beyond the Waygat, that the ſea is open to the North of Nova Zembla all the year; and the moſt knowing people in Ruſſia are of the ſame opinion. Theſe authorities ought certainly to have more weight than ſimple conjectures.

[u] Mr. Dobbs's Account of Hudſon's Bay, p. 69, 70.

The

The notion that approaching to a paſſage under the Pole would deſtroy the uſe of the compaſs, is a popular opinion without any juſt grounds to ſupport it. For it preſumes that the needle is directed by the Pole of the World; which it certainly is not, as appears from the needle's variation, and even the variation of that variation, which if this notion was true could never happen. In Sir Thomas Smith's ſound in Baffin's Bay, the variation was found to be fifty-ſix degrees Weſtward, the greateſt yet known. Captain Wood is very clear upon this point, and maintains, that no danger was to be apprehended from this cauſe [w]. Thoſe who aſſerted, that they had advanced within a degree of the Pole, eſtimated the variation there at five points of the compaſs. Captain Wood, in ſtating the account given of the Dutch ſeamen's voyage by Captain Goulden, omits one very material point, of which we are informed by Mr. Boyle, which is, that one of the Dutch captains coming over to England, Captain Goulden carried him to ſome of the Northern Company, who were perfectly ſatisfied as to the truth of his relation [x]. On the whole, therefore, whether we reſpect reaſon or facts, there are no juſt grounds for apprehenſions on this head, more eſpecially as there are other means by which the true ſituation of a veſſel might be determined, and the difficulty, if any aroſe, would be but of very ſhort continuance. But as ſuch a voyage could not fail of affording many new lights in reſpect to aſtronomy and geography, ſo in this reſpect alſo it muſt neceſſarily aſcertain fully what is at preſent only matter of doubt and conjecture.

[w] Wood's Voyage for the Diſcovery of a North-eaſt Paſſage, p. 139.

[x] See the honourable Mr. Boyle's Hiſtory of Cold, in reſpect to this and a multitude of other curious particulars, which ſhew with how much induſtry and care he ſtruggled to deliver truth from vulgar errors, and fiction.

As notions long received acquire from thence a degree of credit due only to truth; and as new opinions, contrary to these, and in other respects perhaps extraordinary in themselves, meet from these causes with slow and difficult belief, however they may appear to be supported by arguments, authorities, or facts (which it is presumed have been freely and fairly urged in the present case, to a degree that may at least entitle the matter to some attention); let us now proceed one step further. This shall be to shew, that what seems to be so repugnant to the common course of things (*viz.* that near the North Pole the cold should relax, and the ice be less troublesome) is perfectly conformable to the laws of nature, or, which is the same thing, to the will and wisdom of our great Creator If this can be proved, there can be no farther dispute as to the possibility of this passage; more especially when it shall also appear, that this affords a full solution of all the doubts that have been suggested, and at the same time clearly accounts for, and effectually confirms, the facts and reasonings deduced from them, which have been already advanced upon this subject. To come then at once to the point.

Sir Isaac Newton, who it is universally allowed was equally accurate, cautious, and judicious, in his philosophical decisions, hath demonstrated clearly, that the figure of this our earth is not spherical, but of an oblate spheroidal form, the diameter at the equator being the greatest, and at the axis the least of all the lines that can pass through the center. He also determined, by a most curious calculation, the proportion of these diameters to be as two hundred and thirty to two hundred and twenty-nine. These sentiments of his have been experimentally verified by the means which he also pointed out, *viz.* observing the motion of pendulums in very different latitudes, and the actual measurement of a degree at the equator and under the Arctic circle.

This

This laſt evidently proved the depreſſion of the earth's ſurface towards the Pole, which no doubt gradually increaſes. The very learned and ſagacious Dr. Hooke aſſerted, in one of his lectures, and brought very ſtrong reaſons to ſhew, that there is nothing but ſea at the Poles [y]. Theſe points then, being maturely conſidered, will be found to militate in favour of a free paſſage this way, and at the ſame time give much light into other things that have been advanced in the courſe of this enquiry, by ſhewing the true cauſes of thoſe facts that, at firſt ſight, have appeared to many very ſtrange and unaccountable. For example, if there be no land near the Pole, then there can be no bays in which ice can be formed to interrupt the navigation. Again, the rays of the Sun falling on ſo flat a ſurface, and being continually reflected from the water, muſt afford a great degree of heat to the air. At the ſame time this will account for the Sun's being ſeen by the Dutch in Nova Zembla a fortnight earlier than he ſhould have appeared, according to aſtronomical calculations [z]. Many other circumſtances might be mentioned, but theſe will doubtleſs occur to the intelligent, and therefore it is unneceſſary to dwell longer upon them.

The great injuſtice of rejecting opinions, on account of their appearing, at firſt ſight, paradoxical, or ſomewhat inconſiſtent with notions commonly received, having been clearly ſhewn, and the miſchievous conſequences flowing from it by various inſtances pointed out; the foundation of this conjecture, that there may be a paſſage near the Pole, having been fairly ſtated, the popular objections to it clearly removed, the general advantage (that might be expected from thence) placed in a proper light, and the conſiſtence of all the circumſtances relative

[y] Hooke's Poſthumous Works, p. 351.
[z] See Purchas, vol. III. p. 499, 500.

 thereto,

thereto, with the eſtabliſhed courſe of nature, having been alſo rendered evident; there can be nothing more looked for reſpecting this matter merely in the light of a philoſophical ſpeculation. But if ſupporting this had been the only motive, theſe reflections had not employed the time of the writer, or treſpaſſed ſo long upon the reader's patience. What then remains? To demonſtrate, that as the poſſibility, practicability, and facility, of ſuch an undertaking have been inſiſted upon, its national utility ſhould be ſhewn to deſerve conſideration; and that, as it is an object of the greateſt importance to the public welfare, its execution ſhould be no longer delayed. There is unqueſtionably no country in Europe ſo well ſituated for ſuch an enterprize as this. The tranſit from Shetland to the Northern parts of Aſia would, by this way, be a voyage only of a few weeks. The inhabitants of theſe iſlands and of the Orkneys are, and have been for many years, employed in the Greenland fiſheries, and the natives of theſe iſles are the perſons moſtly ſent to the eſtabliſhments in Hudſon's Bay. By theſe means they are inured to cold, to ice, and hard living, and are conſequently the fitteſt for being employed in ſuch expeditions. When this ſhall be once executed with ſucceſs, it will neceſſarily bring us acquainted with new Northern countries, where ordinary cloaths and other coarſe woollen goods will probably be acceptable, new channels of commerce would be thereby opened, our navigation extended, the number of our ſeamen augmented, without exhauſting our ſtrength in ſettling colonies, expoſing the lives of our ſailors in tedious and dangerous voyages through unwholeſome climates, or having any other trade in proſpect than that of exchanging our native commodities and manufactures for thoſe of other countries. This, if it could be brought about, would, in the firſt inſtance, convert a number of bleak and barren iſlands into cultivation, connect them and their inhabitants intimately with Britain, give bread to many thousands, and, by providing suitable rewards for many different species of industry, encourage population, and put an easy and effectual period to the mischiefs and scandal of emigrations. The benefits derived from these discoveries, and the commerce arising from them, will necessarily extend to all parts of our dominions. For however fit the poor people of those islands may be for such enterprizes, or however commodious the ports in their countries may be found for equipping and receiving vessels employed in these voyages, yet the commodities, manufactures, &c. must be furnished from all parts of the British empire, and of course be of universal advantage. These, as they are true, will it is hoped appear just and cogent reasons for wishing, that a project which has dwelt in the mouths and memories of some, and in the judgement and approbation of a few, from the time of Henry the Eighth, should be revived, and at length, for the benefit of his subjects, carried into effect, under the auspices of GEORGE the Third.

I HAVE mentioned in the preceding ſheets[a], that I expected ſome additional inſtances of Dutch ſhips, which had been in high Northern latitudes; but, though I delayed the publication for ſome weeks, they did not arrive time enough to appear with the others. I have however ſince received them from Profeſſor Allamand of Leyden, F. R. S. by means of Mr. Valltravers, F. R. S. &c. and take the earlieſt opportunity to lay them before the public as a valuable addition to the former papers.

To the Honourable DAINES BARRINGTON.

SIR,

HAVING made inquiries (agreeable to your deſire) from Profeſſor Allamand of Leyden, F. R. S. with regard to Dutch navigators, who have reached high Northern latitudes; he has been ſo kind to ſend me the following account, drawn up by Captain William May, a very diſtinguiſhed and experienced ſea officer in the Dutch ſervice, which begins with a letter from Mr. John Walig to his owners, who has been maſter of a Greenland ſhip ever ſince the year 1740. I am, &c.

ROD. VALLTRAVERS.

" To Meſſrs. NIC. and JACOB VAN STAPHORST.

" Helder, Jan. 3, 1775.

" IN anſwer to your letter of the 22d of December, concerning the queſtion, whether we have been nearer to the Pole than 80 deg. and a half, I muſt inform you, that we have been often to 81 deg. near the Seven Iſlands, to the Northward of the North-Eaſt land, and ſome have been in 82 deg.

[a] Page 52, in the additional papers from Hull.

" but

" but then not clear from ice, in which they drove about. I " never heard of any discoveries made there, as they have always " been fishers, who, driving with the ice to the Northward, leave " that direction upon getting room; and when now and then the " sea has been free from ice, that has happened commonly in the " months of June and July. In 1763, I spoke with a Scotch " Captain in Greenland, who told me he had been to 83 deg. " that the sea was then free from ice, but that he had made no " discoveries, without mentioning any more particulars, for we " ask after nothing but Whales. When I spoke to him it was " in July, and then we could get no further North than 79 deg. " 30 min. for the ice. In short, we can seldom proceed much " higher than 80 deg. and a half, but almost always to that " latitude, for it seems that the conjunction of the currents " often fastens the ice there. I fished last year from 80 deg. " 25 min. to 80 deg. 35 min. according to the land we made " afterwards.

" But in the year 1707, Captain Cornelis Gillis, having gone " without any ice far to the Northward of 81 deg. sailed to the " North of the Seven Islands, proceeded from thence East, and " afterwards S. E. remaining to the East of the North East " land, when coming again to latitude 80 deg. he discovered " about 25 miles [b] East, from the country to the N. E. very " high lands, on which, as far as we know, no body has ever " been. As to the season when the Spitzbergen seas may be " expected to be free from ice, I believe, according to my obser- " vations, that the most open sea to the Northward generally " happens in the month of September, but then the nights begin " and make the navigation dangerous. I am, &c.

" JOHN WALIG."

[b] Fifteen to a degree, at the Equator.

A SHORT

A SHORT

ACCOUNT OF NAVIGATORS

WHO HAVE REACHED

HIGH NORTHERN LATITUDES[c].

I WENT to Amſterdam the 26th of March, being the moſt proper time to make the deſired enquiries, and to obtain information from all the commanders that were to depart this year to Greenland; for then you meet ſix, eight, and more together, in houſes where they enliſt their men. I am, however, ſorry to mention, that but few of thoſe commanders keep journals when they are near, or in the ice; but, notwithſtanding this, the accounts they give carry with them ſuch an air of truth, from being confirmed by minute circumſtances, and corroborated by ſo many witneſſes, that theſe relations (I verily believe) may be depended upon as well as ſome journals. I particularly applied myſelf, however, to thoſe to whom a great number of voyages had given experience, and (contrary to my expectations) met with men of candour and penetration. I thought it proper, likewiſe, to take the following extract of a journal, it ſhewing the common form in which ſome of them are kept.

[c] This account was drawn up by Captain William May, in the ſervice of the States, at the deſire of Profeſſor ALLAMAND of Leyden. See p. 94.

Tranſlation of part of a Journal kept on Board the VROW MARIA, Commander MARTIN BREET.

N. B. The ſun's altitudes were taken with an octant, and 12 min. allowed for the ſun's ſemi-diameter, refraction, and dip of the horizon; the longitude from Teneriff, the miles 15 to a degree at the equator, the bearings with a compaſs unrectified.

The 22d of April, 1771, ſailed from the Texel for Greenland. 8th of May, latitude, according to the run, 70 deg. 33 min. longitude 19 deg. 22 min. ſaw the firſt ice.

13 ditto, latitude 74 deg. 50 min. longitude 24 deg. 35. min. met with a border of ice.

14 ditto, latitude by obſervation, 75 deg. 44 min. longitude 26 deg. 13 min. came againſt ſome ice.

15 ditto, latitude 76 deg. 13 min. longitude 25 deg. 40 min. ſaw Spitzbergen, the South Cape bore E. N. E. 14 miles.

N. B. Drove about in the ice, made faſt to a field.

25 ditto, in the morning ſaw the North Foreland, N. E. by E. latitude 79 deg. 12 min. longitude 20 deg. 40 min.

26 ditto, latitude by obſervation 79 deg. 10 min.

27 ditto, againſt the ice.

28 ditto, paſt through ſome ice.

29 ditto, got faſt in the ice, ſaw two ſhips ſailing pretty freely in the E. N. E.

N. B. in the ice till the

7th of June got more room; beat to the Southward and made faſt to a field, ſaw land in the E. N. E. diſtance 14 or 15 miles, ſuppoſed it the Quade-hoek, latitude by obſervation, 79 deg. 58 min. made faſt to the ice till the

11 June, at noon, a violent ſtorm, wind S. W. latitude by obſervation 80 deg. 19 min. In the night drove towards the coaſts, for it blew too hard to carry ſail.

12 ditto, in the morning laid faſt in the ice, the ſtorm continued, and the ſhip ſo much preſt by the ice, that we were obliged to unhang the rudder.

13 ditto, hard preſt by the ice, latitude by obſervation 80 deg. 29 min. Remained preſt by the ice till the

18 ditto, latitude by obſervation 80 deg. 50 min. the ſhip not moveable.

19 ditto, latitude by obſervation 80 deg. 57 min. the ice in great motion.

20 ditto, faſt in the ice again, latitude by obſervation 80 deg. 58 min. calm till the

24 ditto, began to blow a ſtorm; got ſome room in the ice.

25 ditto, having got more room we advanced.

26 ditto, locked up again.

27 ditto, ſaw the land, namely, the Dorre Hoek, S. by E. half E. and the Vlakke Hoek, E. S. E. lay beſet till the

29 ditto, latitude by obſervation 80 deg. 16 min.

30 ditto, wind N. E.

1ſt of July, ſaw water in the W. S. W. which we had not ſeen for many days. In the afternoon got more room.

2 ditto, worked our way through as much ice as we could, wind E. N. E. towards the evening N. made faſt to a field.

3 ditto, at noon, ſaw the land, being the Robbe-bay, bearing S. W. by W. about one mile.

I have left out many little circumſtances reſpecting the wind, tides, &c. as thinking the above ſufficient for aſcertaining the latitudes, and to ſhew the method in which many of the Greenland maſters keep their journals. That year ſeems to have been

 favourable

favourable for getting more to the north, for notwithſtanding Mr. Breet met with ſo much ice, from the latitude of 79 deg. 30 min. to that of 80 deg. 58 min. Captain Jan Klaas Caſtricum, in the ſhip the Jonge Jan, at that very time of the year, and nearly in the ſame longitude, reached 81 deg. 40 min. by the medium of ſeveral obſervations with foreſtaffs, where he fiſhed with ſucceſs in company with Witje Jelles, who ſailed from Hamburg, and found but little ice. There were likewiſe two Engliſh ſhips, who ſailed ſo far to the north, that Caſtricum loſt ſight of them from the maſt head, which two ſhips returned in ſomething more than two days, and the Captains came on board of Caſtricum[d], and aſſured him that they had been to upwards of 83 degrees, and could have gone much further, as they had no obſtructions from ice, but finding no whales, they returned. I ſpoke at the ſame time with other commanders, who, having been in ſight of thoſe ſhips, confirmed Caſtricum's account.

Six of the oldeſt maſters aſſured me (amongſt whom were John Walig, Klaas Keuken, and J. Klaas Caſtricum) that they had known from 1730 to 1742 an old Engliſh commander, whoſe name was Krickrack[e]; it was his cuſtom between the fiſheries, if not obſtructed by ice, to ſail to the northward, and ſome of them affirm, that when they have been at an anchor in Brandewyn's-Bay, he once ſtayed away ten, and at another time twenty days, before his return, and they are very ſure that he reported (and they have reaſons to believe him) that

[d] Captain Caſtricum neither aſked their names, nor thoſe of their ſhips; all that he knew was, he ſaid if he remembered right, they ſailed from England.

[e] From 1730 to 1740, moſt of the maſters of Engliſh ſhips, fitted out for the Greenland trade, were Dutchmen.

he

he had been two degrees, and even more, north of the Seven Iſlands; all I could further learn of this Mr. Krickrack was, that in 1740 he was in the only ſhip ſent from England; that for ſeveral voyages he had the ſame ſhip's company; that in or about 1742 he had the command of a tranſport, on board of which he loſt his life by a muſket ball; they were certain that he kept journals, out of which they think much light might be obtained.

The greateſt part of the Dutch commanders live at the Helder. Mr. Walig and others aſſured me, that the moſt Northern voyage then ever heard of, and on which they could with certainty depend, was that of Jacob Schol in 1700, who had been ſo far North, that on his return he ſailed with a freſh gale of wind, due South, 48 hours, and then fell in with the Seven Iſlands; he conſequently had been (reckoning that run at only four Dutch miles an hour, which they thought too little) in upwards of 84 deg. N. latitude. As Mr. Schol was an inhabitant of the Helder, they told me that they would ſtrive to procure me his papers from his heirs; and, if I miſtake not, they ſaid that they had actually ſeen thoſe papers in their younger da s.

Finding that Mr. Van Keulen had put down (in his chart) the land diſcovered by Captain Gillis, mentioned in Mr. Walig's letter, I went to him, to ſee on what foundation he had placed that diſcovery; but as thoſe papers could not be found, I applied to Mr. Walig, who told me, that Mr Cornelius Gillis had been an inhabitant of the Helder; that Walig, together with Mr. Keuken, Mr. Baſke, and others, ſince dead, had often examined Gillis's papers, maps, &c. and found that he was an enterpriſing man, and very accurate in his remarks and charts; that his grandſon had his journals and other papers in his poſſeſſion; and his grand daughter, who was married to an officer of Walig's ſhip

(who

(who had formerly been a commander) had his charts, ſome of which that officer generally took with him, in order to correct them. I begged hard to have them, if only for twenty-four hours; and next morning Mr. Walig put into my hands the original draughts of all the diſcoveries Mr. Gillis ever made with regard to Spitzbergen, excepting ſome particular drawings of bays and views of land, with permiſſion to keep them in my poſſeſſion till Mr. Walig's return from Greenland; copies of which are here annexed[f], and Mr. Walig promiſed to procure me, if poſſible, all the papers of that old commander before he left the Texel, which I hope to receive in a few days, and ſhall not fail in ſending over every thing I find material. Aſking what particulars Mr. Walig and others remembered out of thoſe papers, they gave the following ſhort account. That Mr. Gillis paſſed more than a degree to the Northward of the Seven Iſlands, without any hindrance from ice, that he proceeded Eaſt for ſome leagues with an open ſea, then bent his courſe S. E. and afterwards South; ſaw in the latitude of 80 deg. to the Eaſt very high land, run through the Eaſt coaſt of the North Eaſt land, and entered the Waygats Streights, came to an anchor in Lamber-bay, and took two whales, and from thence proceeded to the Texel. Mr. Baſke gave alſo an account of his uncle's having, in company with three ſhips, entered Waygat's from the North, and advanced as far as the ſame bay, but found too much ice to get through, which the other three, being young commanders, made a trial of. The North paſſage, however, on their return being ſhut, and it being the beginning of September, they made preparation to leave their ſhips, in order to get over land to Smeerenberg, but the ice luckily giving way, they got out to

[f] Theſe were copies of the draughts of the different coaſts of Spitzbergen, of which Captain Gillis hath taken accurate ſurveys.

the

the Northward. Mr. Baſke, who is a curious man, promiſed me, amongſt other things, his thermometrical obſervations, which, by the converſation I had about them, I have reaſon to think will be accurate.

After having paſſed ſix mornings with a great number of our commanders quartered in different houſes, I find that ſcarcely a year had paſt, but ſome of them have been to 81 deg. North, but rarely found the ſeas free from ice.

This is all the information I have been able to procure during my ſhort ſtay at Amſterdam, which I would have prolonged, if a call to the Hague had not prevented me. I can only add, that waiting upon Mr. Boreel, that gentleman promiſed that he would order a ſearch to be made for the journals of thoſe ſhips which were formerly employed in protecting our Greenland fiſheries.

I muſt, however, not forget to mention a particular that Mr. Van Keulen acquainted me with. He had at his houſe, laſt ſummer, a converſation with a Ruſſian, who had paſt the winter laſt year in Spitzbergen, and gave him the following account. That being in the utmoſt diſtreſs, for want of eatables, on the North Coaſt, he made a trial to get with his boat towards the middle of the iſland, by means of the Bay of Wyde-bay in Gillis's map, into which he proceeded, till, to his great ſurpriſe, he fell into Wybe Janſz's Bay, and ſo came out to the South of Spitzbergen; but he had taken no notice of the depths of water. Being queſtioned as to that particular, he ſaid he was very ſure that he did not paſs through the Waygats.

In all my converſations with our Greenland commanders, I never failed to aſk which courſe they would take to reach high Northern latitudes; the reſult was, that they would never ſeek it to the Weſtward of Spitzbergen, but run out to the North, from the Weſt coaſt of Nova Zembla; Mr. Baſke's reaſons and thoſe of other commanders were,

1ſt. That

1ſt, That all the Weſtern coaſts of the Northern countries were, for the moſt part, free from ice, occaſioned from the winds and tides chiefly coming from the Eaſt, which experience proves.

2d, That the ice comes originally from the Tartarian rivers, for that the ſea never freezes but where it is calm, and at the ſame time a great quantity of ſnow falls.

3d, That near the Seven Iſlands navigators often meet with a great N. E. ſwell, which proves that at ſuch time the ſea, to a conſiderable diſtance to the N. E. is not locked up by the ice.

4th, That the drift wood could not come to the Northward of Spitzbergen, in caſe the ſeas between the North of Aſia and that iſland were frozen; whereas a great quantity of that wood is drove on the North coaſt of Iceland, which is a demonſtration that the currents come from the N. E.

5th, That in ſome of the trees the marks of the axe were very plain, and the colour of the wood ſo freſh, that they certainly had not been ſix months in the ſea.

6th, That ſome whole trees appeared with buds thereon, which they think could not have remained ſo freſh, if the trees had been a year in the ſalt water.

7th, That the Eaſt of Greenland was now diſcovered to the latitude of 79 deg. and a half, that it probably extended further to the N. N. E. which they look upon to be the cauſe of the ſtoppage of ice between that coaſt and Spitzbergen, and the reaſon why they never find a N. W. or Northerly ſwell.

8th, That generally all ſhips, which had once got to the North as far as 82 deg. met with little or no obſtructions from the ice; and more arguments to the ſame purpoſe. There were ſome, however, would rather make the trial between Spitzbergen and the land diſcovered by Mr. Gillis.

N. B. They knew nothing of the papers read before the Royal Society.

To

4

To ROD. VALLTRAVERS, Eſq; &c.

SIR,

PROFESSOR Allamand, being very deſirous that the incloſed might be ſent to you as ſoon as poſſible, has obliged me to draw up with haſte the above account of the informations I received at Amſterdam. In reading it over, and comparing it with my notes, I find no fault as to the facts related, whatever there may be in the manner in which it is drawn up; in caſe the whole or any part of it ſhould be thought worth publiſhing, I hope you will be ſo good as to have it corrected [g].

I could have made it more circumſtantial, as my notes are very full, in particular with regard to the reaſons our Commanders gave for not making the trial to the Weſt of Spitzbergen, &c.

I am informed that Mr. De Bougainville intends to go by the way of Nova Zembla [h].

I am, with profound reſpect,

SIR,

Your moſt obedient humble ſervant,

Leyden,
April 11th, 1775.

WILLIAM MAY.

[g] This hath been done in ſome trifling particulars, relative merely to the ſtile, as Captain May is not a native of England.

[h] This voyage of diſcovery, however, did not take place.

THUS do the Dutch feamen, employed in the Greenland fifhery, agree with our own countrymen, in never having fo much as heard of a perpetual barrier of fixed ice, to the Northward of Spitzbergen, in 80 deg. and a half[h], which indeed is one of their moft common latitudes for catching whales, whilft all of them fuppofe the fea to be generally open in thofe parts, and many of them proceed feveral degrees beyond it.

I fhall only add, that, in my former pamphlet[i], I have mentioned a fact or two, I had reafon to expect from the Rev. Mr. Tooke, Chaplain to the factory at Peterfburgh, which he conceived would ftrongly prove that the fea is open to the Pole, and which I have fince received in a letter from him dated the 26th of May laft.

Mr. Tooke hath been affured by feveral perfons, who have paffed the winter at Kola in Lapland, that in the fevereft weather, whenever a Northerly wind blows, the cold diminifhes inftantly, and that, if it continues, it always brings on a thaw as long as it lafts.

He hath alfo been informed by the fame authority, that the feamen who go out from Kola upon the whale and morfe fifheries early in March (for the fea never freezes there) throw off their winter garments as foon as they are from 50 to 100 werfts[k] from land, and continue without them all the time they are upon the fifhery, during which they experience no inconvenience from the cold, but that on their return (at the end of May) as they approach land, the cold increafes to fuch a feverity, that they fuffer greatly from it.

[h] One of them indeed fays, that the ice frequently *packs* in that latitude, which he fuppofes to arife from the meeting of two currents.

[i] Page 33, note [*s*].

[k] Three werfts make two miles.

This

This account agrees with that of Barentz, whilst he wintered in Nova Zembla [l], and that of the Russians in Maloy-Brun; the North wind cannot therefore, during the coldest seasons of the year, be supposed to blow over ten degrees of ice.

Governor Ellis indeed, whose zeal in prosecuting the attempt of discovering the N. W. passage through Hudson's Bay is so well known, hath suggested to me an argument, which seems to prove the absolute impossibility of a perpetual barrier of ice from 80 deg. and a half to the Pole.

If such a tract hath existed for centuries, the increase, in point of height, must be amazing in a course of years, by the snow, which falls during the winter, being changed into ice, and which must have formed consequently a mountain perhaps equal to the Pic of Teneriff [m]. Now the ice, which sometimes *packs* to the Northward of Spitzbergen, is said commonly not to exceed two yards in height. D. B.

[l] See, Thoughts on the Probability, &c. of reaching the North Pole, p. 83.

[m] Mr. De Luc observes also, that the ice upon the Glacieres is always increasing. See his interesting observations on those mountains of Switzerland.

 OBSER-

OBSERVATIONS

ON THE

FLOATING ICE,

WHICH IS FOUND

IN HIGH NORTHERN, AND SOUTHERN LATITUDES.

SINCE the return of the King's ſhips from voyages of diſcovery, both in high Northern and Southern latitudes, I have found that it hath been a diſputed point, whether the ice which they have met with was formed chiefly from the ſalt or freſh water. I ſhould rather conceive that this doubt muſt have ariſen from what is mentioned by the great Mr. Boyle, in his experiments on heat and cold; or from an obſervation of M. Adanſon, at the end of his voyage from Senegal, becauſe from the quantity of ice merely (at leaſt to the Northward) the early navigators never conceived that it was produced from ſea water.

In full proof of this, not to ſtate the opinion of ſeveral others on the ſame head, I ſhall content myſelf with citing that of Sir Martin Frobiſher, who is well known to have made three ſucceſſive voyages to Greenland, with a further intent of diſcovering the North Weſt paſſage from Europe to the Pacific Ocean.

Ocean. In the ſecond voyage of this celebrated navigator, he obſerves:

"We found none of theſe iſlands of ice ſalt in taſte, whereby it appears that they were not of the ocean water congealed, which is always ſalt, but of ſome ſtanding or little moving lakes; the main ſea freezes not, and therefore there is no *Mare Glaciale*." In his third voyage he moſt anxiouſly repeats this ſame opinion, and in ſtill ſtronger terms, ſo that what he hath thus laid down was not an occaſional obſervation merely, but what he had much reflected upon, and found to be confirmed by his experience in thoſe Northern Seas [n].

This opinion of Sir Martin Frobiſher's ſeems not to have been diſputed by any one, till the time of Mr. Boyle, who obſerves, that there are ſeveral in Amſterdam, who uſed to thaw the ice of ſea-water for brewing, and then cites Bartholinus *De Nivis uſu*. "*De glacie ex aquâ marinâ, certum eſt ſi reſolvatur, ſalſum ſaporem depoſuiſſe, quod non ita pridem expertus eſt Clariſſimus* FINKIUS *in glaciei fruſtis, ex portu noſtro allatis* [o]."

I ſhall not now criticiſe either what falls from Mr. Boyle himſelf, or from Bartholinus, though it is very clear that the ice alluded to by both muſt have probably been formed from freſh water, either in the rivers, or lakes which empty themſelves into the Zuyder Sea, becauſe I ſhall hereafter contradict the aſſertion of Bartholinus, by the actual experiment, which I have tried myſelf during the late hard froſt.

[n] See Hakluyt, Vol. II. p. 62 and 67. In 1776, Mr. Marſhall, Captain of a Greenland ſhip, was ſo good as to bring me a bottle of water, which was melted from ice found floating in the Spitzbergen ſeas, and which had not the leaſt ſaline taſte.

[o] Boyle's Works, Vol. II. p. 264. Folio.

To do juſtice indeed to Mr. Boyle, he afterwards, upon more mature conſideration, ſhews it to be his opinion, agreeable to that of Sir Martin Frobiſher, that the freſh water obtained from ice floating in the ſea proves it could not have been formed from the ocean, "becauſe the main ſea is ſeldom or ever frozen[p]."

The next author who ſuppoſes that congealed ſea-water is by this proceſs rendered ſweet to the taſte, is Monſ. Adanſon, who informs us, that, upon his return from Senegal in 1748, he carried two bottles of ſea-water, taken up on the coaſt of Africa, from Breſt to Paris, which, during an intenſe froſt, was ſo frozen as to burſt the bottles, and the contents afterwards became palatable[q].

To this fact I ſhortly anſwer, either that the bottles were changed, or otherwiſe that Monſ. ADANSON does not mention the circumſtance by which the taſte of the ſea-water was thus altered upon its being diſſolved. Mr. NAIRNE hath been much more accurate in ſtating his experiments with regard to the freezing ſea-water, in a paper read before the Royal Society on the 2d of February, 1776, as he mentions, that, in order to clear the ice from any brine which might adhere to it, he waſhed it in a pail of pump-water for a quarter of an hour, after which he informs the Society, that to his palate it was perfectly free from any taſte of ſalt.

This is moſt undoubtedly the fact, but Mr. Nairne does not ſeem to be aware from what circumſtance the ice thus melted had become freſh water[r]; and indeed I muſt admit, that upon the

[p] Boyle's Works, Vol. II. p. 302.

[q] Voyage au Senegal, p. 190.

[r] As Mr. Nairne, in his letter to Sir John Pringle, ſays that one of his great reaſons for trying theſe experiments was to determine whether the

the firſt experiment which I made with regard to freezing ſea-water, I deduced the ſame inference that he hath done, having waſhed it in freſh water for the ſame reaſon that he did, *viz.* to get rid of the brine which might adhere to the ſurface of the ice.

To determine, therefore, whence this freſhneſs in the thawed ice might ariſe, I placed a large piece of what remained frozen (without being waſhed at all in pump-water) to be diſſolved before the fire, which taſted very ſalt as one might naturally ſuppoſe.

The weather continuing to be very ſevere, I froze more ſea-water, repeating the experiment of freſhening it or not, by leaving, or not leaving it, in pump-water, which always turned out uniformly to be the ſame; and the reaſon of which is the following.

When ſea-water is frozen, it does not form ice ſimilar to that from freſh water, being by no means ſo ſolid or tranſparent, as it conſiſts of thin laminæ or plates, between which the brine is depoſited, and if the ice is accurately examined, the ſmall

the ice which floats in the Northern Seas is formed from the ſalt-water or not, he therefore ſhould have thawed the ice preciſely under the ſame circumſtances with the ſea-water adhering, as the navigators take it up. The truth is, that, if the piece of ice formed from ſea-water is at all large, the adhering ſalt water can ſcarcely affect the taſte at all, and I have melted the central parts of a pretty large maſs, which became very ſalt after diſſolution, though entirely detached from the ſea-water in which it had been frozen. "In the ſevere froſt laſt January (*viz.* 1775), "ſome ſalt-water, being ſet abroad, froze into an ice. which was not "ſolid but *porous*, the hollows being filled with the ſalteſt part of the "water, for the ice when *drained* was quite freſh. The ſalt-water being "again ſet abroad, froze as before, what remained ſtill unfrozen was "now become exceeding ſalt, but the ice drained and diſſolved was "little if at all brackiſh; by this experiment, if another time more fully "repeated, it may be found to what degree the ſaltneſs of water may "be increaſed, by continuing to freeze away the freſh water." Mr. Barker in Phil. Tranſ. Vol. LXVI. p. ii. 1776. p. 373.

portions

portions of brine between the plates may be eaſily diſtinguiſhed. If this brine therefore is removed, the laminæ of ice when diſſolved become ſweet to the taſte, but, if thawed together with the brine intercepted between the laminæ, the taſte is ſalt, nor can the ice be conſiderably diveſted of the brine, by merely leaving it to drain.

Having ſatisfied myſelf thus far from the freezing ſea-water by the natural cold, and under the common circumſtances of expoſing it to the air in ſmall china cups, I applied to Dr. Higgins to proſecute theſe trials with his more ample apparatus, and knowledge of chemiſtry; who was immediately ſo good as to ſuggeſt and try the following experiments, which will throw further light upon this ſubject[s].

"JANUARY 2d[t], 1776. A gallon, Wincheſter meaſure, of ſea-water, which I had freſh imported from Mr. Owen in Fleet-ſtreet, was placed in a ſhallow diſh of Welſh ware, glazed yellow; the depth of the water was three inches and a half in this ſhallow diſh, which I marked A. and placed on a brick wall eight feet high above the ground behind my houſe. This wall on the Eaſtern ſide faces the gardens belonging to five or ſix houſes in the ſame ſtreet with mine; and on the Weſtern ſide of it is the area between my houſe and the elaboratory; and Weſtward of my area is the garden of Meſſ. Wedgwood and Bentley, which I believe is forty feet wide, bounded on the Weſt by high buildings."

[s] It would be great injuſtice to Mr. Lomonoſoff, a Sweediſh chemiſt, not to mention that he ſeems to have tried experiments ſimilar to thoſe which I have made myſelf, and found the reſult to be as I have ſtated it. *Collection Académique*, Tom. XI. p. 5. & ſeq. 4to. *Paris*, 1772. See alſo the Probability of reaching the North Pole diſcuſſed, p. 37. Note [y].

[t] Mr. Nairne began his experiments at the latter end of this month.

"At

" At the ſame time I placed another gallon of the ſame ſea-water in a glaſs body. The column of water in this veſſel was about thirteen inches high, about ſix inches diameter at the baſe, and about three inches at the mouth of the veſſel. I placed this body with the ſea-water cloſe by the veſſel marked A; ſo that both were equally diſtant from the adjoining houſes; and after marking the glaſs body B, I covered the veſſels A and B with glaſs baſons in ſuch a manner, that the air might communicate with the ſurface of the water, but rain or ſnow might be excluded.

" A Thermometer was placed between theſe veſſels.

" From the 2d to the 7th of January, the mercury in the Thermometer ſtood, at various times, as low as thirty-one of Fahrenheit; and Thames water in ſhallow wooden veſſels, placed on the ground, near the wall above-mentioned, was often frozen to the thickneſs of a crown piece. But an earthen oil-jar containing twenty gallons of Thames water, and a like jar containing twenty gallons of diſtilled water, and each covered with a pewter diſh, preſerved the water contained in them from freezing during this interval.

" About the 7th of January, the mercury in the courſe of twenty-four hours did not riſe above thirty-one, but ſometimes ſunk to thirty. Ice was formed in the veſſel marked A; but none in the veſſel marked B. Ice was at the ſame time formed in the great jars containing Thames water and diſtilled water; and to a thickneſs much greater in the Thames water than in the water diſtilled. The ice obtained from the veſſel A was all formed on the ſurface of the water; and conſiſted of thin laminæ adhering to each other weakly, and intercepting in their interſtices a ſmall portion of water, which was ſaline to the taſte. This ice beaten gently with a glaſs peſtle to divide the laminæ,

 then

then drained, and then washed in distilled water, tasted like the ice of fresh water; and being placed in a glass funnel before a culinary fire, so that the water might drain off as soon as formed, it dissolved in half an hour, and not in less time, although the Thermometer placed at the same distance close to the funnel rose to 160; and the side of the funnel next to the fire was hot to the like degree, as nearly as could be ascertained by the touch. The water of the ice thus melted was fresh and palatable, and measured half a pint.

"From the 9th of January to the 11th inclusive, the mercury rose some days to forty, and during three or four hours on other days it sunk and remained at thirty, and sometimes for an hour or less it sunk to twenty-nine. But it did not remain at thirty during any of these days for more than four or five hours, unless at the hours of rest, when no observation was made. During this period, a thin coat of ice, like the former, was produced on the water in the shallow vessel A; but no ice was formed in the vessel B.

"January 12, the Thermometer pointed for several hours between thirty-one at the highest, and twenty-nine at the lowest. A thick crust of ice, of the texture before described, was formed in the vessel A. This ice broken, washed, and dissolved, became fresh water, measuring a pint or more. This quantity of ice, placed in a funnel before a fire, in the circumstances already described, was not all dissolved in an hour and ten minutes. No ice was formed in the vessel B[u].

[u] "The foregoing observations were committed to writing on the days when they were respectively made, but the day of the month was not then accurately noted. It may therefore be found that I have placed some of the foregoing temperatures a day before, or after that on which they were observed."

"January

"January the 13th at night, and 14th in the morning, the Thermometer ſunk for ſome hours below twenty-ſeven, and did not riſe during ſixteen hours above twenty-eight. The water in the veſſel A, remaining after the foregoing congelations, was frozen to the thickneſs of a quarter of an inch in the centre, and three quarters of an inch in the circumference, but no ice was formed at any greater depth in the water. This ice, like the former, was laminated, and when bruiſed and waſhed, it formed freſh water to the quantity of three pints.

"On the ſame day, *viz.* 14th of January, in the morning, the Thermometer pointing below twenty-ſeven, the Thames water in the great jar was frozen to the thickneſs of three or four inches, if not more, contiguous to the jar and the ſurface. The diſtilled Thames water in the other jar was frozen to the thickneſs of two inches, or thereabouts, and contiguous to the jar and ſurface of the water; and the ſea-water in the glaſs body marked B was for the firſt time frozen. On the ſurface, and in the center of this ſurface, the ice was half an inch thick; at the circumference it was an inch thick; and from the circumference and ſurface the ice formed contiguous to the glaſs, in ſuch a manner, that the cruſt was an inch thick near the glaſs and ſurface, but, as it proceeded downwards towards the wider part of the glaſs, it tapered to an edge, terminating within an inch of the bottom of the veſſel.

"Thus all the ice was formed on the ſurface and contiguous to the glaſs, and was thickeſt where the veſſel was narroweſt; that is, the quantity of ice was inverſely as the diameter of the veſſel. This ice reſembled that obtained in the ſhallow veſſel in its laminated ſtructure and ſpongineſs, and in its enveloping a portion of the ſalt-water, with this difference only, that the laminæ ſhot vertically, and from the circumference inclining to-

O 2 wards

wards the centre, not directly, but ſo as to form with the centre an angle of about 15 degrees. This ice bruiſed and waſhed, melted to a pint and a half of pleaſant freſh water. The time and heat were nearly the ſame as I deſcribed above.

" Mr. Barrington at this and former periods obſerved, that the ſeparation of the laminæ of the ice by bruiſing accelerated the effect produced by waſhing; that is, the extrication of the intercepted brine.

" January the 19th at night, the mercury in the Thermometer ſunk to twenty-ſix. The ſea-water, remaining after the foregoing congelations in the flat diſh marked A, was frozen ſo far, that only a pint remained fluid at the bottom. This ice was in all reſpects like the former portions. Bruiſed, waſhed, and melted, as on former occaſions, it gave a quart of freſh water. At the ſame time, the water in B was frozen in the manner before deſcribed, but in a larger quantity, and ſome laminæ of ice ſhot cloſe to the glaſs as far as the bottom of the veſſel. This ice bruiſed and waſhed as formerly, and placed before the fire in a glaſs funnel, melted in a heat of a hundred and ſixty, in an hour and a half, to one quart of freſh water.

" January the 20th, the mercury which ſtood at twenty-ſeven in the morning, and fell to twenty-ſix towards twelve o'clock, fell in a few hours to twenty-four, and, before nine at night, fell to twenty-three. Only a thin coat of ice was formed on the water in A, which I did not diſturb, expecting it to freeze deeper during the night. The water in the veſſel B was frozen to ſome thickneſs at the ſurface, and contiguous to the ſides of the glaſs body, but not at the bottom. Expecting a ſtronger congelation, I ſuffered this alſo to ſtand until the next morning, and conſequently could not determine the quantity of ice formed in it, otherwiſe than by feeling near the ſurface, whereby I preſumed

the

the quantity of ice to be equal to that laſt obtained, and formed in the ſame manner.

" January the 21ſt in the morning, the Thermometer pointed to twenty-eight. The thin cruſt of ice, obſerved on the preceding night, did not appear to be encreaſed or diminiſhed in the veſſel marked A. The laminæ of this ice adhered ſo weakly, that the whole cruſt could not be raiſed without breaking. This ice, bruiſed and well waſhed, diſſolved to near half a pint of water, brackiſh to the taſte. And the ſame day, in the morning, the ice in B was removed, bruiſed, and waſhed; it melted to a pint or more of freſh water.

" From the 21ſt to the 26th of January, the water in the veſſel marked B was frozen twice, and the ice formed each time was bruiſed and waſhed, and melted to freſh water, both portions meaſuring one pint or more.

" From the 26th of January at ſun-ſet, to the 27th at eleven o'clock in the morning, the mercury in the Thermometer ſtood, at the uſual hours of obſervation, between twenty and eighteen. The water remaining after the foregoing congelations in B was frozen ſo far, that only half a pint remained fluid. The ice, bruiſhed, waſhed, and diſſolved, taſted a little brackiſh, and meaſured one pint and a half.

" On the 28th of January the mercury ſtood in the morning and until four o'clock in the afternoon between twenty-two and nineteen, and before eleven o'clock at night it ſunk to ſeventeen. Very little ice was formed in the veſſel B; and what was formed very eaſily crumbled or fell to ſmall flakes in attempting to take it out. I therefore ſuffered it to remain in the liquor until the morning.

" On the 29th of January the mercury ſtood between twenty and twenty-two until ſix o'clock; and between twenty

and

and nineteen, from ſix until twelve at night. The quantity of ice, formed on the preceding day, was not notably augmented or diminiſhed; bruiſed, waſhed, and melted, it yielded two ounces of water, brackiſh to the taſte, in a greater degree than any of the foregoing portions which were waſhed.

"On the 30th of January, finding that the temperature of the preceding evening of the night, and of this day, which was between nineteen and twenty-one, had cauſed no notable congelation in the ſmall quantity of water remaining in B; finding alſo that the reſidue of the water in A admitted of no further congelation worth notice; and conſidering that the ſlender laminæ of ice, lately formed in theſe waters, melted to ſalt-water, and conſequently that no further congelation, capable of ſeparating the freſh water from the brine, even with the aſſiſtance of waſhing, could take place; I mixed the concentrated brine in A with that in B, and found both ſcarcely meaſured a wine pint; ſome ſmall cryſtals were found in the bottom of both veſſels, which ſunk in the brine, and were to the taſte ſea ſalt. It is hence evident that ſome ſea ſalt is formed in cryſtals by the concentration produced by cold acting gradually, and cauſing congelation only on the ſurface of the water, or not affecting that part of it which is contiguous to the bottom of the veſſel.

"The quantity of theſe cryſtals of ſea ſalt was about two grains. I poured them together with the water into a china plate, ſet in a ſand heat, and, by cryſtalization, obtained ſea ſalt and the other ſaline contents of ſea-water, in a dry form, near two ounces, averdupoiſe.

"Now, as this quantity of ſea-water (that is, two gallons), taken on our coaſt, generally yields about ſeven ounces of ſaline matters; it appears, that two-thirds or more of the ſea ſalt, and bitter ſalts of ſea-water, are intercepted in the ice of the ſucceſſive

congelations,

congelations, and are waſhed away by freſh water, applied as above-mentioned. Hence we learn that ſea-water may be freſhened by freezing, provided the brine enveloped between the laminæ of its ice be waſhed away. And in cold countries ſalt might be prepared from ſea-water at a very moderate expence; for by freezing ſhallow ponds of this water, by turning the ice to drain off the brine, and when the brine is reduced to a twentieth part or leſs by evaporation, very little evaporation and fuel will be neceſſary towards the formation of the ſalt [x]. But all the ſalt of the ſea-water employed will not be obtained, becauſe the greater part of it will be retained between the laminæ of the ice, which muſt be rejected; and the concentration by freezing cannot be advantageouſly carried further than is above expreſſed, becauſe at that degree of concentration the cold, and the time neceſſary to cauſe further congelations, muſt be very conſiderable, as will the waſte of ſalt likewiſe, ſince the ice is then ſtrongly ſaline.

" A ſmall portion of the ice, taken at various times from B ſince the 26th of January, was not waſhed, but only left to drain in a funnel; and each portion thus drained during five or ſix days, being ſeparately diſſolved, taſted ſtrongly of ſalt, although the like ice, which was bruiſed and waſhed, yielded freſh water. This proves that waſhing removes the intercepted brine; and that this brine does not ſeparate by draining.

" January the 20th, at eight o'clock in the evening, the Thermometer pointing at twenty-three, in the open air where the Thermometer ſtood, I mixed ſnow with ſmoaking ſpirit of nitre, and placed in the mixture a glaſs half-pint tumbler full of ſea-water; and at the ſame time placed the Thermometer in the

[x] " Wallerius ſays, this art is practiſed in the Northern countries."

mixture.

mixture. In two minutes the mercury ſunk out of the tube quite into the globe. The ſcale extends only twenty-five degrees below O of Fahrenheit; wherefore I could not determine how many degrees lower it would have ſunk on a more extended ſcale. In five minutes, ſome ſlender laminæ of ice began to ſhoot from the circumference of the water, and adhered to the glaſs. The whole water was *not frozen in leſs than an hour*, at which time the mercury in the Thermometer roſe to twenty degrees below O. Having another mixture of the ſame kind ready made, I briſkly removed the tumbler with the ice it contained into the freſh mixture, which, like the former, ſunk the mercury into the globe.

"The ice of ſea-water is more opaque than that of freſh water, when both are naturally congealed. For the elaſtic fluid in common water forms bubbles only in the central parts of the water laſt frozen; but the ice of ſea-water conſiſts of alternate parts of ice and brine; the denſity of which being unequal, and the matter of them being alſo diſſimilar, light cannot be freely tranſmitted, but is partly reflected and refracted, according to Sir I. Newton's Ideas of light.

"In the experiment laſt-mentioned, the ice was commonly opaque; and when it was expoſed to the freſh frigorific mixture, it became like a maſs of ſnow compreſſed, having a ſnowy whiteneſs and opacity, perfect near the ſurface, but not perfect towards the bottom.

"The tumbler, with the ice it contained, was kept in this laſt-mentioned mixture an hour, when the mercury denoted that no further degree of cold could be given by this mixture. The tumbler was then placed in ſnow until the next day, to preſerve the ice for further obſervation. Notwithſtanding the extreme cold to which it had been ſo long expoſed, and the cold medium

in

in which it was placed, the ice was not ſolid like that of freſh water, but, on the contrary, could eaſily be cut through the centre of the maſs with a knife. The ice taſted equally of ſalt through the whole maſs, in the ſame manner as a like quantity of ſea-water. Bruiſed briſkly, waſhed as already deſcribed, and melted, it yielded freſh water to the quantity of four-fifths of the water frozen; wherefore in waſhing very little ice was diſſolved whilſt the ſalt-water intercepted in the ice was removed.

" Mr. Barrington having obſerved that an artificial freezing commences from the bottom and ſides of the maſs of water placed as uſual in the frigorific mixture, but that natural freezing commences on the ſurface and proceeds downwards; and it occuring to me that the ſpecific gravity of incongelable brine is greater than that of the congelable water; and, conſequently, that this greater ſpecific gravity favours the ſeparation of brine from the ice of ſea water, when the freezing commences on the ſurface of ſea-water, and may be an impediment to the ſeparation of the incongelable brine from the ice artificially formed in the ſea-water, when the congelation proceeds from the bottom upwards: On theſe conſiderations it ſeemed that the foregoing experiments indicate, that ice formed in ſea-water cannot, when melted, become freſh water, unleſs it be waſhed in freſh water; but do not fully prove, that ice formed on the ſurface only, and proceeding ſlowly downwards, in ſea-water, may not conſiſt of freſh water, and be freed from brine, by reaſon of the ſpecific gravity of brine and other unnoticed circumſtances. Therefore, on the 21ſt of January, at two o'clock, when the mercury ſtood in the open air at twenty-nine, I made the following experiment, with a view to determine whether ſea-water, frozen artificially from the ſurface downwards in the manner performed by nature, would not yield ice of a ſolid texture capable of melting to freſh water without waſhing, merely by draining; which muſt take place in mountains of ice, if any are formed in the Northern Sea: becauſe, ice being ſpecifically lighter than water, and the acceſs of congealed water being at the baſe, the portions firſt frozen will be raiſed above the water by ſucceeding portions frozen, and thus a mountain of ice may be raiſed, whoſe maſs and height above water will be to the maſſive baſe immerſed in water, inverſely as the ſpecific gravity of ice is to that of water.

"I placed therefore a gallon of ſea-water in a glazed earthen veſſel, whoſe diameter was one-third greater than the depth of the water. In this water I flung a thin glaſs baſon cut from a bolt-head, capable of containing near two quarts of water, in ſuch manner that it might be immerſed two inches deep in the ſea-water. The veſſel containing the ſea-water was ſurrounded with ſnow. I then filled the baſon, which was ſuſpended in the ſea-water, with ſnow preſſed down with a glaſs-peſtle, and poured into the ſnow the uſual quantity of ſtrong nitrous acid.

"In fifteen minutes ſome cryſtals of ice were formed on the interior glaſs baſon, in the part where it was contiguous to the ſurface of the ſea-water. In three hours the whole bottom of the baſon, containing the frigorific mixture, was coated with ice, the thickneſs of which was half an inch or leſs at the bottom of the baſon, increaſing to three-fourths of an inch at the part which correſponded with the ſurface of the water.

"I eaſily ſeparated it entire from the baſon, found it ſomewhat firmer in its aggregation than the ice ſlowly formed by natural freezing, and not compoſed of laminæ like this latter; but ſimilar in texture to the ſalt-water frozen by artificial cold applied in the uſual manner. I placed it on a heap of ſnow, where it remained to drain upwards of ſix hours, but ſtill was wet to the touch on the ſurface, and in the freſh ſurfaces of the fractured parts. I then placed a part of it in a glaſs funnel before the fire, to melt, and found the water ſtrongly ſaline to the taſte, but not near ſo ſaline as equal parts of ſea and river-water mixed.

" Another portion of this ice, which was wrapped up in filtering paper, and left to drain on a heap of dry ſnow during four days, when melted, was ſaline to the taſte, and not ſenſibly different from that which had drained only ſix or ſeven hours. Whence it appeared, that ice formed in the ſea-water, in circumſtances ſimilar to thoſe which attend natural congelation, is, nevertheleſs, ſaline to the taſte.

" The ſeveral portions of water obtained in the foregoing experiments, from the waſhed ice of the ſea-water in A and B, being preſerved in glaſs-ſtopper bottles, were not examined. Although they were freſh to the taſte, it appeared by the quantity of *luna cornea*, which they all formed with ſaturated nitrous ſolution of ſilver, that they were ſtrongly impregnated with marine ſalt, comparatively with Thames and New River water, examined in the like manner.

" Mr. Barrington obſerving, that ſalt in water is an impediment to the congelation of that water, preſumed, that ſalt in water would accelerate the thawing of ice immerſed in it; and that in equal temperatures ice would be thawed in ſea-water ſooner than in freſh water. I therefore made the following experiment.

" January the 20th, when the Thermometer pointed to twenty-three, about nine o'clock at night, I placed five ounces and half a drachm, averdupoiſe, of Thames water in a half pint glaſs tumbler; and the like quantity of the ſame water diſtilled in another half pint glaſs tumbler of equal figure and capa-

 city

city with the foregoing. The tumblers were placed on the wall formerly deſcribed, and left there covered with glaſs until eleven o'clock next morning.

"In the morning, at eleven o'clock, the Thermometer pointed to twenty-eight. The water in both tumblers was frozen quite through, and formed maſſes of ice, tranſparent as cryſtal in every part, except the centre, and near the bottom, which parts were rendered opaque to the thickneſs of half an inch, by a number of air-bubbles locked up in the ice. The diſtilled water had been kept ſeveral days in the jar above deſcribed, whoſe mouth was only covered with an inverted pewter diſh.

"Into a glaſs tumbler, capable of holding a Wincheſter pint or more, I put a wine pint of Thames water; and into another tumbler of the ſame figure and capacity, I poured a pint of ſea-water concentrated, by freezing one fourth of it, the better to repreſent ſea-water of the great oceans, which are not affected by rivers ſo much as the ſea-water uſed in theſe experiments muſt be, as it was taken up near the North Foreland. The ſea-water was thus concentrated for theſe further reaſons: firſt, that the effect of ſalt in the water might be more conſpicuous during the thawing of the ice; and ſecondly, to prevent the firſt portions of ice thawed from diluting the ſalt water to a degree, which never is found in the ocean. I reduced the Sea and the Thames water, contained in theſe tumblers, to the ſame temperature exactly, in the open air; then taking hold of each by the ſummit of the glaſs above the water, I carried them into my ſtudy, and placed them on a carpet fifteen feet equally diſtant from the fire, and three inches from the wainſcot of the wall oppoſite the fire, and equally diſtant from a door on one ſide, and a window, which extends within fourteen inches of the floor, on the other. The tumblers, containing the frozen water, were immerſed in a large a large pan of hot water, close to each other, and near the centre of the pan, the water rising to the height of the ice in the tumblers; after a few minutes the ice was thrown out, by inverting the glasses on clean paper. The two pieces of ice were equal in size, figure, and weight; the weight of each being five ounces averdupoise.

"The moment before the ice was taken out of the tumblers, I found the temperature of the sea and fresh water, placed as above-mentioned, to be equal, and exactly thirty-four; the temperature of the air in that part of the room being forty-six. I plunged the pieces of ice immediately, one in the sea-water, the other in the fresh water. It was at this instant two o'clock in the afternoon. In ten minutes the temperature of the sea-water was thirty-two, that of the fresh water was thirty-three and a half. In half an hour the sea-water raised the mercury to thirty-three, the fresh water raised it to thirty-four and a half.

"At this instant, *viz.* half an hour past two o'clock, I took both the pieces of ice at the same time, weighed them briskly, and replaced them in their respective vessels at the same instant. Of the ice placed in the sea-water, half an ounce was dissolved; of the ice placed in the fresh water, only four drachms and a half were dissolved.

"From half an hour past two o'clock until six I frequently changed the position of the tumblers, making one take the place of the other. At six, the temperature of the sea-water was thirty-six, that of the fresh water was thirty-seven and a half. In the manner already mentioned, the ice was at this time weighed and replaced. Of the ice in sea-water three ounces and four drachms were dissolved; of that in fresh water, only two ounces and eight drachms.

" It is obſervable, that the ſea-water was a degree and a half colder, ever ſince the immerſion of the ice, than the freſh water, acted on by the like maſs of ice, and placed in the like circumſtances; and nevertheleſs the ice was diſſolved much quicker in the colder ſea-water. The quicker ſolution of the ice in ſea-water was evidently the cauſe of the greater degree of cold preſerved in it during four hours; and it already appeared, that ſalt-water is a more powerful ſolvent of ice than freſh water in the like temperature. And, agreeable to Mr. Barrington's ſuggeſtion, the matter which impedes the congelation of water muſt of courſe facilitate the thawing of ice. The nitrous acid furniſhes us with another ſtriking inſtance to this effect; for no cold can be produced to freeze the water in it; and a red-hot ladle cannot thaw ice placed in it, ſo quickly as ice is thawed by nitrous acid.

" At ten o'clock, or in eight hours after the pieces of ice were firſt placed in the Sea and Thames water, the temperature of the ſea-water was thirty-nine, that of the Thames water only thirty-eight. At this time, of the ice in ſea-water four ounces eight drachms were diſſolved; of the ice in Thames water, four ounces only were diſſolved. The ſea-water being at this period warmer than the Thames water, correſponds with the ſmall portion of ice remaining in it, compared with that remaining in the freſh water. The temperature of the room in the place where the tumblers ſtood, being, by reaſon of the fire kept conſtantly in it, forty-four or forty-five, for the laſt ſix hours.

" In twelve hours, or at two o'clock in the morning, the temperature of the room near the veſſels of water being nearly the ſame as formerly deſcribed, the temperature of the ſea-water was forty, the temperature of the freſh water was thirty-nine. Four ounces fifteen drachms of the ice in ſalt-water were diſſolved,

diſſolved, only one drachm remaining; four ounces ten drachms of the ice in freſh water were diſſolved, only ſix drachms remaining.

" At the end of the thirteenth hour, after the immerſion of the maſſes of ice in the freſh and in the ſalt-water, that is, at three in the morning, the temperature of the room was forty-five near the place where the tumblers ſtood. The temperature of the open air was thirty-one. The ice in the ſea-water was melted. The quantity of ice remaining in the freſh water was one drachm, which, in fifteen minutes more, was entirely melted.

" At this period, when the ice in the freſh water was melted, that is, a quarter of an hour paſt three, the mercury ſtood at forty in the freſh water, in the ſalt-water it ſtood at forty-one. In a quarter of an hour after this the mercury ſtood at forty-two in the ſalt-water, and at forty-one in the freſh water. In a quarter of an hour more, the temperature remained unalterable in the ſalt and freſh water, although the temperature of the air between and near the veſſels was forty-five, and the veſſel on the right was placed on the left, and replaced ſeveral times. And both veſſels were at all times equi-diſtant from the wainſcot, which was perfectly cloſe, as were the boards of the floor alſo.

" In a quarter of an hour more, the temperature of the air near and between the tumblers remained forty-five; the temperature of the freſh water was ſcarcely forty-two; the temperature of the ſalt-water was forty-two and a half.

" In a quarter of an hour more, the temperature of the air between the tumblers being forty-four and a half, the temperature of the ſalt-water was forty-three; the temperature of the freſh water was ſomewhat more than forty-two. It was now paſt four o'clock in the morning, on Monday the 22d of January. I went to bed leaving the tumblers in the poſition deſcribed.

" It

" It was obſerved, during the foregoing and other experiments, and it is viſible from the experiments related, that fire, in diffuſing itſelf from warm bodies to contiguous cold bodies, proceeds ſlowly; that cold bodies do not acquire the temperature of the warmer medium in which they are immerſed ſo ſoon as is commonly imagined, but, on the contrary, require a conſiderable time for that purpoſe; and this time is directly as the diameter of the cold body.

" It was inferred from theſe experiments, that a temperate body like water, placed in a cold medium, as in air, cooled to thirty or thirty-one of Fahrenheit, requires many hours before it acquires the temperature of the ſurrounding medium, and before a congelation commences; and that the time neceſſary for the commencement of the congelation is directly as the maſs and ſhorteſt diameter of the water, and the progreſs of the congelation is inverſely as the depth of the water.

" It was alſo obſerved, that as much of a given maſs of water was frozen in five hours in a temperature of twelve degrees below the freezing point, as was frozen in one hour in a temperature fifty degrees below the freezing point; and that long duration of the temperature between twenty and thirty-two is, towards the congelation of water, equivalent to intenſity of cold, ſuch as is marked o, and below o, in Fahrenheit, but of ſhort duration.

" It was moreover obſerved, that water in thick jars covered was not frozen, when water in open veſſels was frozen; that water included in maſſive veſſels of wood, or ſurrounded by any matter except water, to ſome thickneſs, preſerved its temperature, and reſiſted congelation, longer than the like quantity of water expoſed to the cold air; and that water in thick veſſels was not frozen ſo ſoon as a like quantity of water in thin veſſels of like matter, figure, and capacity. It was thence inferred, that fire does not ſo quickly pervade thick bodies as it does thin bodies; and that fire pervades water more freely than it does ſolid bodies, and ſooner diffuſes itſelf from water to air, than from any other body containing water to air.

" Thence it followed, that in reaſoning on the phænomena of congelation, the maſſes of water, the duration of cold temperature in the atmoſphere, and the maſſes of other matter ſurrounding water, are to be conſidered. Deep rivers and lakes do not freeze ſo ſoon as ſhallow rivers and lakes. Large bodies of water are never frozen in any temperature of ſhort duration; but ſhallow waters are often frozen in the ſummer.

" It need not be preſumed, that certain lakes, which are never frozen, communicate with ſubterranean fires, or hot mineral ſtreams; or that they are impregnated with matter which impedes congelation: but it is rather to be preſumed, that as fire ſlowly pervades, enters, or quits bodies, the time neceſſary for its diffuſing itſelf from deep lakes to the cold atmoſphere is greater than ever ſuch temperature of the atmoſphere continues without intermiſſion below the freezing point.

" By the like reaſoning applied to maſſes of earth and other matter which are not ſo quickly pervaded by fire as water is, we can conceive why deep wells and ſprings at or near their iſſuing from the earth are not frozen in this climate even when navigable rivers are ice-bound. We alſo underſtand why the main pipes, buried in our ſtreets, retain the water fluid, when the pipes leading from theſe to the houſes and croſſing the area of each houſe, are choaked with ice; and why hay-bands twiſted round theſe ſmall pipes prevent the freezing, &c.

" On theſe grounds it is preſumed, that no conſiderable congelation ever takes place in the ſea, becauſe this is the greateſt and deepeſt maſs of water we know of; becauſe it is always in motion, and communicates with the water of temperate climates; becauſe ſea-water is not ſo eaſily frozen as freſh water; becauſe the ice found in the ſea is ſolid, and in tranſparency not different from the ice of freſh water; and, laſtly, becauſe this floating ice, which is met with by navigators, both in high northern and ſouthern latitudes, when melted, is palatable to the taſte; whereas the ice formed from ſea-water is very ſaline, if it be thawed without having been waſhed in freſh water.

" It is alſo preſumed, that in the deep Northern ſeas the water near the ſurface will be found warmer than that near the bottom at the approach of ſummer; and will be found colder near the ſurface than at the bottom in the firſt month of the cold ſeaſon, for the reaſons already expreſſed: and in like manner, that, during the firſt ſix or eight hours of a froſt in England, the water in any deep lake will be found colder near the ſurface than at the bottom, but that the water at the bottom will be found colder than that near the ſurface in twenty-four hours after a thaw, provided the air be temperate or nearly ſo."

IT having been proved, from what hath been already urged, as well as by the preceding experiments of Dr. Higgins, that the floating ice, which is obſerved both in high ſouthern and northern latitudes, cannot be probably formed from ſea-water, it may be thought incumbent upon me to ſhew how ſuch quantities can be ſupplied from ſprings, rain, or frozen ſnow.

The rivers which are always found at certain intervals in any large tract of land undoubtedly ſupply conſiderable part of ſuch ice; but there are not wanting other ſources from which theſe floating maſſes may be produced.

The larger and higher ice iſlands[y] I conceive to be chiefly formed on ſhore, after which they are undermined by the rills and melted ſnow, during the ſummer, of which we have an accurate account in the late voyage towards the North Pole[z].

Others

[y] Mr. Wales obſerves, that in the iſlands of ice, near Georgia Auſtralis and Sandwich-land, there are ſtrata of dirty *ice*, which irrefragably proves their having been formed on the land. Remarks on Dr. Forſter's Account, &c. 8vo. London, 1778, p. 106.

With regard to the formation of Ice-iſlands, ſee likewiſe Captain Cook's Voyage, Vol. II. p. 213 and 240, who conceives them to ariſe from congealed ſnow and ſleet in the vallies. Captain Cook alſo ſuppoſes, that the ice-cliffs, at the end of theſe vallies, often project a great way into the ſea, when they are ſheltered from the violence of the wind, p. 242.

[z] "Large pieces frequently break off from the Ice-bergs, and fall "with great noiſe into the water: we obſerved one piece which had "floated out into the bay, and grounded in twenty-four fathoms; it was "fifty feet high above the ſurface of the water, and of the ſame beauti- "ful colour as the Ice-berg." p. 70.

I have likewiſe been favoured with the following account of ice iſlands on the coaſt of Labradore, from Lieutenant John Cartwright, of the Royal Navy, to whom I have not only this obligation. [See the Probability of reaching the North Pole, p. 5.]

Others, which happen to have projected over the ſea, may have had their foundations ſo ſapped by the waves during a ſtorm,.

" DEAR SIR, *Thurſday, Feb. 28, 1776.*

In conformity with my promiſe of yeſterday, I now ſend you, as nearly as I can recollect, my brother's account (who hath reſided four years on the Labradore coaſt) of the formation of thoſe great maſſes of frozen ſnow, ſeen annually in very great numbers on the northern coaſts of America, and by mariners uſually called *Iſlands of Ice.*

Along the coaſt of Labradore, the ſea, in winter, is frozen to a great diſtance from the land [how this ice is produced, will appear, p. 145.]. The north-weſt is the prevailing and coldeſt wind. The ſnow, carried by this or any other weſterly winds over the cliffs of the coaſt, falls becalmed upon the ice at the foot of the ſaid cliffs, drifting up to the very tops of them, although many of them are not inferior to that of Dover, or thoſe about Lulworth. The current of the ſtrong weſtern winds, having paſſed theſe precipices, takes its courſe downwards into the undiſturbed air below; but it is not until it arrives at ſome diſtance from the land, that it can be felt on the ſurface of the ſea. Having the frozen ſurface of the ſea for a baſe, and the precipice for a perpendicular, an hypothenuſe is made by the deſcending direction of the wind. The incloſed triangle, be the cliffs ever ſo high, will be filled with ſnow; becauſe the tops of the adjoining hills, being quite naked, are entirely ſwept clear of ſnow by the violence of the ſtorms, and what would otherwiſe have lain there is carried to the leeward of the hills, and under the ſhelter of the cliffs, where it is depoſited in infinitely greater quantities, than it would fall in without ſuch a cauſe. The hypothenuſe of ſuch triangle is frequently of ſuch a ſlope as that a man may walk up or down without difficulty. By frequent thaws, and the occaſional fall of moiſture interrupting the froſt, during the firſt parts of the winter, the ſnow will, in ſome ſmall degree, diſſolve, by which means it only acquires a greater hardneſs when the froſt returns, and during the courſe of that rigorous ſeaſon it generally becomes a very compact body of ſnow-ice. In the ſpring of the year the icy baſe gives way, and its burden plunges into the ſea, ſometimes entire, ſometimes in many fragments. As the depth of water in many parts is forty, fifty, one hundred fathoms, and upwards, cloſe to the ſhore, theſe bodies of ice, vaſt as is their bulk, will frequently float without any diminution of their contents, although the very large ones do often take the ground, and ſometimes are not ſufficiently reduced by either the penetration of the ſea and the rain-water, or of a whole ſummer's ſun, to get at liberty again before another winter.

The

ſtorm[a], as to have loſt their ſupport; whilſt others again may have been reſt from the maſs to which they before adhered by the expanſive power of the froſt[b].

Great part of the field, or lower ice, I take to be formed by the ſnow falling on the ſands left bare for ſix hours (from half ebb to half flood), which immediately diſſolves upon touching the ſands, and, before the tide returns, becomes ſolid ice; part of theſe pieces are by the wind, or tide, again returned to the ſame ſands, where they again meet with another ſtore of ice, formed during another ſix hours, which, in the courſe of a winter, muſt, by packing, accumulate to immenſe maſſes. That this is not mere conjecture, but the fact, I appeal to Captain James's account of what he himſelf was witneſs of whilſt he wintered at Charlton Iſland, in Hudſon's Bay[c].

The above relation, which my brother gives from his own obſervation, in North latitude, 52 deg. 15 min. accounts very naturally and eaſily for the formation of that ſurpriſing number of the vaſt pieces of ice which is annually ſeen on the Labradore coaſt, and conſiderably to the Southward.

JOHN CARTWRIGHT."

[a] "The ſea has waſhed underneath the ice cliffs, as high as the "Kentiſh Forelands, and the arches overhanging, ſupport mountains "of ſnow, which have lain ſince the creation." Wood's *Voyage*, p. 20.

"Cuncta gelu, canaque æternùm grandine tecta,
"Atque ævi glaciem cohibent, riget ardua montis
"Ætherii facies, ſurgentique obvia Phœbo,
"Duratas neſcit flammis mollire pruinas."

Silius Italicus, Lib. III. l. 480.

[b] "The rocks along the coaſt burſt with a report equal to that of artillery, and the ſplinters are thrown to an amazing diſtance." Mr. Wales, *in Philoſophical Tranſactions*, Vol. LX. p. 125.

[c] For Captain James's account, ſee Boyle, Vol. II as alſo Harris, Vol. II. p. 420. where it is conſiderably abridged, and differs in ſome few circumſtances. It is ſtated, however, that in few hours the ſnow thus frozen will be five or ſix feet thick.

Now

Now if we examine a globe, we ſhall find, that from ſixty to ſeventy degrees of Northern latitude more than half its circumference is land, which is open to a Northern ſea, from which large tract of coaſt much greater quantities of floating ice may be derived than have ever been met with by navigators, without being obliged to ſuppoſe that any part of it is formed from ſea-water.

But it may be ſaid, that our late enterprizing navigators to the Southward have alſo met with as great a quantity of ice in the oppoſite hemiſphere, without ſcarcely diſcovering any land.

To this I anſwer, that their circumnavigation was, at a medium, about fifty-ſeven degrees of Southern latitude, though they made puſhes greatly to the Southward in three points, and in one of theſe to ſeventy-one degrees ten minutes. In the other inſtances, as far as 67 deg. and 67 deg. 30 min.

There is conſequently a very large ſpace in which there may be many a frozen region, which they have not had any opportunity of diſcovering. If, for example, a navigator from the Southern was ſent upon diſcoveries to the Northern hemiſphere, and Europe, as well as Aſia and North America, having been ſunk by earthquakes, was to report that he had circumnavigated at fifty-five degrees North latitude at a medium; made puſhes even to ſeventy-one degrees in different directions, without ſeeing any continent; and that therefore there was no land to the north of fifty-five degrees; his countrymen would be much deceived by ſuch report, becauſe Denmark, Norway, Sweden, Muſcovy, Tartarian Aſia, and part of North America, continued in their preſent ſituation.

Beſides, however, the ice which may come from *Tierra del Fuego*, Captain Cook hath diſcovered two frozen iſlands between Cape Horne and that of Good Hope, which were covered with ice and ſnow [d]. The firſt of theſe, ſituated in fifty-four degrees, is called *Georgia Auſtralis*; and the ſecond, *Sandwich-land*, in fifty-nine degrees, which appeared ſo large, to ſome eyes, that it was conceived to be part of a continent [e].

It is believed alſo, that no ſhip hath been beyond forty-eight degrees to the Southward of New Zealand; and from the coldneſs of the moſt Southern of theſe large iſlands, I cannot but ſuſpect that there is a conſiderable tract of land between it and the Pole.

Having thus endeavoured to account how the floating ice which is met with may be ſuppoſed to be formed from ſnow or freſh water; I cannot but riſk another conjecture, that the time of the year at which attempts are commonly made to make diſcoveries towards the two poles (though favourable in many

[d] Hence whatever land is diſcovered to the ſouth of this latitude muſt produce ice. There is alſo a large tract of land named in ſome maps, the *Gulph of St. Sebaſtian*, which is not far diſtant from *Georgia Auſtralis*, and which poſſibly may have eſcaped Captain Cook. This great navigator alſo conceives, that the ice floats from 70 degrees South, and is detached by accidents from land lying to the South of that parallel, as the currents in the Antarctic Seas always ſet to the North. Cook's Voyage, Vol. I. p. 268.

Captain Furneaux, in 1744, paſſed between Georgia Auſtralis and Sandwich-land (rather ſuppoſed a continent), without ſeeing either of theſe new diſcoveries, though the mountains on both are remarkably high, particularly thoſe in Sandwich-land, one of which, by ſeveral, was conſidered to equal Teneriff.

Captain Furneaux could not have been well more than two degrees from either of theſe countries. See his Track in the lately publiſhed map.

[e] See Captain Cook's voyage, Vol. II. p. 230. where he ſuppoſes land near the South Pole, chiefly oppoſite to the Southern Atlantic, and Indian Oceans, as on thoſe meridians ice is found as far North as 48 deg. It is in this tract of Southern land that Cook ſuppoſes the ice to be chiefly formed, which is met with in the Southern Oceans. Ibid.

other

other circumſtances [f]) is probably the ſeaſon when the greateſt quantity of floating ice will be obſeived.

This ſeems to follow as a neceſſary conſequence from the puſh being never made before Midſummer, and often a month later, which is preciſely the time when the ice begins to break up in the freſh water rivers, &c.

I have accordingly minuted down, from ſeveral voyages into high northern latitudes, the day on which navigators firſt mention ſeeing the floating ice.

The reſult of which is as follows:

Sir Maitin Frobiſher on the 23d of June. Hackluyt, Vol. II. p. 77.

Davis in his firſt voyage, July 19.—In his third, July 2d. Ibid. p. 99.

Pet and Jackman on the 13th of July. Ibid. p. 447.

Burrow, on the 21ſt of July. Ibid. p. 277.

Governor Ellis, July 5th. Voyage to diſcover the Noith Weſt Paſſage, p. 127.

"The ſhores of Hudſon's Bay have many inlets or friths, "which are full of ice and ſnow, and frozen to the ground. "Theſe are broke looſe, and launched into the ſea, by land-"floods, during the months of June, July, and Auguſt." Ibid.

"The firſt floating ice which is obſerved on the coaſt of "Labradore is a joyful preſage to the inhabitants of the "approach of ſummer." Lieutenant Cuitis, in Philoſophical Tranſactions.

"The ice begins to break up the 18th of June." Daniſh Account of Groenland.—*Voyages au Nord*, Vol. I. p. 167.

[f] *Viz.* The nights being ſhorter, and the rigging not being ſo ſubject to be frozen.

"The

" The lakes of Lapland continue frozen on June the 24th." Linſchoten's Voyage, ibid. Vol. IV.

" On the 5th of July, the ſea on two ſides is obſerved to be covered with ice." Ibid. p. 187.

Wood ſees the firſt ice in North latitude ſeventy-five degrees fifty-nine minutes, on June 22d.

On the 17th of Auguſt vaſt pieces of floating ice. Ibid.

" In the month of Auguſt the French obſerve, on the Labra-" dore coaſt, mountains of ice as high as the ſhips." Boyle's Works, Vol. II. p. 303.

" On June 16th, a river in Hudſon's-bay breaks up." Mr. Wales, in Philoſophical Tranſactions, Vol. LX. p. 126.

" The mouth of the Lena is not open till the middle of Auguſt." *Obſervations Géographiques, par* Mr. Engel, p. 229.

With regard to the ice which may be obſerved in Southern latitudes, I ſhall only take notice that Sir Francis Drake, Feuillee, and Clipperton, paſſed Cape Horn, or the Straits of Magellan, during the month of December, without mentioning ice [g], from which it ſhould ſeem that it breaks up chiefly during the months of January, February, and March, anſwering to our July, Auguſt, and September [h].

Three Dutch ſhips, which ſailed on diſcoveries with Commodore Roggewein, in 1721, met with much ice to the South of Cape Horn in the middle of January. The Author of the Narrative afterwards makes this obſervation: " Thoſe mountains of

[g] See Callander's Voyages under theſe three articles.

[h] It may poſſibly break up in ſome years earlier, perhaps in December; but ſome time muſt be allowed for its floating to the north, as far as the latitude of *Tierra del Fuego*. From the inſtances cited, it appears that the earlieſt floating ice which is ſeen in the northern hemiſphere is not obſerved ſooner than the 16th of June, whilſt in much the greater part mention is not made of it till July.

"ice, which are ſeen in the latitude of Cape Horn, prove that "there is land towards the Southern Pole, it being certain that this "ice cannot be formed in the ocean, though the cold is ſo ſevere[i]."

But it may, perhaps, be ſaid, that the ice which breaks up in June, July, and Auguſt, or during the correſpondent months in the oppoſite hemiſphere, may remain floating for years without being much diſſolved.

To this I will not take upon myſelf to ſay that ſome ſuch iſlands, when very large, may not continue more than a year; but I ſhould conceive this not to be very common. Storms and other accidents muſt probably break them into ſmall maſſes which will quickly be thawed; as that able geographer and promoter of diſcoveries, Mr. Bailiff Engel, obſerves that if a piece of ice is faſtened by a cord and let down into the ſea, it is preſently melted[k].

Mr. Wales alſo informs us, that he ſuppoſes moſt of theſe iſlands of ice are ſoon waſted, in the following words: "The "truth is, their motion and diſſolution are apparently ſo very "quick, that I am of opinion it muſt be a pretty large iſland "which is not diſſolved in one ſummer[l]."

How ſoon likewiſe does the ice diſappear, which is diſcharged from our own rivers into the ſea, after our moſt intenſe froſts?

I have omitted ſtating the degree of cold at which the ſea-water I expoſed to the air began to be frozen, and cannot now recover the memorandum which I made at the time. I am pretty confident, however, that the mercury had ſunk only to twenty-ſeven.

[i] Hiſtoire de l'Expedition de trois Vaiſſeaux, &c. *Hague*, 1739, p. 81.
[k] See *Obſervations Geographiques*, p. 224.
[l] Philoſophical Tranſactions, Vol. LX. p. 112.

But though congelation thus took place at five degrees below the freezing point, it is proper that I ſhould ſtate ſome other circumſtances attending the experiment.

The ſea-water which I uſed came from the North Foreland, which is at the mouth of the Thames, and conſequently, not being the ſame with that of the ocean, was more eaſily frozen.

Beſides this, the quantity was ſo ſmall as not to cover a thin china baſon deeper than an inch, both which particulars contribute greatly to the more ſpeedy formation of ice: it need ſcarcely be mentioned alſo, that the liquid to be frozen was in a quieſcent ſtate.

How much a conſiderable degree of motion impedes congelation, may be inferred from what may be obſerved in every river; for as high as the tide hath any force, I doubt much whether any ice is ſcarcely ever formed in the fair open channel, during our moſt intenſe froſts. I attended to the Thames, in this reſpect, during the late ſeverity of the weather, and it ſeemed to me that all the ice floated down from the upper parts of the river; but packing afterwards between the lighters, occaſioned the formation of very large maſſes.

I have little doubt, from theſe circumſtances, but that the open ſea, if it be frozen at all, muſt require a much more intenſe cold than twenty-ſeven; allowing however any greater degree of cold in the high latitudes, it ſeems deducible, from the experiments of Dr. Higgins, that ſea-water cannot be frozen into a ſolid ſtate, if compared with that of ice formed from the water of rivers; nor will ſuch ice when melted become palatable, unleſs it hath been previouſly waſhed in freſh water.

Hence it ſeems to be almoſt demonſtration, that the floating ice met with by navigators, being both ſolid and ſweet to the taſte after diſſolution, cannot be produced from the water of the ocean [m].

I will venture alſo to inſiſt, that if ſuch ice was actually frozen from the ocean, it muſt very quickly be melted, becauſe, as it muſt conſiſt of detached laminæ intercepting the brine, the ſea would ſoon inſinuate itſelf between the interſtices, ſo as to cauſe its diſſolution. If any ice, therefore, ſhould be formed in thoſe parts of bays which are land-locked, have little or no tide, and receive conſiderable quantities of freſh water, when ſuch ice is wafted fairly out to ſea, I ſhould conceive that it muſt diſappear in a very ſhort time.

[m] The ice taken up by Captain Cook, during his circum-navigation in high Southern Latitudes, was ſolid and tranſparent; being placed alſo on the deck for the ſalt-water to drain off, the ice became wholeſome and palatable water.

MISCEL-

MISCELLANEOUS

ESSAYS.

ESSAY I.

WHETHER THE TURKEY WAS KNOWN BEFORE THE DISCOVERY OF AMERICA.

THE earlier writers on ornithology, as Belon, Ray, and Willoughby, had ſuppoſed that the turkey was introduced into Europe from Aſia: M. de Buffon, however, (with other great authorities) hath lately maintained, that we owe this bird to America; and, as he hath more fully entered into the diſcuſſion of this point than any other writer, I ſhall principally conſider the reaſons by which this moſt able naturaliſt ſupports what he hath contended for.

Having taken ſome pains on this ſubject, by examining moſt of the authorities which can afford any light, I ſhall, without heſitation, ſay, that I *rather conceive* this bird was never indigenous in the neighbourhood of Mexico[a]: though I do not mean to aſſert this with any degree of poſitiveneſs; but I am thoroughly convinced, that, whether turkies were found in America by the firſt diſcoverers or not, the Europeans are chiefly indebted to Aſia, and perhaps Africa, for this valuable addition to our tables.

[a] As for Virginia, I admit turkies to have been found in a wild ſtate on that coaſt by the firſt ſettlers in 1584. Hakluyt, Pt. III. p. 274. The vaſt diſtance, however, between Virginia and Mexico is well known; and theſe birds were called turkies in England thirty years before the diſcovery of Virginia.

M. de

M. de Buffon's principal arguments in favour of the American claim are the following:

Hernandez, who wrote the Natural Hiſtory of Mexico, hath mentioned this bird under the name of *Huexolotl.*

Now it is much wiſhed that Hernandez had explained what is the meaning of this Mexican term, as I ſtrongly ſuſpect it ſignifies *The New, The Eaſtern bird*, or of the like import, intimating that it was brought to America by the Spaniards.

But I muſt not diſmiſs this earlieſt and principal authority of M. Buffon's, without dwelling upon ſome material circumſtances, to the deciſion of the point in conteſt.

Hernandez's work was firſt printed at Rome in 1651; and I cannot diſcover at what time he compiled it but by the Dedication, in which it is ſtated that Philip II. had ſent this phyſician to Mexico.

Now this King of Spain began his reign in 1555, and died in 1598; and if we therefore allow twenty-one years as the half of his life, after Charles V. gave up his crown, it ſeems to be a fair conjecture, that Hernandez took notice of this bird in the neighbourhood of Mexico about the year 1576, when he ſpeaks of it alſo as *known to every one* under the name of *Gallus Indicus*, which I hope ſoon to prove means the Eaſtern, and not the Weſtern Indies.

This ſame year alſo, of 1576, was but fifty-one years after the conqueſt of Mexico by Cortez; and if this bird was in that time ſo diſperſed over Europe, as to be known to every one, could the natural hiſtorian of this part of America have omitted ſo material a circumſtance in relation to the animals of the country which he was deſcribing.

As for Columbus's diſcovery of the iſlands in the Gulf of Mexico, neither M. Buffon, or any other writer, hath ever pre-

2 tended

tended that turkies were found upon them; and, on the contrary, *Brown* informs us, that in the present century, "they require a "good deal of care *in Jamaica*, and a moderate climate when "young[b]." Du Tertre also observes, though turkies in the *Leeward Islands* thrive well after they are of a certain size, yet, that if the least dew wets their heads they commonly dye, as likewise from a vertigo, supposed to arise from the intense heat of the sun in that climate[c].

But as the citation from Hernandez is so much relied upon for turkies being indigenous in the neighbourhood of Mexico, it must be recollected that Cortez first visited that country in 1519, did not take the capital till 1521, nor returned to Spain till 1528[d], which is the earliest period that can be reasonably assigned for the introduction of this bird into Europe from America, though no author (as it is believed) hath ever mentioned his bringing with him any live animals.

The inference from this seems to be, that it is much more probable turkies should have been carried with fowls, horses, cows, and sheep, to the West Indies, than that they should have been brought from thence to Europe, as it is well known that a regular supply of wholesome food must be one of the first objects which every new settlement must attend to.

But I will now suppose that Cortez, or any of his followers, had introduced the turkey into Spain in the year 1528; would it not then have received the name of the Mexican bird, or Mexican peacock[e], rather than that of *pago*, which was its old appellation,

[b] History of Jamaica, p. 470.

[c] Histoire des Antilles. T. II. p. 266.—Paris, 1667 Quarto.

[d] Robertson's History of America.

[e] Gage was sent to Mexico in 1625, and traversed not only the Mexican, but adjoining territories; in his account of which journies, he four times mentions *turkies*, together with *fowls* which are known to have

appellation, though now it is more commonly called *pavo*, and the peacock *pavon* [f].

Again, if turkies were firſt introduced from Mexico into Spain, the other parts of Europe muſt have received them from the ſame quarter, which would alſo have termed it either the Mexican or Spaniſh bird at leaſt; but there is no ſynonym in any language of Europe which bears the moſt diſtant alluſion to this circumſtance, nor is there any tradition of ſuch an introduction. On the contrary, we have the authority of Cardinal Perron [g] (a contemporary of Hernandez) that they were in his time drove from Languedoc into Spain in large flocks, " Le " coq d'Inde eſt un oiſeau qui a peuplé merveilleuſement; de Lan- " guedoc ils en menent en Eſpagne, comme des moutons [h]."

By this paſſage, we find that turkies, ſo far from being brought from Spain, were ſent during the ſixteenth century by droves into that country, which is the ſtrongeſt proof (amongſt many others) that we are indebted to Aſia, and perhaps Aſia Minor, for this bird, becauſe the French have long had intercourſe and trade with the Turks, though the Spaniards never have had any communication with them.

The next citation by which M. Buffon ſupports his opinion, is from Sperlingius's Zoologia Phyſica, in the following words:

have been introduced from Europe, and originally Aſia. It is remarkable alſo, that he always meets with *turkies and fowls* near ſome towns, and not in the uninhabited tracts through which he paſſed. Now if turkies were wild in the Mexican empire in 1576, when Hernandez may be ſuppoſed to have wrote, can it be conceived that they were entirely confined fifty years afterwards to the cultivated parts of the country? See Gage's New Survey of the Weſt Indies, London, 1648, p. 23. 75. 105. 125.

[f] See the Royal Dictionary of the Caſtilian language, Madrid, 1726.

[g] Cardinal Perron died in 1620.

[h] Perroniana, p. 67.

" ante

"ante centum, et *quod excurrit*, annos, delata hæc avis (ſc. Gall. "Pavo) ex Nova India in Europam [i]."

I really am not without my doubts, whether by *Nova India* Sperlingius does not mean ſome of the diſcoveries of the Portugueſe in the Eaſt Indies; but, allowing him to ſpeak rather of America, let us examine this aſſertion, for which he cites no authority whatſoever.

Sperlingius's Zoologia Phyſica was printed at Leipſic in 1661; and from the pretence to great accuracy in ſpeaking of 101 years rather than a round 100, the turkey muſt have been firſt brought to Europe from Nova India during the year 1560; whereas four young *turkies* [k] (and conſequently bred in England) were dreſſed at a ſerjeant's feaſt in 1555 [l], which, by the way, was but twenty-ſeven years after Cortez's firſt return to Spain.

But I ſuſpect at leaſt, that I find a ſtill earlier mention of turkies in England, for capons of *Greaſe* (Greece probably) made part of an entertainment in the ſixth year of Edward IV. A. D. 1467 [m]; it being highly probable that this bird was common to two countries lying ſo near to each other, as Greece and Aſia Minor.

Sperling, however, printing his work at Leipſic, muſt be ſuppoſed to have been a native of Saxony; and how are we to expect an accurate account of the introduction of turkies into Europe from an inland part of that empire, which never had the leaſt intercourſe with America? I ſhall alſo prove hereafter, that ſuppoſing the paſſage cited to relate to America, and not to

[i] P. 366.

[k] They are ſo called, and undoubtedly, as Willoughby obſerves, becauſe they were ſuppoſed to have been introduced into England from that quarter.

[l] Dugdale's Orig. Jur. p. 135.

[m] Leland's Itinerary, vol. VI. p. 5.

India,

India, we ſhall find this writer to be contradicted by the terms now uſed in Germany when the turkey is ſpoken of. I am confident, moreover, that this whole treatiſe of Zoologia Phyſica is ſuch a publication, as M. Buffon would neither read nor cite for any other purpoſe; eſpecially as *Sperling* ſuppoſes the bird in queſtion to be a monſtrous production between the peacock and common hen, both of which were firſt brought to Europe from Aſia; as alſo that there is frequently intercourſe between turkies and ducks [n].

Buffon next endeavours to prove, that the turkey does not come from Aſia but America, by travellers agreeing that few or none are found over that vaſt and firſt-mentioned continent.

Before I enter into a diſcuſſion of this laſt argument, inſiſted upon by ſo ingenious and able an ornithologiſt, I ſhall premiſe, that moſt of his authorities relate to the S. E. parts of Aſia, and not to Aſia Minor, or Indoſtan, from whence I rather ſuppoſe the turkey was firſt brought into Europe.

In the next place, though ſome of theſe travellers have paſſed through conſiderable tracts of this quarter of the globe, it is no more to be inferred, becauſe they did not obſerve turkies in their route, that therefore they are not to be found in other parts of Aſia, than if an Aſiatic had made a complete tour of Great Britain fifty years ago, without ſeeing *Guiney-hens*, that the Engliſh were therefore without that bird. I mention fifty years ago, becauſe *Guiney-hens* ſince that time have become much more common in this country [o].

This

[n] Though I disbelieve this, together with M. Buffon, yet I have frequently been informed that ducks, hatched under a hen, prefer them to the females of their own ſpecies, or rather genus. Suppoſing this to be true, where birds do not differ generically, as ducks and hens do, perhaps the hatching the eggs of one ſpecies under that of another is the moſt likely means to produce a mixed breed.

[o] As M. Buffon's moſt poſitive authority for this negative ſort of proof is Tavernier, I ſhall now endeavour to ſhew that little is to be inferred from

This ſeems to be a general anſwer to all ſuch negative authorities, becauſe the traveller certainly deſerves little or no credit, but in what relates to particulars ſeen or not ſeen by him, and in his own route.

Whenever any of theſe writers, however, happen to aſſert, that turkies are to be found in Aſia, M. Buffon will not give them credit, as in the caſe of Du Halde, whom he believes, when he ſays, that "*the Chineſe have them not, but from other countries*[p]," becauſe he ſpeaks of what he had been *an eye-witneſs of.* But M. Buffon pays no regard to the ſame authority, when he ſtates that theſe birds are very common in the Eaſt Indies, becauſe Du Halde is ſuppoſed to have received this account from others. Now I have always underſtood, that Du Halde had never been in China, or any other part of Aſia, having compiled his hiſtory from materials collected by others who had viſited that moſt extraordinary empire.

M. Buffon having endeavoured to prove that no turkies have been found in Aſia, in order to ſupport the excluſive claim of America, hath baniſhed this ſort of poultry likewiſe from Africa, aſſerting, upon the authority of Boſman, that thoſe which they have near Senegal were originally brought from Europe[q].

from the teſtimony of this traveller, who, indeed, does take upon himſelf to aſſert, that there are *no turkies in all Aſia*, though he never was but once in any part of the Indies, *viz.* in 1649, when he failed from Gombroon, in Perſia, to Suratte, Ceylon, and Batavia. But this is not all, for he hath refuted himſelf by the publication of his brother's account of the kingdom of Tunquin, where there is a print repreſenting the ceremony of a funeral in that part of Aſia, and the animals which are to be ſacrificed, amongſt which there is a Turkey-cock. See the third volume of Tavernier's Travels.

[p] Buffon's Orn. t. II. p. 150. Theſe *other countries*, however, moſt probably refer to other parts of Aſia.

[q] Hiſt. Nat. des Oiſ. t. II. p. 151. 158.

Boſman's

Bofman's Voyage to Africa was firft printed at London in 1705; and I conclude, that fuch turkies as he happened to fee at that time on the coaft of Guiney might not be in a wild ftate, but fupplied from Europe.

It fhould feem, however, that above a century before this the fame coaft abounded with them: for in Thomas Candifh's Voyage in 1588, he informs us, "That we found in this ifland (*viz.* St. Helena) great ftore of *Guiney cocks*, which we call *turkies*[r]."

Thefe birds were therefore either indigenous in St. Helena, "being found *in great ftore*[s];" or muft have been brought early in the fixteenth century by the Portuguefe from the coaft of Guiney[t], or the Eaft Indies, of both which they were the firft difcoverers, as well as of the ifland of St. Helena.

There is one circumftance, indeed, rather in favour of the Eaft Indies, which is, that a turkey to this day is called in the Portuguefe language *peru*, whilft it goes by the fame name in many parts of India; nor can it be contended that the bird is thus named from that part of South America, becaufe the Portuguefe had never any connexions with Peru. Befides which it never

[r] Hakluyt, Pt. II. p. 825.

[s] Four years before this, *viz.* in 1584, Mr. William Barrett touched at this ifland, and found there only two Portuguefe hermits. Turkies therefore could have been fcarcely introduced merely for their fuftenance; and if the Portuguefe had intended to make the fame ufe of the ifland that we do, they would have left there more ufeful members of fociety. Hakluyt, Pt. II. p. 280.

[t] So early as the year 1453, and confequently long before the difcovery of any part of America, a Venetian named *Alvife da Mofto*, fpeaks thus of birds, which he found on the coaft of Senegal. "There are alfo in this "country fome large birds, which we call *hens of Pharaoh*, and which "come to us (fc. the Venetians) from the *Levant*." Ramufio, v. 1. p. 104. B. Venezia, 1588. I fhall afterwards take notice, that one of the Turkifh fynonyms for this bird is *Mefry*, or of *Egypt*.

hath been insisted upon by any one, that turkies were found indigenous in that part of the globe.

But I have another authority to produce, that this bird abounded during the seventeenth century in the great island of Madagascar, so much nearer to the coast of Asia than St. Helena.

De la Croix, who published his General History of Africa in 1688, informs us, that there are many turkies in the *woods* of Madagascar [u], which therefore it should seem most highly probable were indigenous, because the Portuguese were merely the first discoverers of that island; and, though the French did begin a small settlement in 1640, yet it was soon abandoned. De la Croix may be supposed to have received this account from some of these settlers, who clearly speak of them as in a wild state; whilst otherwise it would have been highly natural to mention, that these birds had multiplied greatly since their first introduction from Europe.

Let us now examine how this bird is called in most of the European languages, as it must afford so strong a proof of the country from whence it was first introduced, especially if most of these concurr in pointing to Asia, or Africa, for its origin, whilst none bear the most distant allusion to America.

The Spanish term is not Pavon *de las Indias*, as M. Buffon states, but simply *pavo*, and formerly *pago*. If moreover the name were Pavon de las Indias, it would not signify the West Indies, as in all European languages the addition of *Western* is necessary, and for the following reason, besides the constant usage.

The country called India, during the earlier centuries, comprehended only the territory of the Great Mogul (properly the present Hindostan) but when the Portuguese had discovered the

[u] "Beaucoup des coqs d'Inde dans les bois." Relation Universelle Afrique, tom. IV. p. 426. *Lyon*, 1688.

two

two great peninſulas which lie to the South, theſe three immenſe territories went by the name of the *Indies* for pre-eminence. When America therefore is referred to, it muſt be termed the *Weſt Indies*, to diſtinguiſh it from the Aſiatic India, ſo long in poſſeſſion of that appellation.

I ſuſpect, however, that the turkey was never termed Pavo de las *Indias*, becauſe we ſhall find that in moſt of the European tongues it is ſtiled Cock of *India* and not of the *Indies*.

In France, therefore, the name is Coq-d'Inde [not des Indes], Indar, Paon d'Inde, Dindon [x]. In Italian, Gallina Indiana.

Buffon gives us the German name of *Indianiſcher hahn*, or the *cock of India*, but he omits the more common appellation of *Welſcher hahn*, or the cock from Italy; as alſo *Kalekutiſcher hahn* [y], or the cock from Calcutta [z]. Nor is it at all extraordinary, that this bird ſhould paſs under different names in different parts of the ſame empire, as the turkey to this day is called in Scotland *Bubble-Jack*, [or *Snotty-Jack*], from the caruncle which projects and hangs down beyond the bill of the male bird.

The Portugueſe ſynonym is *peru*, which I am informed is the name for a turkey in the Eaſt Indies, whilſt that of the Swedes and Danes is *kalkohn*; in all which terms there is not the leaſt alluſion to its firſt coming from Mexico, or being diſperſed from Spain into the different parts of Europe and Aſia. In the modern Greek this bird is called *Yana*.

[x] Cotgrave's Dictionary.

[y] The moſt common name in Sileſia is *auer hahn*, which I am told ſignifies the *wild hen*. In Bavaria and the Palatinate, it is called *Trutt hehn*. See Schoeffer's Ornithology. The Synonyms of *Welſcher* and *Kalekutiſcher* are to be found in Johnſton's Natural Hiſtory, printed at Amſterdam in 1657.

[z] Barboſa viſited Bengal in 1518, and ſpeaks of ſeeing there "Galline "grandiſſime, e ſmiſurate," by which he poſſibly means theſe Calcutta turkies. Ramuſio, Vol. I. *Gallus decumanus*, quem Geſnerus *gallopavum* vocat. De-Bry, Hiſt. Orient. Pt. 6.

I ſhall now mention ſome of the Aſiatic names for a turkey.

I find by an Italian and Turkiſh Dictionary, printed at Rome in 1641, that this bird is termed in that language *Hind Taughi*[a]; and in Arabic *Deek Hindy*, both ſignifying the cock of *India*; in ſome parts of Aſia Minor alſo, I am informed that it is ſtiled *Meſry* or *Myſyr*, ſignifying the bird from Egypt.

It will ſcarcely therefore be contended that the Turks (who muſt have had this bird in conſiderable numbers before 1641, ſo that it had obtained an Arabic as well as Turkiſh name) by the term *Hindy* mean the Weſt Indies[b], about which they were then, and continue to be ſo ignorant, eſpecially as America in their language is called *Yeni dunia*[c]; beſides that ſome of them conceive the bird to have been introduced from Egypt by the term of *Meſry* or *Myſyr*, it having probably been brought from India to Suez, and from thence to Cairo.

I ſhall cloſe the different ſynonyms by our name of *turkey*, which I have proved to have been uſed in England ſo long ago as the year 1555, becauſe the chickens or powts made part of a ſerjeant's feaſt in that year.

Turkies had ſo increaſed in England within twenty-five years from this, that Caius in his account of our *rarer* animals (printed in 1570) omits mention of them, though he is very particular in the deſcription of a *Guinea hen*, ſtiling it Meleagris. At the latter end of the ſame century they were driven by the carriers from Kent to London, as they are now from Norfolk[d].

[a] It had therefore obtained this name in Turkey, twenty years before (according to Tavernier) it was ſcarcely heard of in any parts of Aſia.

[b] *Hind* or *Hend*. Les Indes *Orientales*. Herbelot.

[c] Or the *New World*, the Arabs uſing the ſame term, though they ſometimes ſay alſo *Amerik*.

[d] See Shakeſpear's Henry IV. Pt. I. By a proclamation in 1633, their price at different growths is ſettled. Rymer, Vol. VIII. Pt. IV. p. 53. Some horſes left near Buenos Ayres, by the Spaniards, in thirty years filled the country for twenty leagues round. Hakluyt, Pt. III. p. 7.

But Buffon himſelf ſupplies us with a more deciſive proof againſt the claim of America, by aſſerting that turkies were firſt known in France during the reign of Francis the Iſt, and in England during that of Henry the VIIIth.

As for what he advances in relation to France, it reſts upon a tradition which I ſhall have no reaſon to controvert, as this tradition does not ſettle whence they were ſo introduced. Francis the Iſt, however, dying in 1547, which was but nineteen years after Cortez's firſt return to Spain, it is not very probable that they ſhould have come from America.

With regard to their being firſt known in England during the reign of Henry the VIII. this depends upon the following old verſe:

> Turkies, carps, hops, pickarel, and beere,
> Came into England in one yeare.

Theſe old lines are certainly erroneous with regard to ſome of the particulars; but are generally agreed to have been made from the tenth to the fifteenth year of Henry the Eighth, or from 1519 to 1524; the lateſt of which is before Cortez's firſt return to Spain, and conſequently we muſt have been ſupplied with theſe birds from ſome other quarter than that of Mexico. It is to be obſerved alſo, that they are thus early called *Turkies.*

I have indeed preſumed to ſuggeſt a ſtill more early introduction of turkies into England, under the name of *Capons of Greaſe*; nor is it impoſſible that Fitz Steven who wrote in the time of Henry the IId. alludes to them under the term of Afra Avis, which ſeems to have formed ſome part of an entertainment, during the Thirteenth Century, at a London Feaſt.

Some alſo have relied much on their not being mentioned in our oldeſt bills of fare; but it muſt be recollected that we have

have very few of these till the Sixteenth Century; as also, that the place where the feast is given, and the time of year, is very material. If at a distance from London, these dainties could not be procured; whilst the autumn *only* produced the chickens or powts, which were then only eaten by our ancestors, as they had not discovered that a grown turkey becomes only a delicacy by having been kept for a fortnight or three weeks.

Having thus endeavoured to shew that M. Buffon is not supported by any of his authorities in the turkey's not being known till the discovery of America, it would be uncandid to suppress a stronger proof on his side of the question than any which he hath produced, and which I happened to stumble upon in my researches on this question.

Peter Gyllius, who was a native of France, and published a translation of Ælian's Miscellaneous History in 1535, together with a few remarks of his own, hath described the turkey; saying, that the living specimens had been brought *ex Novo Orbe.*

Though, perhaps, there may be doubts whether this expression alludes to America, or the discoveries of the Portuguese in Asia, yet I will admit it to refer to the former, according to Gyllius's meaning; but still I conceive he must have been deceived from the following circumstances.

Gyllius was born in 1490, and died in 1555, having travelled for forty years of his life, and, amongst other parts of the world, to Constantinople, of which he hath printed a description, together with that of the Bosphorus Thracius. As he does not mention *where* he saw these birds, it is not improbable that this might have happened in Turkey; and can it be otherwise supposed that they could have been brought to any part of Europe (except Spain), within eight years from Cortez's first return from

 Mexico,

Mexico, which happened in 1527, whilſt Gyllius's work was publiſhed in 1533? It is highly probable alſo, that this aſſertion was made many years before it appeared in print.

There is another very deciſive circumſtance with regard to his meaning either to refer to the Eaſt Indies by *Novus Orbis*, or otherwiſe being miſtaken in ſuppoſing that the birds came from America, which is, that the cock is deſcribed to be of the dark colour obſerved commonly in wild birds, whilſt the hen was *white*.

Now ſuch a change of colour ariſes from birds and other animals being long domeſticated and pampered; nor can it probably be produced in ſo ſhort a ſpace of time as eight years, allowing their importation from America as early a date as poſſible.

Whilſt birds remain in a wild ſtate, the leaſt deviation from the common plumage becomes a phænomenon, and is depoſited in the Muſeums of the curious; but the conſtant ſupply of palatable food, together perhaps with a better protection from the inclemencies of the weather, produces daily *varieties* in all our poultry, as it does in Canary birds [e].

I ſhall now urge another argument of ſome preſumption againſt the Mexican claim. Wherever birds are found indige-

[e] The darker colour in all wild birds, and which conſequently are not protected by man, is a moſt providential circumſtance againſt their being diſcovered by their numerous enemies. In birds of the gayeſt plumage therefore, the young of both ſexes do not aſſume their bright and gloſſy feathers, till the third year; nor does the female at any age, who would be otherwiſe ſeen whilſt ſitting. No colour, however, points out a bird ſo much to it's purſuers as that of white; and Columella, for that reaſon, adviſes againſt the white breed of chickens, as being more eaſily ſeen by hawks. De Re Ruſtica, l. viii. c. 2. As for the Ptarmigan, it is an exception which proves the juſtice of the general obſervation, becauſe it becomes white only, when the ground is covered with ſnow.

nous,

nous, they are in the climate beſt ſuited to their wants, and moſt favourable to the increaſe of their ſpecies. The mother bird therefore moſt aſſiduouſly exerts and attends to the great duties of incubation, and rearing her young. Theſe ſame birds, however, removed to other climates, often neglect, or ſeem inſenſible of this moſt providential impulſe, which I conceive to ariſe from a ſuppoſition that their neſtlings cannot be reared.

In our own latitudes we find this almoſt conſtantly with regard to pea and Guiney hens, whilſt, on the other hand, a duck removed to a tropical climate will ſeldom hatch her eggs or rear her young.

A French gentleman, therefore, named Moriſette, who for ſome years hatched chickens in ovens near Lambeth Marſh, gave me the following account:

The firſt time he went to Batavia, he was at dinner with a large company, when a man came in out of breath, to inform them, that he had found a duck ſitting upon her eggs, on which every one but himſelf immediately left the room to ſee this uncommon ſight. After this Mr. Moriſette having been employed both by the Engliſh, Dutch, French, and Portugueſe, viſited almoſt every part of the Eaſt Indies, where he found that ducks would not ſit for any time, and which is the occaſion of the Chineſe (who live ſo much upon this bird) making uſe of ovens for this purpoſe, and contriving that the young ones ſhall burſt the egg, whilſt the gleanings of the rice harveſt float upon the water[f].

[f] I rather ſuſpect, for the ſame reaſon, that hens do not ſit cloſe in Egypt, though this moſt uſeful of all poultry is admitted to breed well in almoſt every climate, and to be an exception to the general obſervation which I have ventured to make.

To

To apply this general obſervation to the inſtance of the turkey. Mexico is not only ſituated within the tropicks, but the continent in that part being narrow between the two ſeas, I ſhould ſuppoſe that the climate muſt be nearly the ſame with that of Jamaica, where Brown informs us "that turkies require a good "deal of care, and a moderate climate when young[g]", which ſeems to imply neglect commonly in the mother bird. On the other hand, turkies are very attentive to their parental duties in all the more moderate climates of Europe, which circumſtance affords ſome preſumption that we derive this bird originally from the Northern parts of Indoſtan, which are not only out of the Tropic, but being inland have often very conſiderable degrees of cold.

I therefore conceive, that if Gyllius ſpeaks of America by the term of *Novus Orbis*, he was impoſed upon by thoſe who ſhewed him theſe then extraordinary birds, as we know well how every one's curioſity muſt have been raiſed with regard to the productions of that lately diſcovered quarter of the globe. To this it may be added, that Belon, who writes expreſsly on birds (and therefore deſerves much more credit on the point in controverſy) ſo far from imagining that turkies came from America, gives us his opinion, that they were known to the ancients. Now Belon was a Frenchman as well as Gyllius, and only publiſhed his Ornithology in 1555, or twenty years after Gyllius's work.

I have thus ſtated, for the deciſions of others, this new authority on the ſide of America, together with the circumſtances which may invalidate it: if, upon the whole, my arguments ſhould not be deemed irrefragable againſt the turkey's being found indigenous in Mexico, yet I flatter myſelf that I have fully proved that this bird was not peculiar to America, as M. Buffon hath contended.

g Hiſtory of Jamaica, p. 470. See alſo ante, p. 129, where there is a citation from Du Tertre to the ſame import.

Having thus endeavoured to prove that the turkey (whether indigenous or not in the neighbourhood of Mexico) could not have been firſt introduced into Europe from that quarter of the globe; I ſhall next conſider another queſtion of ſome moment amongſt the ornithologiſts, whether it was the *meleagris* of the ancients.

Moſt of the earlier writers on this part of Natural Hiſtory have rather ſuppoſed the meleagris to be the ſame bird; but M. de Buffon contends that the meleagris was the *Peintade* or Guiney hen.

I will not pretend to pronounce with any poſitiveneſs on this point; but I muſt own that I rather conceive, neither the one nor the other were commonly known to the ancients, at leaſt to the Romans, nor were perhaps uſed by them or the Greeks as poultry.

My firſt reaſon for this is, that I do not conceive how theſe very uſeful birds, having been once introduced into Italy, could have been loſt, as both turkies and Guiney hens were undoubtedly for ſo many centuries: whereas the peacock, by no means ſo neceſſary as either of them, was continued from the time of the Romans to the preſent century. It is agreed likewiſe that the common hen was originally introduced from Aſia.

But it may be ſaid, that this argument is not to hold againſt poſitive deſcriptions of the bird, which I agree to; but let us examine what theſe deſcriptions are.

Ovid, in his Eighth Book of the Metamorphoſes, transforms the ſiſters of Meleager into theſe birds, in the following lines.

—— natis in corpore pennis
Allevat, & *longas* per brachia porrigit *alas*,
Corneaque ora facit, *verſaſque per aera* mittit.

Now

Now Ovid is known to be very accurate in the deſcription of the animals into which every one is changed[h]; and yet, of the only three circumſtances mentioned in this deſcription, two of them are not the leaſt applicable to the Guiney hen, for this bird hath very ſhort wings, and conſequently ſeldom takes any flights. Even the third circumſtance of *corneaque ora facit* perhaps implies nothing more than the change of the human mouth into a bird's bill.

Varro ſpeaks of the Meleagris after mention of the *Gallina ruſtica*, which he ſays was then rare at Rome, and ſcarcely ever ſeen but in a cage. He then obſerves that they are like the African hens, *aſpectu ac faciè incontaminatâ*[i], which brings him to the deſcription of the *Gallina Africana*; Gallinæ Africanæ ſunt *grandes*, variæ, gibberæ quas μελεαγρίδας appellant Græci.

Now when the reſemblance to fowls is mentioned, it certainly cannot be ſaid of the *Guiney hen*, that they are comparatively *large*, or grandes.

Columella thus alludes to the meleagris:

Africana eſt, (quam plerique Numidicam dicunt) Meleagridi ſimilis, niſi quod *rutilam* galeam & criſtam in capite gerit quæ utraque ſunt in Meleagride *cærulea*[k]." Now a Guinea hen hath neither creſt nor comb; and as for the horny nob on its head, it is red and not blue. Columella by this paſſage likewiſe only ſays, that the African hen is *like* the meleagris, except as to the colour of its creſt and comb, and not that it is the ſame bird.

[h] I ſhould therefore wiſh, that if an elegant edition of the Metamorphoſes ſhould be printed, it might be beautified and illuſtrated by coloured engravings from ſpecimens in Sir Aſhton Lever's moſt capital Muſeum.

[i] De Re Ruſtica, l. iii. c. 9. I muſt own that I have no clear idea of what Varro means by *facie incontaminatâ*.

[k] Columella de Re Ruſtica, l. viii. c. 2.

As the African hen is here likewife fpoken of, and faid to have been more commonly called the Numidian hen, it explains that Martial cannot allude to the *peintade* in the following lines. After having ftated that his friend Fauftinus's villa was a mere farm, the poet enumerates his poultry:

"Vagatur omnis turba fordidæ cortis;
"Argutus anfer, gemmeique pavones
"Nomenque debet quæ rubentibus pennis,
"Et picta perdix, *Numidicæque* guttatæ,
"Et impiorum phafiana Colchorum,
"Rhodias fuperbi fœminas premunt galli."

Martial, L. iii. Ep. 58.

I cannot but rather think that Martial defcribes thefe birds from a picture, than what were before his eyes in the farm-yard (for fo I tranflate *fordidæ cortis*) becaufe the Phænicopterus, or Flamingo, is plainly alluded to by

Nomenque dedit quæ rubentibus pennis;

and though fome of the Roman Epicures were fond of the flamingo's tongue, yet it cannot be well conceived that they were reared as poultry. But the moft material part is to determine what the poet means by

Numidicæque guttatæ.

As I have juft now proved from the words of Columella, that the African and Numidian hen were the fame bird, and that it differed in moft material circumftances from the *peintade*, I cannot underftand any thing more to be implied by this expreffion, than the common fowl from Numidia, fpotted in a rather particular manner, as the *penciled and partridge hens* are with us, the varieties being fo numerous; but ftill with fome care fuch a beautiful breed may be continued for a confiderable time. In this fame poem, therefore, we find mention of the

U fowl

fowl from Rhodes, whilſt Varro and Columella likewiſe recommend the ſorts which came from Africa and Media.

Another circumſtance which inclines me to think that our Guiney hens were little known to the ancients, is that neither the moſt diſagreeable noiſe, which they are perpetually making, nor their moſt envious and quarrelſome diſpoſition, are noticed by any of the writers who may be ſuppoſed to have alluded to them.

Pliny ſpeaks twice of the Meleagris, which he ſays were not ſoon introduced to the Roman tables, *propter ingratum virus*. We know, however, of no diſagreeable or poiſonous taſte in the Guiney hen at preſent, but, on the contrary, eſteem it to be a bird of excellent flavour.

In his thirty-ſeventh Book, and ſecond Chapter, the ſame naturaliſt cites Cteſias for ſaying, that near a place called Sicyone in Africa, and the river of Crathis, which empties itſelf into the ocean, there were birds called Meleagrides and Penelopes [l]; whilſt a few lines afterwards he referrs to Sophocles the Tragedian, for ſaying that amber is made by the tears of the Meleagrides *beyond India*. There ſeems, therefore, to be as little agreement amongſt the ancient Romans about the place theſe birds were brought from, as in their deſcription of them.

It appears from this great uncertainty in deſcribing the Meleagris by the Roman writers, that, if known at all by them, it was not conſidered as poultry, becauſe, if that was the caſe, they muſt have continued in Italy till the ſixteenth century, when they were firſt introduced from Africa [m], and as I ſhould ſuppoſe from the Coaſt of Guiney, according to their Engliſh name. Nor can I hear that they are at preſent found in a wild ſtate

[l] Ariſtotle conſiders the bird of this name, as a ſea eagle. L. viii. c. 3.

[m] We are informed likewiſe by Margrave, that they were firſt brought to Braſil from the ſame quarter.

upon the Northern parts of that vaſt continent [n]. On the contrary, Athenæus mentions, that they were brought from Ethiopia, and carried about in cages at a proceſſion of Ptolemy Philadelphus [o]. Photius alſo informs us, that ſome of them were to be found on an iſland of the river Nile, and probably the upper part of that river [p].

I ſhould for theſe reaſons rather ſuppoſe, that when the Romans ſpeak of Volucres Libycæ or Numidicæ, they only refer to a variety of the common fowl, the plumage of which might ſomewhat reſemble that of the Guiney hen, as we now diſtinguiſh them by the name of Bantam, &c.

I am by no means ſo clear that Guiney hens were not conſidered as poultry by the Greeks, though their having been introduced to Europe from the Coaſt of Guiney makes me ſuſpect that they were not, becauſe this delicacy could not have been wanting for the tables of the emperors when they reſided at Conſtantinople, and conſequently the breed could not be entirely

[n] Dr. Shaw takes no notice of the *peintade* amongſt the birds in the neighbourhood of Algiers, but on the contrary gives an engraving and deſcription of the *Rhaad* or *Saf-ſaf*, which anſwers almoſt in every circumſtance with Columella's account of the Meleagris. The *Rhaad* is of the ſize of a capon, and hath a tuft of *blue feathers* on its head; having no hind claw, it may properly be conſidered as a buſtard; and there is a ſpecimen of the leſſer ſpecies of this bird in Sir Aſhton Lever's Muſeum, which Dr. Shaw obſerves hath no tuft of blue feathers behind the head; it is alſo elegantly mottled with brown and white.

I had an opportunity of ſhewing Dr. Shaw's engraving and deſcription of the Rhaad, to a lady who had lived many years at Tunis, and who told me that ſhe believed it to be what was there more commonly called the *Hen of Carthage*, becauſe it was generally brought from thence, and eſteemed a good bird for the table. From theſe circumſtances it is not improbable that the Rhaad may be the Meleagris of the Romans, their intercourſe being chiefly with the neighbourhood of Carthage, after their conqueſt of that part of Africa.

The ſame lady informed me that they had no Guiney hens at Tunis but what came from Italy.

[o] Athenæus, L. IX.

[p] P. 1366. Rhotomagi, 1653.

 loſt

loſt in that part of the world. We find alſo, by what hath before been mentioned from Athenæus, that Ptolemy Philadelphus was obliged to ſend to Ethiopia for them, inſtead of Greece.

There is, however, ſo particular a deſcription of the Guiney hen in the 14th book of the ſame writer, that there cannot be the leaſt doubt of this bird being referred to, and I ſhall therefore tranſlate the whole paſſage:

" Clytus of Miletus[q], a diſciple of Ariſtotle, mentions theſe " particulars about the meleagris. They are to be found near the " temple of Minerva in Ærus[r]; and they are ſo negligent of " their young, that it is neceſſary for the prieſts to look after " them. They are about the ſize of a grown fowl, have a head " rather ſmaller than in proportion to their body, which is ſmooth " (or naked), and hath upon it a fleſhy hard and round knob, " which riſes above the head like a ſmall ſtake[s], and of the " colour of wood[t]. Near the cheeks lies a long piece of fleſh " like a beard, which begins from the mouth, and is redder " than in hens; but it hath not the comb of the latter (or as " ſome call it *the beard*), but appears to be mutilated in that part. " The beak is larger and ſharper than that of a hen; the neck " is blacker, thicker, and ſhorter; the whole body is variegated, " being black intermixed with white ſpots larger than a wart[u], " which are ſurrounded with ſmall black circles or rhomboids, " producing that variety of plumage by a mixture of white and " black; the wing feathers are diſtinguiſhed by white and ſerrated " lines, which are parallel. They have no ſpur on their legs like " cocks; and the female can ſcarcely be diſtinguiſhed from the male."

This deſcription upon the whole cannot be applied to any other bird but the Guiney hen; and yet it is very remarkable

[q] The town of Ionia ſo called, not that of Calabria.

[r] Some place near Miletus probably.

[s] Πατταλον. [t] Ξυλοειδες. It is, however, of a red colour. [u] Φακων.

that

that the comparifon is made throughout with the common hen, rather than the partridge or the pheafant[x]; as alfo, that neither Clytus, nor the *deipnofophift* himfelf, takes notice that the bird is good for the table.

I fhould therefore conceive that even amongft the Greeks, though the bird had been feen by them, yet that it was very rare, and not fuppofed to be a palatable food. It confequently fared the fate of other uncommon animals, which are not confidered as ufeful, and was foon loft.

It requires a confiderable time to remove our early ideas with regard to animals being improper for the table. In many parts of Ireland they will not eat landrails; and the Highlanders of Scotland reject both eels and pike.

P. S. After the preceding part of this effay was printed, I have happened to meet with authorities, which, perhaps, add fome confirmation to what I have before contended.

Liebaut publifhed the firft edition of his Maifon Ruftique in 1582, and hath a particular chapter upon turkies, under the name of Poules d'Inde, againft the rearing of which he advifes *whether they were brought from the iflands of India lately difcovered by the Spaniards or Portuguefe*, becaufe they are more chargeable than a mule.

It appears by this paffage, that in 1582, and perhaps fome years before the actual publication of this work, there were doubts whether turkies had been introduced by the Portuguefe or the Spaniards, and as it fhould feem, whether from the Philippines, or any of the *iflands* firft known to the Portuguefe in the Eaft Indies, for the expreffion is *India*; and as to America, the firft fettlements of the fame nation were upon the continent of Brazil.

[x] The *peintade* likewife hath no fpur, and therefore differs in that very effential particular from the common cock.

Liebaut

Liebaut was a Doctor of Physic, and no work hath gone through more editions, or been translated into more languages; the authority therefore, as to this doubt, is more considerable, than if taken from most modern publications upon the subject of rural œconomy. It is to be remarked also, that he makes no mention of the Guiney hen, which proves that bird to have been as scarce in France at that time, as I have supposed it to be in England.

I shall take this same opportunity of stating from Camoens what affords some degree of confirmation with regard to turkies being found on the Southern coast of Africa, at the beginning of the sixteenth century, by his mentioning that the women of the *Cape* brought to the Portuguese both *hens* and sheep [y].

Camoens was born in 1517; and as he went himself a voyage to the East Indies, and made Vasco da Gama's expedition the subject of an Epic Poem, it is highly probable that he had received the account of this interview from some of those who had sailed on that famous enterprize.

But it may be asked, why these *galinhas* (or hens) mentioned by the Poet, are conceived to be turkies? to which I answer, that all the Naturalists have agreed that the common cock came originally from Asia; and there having been no intercourse between that vast continent and the Southern promontory of Africa before the time of Vasco da Gama, it affords a presumption that the birds alluded to are turkies, and not hens [z].

[y] Estes, como na vista prazenteyros
Fossem, humanamente nos trataraon,
Trazendonos, *galinhas*, & carneyros.

Lusiadas, Canto V. St. 64.

[z] They could not likewise be *peintades*, because none of the early travellers mention those birds being wild in the neighbourhood of the Cape of Good Hope.

I have

I have in the outſet of this Eſſay admitted, that turkies were found in a wild ſtate upon the coaſt of Virginia at the latter end of the ſixteenth century; and though I have conceived from many proofs that they were not indigenous in the neighbourhood of Mexico, I do not pretend to aſſert this with the poſitiveneſs uſed by Mr. de Buffon, in relation to their being unknown in Europe till the diſcovery of America, the contrary of which I hope to have fully evinced. If M. de Buffon had not thus excluded Aſia and Africa, the controverſy would have turned out, as if the point to be diſcuſſed was, whether tobacco and potatoes were not peculiar to the New World. Now it is certain that both theſe plants are of American growth, but not excluſively ſo, for in 1584, Cavendiſh received potatoes from the inhabitants of Capul, which is an iſland not far from Manilla[a]; and in 1616, Schouten was ſupplied with tobacco from the coaſt of New Guiney[b].

[a] See Calander's Collection of Voyages, Vol. I. p. 459.
[b] Ibid. Vol. II.

ESSAY

ESSAY II.

ON THE REIN-DEER.

IT hath been a generally received opinion, that the rein-deer[a] will not live for any time ſouth of Lapland, or that part of North America which, though of a more ſouthern latitude, equals Lapland in the rigour of its climate.

Queen Chriſtina of Sweden had procured five and twenty of theſe quadrupeds, which ſhe propoſed to ſend to Oliver Cromwell, and which might long ſince have proved the contrary, had they reached this country.

Whitelock was then ambaſſador from England at that court, and endeavoured to prevail upon four Laplanders, who brought the reins as far as Stockholm, to attend them to England, which they refuſed to do, but ſaid they would take care of them during the winter. The Laplanders, however, were very negligent in their charge, for ſoon afterwards fifteen were killed by the wolves, and the remaining ten did not long ſurvive, the climate of Stockholm being conſidered as too warm[b].

Buffon,

[a] Rennthier (which is uſually pronounced rein-deer) ſignifies an animal formed for running, from the Teutonic word *rennen* to run. Buſching's Geography, Vol. I. p. 345.

[b] See the Journal of Whitelock's Swediſh embaſſy, Vol. I. p. 442. I ſhall here ſtate ſome other inſtances, however, of reins being brought to more ſouthern countries, where they ſeem to have lived a conſiderable time.

Sir

Buffon (who is one of the lateſt naturaliſts that hath deſcribed the Rein-deer) mentions, that three or four were not long ſince carried to Dantzic, where they ſoon died, as the temperature of the air was too mild for them [c]; and in another part of the ſame article, he regrets the impoſſibility of ſeeing this quadruped alive in France, on which account he only engraves the ſkeleton, having procured a drawing from a ſpecimen in the Muſeum of the Royal Society. Pontoppidan alſo ſays, that it will always be a vain attempt to naturalize this animal in other countries, as no nouriſhment can be found any where elſe which will keep them alive, ſo that they have all periſhed [d].

Notwithſtanding, however, this moſt prevailing opinion, it is contradicted, by the fact of a buck Rein-deer having lived near three years at Homerton (not far from Hackney), in the cloſe of Mr. Heyde, a merchant, and which died only in 1773, very ſuddenly, having been the preceding day in perfect health. He was ſent to England from Norway with a doe, which did not

Sir Hierom Bowes, who was ambaſſador from Queen Elizabeth to the court of Ruſſia, brought over with him certain *fallow deer*, which being yoked together drew a man ſitting in a ſled, which deer I ſuppoſe muſt have been reins. Camden's Annals, A. D. 1584.

Geſner, indeed, informs us, that the king of Sweden (though ſo near to Lapland) cauſed ten of theſe deer to be driven conſtantly upon the higheſt mountains, in the neighbourhood of the place where they were kept, becauſe they could not endure the heat of that part of Sweden. The ſame author, however, mentions, that a rein was preſented to the duke of Saxony in 1561. Scheffer likewiſe, who was never in Lapland, and printed his work at Straſburgh, gives us the figure of a rein-deer which he himſelf had ſeen. After theſe inſtances, and that mentioned above, I may boldly pronounce the notion, that this ſpecies of deer will not live to the ſouthward of Lapland, to be a vulgar error.

[c] Buffon, Tom. XII. p. 98, citing Regnard.

[d] Pt. II. p. 210.

live more than a year; and Mr. Heyde hath this autumn [1773] received a male and female, which were in November laſt very healthy. Leemius obſerves, that in Finmark they are ſubject to the epilepſy [e].

Every written voyage to the higher northern latitudes makes mention of this very uſeful quadruped, whilſt Scheffer, Buffon, Hoffberg, and Leemius, have given us its natural hiſtory.

Leemius is the laſt of theſe, who publiſhed at Copenhagen his account of Finmark Lapland in 1767, and reſided in that country more than ten years; he is therefore more to be depended upon than any of the others, who it is believed never ſaw the animal alive; at leaſt the upper antlers, as engraved by Hoffberg, more reſemble thoſe of the Elk than of the rein-deer. There is, however, a very good repreſentation of the rein-deer in Pennant's Synopſis of Quadrupeds.

As Leemius's work, hath ſcarcely found its way yet into the more ſouthern parts of Europe, I ſhall make ſome extracts from it, with regard to this animal, with which he had ſo frequent opportunities of being thoroughly acquainted.

It is agreed by all naturaliſts to be peculiar to the female Rein-deer, that they ſhould have horns as well as the male: Leemius however remarks, that this is not always the fact, ſome having none at all, as likewiſe that they loſe them entirely after parturition [f].

The projecting brow antler alſo is not obſerved in any other ſpecies of deer, the uſe of which I ſhould conceive to be a proper defence againſt that arch enemy the wolf; and Leemius accordingly

[e] See alſo Amœn. Acad. Vol. IV. p. 144.

[f] P. 142.—Scheffer cites Olaus for the rein's, having a third horn in the middle of their heads, and confirms this on his own authority. See p. 324. c. 28; as alſo for their attaining their full ſize in the fourth year.

mentions

mentions an inſtance of one Rein having drove away two of theſe maroders. When the reins, however, uſe their antlers againſt their own ſpecies in the rutting time, the horns are frequently ſo entangled, that they cannot be ſeparated but by the aſſiſtance of the Rein herd[g].

If it be aſked why every ſpecies of deer hath not the ſame protection? the anſwer ſeems to be, that the ſwiftneſs of the other kinds enables them to eſcape their purſuer.

Though the northern naturaliſts ſpeak of the expedition alſo, with which the Rein-deer will draw the traineau; yet I beg leave to ſay, from having ſeen three of theſe animals, that they are rather of a make calculated for the collar, than for extraordinary ſwiftneſs; and I have little doubt but that they are the floweſt of their whole genus[h], except the Elk, whoſe antlers are alſo of a moſt peculiar form, as well as ſtrength.

I ſhould conceive likewiſe, that the Elk makes uſe of theſe extraordinary horns to remove the thick underwood and briars in which this quadruped lives, not being ſo fleet as the reſt of its genus are: the antlers therefore are exceſſively wide, as well as ſhallow, and the ſagged terminations ſeem not improper to perform the office of a ſaw.

I know well that ſome naturaliſts, not being able to find out the uſe of particular parts in ſeveral animals, have rather ridiculed the attempt to diſcover for what purpoſe they are deſigned: I am perſuaded, however, that this ariſes from ignorance of the habits of the animal (which is the intereſting part of Natural Hiſtory); nor is it leſs true, becauſe it hath been often advanced, *that nature does nothing in vain.*

[g] Leemius, c. 9.

[h] Outhier obſerves, that they move but very ſlowly except the track is very even. Voyage au Nord, p. 142.

Buffon makes but one article of the Rein and Elk; he alſo obſerves, that when the latitude begins to be too warm for the former, the Elks are firſt to be diſcovered. North America furniſhes, however, an exception to this obſervation, becauſe Reins are found in Newfoundland, 50° N. lat. and the Hudſon's-bay Company have a noble ſpecimen of Elk's horns in their hall, which was ſent them from their forts, ſome of which are nine degrees to the northward; at the ſame time that the ſituation is ſo much more inland, and conſequently from that circumſtance alſo the temperature more cold than might be expected, merely from the fort's being nine degrees nearer to the Pole. On the other hand *Iſbrand Ides* met with a great many Reins not far from Nezzinſkoi, which is only in N. lat. 50. at no great diſtance from the Eaſtern Ocean.

I ſhall now mention two or three particulars from Leemius, with regard to the Rein, which have not been noticed by other naturaliſts.

They are extravagantly fond of human urine, and lick up the ſnow with the greateſt avidity when the upper part hath been ſtained by it; poſſibly, however, the opening the way to their favourite lichen may be in part the occaſion of their immediately finding out ſuch ſpots.

We have the ſame authority for their killing a vaſt number of mice, which are called in the Lapland language *Godde Saepaw*, and *Lemæner* in the Norwegian. As their make, however, is not deſcribed, and as I can find no names which bear the leaſt affinity in the Fauna Suecica, it is impoſſible to ſettle the ſpecies. Poſſibly alſo the Reins only uſe this food when they can procure no other; it is for the ſame reaſon that the Lapland gulls are ſaid likewiſe to feed on mice, and the crows to tear the linen which is hung to dry. Leemius, in other parts of his work, mentions, that they devour the heads of theſe mice only, with the greateſt avidity; which alſo may ariſe from want of other food, as it is believed that no other quadruped (which chews the cud) deſtroys animals for the purpoſe of ſuſtenance.

All deſcribers of the Rein have taken notice of the cracking noiſe which they make when they move their legs, which Hoffberg attributes to the animals ſeparating and afterwards bringing together the diviſions of their hoof; but he does not aſſign the cauſe of the Reins ſo doing, which I conceive to be the following[k].

The Rein inhabits a country which is covered with ſnow for great part of the year; the hoof therefore of this quadruped is moſt admirably adapted to the ſurface which it is moſt commonly to tread.

The under part is entirely covered with hair, in the ſame manner that the claw of the Ptarmigaw is with feathery briſtles, which is almoſt the only bird that can endure the rigour of the ſame climate.

The hoof, however, is not only thus protected; the ſame neceſſity which obliges the Laplanders to uſe ſnow ſhoes makes the extraordinary width of the Rein's hoof to be equally convenient in paſſing over ſnow, as it prevents their ſinking too deep, which they would be ſubject to eternally, did the weight of their body reſt only on a ſmall point.

[k] M. Buffon ſuppoſes that the Elk makes the ſame ſnapping noiſe with the Rein, which, if true, ſeems to ariſe from its having the ſame occaſion to traverſe large tracts of ſnow. I can only ſay that I ſaw a live Elk about ten years ago, which belonged to Lord Rockingham, and that, though I put this awkward quadruped in motion, I did not hear any ſuch noiſe. Sir Jerom Eowes, who was ambaſſador from Queen Elizabeth to the Duke of Muſcovy, brought with him from thence an Elk. Cambden's Annals, 1583.

This

This quadruped hath therefore an inſtinct to uſe a hoof of ſuch a form in a ſtill more advantageous manner, by ſeparating it when the foot is to touch the ground, ſo as to cover a larger ſurface of ſnow. The inſtant, however, the leg of the animal is raiſed, the width of the foot becomes inconvenient, eſpecially when it is going againſt the wind; the hoof, therefore, is then immediately contracted, and the colliſion of the parts occaſions the ſnapping, which is heard upon every motion of the Rein.

Another reaſon, poſſibly, for this noiſe, may ariſe from Lapland's being not only covered with ſnow great part of the year, but alſo for ſome time under a perpetual night; the Rein is a gregarious animal, and often obliged to go a great way for ſuſtenance, probably therefore the cracking which they perpetually make, may ſerve to keep them together when the weather is remarkably dark. Bells round ſheep are known to be very convenient for the ſame purpoſe, when they graze upon a wide extended down.

Leemius mentions another very ſingular circumſtance with regard to the Lapland wolves; which is, that, when they have killed the Rein, they always place the carcaſe with the head towards the Eaſt, and that the ſkeletons are conſtantly found in ſuch poſition. This fact, indeed, is ſo extraordinary, that it ſhould not be too lightly credited; animals, however, have undoubtedly their reaſon for chooſing or declining certain aſpects: the martin, for example, ſeldom builds its neſt againſt the ſouth.

Though I have ſtated ſo many particulars from this writer, not only becauſe he is the lateſt Naturaliſt who hath deſcribed the Rein, but becauſe he reſided ten years in Finmark; yet I cannot but take notice of one paſſage in his work, in which I conceive he muſt be entirely miſtaken.

Leemius

Leemius affirms, in his ninth chapter, that the Reins lofe their horns in the fpring, which is not only contradicted by what Hoffberg and Buffon have advanced, but by the fact, for Mr. Heyde's buck dropt his horns for two fucceffive winters, but *refumed them in the fpring*. In one of thefe years they continued to be no more than ftumps till the 30th of January, when they began to fhoot; on the 24th of February they were five or fix inches high, covered with a deep pile of velvet.

At the fame time Leemius not only afferts this to happen otherwife, but the engravings which accompany his work reprefent the deer amongft fnow with their horns on [l].

In juftice to Leemius, however, I fhould add [m], that though Hoffberg and Buffon take notice that the Rein lofes his horns at the approach of winter [n], yet other naturalifts have fuppofed that they were of ufe in removing the fnow which covers the lichen they are faid to be fo fond of, and which is utterly inconfiftent with this quadruped being deprived of them during the winter. Leemius indeed exprefsly informs us, that they procure the lichen by means of their feet [o].

[l] Moft of the Reins, however, which draw fleds, have been gelt; and it is obfervable that our fallow deer, which undergo the fame operation for the fake of *haver* venifon, never lofe their horns afterwards.

[m] Leemius is alfo fupported by Le-Brun in this particular. See his Travels, Vol. I. p. 11.

[n] Yet in another part of the fame differtation, Hoffberg mentions, that the Reins are faftened to the fled in the winter by their horns. See Am. Acad. p. 167. Vol. IV.

[o] P. 141. De la Motraye takes notice of the fame circumftance; and that their hoofs are formed like mufcle fhells fet on their edge and confequently very convenient for fcooping away the fnow which covers the lichen, called by the Sweeds *Steenmoffa*, and by the Laplanders *Vеекle*. Reins are alfo fond of another mofs which hangs down from the branches of pines [in Sweedifh Laa, and in the Lap language Loppo] which they fhake off with their antlers. With regard to the firft circumftance, I find that Motraye is confirmed by the fpecimen of a rein's leg in Sir Afhton Lever's Mufeum, as the hoofs are of the form defcribed, and at leaft two inches and a half high, very thin, and tapering in the form of a fcoop.

As

As I have very frequently viſited Mr. Heyde's Rein, I ſhall now mention ſome few particulars I happened to obſerve myſelf with regard to this quadruped, which is ſo ſeldom to be ſeen to the ſouthward of the Baltic.

This animal was kept in a cloſe of about an acre, the graſs of which was rich; and he conſtantly fed upon it during the whole year [p], though he was much fonder of the lichen, which was ſent over from Norway: by holding a little of it in my hand, I could at any time bring him to me. No animal, indeed, could be better humoured, as he would even permit his antlers to be handled when the blood veſſels were moſt turgid. He likewiſe permitted me to meaſure his height, which was three feet two inches and a half, being in his ſixth year, and of full growth. Now Leemius obſerves, that the doe is not ſo large as the buck; and I have meaſured the ſpecimen of a Doe-rein, lately ſent to the Royal Society from Hudſon's-bay, which is about three feet in height. I ſtate this compariſon, becauſe it makes me doubt with regard to the juſtneſs of an obſervation of M. de Buffon, who in his article (Rein-deer) ſuppoſes that all American animals are leſs than the ſame ſpecies in other parts of the globe. Mr. Pennant alſo takes notice, that the American Elk is larger than the European [q].

I once ſaw this Rein in Mr. Heyde's garden, where there was a conſiderable variety of flowering ſhrubs and foreſt-trees, all of which he browzed upon except the elder; he alſo drank a great deal of water out of a pond.

I have therefore little doubt but that this quadruped will live without the Lapland lichen [r], to which it only hath, perhaps,

[p] He was fond alſo of bread and oats.

[q] Synopſ. Quad. p. 42.

[r] Pontoppidan ſays, the Rein is very fond of birch catkins, Pt. II. p. 10.

recourſe,

recourse, because there is in those latitudes no other sustenance during the winter.

I have, indeed, procured some of this lichen, which I have tasted, and conceive from thence it may be a nourishing food either to man or beast; it is, however, by no means peculiar to Lapland, as we have much of the same on our own heaths. In one respect, indeed, the Rein fares better in England than in Lapland, as Hoffberg and all other naturalists speak much of its suffering from an insect, which they term the Oestrus Tarandi [s]. We have, perhaps, the same gad-fly in England, but they are not so numerous, and Mr. Heyde's Rein did not seem to feel much inconvenience from this persecution [t].

Le Brun observes [u], that the Rein carries his head so high, that the horns touch the back; and it is not therefore improbable that these antlers may be given them as a means of removing these very troublesome insects.

The same traveller takes notice, that the chiefs of the Samoieds have sometimes six or eight of them to draw their traineaus, and that they never sweat, notwithstanding their being often much pressed, but pant with their tongues out, just as grey-hounds do after a severe course.

Leemius also informs us, that after being hard driven they lose their sight frequently for three or four days [x].

I have before observed, that Mr. Heyde's buck rein was very good humoured; possibly, however, if he had been harnessed, I should not have found him so tractable, for on account of its

[s] These insects pierce the skin of the Rein in such a manner, that the Laplanders would have no hopes of selling it, if they did not fill up the holes in order to defraud the purchaser. Leemius, p. 68.

[t] That most able entomologist, Mr. Hudson, F. R. S. informs me, that he hath seen the *Oestrus Tarandi* in England.

[u] Vol. III. p. 25.

[x] P. 52.

greater docility, a gelt Rein bears a much better price in Lapland, and another caufe for the advanced value is, that the operation being performed but aukwardly, the owners frequently lofe them: for the fame reafon the poorer Laplanders only harnefs the doe [y].

[y] Leemius, p. 151.

ESSAY

ESSAY II.

ON THE BAT, OR RERE-MOUSE.

THE Bat is so disagreeable an animal, that we are generally desirous of avoiding it rather than examining into its habits; the consequence of which aversion is, that we are more ignorant with regard to its natural history, than perhaps of any other animal of the same size.

Hideous as it may appear to our eyes, yet, if we are to believe Johnson[a] (who is a writer of merit), there is a perpetual alliance between them and pigeons, insomuch, that if the head of a Bat is fixed upon the top of a pigeon-house, the pigeons will never leave it. I profess, however, that I cannot hear this animal hath any other friend or ally, and they must naturally be dreaded by moths or other insects of the night[b], as much as hawks are the terror of our smaller birds; nature is one perpetual scene of warfare, for the sake of food, and Bats again become the prey of owls.

A friend of mine kept one for ten days, and was much amused with its manner of taking flies on which it chiefly lived[c];

[a] Nat. Hist 1657, folio. Amsterdam.

[b] Or to speak more accurately of the evening and morning twilights, as Bats are seldom seen at midnight. Bats, however, are also fond of bacon, and perhaps other meats: in the East Indies likewise some species devour both fruits and leaves of the trees. Linschoten's Voyages. Others prey on fish.

[c] Gesner says, that Bats will live many days without any sustenance.

Linnæus hath claſſed it with his primates, at the head of which ſtands *Man:* a more natural arrangement, perhaps, might have exalted this animal to the *order of angels*, as they are depicted with wings as well as teats.

I never met with any one who had taſted a Bat; and, indeed, with us they are ſo diminutive, that the morſel ſhould be as delicate as it is ſmall. In the iſland of Mauritius, however, where they are very large[d], the ſeamen conſider them as dainties. "They are innumerable, and ſome as large as goſhawks, and "the ſeamen caſe them as rabbits; they hang in ſwarms on the "boughs of the trees, by claws fixed at the extreme part of their "wings, and their monkey faces turned downwards[e]." In the time of falconry they were given to hawks as a remedy for the falling-ſickneſs.

From its likeneſs to a mouſe, the ſynonym is formed in many languages, the French terming it *chauve-ſouris* and *rat-pennade*. The Dutch, Vleermuys. The Germans, Fleder-mauſch. The Danes, Flaggermuus. The Swedes, Flader-mus. The Spaniards, *Mur*-cielago. As for our modern name of *Bat*, I do not know whence we apply it to this animal, but it was anciently called *reremouſe*, from the Anglo-Saxon hꞃeꞃemuꞅ. Our blaſoners alſo uſe this word. In the Greek and Latin, however, the name is taken from its appearing only during the night νυκτερις & veſpertilio.

"Seroque trahunt a veſpere nomen." Ovid.

Different ſpecies, or varieties of Bats, are found in moſt quarters both of the Old and New World; but for an enumeration of theſe

[d] A ſpecimen from that iſland may be ſeen in Sir Aſhton Lever's moſt capital Muſeum. Kircher, in his China Illuſtrata, gives us an engraving of a Bat of Indoſtan, whoſe head exactly reſembles in ſize and figure that of a cat, and is therefore called the *Flying Cat*.

[e] Herbert's Travels, p. 360.—Le chauve-ſouris eſt fort au gré des Indiens, ils ſont fort grandes & ſont beaucoup de degat aux fruits & aux arbres. Linſchoten, p. 124.

I ſhall

I ſhall refer to Mr. Pennant's moſt excellent Synopſis of Quadrupeds, and after obſerving, that ſome of thoſe in America are ſuppoſed to ſuck the blood of perſons aſleep, I ſhall confine myſelf to thoſe of our own iſland [f].

That moſt able naturaliſt Mr. Ray takes notice of but one ſpecies, though Mr. Pennant conceives that we have four [g]. Nothing can exceed both the diligence and accuracy of Ray, but the common averſion to theſe animals ſeems to have prevented both him and others from either catching or examining many ſpecies.

Having but two teats, it is ſuppoſed that they never produce more than two young ones, which, according to Pliny [h], they fly about with on their back.

If this is true at all, I ſhould ſuppoſe that it only takes place when the young are to be taught to fly [i], as they may be more eaſily launched from their parent's back into the air, than from any other place. They cannot riſe at all from the ground

[f] Belon ſays, that thoſe which frequent the great pyramid have tails as long as thoſe of mice.

[g] Synopſis of Quadrupeds; *viz.*

1ſt, Buffon's *Chauve-ſouris à cheval*; ſo called, becauſe it hath a membrane at the end of the noſe, in form of a horſe-ſhoe. This ſpecies, however, wants the little internal ear, which Mr. Pennant hath obſerved in all other Bats, and which is ſhut during ſleep, whilſt the other is open. M. Buffon mentions, that this ſpecies is not uncommon in Burgundy; and Mr. Pennant hath been informed that they are likewiſe to be found in Kent

2d, *La Noctule* of Buffon, the extent of whoſe wings is thirteen inches. Numbers of this ſecond ſpecies have been taken under the eves of Queen's College Cambridge.

3d, The common, or *ſhort-eared Bat.*

4th, The *Long-eared Bat*, with ears of more than an inch in length, which are at the ſame time ſo thin as to be pellucid. The body, however, and tail is but one inch and three quarters long, whereas thoſe of the preceding ſpecies are two inches and a half in length.

[h] Pliny, l. x. c. 61.

[i] According to Johnſtone the young are quite naked. Thaumatographia, p. 269.

according

according to Linnæus[k]; and in this ſituation therefore they ſeem to be diveſted of every pretenſion to be deemed birds, if their being viviparous, and having no beaks, did not ſufficiently exclude them, as well as their want of feathers. As to their having wings, a flying fiſh, or the flying ſquirrel, might for the ſame reaſon be conſidered as birds.

But the moſt intereſting part in relation to this animal, is its ſtate of torpidity during the winter, to which it is induced probably from want of flying-inſects for its food[l], as ſeems to be the caſe with the ſwallow tribe.

In this part of the Natural Hiſtory of this animal, I am much indebted to the communication of a moſt ingenious correſpondent[m], who knows where to find them torpid at any time during the winter, and more particularly in a large cavern near Torbay[n].

The prevailing notion that they hang always in cluſters touching each other is not true, as this depends entirely upon their having

[k] I conceive, however, Buffon to be more accurate when he informs us that, "elles s'elevent de terre avec peine," which is alſo the caſe with the *Swift*, on account of the legs of that bird being ſo ſhort, that the Greek ſynonym is *απȣς*. Linnæus alſo ſtates two other particulars with regard to Bats, of which I ſhould much doubt. He ſays, that an Aſiatic ſpecies (which he ſtiles *Vampyrus*) is *phlebotomus felicisſimus in pleuritide*, and ſuppoſes the common ſort (named by him *murinus*) to be poiſonous

[l] Sleep therefore appears to be providential, not only for the refreſhment ariſing from relaxation, but from the ſaving of food, becauſe all animals, whilſt awake, are very apt to eat, and this is the caſe with the Greenland fiſhers who have perpetual day.

[m] Mr. Corniſh, ſurgeon, at Totneſs in Devonſhire.

[n] Homer had obſerved them in the ſame ſtate, and afterwards iſſuing from a cavern;

Ως δ' οτε νυκτεριδες, μυχῳ αντρȣ θεσπεσιοιο,
Τριζȣσαι ποτεονται, επει κε τις αποπεσησιν
Ορμαθȣ εκ πετρης, ανα αλληλῃσιν εχονται. Odyſſ. Ω. l. 7.

a proper opportunity of adhering to the place from which they are ſuſpended; they ſometimes, therefore, are in contact, and often at conſiderable diſtances, but always fix themſelves by both their feet.

Martial ſays of the dormouſe, that it is fatter during its ſtate of torpidity than when it revives [o]. I therefore begged to know from Mr. Corniſh, whether this was the caſe with Bats during the winter, who informs me that the fact does not hold with regard to the one or the other, and that bats mute [p], whilſt they are thus ſuſpended. Both dormice and bats loſe from five to ſeven grains in weight during a fortnight, whilſt in a ſtate of torpidity.

Bats on the whole fare better during a hard than a mild winter, for warm weather not only awakens them, but promotes their power of digeſtion, whilſt at the ſame time they cannot procure the food of which they are in ſearch. This holds likewiſe with regard to bees, which are better preſerved in a dark room than if expoſed to the air whilſt torpid, becauſe ſometimes they are awakened by the mild temperature of the weather, when there are no flowers for their ſupport.

As Bats mute whilſt torpid, there is alſo a circulation of the blood, for Mr. Corniſh having applied a thermometer to the body of one perfectly aſleep, which ſtood at 36, the heart beat

[o] Tota *mihi* (ſc. gliri) dormitur hyems, & pinguior illo
Tempore ſum, quo me nil niſi ſomnus alit.

As the Romans conſidered dormice as a delicacy for their tables, and Varro hath made them an article of the farmer's attention, I thought this obſervation of the poet might have been relied upon.

[p] This evacuation, however, becomes leſs and leſs the longer the animal ſleeps; and as the inteſtinal tube empties, the fæces become harder and harder. The guts alſo are very weak after a torpidity of ſome continuance, nor can they be extracted without breaking. The blood is vivid and black, in proportion to the continuance of the animal in a ſleeping ſtate. A correſpondent of Geſner's informed him, that he had ſeen ſuch a quantity of bats dung in *Miſnia*, that carts would have been neceſſary to have carried it off.

60 times in a minute[q]; the ſame Bat being awakened ſo as to fly weakly; the thermometer applied in the ſame manner roſe to 38, and the heart beat 100 times in a minute.

They have been, however, obſerved to continue in their torpid ſtate when the thermometer, placed in the air, hath been at 48[r], which is ten degrees warmer than the animal when awakened according to this experiment.

Moſt of the Bats rouſed by irritation have not ſurvived more than three days, but then it is ſtated that the weather became colder. Frequent attempts have been made to revive them after this ſeeming death, but they have all proved ineffectual.

Having deſired Mr. Corniſh to make ſome experiments with an air-pump on torpid bats, he informs me that his apparatus for that purpoſe is not ſo good as it ſhould be, but that he is of opinion from ſome imperfect trials, that they are not ſo ſoon affected by want of air, as other animals, which do not ſleep during the winter.

That diſtinguiſhed anatomiſt Mr. John Hunter, having occaſion to diſſect bats during the winter, applied to me to procure him ſome from Devonſhire, knowing that I had a correſpondence with Mr. Corniſh, who could at any time reſort to their lurking places.

I accordingly requeſted Mr. Corniſh to ſend up a dozen of bats in their ſtate of torpidity, which he was ſo obliging as to do by the next conveyance; but though he had packed them with the greateſt care, they died, as Mr. Corniſh apprehended, before they reached London. The motion of the carriage pro-

[q] Mr. Corniſh, however, is not poſitive that there is any circulation in the capillaries. He ſuppoſes, indeed, that the animal reſpires, though moſt ſlowly and weakly.

[r] Mr. Corniſh hath known inſtances of their venturing out when the thermometer was only at 42 in the open air. The pulſation in a Bat, during the ſummer, is from 2 to 300, and the ball of the thermometer being laid in its body, hath ſometimes riſen 8 degrees.

 bably

bably occaſioned this diſappointment, as alſo that they did not hang in their uſual attitude, nor in the proper temperature of air. If they had continued to live, Mr. Corniſh informed me, that though one could perceive no motion in them, yet if placed in contact with a proper crevice, they would however fix themſelves by their claws.

Theſe bats were kept for ſome time by Mr. Hunter before he would abſolutely pronounce them to be dead, and afterwards, at Sir Aſhton Lever's, before they were *ſet up*; but though they never ſhewed any ſigns of life, yet their bodies did not putrify. The ſame thing I had occaſion to obſerve with regard to ſome torpid martins which were ſent to me from Somerſetſhire, and which I wiſhed Mr. Hunter to diſſect. Theſe birds alſo did not revive, but no ſigns likewiſe of putrefaction appeared, though they were kept a conſiderable time.

And here it may be obſerved, that a moderate heat, ſuch as the boſom or hand, is the moſt likely to bring torpid animals to life, which are often killed by being placed too near the fire, from the common prejudice, that one cannot have too much of a good thing.

For a more immediate teſt of life in the animal, it will ſhrink either upon the touch, or holding a lighted candle near it.

ESSAY III.

ON THE SUDDEN DECAY OF SEVERAL TREES IN ST. JAMES'S PARK.

SEVERAL years ago I happened to be at a country-houſe where a narrow canal was filled, on the ſides of which grew ſome limes of about forty years growth, and which continued to be in a flouriſhing ſtate. The next ſummer all theſe trees died, which was ſuppoſed to ariſe from the canal's being filled with ſome materials of a noxious nature to them: but as I was on the ſpot when the alteration was made, I knew that there was nothing uncommon in the ſtrata of the ſoil which had been uſed for this purpoſe; I therefore began to ſuſpect the real cauſe of this accident, and determined to obſerve what might be the event under ſimilar circumſtances, if a proper opportunity ſhould offer.

It is well known that Roſamond's Pond, as well as ſome ſmaller ones within the iſland of St James's Park, have lately been filled up; and it is as well known that every tree which grew very near to their margins hath died within the enſuing year, which therefore ſeems to be owing to the following cauſe.

When a tree is planted at a diſtance from water, the roots ſpread equally in every direction, in order to receive the moiſture which is neceſſary to carry on its growth and vegetation. When it is however placed very near to the water's edge, the roots on that ſide are chiefly protruded, to meet with the nouriſhment ſo immediately at hand, and for the ſame reaſon become vaſtly larger than thoſe which are extended in any other direction.

If therefore in proceſs of time the water is dried up, the tree is left without any other ſupply than that which is commanded by one which is ſurrounded with a dry ſoil, at the ſame time that the principal roots are only to be found on one ſide; ſo that the tree is deprived of at leaſt half the nouriſhment which was neceſſary for its ſupport. But it is not only where ponds or ditches have been filled, that the trees in St. James's park have ſuffered, for many of the limes on the ſides of the Mall are decaying very faſt, and that from year to year, when they were before in a moſt flouriſhing ſtate. I ſhould ſuppoſe, that this alteration ariſes from the central walk becoming convex inſtead of concave, by a vaſt quantity of freſh gravel, which hath alſo been laid on the two ſide-walks. The conſequence of which is, that almoſt all the rain which falls never reaches the roots, having ſo much a thicker ſurface to penetrate through than when the limes were originally planted, as alſo by being carried off immediately to the ſide drains, by the proper convexity of the Mall, in its preſent ſtate. Even under the moſt favourable circumſtances much rain muſt fall to moiſten an inch of ſoil, from which the capillary parts of the roots are far removed, being probably more than at twelve times that depth.

It appears alſo, by what has happened in St. James's Park, that ſuch loſs of water is certain death to many ſorts of trees, which are not aquatics, and that their age is no greater protection than their ſpecies. Some of the elms near Roſamond's Pond may be pronounced to have been at leaſt two hundred years old; the limes, horfe-chefnuts, and birches[a], which have fhared the fame fate, were not indeed of the fame antiquity, but were in a very flourifhing ftate. I fhould therefore hope that what hath been experienced in St. James's Park will prove a warning to thofe who may intend to dry ponds near which trees grow that they would be forry to lofe; for though the filling up Rofamond's Pond is in moft refpects a very ftriking improvement, as well as the other alterations which are now carrying on, yet I fhould fuppofe that a landfchape painter would wifh the pond reftored, with all its inconveniences, provided thofe very capital trees could be replaced, which were fo great an ornament from every point of view in the two parks. As thefe public walks are not only fo ornamental, but contribute fo much to the health of the inhabitants of the metropolis, I fhall take the liberty of objecting to the new trees which have lately been planted there, and which are almoft entirely elms. It is admitted that thefe young trees are in a very promifing condition; but they want that moft effential requifite in plantations of

—feris factura nepotibus umbram;

for the roots of elms fpread fo very near to the furface, that they are very apt to be blown down by high winds, when they are become of a confiderable fize; nor have I obferved any other tree which fuffers fo frequently in this refpect, if the birch be excepted.

I could wifh therefore that as faft as the limes decay, frefh trees of the fame fort were introduced, as they grow to an immenfe fize and age, there being fome in Sir Laurence Dundafs's park, in Hertfordfhire, which muft have been planted for many centuries,

[a] I allude to the trees of thefe forts which grew within the Decoy.

 and

and which, till they are examined at a ſmall diſtance, one ſhould conceive to be ancient beeches. We know alſo that they throve remarkably well on the ſame ſpot before the gravel laid upon the Mall prevented the roots from receiving the proper quantity of moiſture, whilſt at the ſame time their coming ſo early into leaf, and the fragrance of their flowers, make them peculiarly proper for the public walks of a metropolis.

ESSAY IV.

On the periodical Appearing and Disappearing of certain BIRDS, at different Times of the Year[a].

To WILLIAM WATSON, M.D. F.R.S.

DEAR SIR,

AS I know, from some conversation we had on this head, that you consider the migration of birds as a very interesting point in natural history, I send you the following reflections on this subject as they have occured to me upon looking into most of the ornithologists who have written on this question.

It will be first necessary in the present, as in all other disputes, to define the terms on which the controversy arises. I therefore premise that I mean, by the word Migration, a periodical passage by a whole species of birds across a considerable extent of sea.

I do not intend therefore to deny that a bird, or birds, may possibly fly now and then from Dover to Calais, from Gibraltar to Tangier, or any other such narrow strait, as the opposite coasts are clearly within the bird's ken, and the passage is no more adventurous than across a large fresh-water lake.

[a] This Essay was first printed in the LXIId vol. of the Philosophical Transactions; but is now reprinted, with considerable additions.

I as

I as little mean to deny that there may be a periodical flitting of certain birds from one part of a continent to another: the Royston Crow, and Rock Ouzel, furnish instances of such a regular migration.

What I mean chiefly to contend therefore is, that it seems to be highly improbable, birds should, at certain seasons, traverse large tracts of sea, or rather ocean, without leaving any of the same species behind, but the sick or wounded.

As this litigated point can only receive a satisfactory decision from very accurate observations, all preceding naturalists, from Aristotle to Ray, have spoken with much doubt concerning it.

Soon after the appearance of Monf. Adanson's Voyage to Senegal, however, Mr Collinson first, in the Philosophical Transactions [b], and after him the most eminent ornithologists of Europe, seem to have considered this traveller's having caught four European Swallows on the 6th of October, not far from the African coast, as a decisive proof, that the common swallows, when they disappear in Europe, make for Africa during the winter, and return again to us in the spring.

It is therefore highly incumbent upon me, who profess that I am by no means satisfied with the account given by Monf. Adanson of these European swallows, to enter into a very minute discussion of what may, or may not, be inferred from his observation according to his own narrative.

I shall first however consider the general arguments, from which it is supposed that birds of passage periodically traverse oceans, which indeed may be almost reduced to this single one, viz. we see certain birds in particular seasons, and afterwards we see them not; from which circumstances it is at once inferred, that the cause of their disappearance is, that they have crossed large tracts of sea.

[b] Part II. 1760, p. 459, & seq.

The

The obvious anſwer to this is, that no well-atteſted inſtances can be produced of ſuch a migration, as I ſhall endeavour to ſhew hereafter; but, beſides this convincing negative proof, there are not others wanting.

They who ſend birds periodically acroſs the ſea, being preſſed with the very obvious anſwer I have before ſuggeſted, have recourſe to two ſuppoſitions, by which they would account for their not being obſerved by ſeamen during their paſſage.

The firſt is, that they riſe ſo high in the air that they become inviſible[c]; but unfortunately the riſing to this extraordinary height, or the falling from it, is equally deſtitute of any ocular proof, as the birds being ſeen whilſt croſſing an ocean.

I have indeed converſed with ſome people, who conceive they have loſt ſight of birds by their perpendicular flight; I muſt own, however, that I have always ſuppoſed them to be ſhort-ſighted, as I never loſt the ſight of a bird myſelf, but from its horizontal diſtance, and I doubt much whether any bird was ever ſeen to riſe to a greater height than perhaps twice that of St. Paul's croſs[d].

There

[c] It is well known that ſome ornithologiſts have even ſuppoſed that they leave our atmoſphere for that of the moon. See Harl. Miſcell. vol. II. p. 561.

> A bird of paſſage, loſt as ſoon as found;
> Now in the moon perhaps, now under ground.
>
> Pope.

[d] Wild-geeſe fly at the greateſt height of any bird I ever happened to attend to; and from comparing them with rooks, which I have frequently looked at, when perched on the croſs of St. Paul's, I cannot think that a wild-gooſe was ever diminiſhed, to my ſight at leaſt, more than he would be at twice the height of St. Paul's, or perhaps 300 yards. Mr. Hunter, F. R. S. informs me, that the bird which hath appeared to him as the higheſt flier, is a ſmall eagle on the confines of Spain and Portugal, which frequents high rocks. He hath firſt ſeen this ſpecies

There ſeems to be but one method indeed, by which the height of a bird in the air may be eſtimated; which is, by comparing its apparent ſize with its known one, when very near us; and it need not be ſaid that this method of calculating muſt depend entirely upon the ſight of the obſerver, who, if he happens not to ſee objects well at a diſtance, will very ſoon ſuppoſe the bird to be loſt in the clouds.

There is alſo another objection to the hypotheſis of birds paſſing ſeas at ſuch an extraordinary height, ariſing from the known rarefaction of the air, which may poſſibly be inconvenient for reſpiration, as well as flight; and if this was not really the caſe, one ſhould ſuppoſe that birds would frequently riſe to ſuch uncommon elevations, when they had no occaſion to traverſe oceans.

The Scotch Ptarmigan frequents the higheſt ground of any Britiſh bird, and it takes but very ſhort flights.

But it is alſo urged by ſome, that the reaſon why ſeamen do not regularly ſee the migration of birds, is becauſe they chooſe the night, and not the day, for the paſſage [e].

Now though it may be allowed, that poſſibly birds may croſs from the coaſt of Holland to the Eaſtern coaſt of England (for example) during a long night, yet it muſt be dark nearly as long as it is within the Arctic circle to afford time for a bird to paſs from

ſpecies of eagle from the bottom of a mountain, and followed it to the top, when the bird hath riſen ſo high as to appear leſs than he did from the bottom. Mr. Hunter however adds, that he could ſtill hear the cry, and diſtinguiſh the bird.

[e] Mr. Cateſby ſuppoſes that they may thus paſs in the night-time, to avoid birds of prey. Phil. Tranſ. Abr. Vol. II. p. 887. But are not owls then ſtirring?

On the other hand, if they migrate in the day-time, kites, hawks, and other birds of prey, muſt be very bad ſportſmen not to attend (like Arabs) theſe large and periodical caravans.

the Line to many parts of Europe, which Monf. de Buffon calculates may be done in about eight or nine days [f].

If the paffage happened in half the nights of the year which have the benefit of moonlight, the birds would be difcovered by the failors almoft as well as in the day-time; to which I muft add that feveral fuppofed birds of paffage (the Fieldfare in particular) always call when on their flight, fo that the feamen muft be deaf as well as blind, if fuch flocks of birds efcape their notice.

Other objections however remain to this hypothefis of a paffage during the night.

Moft birds not only fleep during that time, but are as much incapacitated from diftinguifhing objects well as we are in the abfence of the fun: it is therefore inconceivable that they fhould choofe owl-light for fuch a diftant journey.

Befides this, the Eaftern coaft of England, to which birds of paffage muft neceffarily firft come from the continent, hath many light-houfes upon it; they would therefore, in a dark night, immediately make for fuch an object, and deftroy themfelves by flying with violence againft it, as is well known to every bat-fowler.

Having endeavoured to anfwer thefe two fuppofitions, by which it is contended that birds of paffage may efcape obfervation in their flight; I fhall now confider all the inftances I have been able to meet with of any birds being actually feen whilft they were croffing any extent of fea, though I might give a very fhort refutation to them, by infifting, that if this was ever experienced, it muft happen as conftantly in a fea which is much navigated,

[f] In the preface to the firft volume of his lately publifhed Ornithology, p 32. Brown fuppofes, however, that a hawk had purfued a woodcock at no greater rate than 30 miles in an hour. Treatife on Falconry, 1608.

as

as the return of the ſeaſons, or the motions of a ſtated carrier.

I cannot do better than to follow theſe according to chronological order.

The firſt in point of time is that which is cited by Willoughby [g], from Bellon, whoſe words are thus tranſlated, "When we "ſailed from Rhodes to Alexandria, many quails flying from the "North towards the South were taken in our ſhip, whence I "am perſuaded that they ſhift places; for formerly, when I "ſailed out of the Iſle of Zant to Morea, or Negropont, in the "ſpring, I had obſerved quails flying the contrary way to N. "and S. that they might abide there all ſummer, at which time "alſo a great many were taken in the ſhip."

Let us now conſider what is to be inferred from this citation.

In the firſt place, Bellon does not particularize the longitude and latitude of that part of the Mediterranean which he was then croſſing; and in his courſe from Rhodes to Alexandria, both the iſlands of Scarpanto and Crete could be at no great diſtance: theſe quails therefore were probably flitting from one iſland of the Mediteranean [h] to another.

The ſame obſervation may be made with regard to the quails which he ſaw between Zant and Negropont, as the whole paſſage is crouded with iſlands; they therefore might be paſſing from

[g] B. II. c. 11. § 8.

[h] One of the Mediterranean iſlands is ſuppoſed to have obtained its ancient name of Ortygia from the numbers of quails. The Mediterranean birds alſo flit from the iſlands to the continent.

> Ουδε μεν ορνιθων αγελαις ηπειροθεν αδην,
> Εκ νησων οτε πολλαι επιπλησσωσιν αρουραις,
> Ερχομενου θερεος χαιρει. ARATUS—

who is known to have attended particularly to the flights of birds, as they afforded prognoſtics of the weather.

iſland to iſland, or headland to headland, which might very probably lie Eaſt and Weſt, ſo as to occaſion the birds flying in a different direction from that in which they paſſed the ſhip before.

I have therefore no objection to this proof of migration, if it is only inſiſted upon to ſhew that a quail ſhifts its ſtation at certain ſeaſons of the year; but cannot admit that it is fair from hence to argue that theſe birds periodically croſs large tracts of ſea.

Bellon himſelf ſtates, that when the birds ſettled upon the ſhip, they were taken by the firſt perſon who choſe to catch them, and therefore they muſt have been unequal to the ſhort flight which they were attempting. Mr. Burnaby therefore obſerves, that the wild pigeons in their migration (though a bird diſtinguiſhed for their flight) ſettle on the trees of Rhode Iſland in ſuch numbers as ſometimes to break the branches; and that they ſeem ſo fatigued with their flight, as not to be driven away but by extraordinary noiſes[i].

It is very true that quails have been often pitched upon as inſtances of birds that migrate acroſs ſeas, becauſe they are ſcarcely ever ſeen in winter: it is well known, however, to every ſportſman, that this bird never flies 300 yards at a time, and the tail being ſo ſhort, it is highly improbable they ſhould be equal to a paſſage of any length.

We find therefore, that quails, which are commonly ſuppoſed to leave our iſland in the winter, in reality retire to the ſea coaſts, and pick up their food amongſt the ſea weeds[k].

I have happened lately to ſee a ſpecimen of a particular ſpecies

[i] Burnaby's Travels in N. America, p. 132.

[k] See Br. Zool. Vol. II. p. 210. 2d ed octavo. Thus Bellon alſo informs us, that the ortygometre (or raile) is frequently ſeen in France during the winter.

of quail, which is defcribed by Dr. Shaw[l], and is diftinguifhed from the other kinds by wanting the hind-claw. Dr. Shaw alfo ftates that it is a bird of paffage. Now if quails really migrate from the coaft of Barbary to Italy, as is commonly fuppofed, whence can it have arifen that this remarkable fpecies hath efcaped the notice of Aldrovandus, Olina, and the other Italian ornithologifts?

When I had juft finifhed what I have here faid with regard to the migration of quails, I had an opportunity of feeing the fecond volume of Monf. de Buffon's ornithology[m]; where he contends, that this bird leaves Europe in the winter.

It is incumbent upon me, therefore, either to own I am convinced by what this moft ingenious and able naturalift hath urged, or to give my reafons why I ftill continue to diffent from the opinion he maintains.

Though M. de Buffon hath difcuffed this point very much at large, yet I find only the following facts or arguments to be new.

He firft cites the Memoirs of the Academy of Sciences[n], for an account given by M. Godeheu of quails coming to the ifland of Malta in the month of May, and leaving it in September.

The firft anfwer to this obfervation is, that the ifland of Malta is not only near to the coaft of Africa, but to feveral of the Mediterranean iflands; it therefore amounts to no more than the flitting I have before taken notice of[o].

Buffon

[l] Phyf. Obf. on the Kingdom of Algiers, ch. 2. See alfo an engraving and defcription of such a quail which is found in Luconia, one of the Philippine Iflands. Sonneratte's Voyage. Paris, 1776, 4to.

[m] See p. 459, & feq.

[n] Tom. III p. 91 and 92.

[o] Both Monf. de Godeheu and M. de Buffon feem to conceive that the quail fhould fly in the fame direction as the wind blows, but birds on the

Buffon next suppofes that a quail only quits one latitude for another, in order to meet with a perpetual crop on the ground.

Now can it be conceived that there is fuch difference between the harveft on the coaft of Africa, and that of the fmall quantity of grain which grows on the rocky ifland of Malta, that it becomes inconvenient to the bird to ftay in Africa as foon as May fets in; and neceffary, on the other hand, to continue in Malta from May till September.

Buffon then conjectures that quails make their paffage in the night, as well as conceives them to be of a remarkably warm temperature [p], and fays that "*chaud comme une caille*" is in every one's mouth [q].

Now in the firft place their migration during the night is contrary to Belon's account, which M. de Buffon fo much relies upon, and which rather implies that the birds were caught in the day-time.

In the next place I apprehend that "*chaud comme une caille*" alludes to the very remarkable falacioufnefs of this bird, and not to the conftant heat of its body.

the wing from point to point, which are at a confiderable diftance, fly againft the wind, as their plumage is otherwife ruffled. See alfo Marten's Voyage to Spitzbergen, who obferves the fame, as likewife with regard to the fwimming of whales, for which indeed there is not the fame reafon.

[p] As this is given for a reafon why the African quails pafs Northward. Q. What is to become of the Swedifh quails during the fummer? Varro gives us a very particular account of this migration:

"De illo genere funt turdi adventitii, ac quotannis trans mare in Italiam advolant circa æquinoctium autumnale, et eodem revolant ad æquinoctium vernum. Et alio tempore turtures ac *coturnices* immani numero. Hoc ita fieri apparet in infulis propinquis Pontia, Palmatia, Pandataria, ibi enim cum primâ volaturâ veniunt, *morantur paucos dies requiefcendi causâ*; idemque faciunt cum ex Italiâ trans mare remeant." Varro de Re Rufticâ, l. III. c. 5.

[q] All birds indeed are warmer by four degrees than other animals. See fome ingenious thermometrical experiments by Mr. Martin of Aberdeen, Edinb. 1771, 12mo.

Buffon proceeds to obſerve, that if quails are kept in a cage, they are remarkably impatient of confinement in the autumn and ſpring, whence he infers that they then want to migrate[r]; he alſo adds, in the ſame period, that this uneaſineſs begins an hour before the ſun riſes, and that it continues all the night.

This great naturaliſt does not ſtate this obſervation as having been made by himſelf, and it ſeems upon the face of it to be a very extraordinary one.

No one (at leaſt with us) ever keeps quails in a cage except the poulterers, who always ſell them as faſt as they are fat, and conſequently can give no account of what happens to them during ſo long an impriſonment as this obſervation neceſſarily implies.

No ſuch remarkable uneaſineſs hath ever been attended to in any other ſuppoſed bird of paſſage during its confinement: but, allowing the fact to be as Buffon ſtates, he himſelf ſupplies us with the real cauſe of this impatience.

He aſſerts, that quails conſtantly moult twice[s] a year, *viz.* at the cloſe both of ſummer and winter; whence it follows, that the

[r] It may alſo ariſe from this bird's being of ſo quarrelſome a diſpoſition, and conſequently moſt likely to fight with its fellow priſoners when they are all in greateſt vigour after moulting, and on the return of the ſpring.

Buffon allows that they will fight for a grain of millet, and adds, "car "parmi les animaux il faut un ſujet reel pour ſe battre" M. de Buffon hath never been in a cockpit.

[s] I have often heard that certain birds moult twice a year, ſome of which I have kept myſelf without their changing their feathers more than once.

I ſhould ſuppoſe that this notion ariſes from ſome birds not moulting regularly in the autumn every year; and when the change takes place in the following ſpring, they very commonly die. I can ſcarcely think that many of them are equal to two illneſſes of ſo long a continuance, which are conſtantly to return within twelve months.

I ſhould

the bird, in autumn and the ſpring, muſt be in full vigour upon its recovery from this periodical illneſs: it can therefore as little brook confinement, as the phyſician's patient upon the return of health after illneſs.

Thus much I have thought it neceſſary to ſay in anſwer to M. de Buffon, who "dum errat, docet," who ſcarcely ever argues ill but when he is miſinformed as to facts, and who often, from ſtrength of underſtanding, diſbelieves ſuch intelligence as might impoſe upon a naturaliſt of leſs acuteneſs and penetration.

The next inſtance of a bird being caught at any diſtance from land, is in Sir Hans Sloane's Voyage to Jamaica, who ſays, that a lark was taken in the ſhip 40 leagues from the ſhore: this therefore was certainly an unfortunate bird, forced out to ſea by a ſtrong wind in flying from headland to headland, as no one ſuppoſes the ſkylark to be a bird of paſſage.

The ſame anſwer may be given to a yellow-hammer's ſettling upon Haſſelquiſt's ſhip in the entrance of the Mediterranean, with this difference, that either the European or African coaſt muſt have been much nearer than 40 leagues [t].

The next fact to be conſidered is what is mentioned in a letter of Mr Peter Collinſon's, printed in the Philoſophical Tranſactions [u].

He there ſays, "That Sir Charles Wager had frequently in-"formed him, that in one of his voyages home in the ſpring, as "he came into ſoundings in our chanel, that a great flock of

I ſhould therefore rather account for the extraordinary briſkneſs of a quail in autumn and the ſpring, from its recovery after moulting in the former, and from the known effects of the ſpring as to moſt animals in the latter.

[t] See Haſſelquiſt's Travels. Crantz mentions that a Redpoll forced out by a ſtorm hath been taken in a ſhip which was 40 leagues from Greenland. Vol. I. p. 77.

[u] 1760. Part II. p. 461.

"ſwallows

" ſwallows almoſt covered his rigging; that they were nearly " ſpent and famiſhed, and were only feathers and bones; but " being recruited by a night's reſt, they took their flight in the " morning."

The firſt anſwer to this is, that if theſe were birds which had croſſed large tracts of ſea in their periodical migrations, the ſame accident muſt happen eternally, both in the ſpring and autumn, which is not however pretended by any one.

In the next place, the ſwallows are ſtated to be ſpent both by famine and fatigue; and how were they to procure any flies or other ſuſtenance on the rigging of the admiral's ſhip, though they might indeed reſt themſelves?

Sir Charles, however, expreſſly informs us, that he was in the channel, and within ſoundings: theſe birds, therefore (like Bellon's quails) were only paſſing probably from headland to headland; and being forced out by a ſtrong wind, were obliged to ſettle upon the firſt ſhip they ſaw[x], or otherwiſe muſt have dropped into the ſea, which I make no doubt happens to many unfortunate birds under the ſame circumſtances.

As the birds which thus ſettled upon Sir Charles Wager's rigging were ſwallows, it very naturally brings me now to conſider the celebrated obſervation of Monſ. Adanſon, under all its circumſtances,

[x] Mr. Franklin of Tobago informs me, that being 60 or 70 leagues from the coaſt of Portugal, at the latter end of December, many birds of different ſorts, blown from the land, ſettled on the ſhip, and, amongſt the reſt, a Woodcock and Skylark. The Skylark was taken up by Mr. Franklin himſelf, and was ſo fatigued that it inſtantly ſhewed an inclination to ſleep; after which, being put into a cage, the bird not only recovered, but became the next day remarkably tame. A hawk which would not ſettle on the ſhip was obſerved to drop into the ſea. " For it " often happens, that birds not natives of our iſland are, through ſtorms, " or other accidental cauſes (unknown to us), brought over hither," Edwards's Gleanings in the article *Roſe-colour'd Ouſel.*

cumſtances, as it hath been ſo much relied upon, and by naturaliſts of ſo great eminence.

Monſ. Adanſon is a very ingenious writer, and the publick is much indebted to him for many of the remarks which he made whilſt he reſided in Senegal. I may, however, I think, preſume to ſay, that he had not before his voyage made ornithology his particular ſtudy; proofs of which are not wanting in other parts of his work, which do not relate to ſwallows. For example, he ſuppoſes, that the Canary birds which are bred in Europe are white, and that they become ſo by our climate's being more cold than that of Africa.

" J'ai remarqué que le ſerin qui devient tout blanc en France, " eſt à Teneriffe d'un gris preſque auſſi foncé que celui de la li- " notte; ce changement de couleur provient vraiſemblablement " de la froidure de notre climat [y]."

Mr. Adanſon in this paſſage ſeems to have deduced two falſe inferences from having ſeen a few white Canary birds in France, which he afterwards compares with thoſe of Teneriff, and ſuppoſes the change of colour to ariſe merely from alteration of climate: it is known, however, almoſt to every one, that there is an infinite variety in the plumage of the European Canary birds, which, as in poultry, ariſes from their being pampered with ſo much food, as well as confinement [z].

Monſ.

[y] Voyage au Senegal, p. 13. Shells ſeem to be the part of natural hiſtory which chiefly engaged Mr. Adanſon's attention.

[z] In the ſame paſſage, he compares the colour of the African Canary bird to that of the European linnet, and ſays it is *d'un gris preſque auſſi foncé*, whereas the European linnet is well known to be brown, and not grey. The linnet affords a very deciſive proof that the change of plumage does not ariſe from the difference of climate, but the two cauſes I have aſſigned. The cock bird, whilſt at liberty, hath a red breaſt: yet if it is either bred up in a cage from the neſt, or is caught with its red plumage, and afterwards moults in the houſe, it never recovers the red feathers.

That

Monſ. Adanſon, in another part of his voyage [a], deſcribes a Roller, which he ſuppoſes to migrate ſometimes to the Southern parts of Europe.

This circumſtance ſhews that he could not have looked much into books of natural hiſtory, becauſe the principal ſynonym of this bird is *Garrulus Argentoratenſis* [b]; and Linnæus informs us that it is found even in Sweden [c].

The ſtrong characteriſtic mark of the Roller is the outermoſt feathers of the tail, which able naturaliſts deſcribe as three fourths of an inch longer than the reſt [d]. Monſ. Adanſon, however, compares their length, not with the other feathers of the tail, but with the length of the bird's body, which is by no means the natural or proper ſtandard of compariſon.

The reaſon of my taking notice of theſe more minute inaccuracies in Monſ. Adanſon's account of birds, ariſes from Mr. Collinſon's relying upon his obſervations with regard to ſwallows being ſo abſolutely deciſive, becauſe he is repreſented to be ſo able a naturaliſt.

I ſhall now ſtate (very minutely) under what circumſtances theſe ſwallows were caught, and what ſeems to be the true inference from his own account.

He informs us, that four ſwallows ſettled upon the ſhip, not 50 leagues from the coaſt of Senegal, on the 6th of October; that

That moſt able naturaliſt Monſ. de Buffon, from having ſeen ſome cock linnets which had thus moulted off, or perhaps ſome hen linnets (which have not a red breaſt) conſiders them as a diſtinct ſpecies, and compares their breeding together in an aviary to that of a Canary bird and Goldfinch. Ornith. p. xxii.

[a] P. 16.

[b] Or of Strasburgh. Ray's Synopſis.

[c] Faun. Suec. 94.

[d] Willoughby, p. 131. Br. Zool. Vol. II. in Append.

theſe birds were taken, and that he knew them to be the true ſwallow of Europe [e], which he ſuppoſes were then returning to the coaſt of Africa.

I ſhall now endeavour to ſhew that theſe birds could not be European ſwallows; nor, if they were, could they have been on their return from Europe to Africa.

The word *hirondelle*, in French, is uſed as a general term for the four [f] ſpecies of theſe birds, as the term *ſwallow* is with us.

Now the four ſwallows thus caught and examined by Monſ. Adanſon were either all of the ſame ſpecies, or intermixed in ſome other proportion.

Would not then any naturaliſt in ſtating ſo material a fact (as he himſelf ſuppoſes it to be) have particularized of what ſpecies of ſwallow theſe very intereſting birds were?

Should not Monſ. Adanſon alſo have taken care to diſtinguiſh theſe ſuppoſed European ſwallows from a ſpecies of the ſame tribe, which bears a general reſemblance to thoſe of Europe, and is not only deſcribed, but engraved by Briſſon, under the name of *Hirondelle de Senegal* [g]?

Monſ. Adanſon however concludes his account of the ſuppoſed European ſwallow, whilſt it continues on the coaſt of Senegal, by

[e] I have before endeavoured to ſhew that Monſ. Adanſon does not always recollect with accuracy the plumage of the moſt common European birds, by what he ſays with regard to the linnet. I need ſcarcely obſerve alſo that the 6th of October, when theſe ſwallows were caught, is too early for their migration ſo far ſouthward from any part of Europe.

[f] *Viz.* the ſwallow κατ' ἐξοχὴν, the martin, the ſand martin, and the ſwift: I omit the goat-ſucker, becauſe this bird, though properly claſſed as a ſpecies of ſwallow by ornithologiſts, is not ſo conſidered by others.

[g] See Briſſon, Tom. II. pl. xlv. Sonnerat alſo hath given a deſcription and engraving of the ſwallow of Antigue [ſome iſland between the Philippines and N. Guinea] which much reſembles our martin, except that the throat is yellow.

a circumſtance which ſeems to prove to demonſtration of what ſpecies the four ſwallows caught in the ſhip really were.

He ſays that they rooſt on the ſand, either by themſelves, or at moſt only in pairs, and that they frequent the coaſt much more than the inland parts [h].

Theſe ſwallows therefore, if they came from Europe, muſt have immediately changed at once their known habits: and is it not conſequently moſt clear that they were of that ſpecies which Briſſon deſcribes under the name of *Hirondelle de rivage du Senegal?*

But though it ſhould be admitted, notwithſtanding what I have inſiſted upon, from Monſ. Adanſon's own account, that theſe were really ſwallows of the ſame kind with thoſe of Europe; yet I muſt ſtill contend that they could not poſſibly have been on their return from Europe to Africa, becauſe the high road for a bird from the moſt Weſtern point of Europe to Senegal is along the N. Weſt coaſt of Africa, which projects greatly to the Weſtward of any part of Europe.

What then could be the inducement to theſe four ſwallows to fly 50 leagues to the Weſtward of the coaſt of Senegal, ſo much out of the proper direction?

It ſeems to me therefore very clear, that theſe ſwallows (whether of the European kind or not) were flitting from the cape de Verde iſlands to the coaſt of Africa, to which ſhort flight, however, they were unequal, and were obliged, from fatigue, to fall into the ſailors hands.

[h] Voyage au Senegal, p. 67. I wiſh Monſ. Adanſon had alſo informed us whether theſe ſwallows had the ſame notes with thoſe of Europe, which is a very material circumſtance in the natural hiſtory of birds, though little attended to by moſt ornithologiſts. Julius Pollux, in his Onomaſticon, gives us the different terms for the notes of many birds, that of the χελιδων (or martin) is ψιθυριζειν. l. V. ch. 14.

Monſ.

Monſ. Adanſon likewiſe mentions [l] that the ſhip's company caught a Roller on the 26th of April, which he ſuppoſes was on its paſſage to Europe, though he was then within ſight of the coaſt of Senegal: this bird, however, muſt be admitted not to have had ſufficient ſtrength to reach the firſt ſtage of this round-about journey, and was therefore probably forced out to ſea by a ſtrong wind, in paſſing from head-land to head-land.

But I muſt not diſmiſs what hath been obſerved with regard to the ſwallows ſeen by Monſ. Adanſon at Senegal [k], without endeavouring alſo to anſwer what M. de Buffon hath not only in-

[l] Voyage au Senegal, p. 15.

[k] Since this eſſay was printed in the Philoſophical Tranſactions, I have had an opportunity of examining the Planches Enluminées, which are ſaid to be publiſhed under the inſpection of M. de Buffon, and which ſeem to afford a demonſtration of M. Adanſon's inaccuracy, in ſuppoſing either the Roller or Swallows which were caught in his ſhip near the coaſt of Senegal to be the ſame with thoſe of Europe *.

In the 8th of theſe plates there is a coloured figure of a bird, called le Rollier d'Angola, which agrees exactly with M. Adanſon's deſcription; but he truſted too much to his memory when he pronounced it to be the Garrulus Argentoratenſis of Willoughby, and therefore ſuppoſed it to be on its paſſage to Europe. This bird hath indeed, in many reſpects, a very ſtrong reſemblance to the European Roller, but it differs moſt materially in the length of the two exterior feathers of the tail, as well as in the colour of the neck, which in the African Roller is of a moſt bright green, and in the European of rather a dull blue.

In the 310th plate of the ſame publication there is likewiſe a coloured repreſentation of the Hirondelle *à ventre roux du Senegal*, which very much reſembles the European ſwallow, but the tail differs materially, as the forks (in the Senegal ſpecimen) taper from the bottom of the two exterior feathers to the top, at three regular diviſions or nitches, whereas in the European they are nearly of the ſame width throughout.

The convincing proof, however, that the Hirondelle à ventre roux du Senegal differs from our chimney ſwallow is, that the rump is entirely covered with a bright orange or cheſnut, which in the European ſwallow "is of a very lovely but dark purpliſh colour †."

* Voyage au Senegal, p. 9. † Willoughby, p. 312.

ferred

ferred from it, but hath endeavoured to confirm by an actual experiment[l].

M. de Buffon, from the many inſtances of ſwallows being found torpid even under water, very readily admits, that all the birds of this genus do not migrate, but only that ſpecies which was ſeen by Monſ. Adanſon in Africa, and which he generally refers to as the chimney ſwallow[m]; but, from the outſet, ſeems to ſhew that he hath himſelf confounded this ſpecies with the martin.

"Prenons un ſeul oiſeau, par exemple, l'hirondelle, celle que "tout le monde connoit, qui paroit au printems, diſparoit en "automne, & fait ſon nid avec de la terre contre les fenetres, ou "dans les cheminees," p. 23.

It is very clear that the deſign in this period is to ſpecify a particular bird in ſuch a manner that no doubt could remain with any one about the ſpecies referred to; and from other paſſages which follow, it is as clear that Monſ. de Buffon means to allude to the ſwallow *κατ' ἐξοχην*.

Though this was certainly the intention of this moſt ingenious naturaliſt, it is to me very evident that the martin, and not the

[l] See the two prefatory diſcourſes on his ſixteenth volume of natural hiſtory.

[m] So little do naturaliſts know of this very common bird, that I believe it hath never yet been obſerved by any writer, that the tail-feathers are much longer in the cock than hen ſwallow, which are conſidered as its moſt diſtinguiſhing marks. I venture to make this remark upon having ſeen the difference in two ſwallows which are in Mr. Tunſtall's collection, F. R S. as alſo in two others, which have lately been preſented to the Muſeum of the Royal Society by the directors of the Hudſon's Bay company

Theſe very long feathers would be very inconvenient to the hen during incubation; and they are likewiſe confined to the cock *widow-bird*, as, from their more extraordinary length, they would be ſtill more ſo. The ſame holds with regard to moſt (if not all) of the humming birds.

ſwallow,

ſwallow, was in his contemplation, becauſe he firſt ſpeaks of the bird's building againſt windows, before he mentions chimnies, and therefore ſuppoſes that either place is indifferent; which is not the caſe, becauſe the ſwallow ſeldom builds on the ſides of windows, or the martin in chimnies.

There are perhaps three or four martins to one ſwallow in all parts; and from their being the more common bird of the two, as well as from the circumſtance of their building at the corner of windows (and conſequently being eternally in our ſight) nineteen out of twenty, when they ſpeak of a ſwallow, really mean a martin [n].

I only take notice of this ſuppoſed inaccuracy in Monſ. de Buffon, becauſe, if that able naturaliſt does not ſpeak of the different ſorts of ſwallows with that preciſion which is neceſſary upon ſuch an occaſion, why ſhould he rely ſo entirely upon the impoſſibility of M. Adanſon's being miſtaken?

I ſhall now ſtate the experiment of Monſ. de Buffon, to prove that the ſwallow is not torpid in the winter, and muſt therefore migrate to the coaſt of Senegal [o].

[n] In the ſame manner the generical name in other languages, for this tribe of birds, always means the martin, and not the ſwallow.

Thus Anacreon complains of the χελιδων for waking him by its twittering.

Now if it be conſidered that there was only the kitchen chimney in a Grecian houſe, it muſt have been the martin which built under the eves of the bed-chamber window, that was troubleſome to Anacreon, and not the ſwallow.

Ovid alſo ſpeaking of the neſt of the *hirundo*, ſays,

—luteum ſub trabe figit opus.

by which he neceſſarily alludes to the martin, and not the ſwallow.

Garrula quæ *tignis* nidum ſuſpendit hirundo.

Virg. Georg. l. IV.

[o] Plan de l'ouvrage, p. 15.

He

He ſhut up ſome ſwallows (*hirondelles*) in an ice-houſe, which were there confined "plus ou moins de temps;" and the conſequence was, that thoſe which remained there the longeſt died, nor could they be revived by expoſing them to the ſun; and that thoſe, "qui n'avoient ſouffert le froid de la glaciere que pendant "peu de tems," were very lively when permitted to make their eſcape.

M. de Buffon does not, in this account of his experiment, ſtate the time during which the birds were confined; but as the trial muſt have been made in France, the ſwallows which he procured could not be expected to be torpid either in an ice-houſe[p] or any other place, becauſe the ſeaſon for their being in that ſtate was not yet arrived.

I cannot alſo agree with M. de Buffon, that thoſe birds which were ſhut up the longeſt time died through cold, as he ſuppoſes, but for want of food, as he neither ſupplied them with any flies, nor, if he had, could the ſwallows have caught them in the dark: a very ſhort faſt kills theſe tender animals, which are feeding every inſtant when on the wing.

It therefore ſeems not to follow from this experiment, that ſwallows muſt neceſſarily migrate (as M. de Buffon ſuppoſes) to the coaſt of Senegal.

[p] The very name of an ice-houſe almoſt ſtrikes one with a chill; I placed, however, a thermometer in one near Hyde Park Corner on the 23d of November, where it continued 48 hours, and the mercury then ſtood at 43½ by Fahrenheit's ſcale.

This is therefore a degree of cold which ſwallows ſometimes experience whilſt they continue in ſome parts of Europe, without any apparent inconvenience; and it ſhould ſeem that the cold vapours, which may ariſe from the included ice, ſink the thermometer only 7 or 8 degrees, as the temperature in approved cellars is commonly from 50 or 51 throughout the year.

Swallows are ſeen during the ſummer in every part of Europe from Lapland to the Southern coaſt of Spain; nor is Europe vaſtly inferior in point of ſize to Africa.

If ſwallows therefore retreat to Africa in the winter, ſhould not they be diſperſed over the whole Continent of Africa during that ſeaſon, juſt as they are over every part of Europe during the ſummer?

But this moſt certainly is not ſo: Dr. Shaw, who was a very good naturaliſt and attended much to the birds in the neighbourhood of Algiers (as appears by his account of that country), makes no mention of any ſuch circumſtance; nor have we heard of it from any other traveller [q].

It muſt be admitted indeed, that Herodotus, ſpeaking of a part of upper Egypt (which he had never ſeen), ſays, that kites and ſwallows never leave it [r]; this, however, totally differs from Monſ. Adanſon's account, who informs us that they diſappear in Senegal on the approach of ſummer [s].

[q] It may alſo be obſerved here, that credit is in ſome meaſure given to M. Adanſon's eyeſight, againſt that of all the Engliſh, French, Dutch, Portugueze, and Danes, who have been ſettled not far from Senegal for above a century, many of which have ſpent great part of their lives there, and whoſe notice European ſwallows ſeen during the winter muſt have probably attracted. I do not mean by this to deny that ſuch ſwallows may not be obſerved at Senegal, I only doubt their periodical migration.

[r] *Ικτινοι δε και χελιδονες δι ετεος εοντες ȣκ απολειπȣσι.* Euterpe, p. 98. ed. Gale.

[s] On the contrary they appear, and diſappear, at the ſame ſeaſons as with us, both in the tropical parts of America and Aſia. With regard to America, I ſhall cite Hughes's Hiſtory of Barbadoes, p. 75. and, with relation to Aſia, a gentleman long reſident in Bengal, who informs me that ſwallows are often found in the banks of the Ganges during the winter, and in their torpid ſtate. They alſo conceal themſelves in the rocks of Barbadoes, according to Hughes.

It ſeems to follow therefore, from this ſilence in others, that ſwallows cannot be accommodated for their winter reſidence in any part of the vaſt continent, except in the neighbourhood of Senegal. But this is not the whole objection to ſuch an hypotheſis.

If the ſwallows of Europe, when they diſappear in thoſe parts, retreat to the coaſt of Senegal, what neceſſarily follows with regard to a Lapland ſwallow?

I will ſuppoſe ſuch a bird to have arrived ſafely at his winter quarters upon the approach of that ſeaſon in Lapland; but it muſt then, according both to Monſ. Adanſon's and de Buffon's account, return to Lapland in the ſpring, or at leaſt ſome other ſwallow from Senegal fill its place.

Such a bird immediately upon its arrival on the Southern coaſt of Spain would find the climate and food which it deſired to attain, and all proper conveniences for its neſt: what then is to be its inducement for quitting all theſe accommodations which it meets with in ſuch profuſion, and puſhing on immediately over ſo many degrees of European continent to Lapland, where both martin and ſwallow can procure ſo few houſes to build upon? What alſo is to be the inducement to theſe birds, when they have arrived at that part of the Norwegian coaſt which is oppoſite to the Ferroe iſlands, to croſs degrees of ſea, in order to build in ſuch ſmall ſpots of land, where there are ſtill fewer habitations?

The next fact I have happened to meet with, of a bird's being ſeen at a conſiderable diſtance from the ſhore, is in Dr. Forſter's lately publiſhed tranſlation of Kalm's account of N. America[t].

[t] Vol. I. p. 24.

We are there informed that a bird (which Kalm calls a ſwallow) was ſeen near the ſhip on the 2d of September, and, as he ſuppoſes, 20 degrees from the continent of America [u].

It appears however, by what he before ſtates in his journal, that the ſhip was not above 5 degrees from the iſland of Sable.

Beſides, if it is contended that this was an European ſwallow on its paſſage acroſs the Atlantic on the 2d of September, it is too early even for a ſwift to have been on its migration, which diſappears with us ſooner than the three other ſpecies of European ſwallows [x].

Only three more inſtances have occurred of birds being ſeen in *open* ſea that have been deſcribed with any ſort of preciſion, which I ſhall juſt ſtate, as I would not decline giving the beſt anſwer I am able to every argument and fact which may be relied upon, by thoſe who contend that birds periodically migrate acroſs oceans. Dr. Shaw mentions, that whilſt his ſhip was at anchor under mount Carmel, he obſerved many ſtorks paſſing, but as

[u] It may not be improper here to obſerve, that in all inſtances of birds being ſeen at ſea any great diſtance from the coaſt, it is not improbable that they may have before ſettled on ſome other veſſel, or perhaps on a piece of wreck. In a paſſage from Newfoundland to England Mr. Thomas Butts fell in with floating ice on which were hawks and other fowls to reſt themſelves, being weary of flying over far from the main. Hakluyt, part III. p. 131. In and after a ſtorm, blackbirds, ſtarlings, and all ſorts of ſmall birds, are driven from the ſhore, and make for the ſhips to ſave themſelves, whilſt others fly about till they are ſpent, fall into the ſea, and are drowned. Marten's Voyage to Spitzbergen, p. 31.

By accidents of this ſort even butterflies have ſometimes been caught by the ſailors at 40 leagues diſtance from any land. See Monſ. l'Abbé Courte de la Blanchadiere's Voyage to Brazil, Paris, 1759, 12mo. p. 169.

[x] The bird mentioned by Kalm was probably an American ſwallow, forced out to ſea by ſome accidental ſtorm there are ſeveral ſpecies of them, and they ſeem to bear a general affinity to thoſe of Europe.

the

the veſſel was ſo near the coaſt, this ſeems to be only a flitting from headland to headland.

On the 30th of March, 1751, Oſbeck, in his voyage from Sweden to China[y], met with a ſingle houſe-ſwallow near the Canary Iſlands, which was ſo tired that it was caught by the ſailors: Oſbeck alſo ſtates, that though it had been fine weather for ſeveral preceding days, the bird was as wet as if it had juſt emerged from the bottem of the ſea.

If this inſtance proves any thing, it is the ſubmerſion and not the migration of ſwallows ſo generally believed in all the northern parts of Europe. It would ſwell this Eſſay to a moſt unreaſonable ſize, to touch only upon this litigated point; and I ſhall, for the preſent, ſuppreſs what hath happened to occur to me on this controverted queſtion.

Oſbeck afterwards, in the courſe of his voyage, mentions, that a ſwallow (indefinitely) followed the ſhip, near Java, on the 24th of July, and another on the 14th of Auguſt, in the Chineſe ſea, as he terms it.

After what I have obſerved before with regard to other inſtances of the ſame ſort, I need ſcarcely ſay that this naturaliſt does not ſtate of what ſpecies theſe ſwallows were; and that, from the latitudes in which they were ſeen, they muſt have been ſome of the Aſiatic kinds.

I cannot, however, diſmiſs this article of the ſwallow, without adding ſome general reaſons, which ſeem to prove the great improbability of this or any other bird's periodically migrating over wide tracts of ſea; and I the rather do it in this place, becauſe the ſwallow is commonly pitched upon as the moſt notorious inſtance of ſuch a regular paſſage.

y See the lately publiſhed tranſlation of this voyage.

This

This ſeems to ariſe from its being ſeen in ſuch numbers during the ſummer, from its appearing almoſt always on the wing, and from its feeding in that poſition: from which two latter circumſtances it is ſuppoſed to be the beſt adapted for ſuch diſtant migrations.

And firſt, let us conſider, from the few facts or reaſons we have to guide us in the diſcuſſion, what length of flight either a ſwallow or any other bird is probably equal to.

A ſwallow, it is true, ſeems to be always on the wing; but I have frequently attended, as much as I could, to the motions of a particular one; and it hath appeared to me, that the bird commonly returned to its neſt in eight or ten minutes: as for extent of flight, I believe I may venture to ſay, that theſe birds are ſeldom a quarter of a mile from their mate or young ones; they feed whilſt on the wing, and are perpetually turning ſhort round to catch the inſects, who endeavour to illude them as a hare does a greyhound.

I have ſometimes ſeen ſwallows in a church, into which they had entered through a broken window; theſe birds fled backwards and forwards for perhaps ten minutes; but then always perched to reſt themſelves. It therefore ſeems to me, that ſwallows are by no means equal to long flights, from their practice during their ſummer reſidence with us.

I have long attended to the motions of birds; and it hath always appeared to me, that they are never on the wing for amuſement (as we walk or ride), but merely in ſearch of food.

The only bird which I have ever obſerved to fly without any particular point of direction, is the rook, which will, when the wind is high,

"Ride in the whirlwind, and *enjoy the ſtorm*."

They

They never paſs, however, at this time, from point to point, but only tumble in the air, merely for their diverſion.

It ſeems, therefore, that birds are by no means calculated for flights acroſs oceans, for which they have no previous practice: and they are, in fact, always ſo fatigued, that, when they meet a ſhip at ſea, they forget all apprehenſions, and deliver themſelves up to the ſailors.

Let us now conſider another objection to the migration of the ſwallow, which Monſ de Buffon ſuppoſes may croſs the Atlantic to the Line in eight days [z]; and this is not only from the want of reſt, but of food, during the paſſage.

A ſwallow, indeed, feeds on the wing; but where is it to find any inſects, whilſt it is flying over a wide expanſe of ſea? This bird, therefore, if it ever attempted ſo adventurous a paſſage, would ſoon feel a want of food, and return again to land, where it had met with a conſtant ſupply from minute to minute.

I am aware it may be here objected, that the ſwallow leaves us on the approach of winter, when ſoon no flying inſects can be procured: but I ſhall hereafter endeavour to ſhew, that ſome ſpecies of theſe birds are then torpid, and, conſequently, can want no ſuch food.

Another objection remains to the hypotheſis of migration, which is, that birds, when flying from point to point, endeavour always to have the wind againſt them [a], as is periodically experienced by the London bird-catchers in March and October, when they lay their nets for ſinging birds [b].

[z] Diſcours ſur la nature des oiſeaux, p. 32.

[a] Kalm, in his voyage to America, makes the ſame obſervation, with regard to flying fiſh; and Valentine ſays, that if the wind does not continue to blow againſt the bird of paradiſe, it immediately drops to the ground.

[b] Theſe birds, as it ſhould ſeem, are then in motion, becauſe, at thoſe ſeaſons, the ground is plowed either for the winter or lent corn.

Let us ſuppoſe, then, a ſwallow to be equal to a paſſage acroſs the Atlantic in other reſpects; how is the bird to be inſured of the wind's continuing for days in the ſame quarter; or how is he to depend upon its continuing to blow againſt his flight with moderation? For who can ſuppoſe that a ſwallow can make his way to the point of direction, when buffeted by a ſtorm blowing in the teeth of his intended paſſage[c]?

Laſtly, can it be conceived that theſe, or any other birds, can be impelled by a providential inſtinct, regularly to attempt what ſeems to be attended with ſuch inſuperable difficulties, and what moſt frequently leads to certain deſtruction?

But it will ſtill be objected, that, as ſwallows regularly appear and diſappear at certain ſeaſons, it is incumbent upon thoſe who deny their migration to ſhew what becomes of them in Europe during our winter.

Though it might be anſwered, that it is not neceſſary thoſe, who endeavour to ſhew the impoſſibility of another ſyſtem or hypotheſis, ſhould from thence be obliged to ſet up one of their own; yet I ſhall, without any difficulty, ſay, that I at leaſt am convinced ſwallows (and perhaps ſome other birds) are torpid during the winter.

I have not, I muſt own, myſelf ever ſeen them in this ſtate; but, having heard inſtances of their being thus found from others of undoubted veracity, I have ſcarcely the leaſt doubt with regard to this point.

It is, indeed, rather difficult to conceive why ſome ornithologiſts continue to withhold their aſſents to ſuch a cloud of wit-

[c] I have myſelf attended to ſwallows during a high wind, and have obſerved that they fly only in ſheltered places, whilſt they almoſt touch the ſurface of the ground. The ſea-fowl even, on the approach of a hurricane, fly to the land for ſhelter. Voyage to the iſland of Mauritius, in 1768, p. 169.

neſſes,

nesses, except that it perhaps contradicts a favourite hypothesis which they have already maintained.

Why is it more extraordinary that swallows should be torpid during the winter, than that bats are found in this state [d], and so many insects which are the food of swallows?

But it may be said, that as the swallows have crowded the air during the summer in every part of Europe since the creation, and as regularly disappear in winter, why have not the instances of their being found in a sleeping state been more frequent?

To this it may be answered, that though our globe may have been formed so many centuries, yet the inhabitants of it have scarcely paid any attention to the study of natural history but within these late years.

As for the antient Greeks and Romans, their dress prevented their being so much in the fields as we are; or, if they heard of a rather extraordinary bird in their neighbourhood, they had not a gun to shoot it: the only method of attaining real knowledge in natural history depends almost entirely upon the having frequent opportunities of thus killing animals, and examining them when dead.

If they did not stir much in their own country, much less did they think of travelling into distant regions; want of bills of exchange, and of that curiosity which arises from our being thoroughly acquainted with what is near us at home, probably occasioned this; to which may also be added, the want of a variety

[d] And yet how few can go to the places where bats are to be found thus torpid during the winter! I speak this from having been obliged to send as far as Totness in Devonshire for some, which were wanted in that state by Mr. Hunter, F.R.S.

of languages: ſcarcely any Greek ſeems to have known more than his own tongue, nor Roman more than two [e].

Ariſtotle, indeed, began ſomething like a ſyſtem of natural hiſtory; and Pliny put down, in his common place-book, many an idle ſtory; but, before the invention of printing, copies of their works could not be ſo generally diſperſed, as to occaſion much attention to what might be intereſting facts for the ornithologiſt.

In the ſixteenth century, Geſner, Belon, and Aldrovandus, publiſhed ſome materials, which might be of uſe to future naturaliſts; but, in the ſeventeenth, Ray and Willoughby firſt treated this extenſive branch of ſtudy with that clearneſs of method, perſpicuity of deſcription, and accuracy of obſervation, as hath not, perhaps, been ſince exceeded. The works of theſe great naturaliſts were ſoon diſperſed over Europe, and the merit of them acknowledged; but it ſo happened, that Sir Iſaac Newton's amazing diſcoveries in natural philoſophy making their appearance about the ſame time, engaged entirely the attention of the learned.

In proceſs of time, all controverſy was ſilenced by the demonſtration of the Newtonian ſyſtem; and then the philoſophical part of Europe naturally turned their thoughts to other branches of ſcience.

Since this period, therefore, and not before, natural hiſtory hath been ſtudied in moſt countries of Europe; and conſequently the finding ſwallows in a ſtate of torpidity, or on the coaſt of Senegal,

[e] It need be ſcarcely here mentioned alſo, that their navigation was confined to the Mediterranean, from the compaſs not having been then diſcovered.

Q. Ennius tria corda ſe habere dicebat, quod loqui Græcè, Oſcè, et Latinè ſciret. Aulus Gellius, LXVII. c. 17.

Linguâ doctus utrâque.—Martial.

Linguas edidiciſſe duas.—Ovid.

Senegal, during the winter, begins to be an intereſting fact, which is communicated to the world by the perſon who obſerves it.

The annual publications of the Royal Society, as likewiſe the periodical ones of other ſcientific academies, have alſo afforded an immediate and convenient opportunity of laying ſuch facts before the publick, which would neither have been printed, nor perpetuated in detached pieces.

To this I may add, that the common labourers, who have the beſt chance of finding torpid birds, have ſcarcely any of them a doubt with regard to this point; and conſequently, when they happen to ſee them in this ſtate, make no mention of it to others, becauſe they conſider the diſcovery as neither uncommon or intereſting to any one.

Molyneux, therefore, in the Philophical Tranſactions [f], informs us, that this is the general belief of the common people of Ireland with regard to land-rails [g]; and I have myſelf received the ſame anſwer from a perſon who, in December, found ſwallows in the ſtump of an old tree [h].

Another reaſon why the inſtances of torpid ſwallows may not be expected ſo frequently is, that the inſtinct of ſecreting themſelves at the proper ſeaſon of the year likewiſe ſuggeſts to them,

[f] Phil. Tranſ. abr. vol. II. p. 853.

[g] The Rev. Dr. De-Salis (who hath been in moſt parts of Ireland) informs me that the following lines are commonly repeated in many parts of that country.

"The bat, the bee, the butterfly, and the ſwallow,
"The corn-creak *, and the ſtonechat, all ſleep the winter thorough.

[h] Vel qualis gelidis plumâ labente pruinis
Arboris immoritur trunco brumalis hirundo."

CLAUDIAN.

* i. e. Our landrail.

its being neceffary to hide themfelves in fuch holes and caverns as may not only elude the fearch of man, but of every other animal which might prey upon them; it is not therefore by any common accident that they are ever difcovered in a ftate of torpidity.

Since the ftudy of natural hiftory, however, hath become more general, proofs of this fact are frequently communicated, as may appear in the Britifh Zoology [i].

That it may not be faid, however, I do not refer to any inftance which deferves credit, if properly fifted, I beg leave to cite the letter from Mr. Achard to Mr. Collinfon, printed in the Philofophical Tranfactions [k], from whence it feems to be a moft irrefragable fact, that fwallows [l] are annually difcovered in a torpid ftate on the banks of the Rhine. I fhall alfo refer to Dr. Birch's Hiftory of the Royal Society [m], where it is ftated, that the celebrated Harvey diffected fome, which were found in the winter, under water, and in which he could not obferve any circulation of the blood.

Affuming it, therefore, from thefe facts, that fwallows have been found in fuch a ftate, I would afk the partifans of migration,

[i] See vol. II. p. 250. Brit. Zool. ill. p. 13, 14. As alfo Mr. Pennant's Tour in Scotland, p. 199.

[k] 1763. p. 101.

[l] "Swallows or martins," are Mr. Achard's words, which I the rather mention, becaufe Mr. Collinfon complains that the fpecies is not fpecified.

Mr. Collinfon himfelf had endeavoured to prove, that fand martins are not torpid, Phil. Tranf. 1760, p. 109. and concludes his letter, by fuppofing that all the fwallow tribe migrates, therefore the fwift is the only fpecies [illegible], for his friend Mr. Achard [illegible] to demonftration, that fwallows or martins are torpid; he does not, indeed, precifely ftate which of them.

[m] Vol. IV. p. 537.

whether

whether any inſtance can be produced where the ſame animal is calculated for a ſtate of torpidity and, at the ſame time of the year, for a flight acroſs oceans?

But it may be urged, poſſibly, that if ſwallows are torpid when they diſappear, the ſame thing ſhould happen with regard to other birds, which are not ſeen in particular parts of the year.

To this I anſwer, that this is by no means a neceſſary inference: if, for example, it ſhould be inſiſted that other birds beſides the cuckow are equally careleſs with regard to their eggs, it would be immediately allowed that the argument ariſing from ſuch ſuppoſed analogy could by no means be relied upon.

It is poſſible, however, that ſome other birds, which are conceived to migrate, may be really torpid as well as ſwallows; and if it be aſked why they are not ſometimes alſo ſeen in ſuch a ſtate during the winter, the anſwer ſeems to be, that perhaps there may be a hundred ſwallows to any other ſort of bird, and that they commonly are found ſleeping in clusters.

If a ſingle bird of any other kind happens to be ſeen in the winter, without motion or apparent warmth, it is immediately conceived that it died by ſome common accident.

I ſhall, however, without any reſerve, ſay, that I rather conceive the notion which prevails with regard to the migration of many birds, may moſt commonly ariſe from the want of obſervation, and ready knowledge of them, when they are ſeen on the wing, even by profeſſed ornithologiſts.

It is an old ſaying, that "a bird in the hand is worth two in "the buſh;" and this holds equally with regard to their being diſtinguiſhed, when thoſe even who ſtudy natural hiſtory have but a tranſient ſight of the animal [n].

If,

[n] An ingenious friend of mine makes always a very proper diſtinction between what he calls in-door and out-door naturaliſts.

Thomas

If, therefore, a bird, which is ſuppoſed to migrate in the winter, paſſes almoſt under the noſe of a Linnæan, he pays but little attention to it, becauſe he cannot examine the beak, by which he is perhaps to claſs the bird. Thus I conceive, that the ſuppoſing a nightingale to be a bird of paſſage ariſes from not readily diſtinguiſhing it, when ſeen in a hedge, or on the wing [o]. This bird is known to the ear of every one, by its moſt ſtriking and capital notes, but to the eye of very few indeed; becauſe the plumage is dull, nor is there any thing peculiar in its make.

The nightingale ſings perhaps for two months [p], and then is never heard again till the return of the ſpring, when it is ſuppoſed to migrate to us from the continent, with redſtarts, and ſeveral other birds.

That it cannot really do ſo, ſeems highly probable, from the following reaſons.

This bird is ſcarcely ever ſeen to fly above twenty yards, but creeps at the bottom of the hedges, in ſearch of maggots, and other inſects, which are found in the ground.

If the ſwallow is not ſupplied with any food during its paſſage acroſs oceans, much leſs can the nightingale be ſo accommodated; and I have great reaſon to believe, from the death of birds in a cage, which have had nothing to eat for twenty-four hours, that theſe delicate and tender animals cannot ſupport a longer faſt, though uſing no exerciſe at all.

Thomas Willifel, who aſſiſted Ray and Willughby much with regard to the natural hiſtory of the animals of this iſland, never ſtirred any where without his gun and fiſhing tackle.

[o] No two birds fly in the ſame manner, if their motions are accurately attended to.

[p] Whilſt it ſings even, the bird can ſeldom be diſtinguiſhed, becauſe it is then almoſt perpetually in hedges, when the foliage is thickeſt, upon the firſt burſt of the ſpring, and when no inſects can as yet have deſtroyed conſiderable parts of the leaves.

To this I may alſo add, that thoſe birds which feed on inſects are vaſtly more feeble than thoſe whoſe bills can crack ſeeds, and conſequently, leſs capable of bearing any extraordinary hardſhips or fatigue.

But other proofs are not wanting that this bird cannot migrate from England.

Nightingales are very common in Denmark, Sweden, and Ruſſia [q], as alſo in every other part of Europe, as well as Aſia, if the Arabic name is properly tranſlated. Kempfer likewiſe informs us that they are found in Japan, and much prized there.

Now, if it is ſuppoſed that many of theſe birds which are obſerved in the ſouthern parts of England, croſs the German-ſea, from the oppoſite corſt of the continent; why does not the ſame inſtinct drive thoſe of Denmark to Scotland, where no ſuch bird was ever ſeen or heard [r]?

But theſe are not all the difficulties which attend the hypotheſis of migration; nightingales are agreed to be ſcarcely ever obſerved to the weſtward of Dorſetſhire, or in the principality of Wales [s], much leſs in Ireland.

I have alſo been informed, that theſe birds are not uncommon in Worceſterſhire, whereas they are exceſſively rare (if found at all) in the neighbouring county of Hereford.

[q] See Dr. Birch's Hiſtory of the Royal Society, vol. III. p. 189. Linnæi Fauna Suecica. and Biographia Britannica, art. FLETCHER; where it is ſaid, that they have in Ruſſia a greater variety of notes than elſewhere.

[r] Sir Robert Sibbald, indeed, conceives the nightingale to be a bird of North Britain; but, if I can depend upon many concurrent teſtimonies, no ſuch bird is ever ſeen or heard ſo far northward at preſent, nor could I ever trace them in that direction further than Durham.

[s] I have, however, frequently ſeen the nightingale's congener (and ſuppoſed fellow-traveller) the redſtart in Wales.

Whence

Whence therefore can it arise, that this bird should at one time be equal to the crossing of seas, and at other times not travel a mile or two into an adjacent county? Does it not afford, on the other hand, a strong proof, that the bird really continues on the same spot during the whole year, but happens not to be attended to, from the reasons I have before suggested?

I am therefore convinced, that if I was ever to live in the country during the winter, I should see nightingales, because I should be looking after them; and I am accordingly informed, by a person who is well acquainted with this bird, that he hath frequently observed them during this season [t].

If it be asked, why the nightingales are all this time mute? the answer is, that the same silence is experienced in many other birds, and this very muteness is, in part, the cause why the bird is not attended to in winter.

I must now ask those who contend for the migration of a nightingale, what is to be its inducement for crossing from the continent to us? A swallow, indeed, may want flies in winter, if it stays in England; but a nightingale is just as well supplied with insects on the continent, as it can be with us after its passage [u].

I must

[t] I find they have also been seen in France during the winter. See a treatise, intitled, Aedologie, Paris, 1751. p. 23.

[u] I have omitted the mention of a more minute proof, that this bird cannot migrate from the continent, from the having kept them for some years in a cage, and having been very attentive to their song.

Kircher (in his Musurgia) hath given us the nightingale's notes in musical characters, from which it appears that the song of a German nightingale differs very materially from that of an English one: now, if there was a communication by migration between the continent and England, the song of these birds would not so materially differ, as I may, perhaps, shew, by some experiments I have made, in relation to the notes of birds.

I have

I muſt alſo aſk, in what other part of the world this bird is ſeen during the winter: muſt it migrate to Senegal with the ſwallow?

I am perſuaded likewiſe, that the cuckow never leaves this iſland any more than the nightingale: this bird is either probably torpid in the winter, or otherwiſe is miſtaken for one of the ſmaller kind of hawks [x]; which it would be likewiſe in the ſpring, was it not for its very particular note at that time, and which only laſts during courtſhip, as it does with the quail.

If there is fine weather in February, this bird ſometimes makes this ſort of call to its mate, whilſt it is ſuppoſed to continue ſtill on the continent.

An inſtance is mentioned by Mr. Bradly [y], of not only a ſingle cuckow, but ſeveral, which were heard in Lincolnſhire during the month of February; and that able naturaliſt Mr. Pennant informs me, another was heard near Hatcham in Shropſhire, on the 4th of February [z]. I have received a ſimilar account from Welſhpool, in Montgomeryſhire, but of the laſt week of the ſame month, 1779, as alſo from Argyleſhire.

I have before mentioned, that Mr. Fletcher, who was embaſſador from England to Ruſſia in the time of Queen Elizabeth, obſerved that the ſong of the Ruſſian nightingale differed from that of the Engliſh.

[x] Mr. Hunter, F. R. S. informs me, that he hath ſeen cuckows in the iſland of Belleiſle during the winter, which is not ſituated ſo much to the ſouthward, as to make it improbable that they may equally continue with us.

[y] Works of Nature, p. 77.

[z] Mr. Pennant received this account from Mr. Plimly, of Longnor in Shropſhire, and Amis the Poulterer in Bond-ſtreet hath told me that he hath procured cuckows during the winter. See likewiſe Willughby, art. CUCKOW.

Thus likewiſe Mr. Edwards informs us, that the ſea fowls near the Needles, which are commonly ſuppoſed to migrate in winter, appear upon the weather's being very mild. Eſſays, p. 197.

It is amazing how much the being intereſted to diſcover particular objects contributes to our readily diſtinguiſhing them.

I remember the being much ſurprized that a greyheaded gamekeeper always ſaw the partridge on the ground before they roſe, when I could not do the ſame; he told me, however, that the reaſon was, I lived in a time when the ſhooter had no occaſion to give himſelf that trouble.

He then further explained himſelf, by ſaying, that when he was young, no one ever thought of aiming at a bird on the wing, and conſequently they were obliged to ſee the game before it was ſprung. He added, that from this neceſſity he could not only diſtinguiſh partridges, but ſnipes and woodcocks, on the ground.

Another inſtance of the ſame kind, is the great readineſs with which a perſon who is fond of courſing finds a hare ſitting in her form: thoſe, however, who are not anxious about ſuch ſport, can ſcarcely ſee the hare when it is under their noſe, and pointed out to them.

But more apparent objects eſcape our notice, when we are not intereſted about them.

Aſk any one, who hath not a botanical turn, what he hath ſeen in paſſing through a rich meadow, at the time it is moſt enamelled with plants in flower; and he will tell you, that he hath obſerved nothing but graſs and daiſies. If moſt gardeners even are in like manner aſked whether the flowers of a bean grow on every ſide of the ſtalk, they will ſuppoſe that they do; whereas they, in reality, are only to be found on one ſide.

The mouths of flounders are often turned different ways, which one would think could not well eſcape the obſervation of the London fiſhmongers; yet, upon aſking ſeveral of them whether they had attended to this particular, I found they had not, till I ſhewed them the proof in their own ſhops.

A fiſh-

A fiſhmonger, however, knows immediately whether a fiſh is in good eating order or not, on the firſt inſpection: becauſe this is a circumſtance which intereſts him.

I ſhall, however, by no means ſuppreſs two arguments in favour of migration, which ſeem to require the fulleſt anſwer that can be given to them.

The firſt is, that there are certain birds, which appear during the winter, but diſappear during the ſummer; and it may be aſked, where ſuch birds can be ſuppoſed to breed, if they do not migrate from this iſland. Theſe birds are in number four; viz. the ſnipe, woodcock, red-wing, and fieldfare.

As for the ſnipe, I have a very ſhort anſwer to give to the objection, as far as it relates to this bird; becauſe it conſtantly breeds in the fens of Lincolnſhire, Wolmar foreſt, and Bodmyn downs; it is therefore highly probable that it does the ſame in almoſt every county of England.

I muſt own, however, that, till within theſe few years, I conceived the neſt of a ſnipe was as rarely ſeen in England as that of a woodcock or fieldfare; and that able ornithologiſt Mr. Edwards ſuppoſes this to be the fact, in the late publication of his ingenious Eſſays on Natural Hiſtory [a].

Woodcocks likewiſe are known to build in ſome parts of England every year; but, as the inſtances are commonly thoſe of a ſingle neſt, I would by no means pretend to draw the ſame proof againſt the ſummer migration of this bird, as in the former caſe of the ſnipe. It is remarkable, however, that Belon aſſerts, without the leaſt doubt of the fact, that in France the woodcocks leave the plains for the mountains, in order to make their neſts [b]; and Willughby fluſh'd them in the months of June and July on mount Jura.

[a] P. 72.

[b] Belon, p. 273.

I will moſt readily admit, that theſe accidental facts are rather to be accounted for, perhaps, from the whimſy or ſillineſs of a few birds, which occaſions their laying their eggs in a place where they are eaſily diſcovered, and contrary to what is uſual with the bulk of the ſpecies.

I remember to have ſeen a duck's neſt once on the top of a pollard willow, near the decoy in St. James's Park; it would not be, however, fair to infer from ſuch an inſtance that all ducks would pitch upon the ſame very improper ſituation for a neſt, upon which it is difficult to conceive how a web-footed bird could ſettle. Some ſilly birds likewiſe now and then chooſe a place for building, which cannot eſcape the obſervation of either man or beaſt, as they paſs by[c].

I therefore ſuppoſe that the few inſtances of woodcocks neſts having been found in England, ariſe either from one or other of theſe two cauſes; and all which they ſeem to prove is, that our climate in ſummer is not abſolutely improper for them.

It is to be obſerved, however, that Mr. Cateſby conſiders ſuch inſtances as of equal force againſt the migration of the woodcock as of the ſnipe[d]. Willughby alſo ſays, that Mr. Jeſſop ſaw young woodcocks ſold at Sheffield (which rather implies a certain number being brought to market), and that others had obſerved the ſame elſewhere[e].

We are, indeed, informed by Scopoli[f], that they breed conſtantly in Carniola, which is conſiderably to the ſouthward of

[c] See alſo other inſtances of neſts imprudently placed by birds, Phil. Tranſ. vol. LXIV. part I. p. 199. as alſo vol. LXV, part I. p. 263.

[d] Phil. Tranſ. Abr. vol. II. p. 889.

[e] B. III c. 1. The ſame able ornithologiſt obſerved Woodcocks which were brought to market during the month of Auguſt at Nuremberg; from whence he concludes, that they continue in that part of Germany throughout the year, which is only in 49½ North Latitude.

[f] Ornith. Leipſig, 1769.

any

any part of England: our country therefore is certainly not too hot for them.

Woodcocks appear and disappear almost exactly about the same time in every part of Europe, and perhaps Africa[g]: heat and cold, therefore, seem not to have any operation whatsoever with regard to the supposed migration of this bird.

But it may be said, what signifies proving the probability of woodcocks breeding in England, if it is not a known fact that they do so?

To this it should seem there are several answers, as it is equally incumbent upon those who contend for migration, to shew that these birds were ever seen on such passage.

Another answer is, ask ninety-nine people out of a hundred, whether snipes ever make a nest in England; and they will immediately say, that they do not; so little are facts or observations of this sort attended to[h].

But

[g] Shaw's Travels, Phys. Obs ch ii.

[h] I have scarcely ever been in company when this subject hath been started but that some of those who were present have mentioned instances of woodcocks nests being found in different parts of England, and a Sussex farmer near Cuckfield hath kept several, feeding them on worms. A pair of such woodcocks were given by this farmer to Lord Montague in December 1778. They were cock and hen, being called by the name of Derby and Joan; but one of them, after having survived the journey to London, and continued there a few days, died before it could be sent to Cowdry.

In an aviary of the Infant Don Lewis's at St. Ildelfonso, there were many woodcocks [chocas] which had been kept there several years. In this aviary there was a fountain, as also a pine tree, and some shrubs, to keep the ground always moist, whilst the woodcocks were likewise frequently supplied with fresh sods from the neighbouring forest, as full of worms [*lombrices*] as they could be procured. Though these worms hid themselves in the sods, yet the woodcocks, by their smell, soon found them out, darting their bills into the sods only as far as the nostrils; after

But I shall now endeavour to give some other reasons why woodcocks may not only continue with us during the summer, but also breed in large tracts of wood or bog, without being observed.

In the other parts of Europe all birds almost are considered as game, or, at least, are eaten as wholesome food; Ray therefore mentions, that hawks and owls are sold by the poulterers at Rome: every sort of small bird also is equally the foreign fowler's object[1].

after which, holding up their heads quite perpendicular, they swallowed the worm without the least perceptible motion in the throat. Historia Natural de España por Gulielmo Bowles. Madrid, quarto, 1775. p. 454. A friend of mine also saw several woodcocks in the menagery of Versailles during the month of August, 1748. Gisner likewise cites Longolins, who had often seen woodcocks fattened with meal, dried figs, and water, which, "rostris longissimis hauriunt potius quam ducunt."

I should by no means despair of having a breed of woodcocks in an aviary if they were taken young from the nest, and brought up by hand; for, if there is no awe of man, why should we expect this only from Canary birds? On this idea I prevailed upon a bird-catcher, who reared young robins in the house, to put the next year a cock and hen of such a brood into a breeding cage. In this experiment I prevailed with some difficulty; but, to the bird-catcher's great surprise (though not so to mine), five nestlings were not only hatched, but grew to be of their full size.

When birds are thus brought up, they not only have no dread of man, but consider him as their parent and benefactor, of which I have seen the following proof.

Mr. Morisette (a French Gentleman who had traded several years in the East Indies) took a house in Lambeth Marsh, where he raised many chickens by ovens. These chickens not only rejoiced upon seeing any one come into their little garden, but would frequently run up one's legs; and Mr. Morisette was obliged to make an old woman frequently sit amongst them, as otherwise they pined, and did not feed heartily.

[1] In one of Boccace's Novels, a lover, who lives at Florence, dresses a falcon for the dinner of his mistress. Giornata V. Novel. IX. Aristotle likewise informs us that young hawks are very fat and sweet. De Hist. An. l. vi. c. 7.

2 An

An Englifhman does not confider, on the other hand, perhaps, twelve kinds of birds worthy his attention, or expence of powder, none of which are ever fhot in our woods during the fummer, nor are birds then difturbed by felling either coppice or timber.

But it will be faid, why are not woodcocks fometimes feen, however, as they may be fuppofed to leave their cover in fearch of food?

To this I anfwer, that woodcocks fleep in the day-time, whilft with us in the winter, and feed during the night[k]. Whenever a woodcock, therefore, is flufhed, he is roufed from his fleep by the fpaniel or fportfman, and then takes wing, becaufe there are no leaves on the trees to conceal the bird.[l]

Whoever hath looked attentively at a woodcock's eye, muft fee that, from the appearance of it, the fight muft be more calculated to diftinguifh objects by night than by day[l].

The fact therefore is notorious to thofe who cut glades in their woods, and fix nets for catching thefe birds, that they never ftir but as it begins to be dark, after which they return again by day-break, when their fight even then is fo indifferent that they ftrike againft the net, and thus become entangled.

No one with us ever thinks of fixing or attending fuch nets in fummer for woodcocks, becaufe it is not then fuppofed that there

[k] Almoft all the wild fowl of the duck kind alfo fleep in the day-time, and feed at night. Virgil therefore is miftaken when he fuppofes that aquatic birds fleep at the fame time with thofe of the land.

—— pictæque volucres
Quæque *lacus latè liquidos*, quæque afpera dumis
Rura tenent, *fomno pofitæ* fub nocte filenti
Lenibant curas, &c.

[l] I conceive alfo, it is from the eye's looking fo dull that this bird is generally confidered as being fo foolifh hence the Africans call the woodcock *hammar el hadgel*, or the partridge's afs. Shaw's Phyf. Obf. ch. ii.

is any such bird in the island; if they tried this experiment, however, I must own that I believe they would have sport [m].

Dr. Reinhold Forster, F. R. S. who is an able naturalist, informed me, that the fowlers in the neighbourhood of Dantzick kill many woodcocks about St. John's day (or Midsummer) in the following manner, and that they continue to do so till the month of August.

They wait on the side of some of the extensive woods in that neighbourhood, before day-break, for the return of the woodcock from his feeding in the night-time, and always depend upon having a very good chance of thus shooting many of them.

The Dantzickers, however, might be employed the whole summer near these woods in the day-time, without ever seeing such a bird; and it seems therefore not improbable, that it arises from our not waiting for them at twilight or day-break, that they are never observed by Englishmen in the summer. If this bird should, however, be seen in the night, it is immediately supposed to be an owl, which a woodcock does not differ much from in its flight.

m I would ask those who will probably laugh at the very idea of such sport (which I do not, however, absolutely insure), whether, if I was to send them to any part of the British coast to catch the true anchovy, or tunny fish, they would not suppose equally that it was a fool's errand.

Notwithstanding, however, this incredulity, I can produce the authority of both Ray (Syn. Pisc. p. 107.) and Mr Pennant (Brit. Zool. ill. p. 34. 36.) that the true anchovy is caught in the sea not far from Chester, and the tunny fish on the coast of Argyleshire, together with the herrings, where they are called *mackrel sture*.

Is it not amazing, however, that a fish of such a size as the tunny should never have been heard of, even by the Scotch naturalist Sir Robert Sibbald?

Few will suppose, that the largest of the British Grouse (commonly called *Black Game*) are to be found but at a great distance from London; yet I have myself within the space of two hours seen two different broods of these birds in the neighbourhood of the New Forest in Hampshire.

To

To theſe reaſons for woodcocks not being obſerved, it may be added, that the bird is commonly mute, and conſequently ſeldom diſcovers itſelf by its call.

If it be ſtill contended, that the neſt or young muſt ſometimes be ſtumbled upon, though in the centre of extenſive woods, or large bogs, the ſiſkin (or aberdavine [n]) is a much more extraordinary inſtance of concealing its neſt and young.

The plumage of this bird is rather bright than otherwiſe, and the ſong, though not very pleaſing, yet is very audible, both which circumſtances ſhould diſcover it at all times; yet [o]Kramer informs us, that, though immenſe numbers breed annually on the banks of the Danube, no one ever obſerved the neſt.

This bird is rather uncommon in England; ſo that if I aſk when the neſt was ever found within the verge of the iſland, it may be conſidered as rather an unfair challenge.

There is another bird, however, called a redpoll [p], which is taken in numbers during the Michaelmas and March flights by the London bird-catchers, whoſe neſt, I believe, hath ſeldom been ſeen in the ſouthern parts of England, though I have ſeen them in pairs during the ſummer, both in the mountainous parts of Wales and highlands of Scotland [q].

But I ſhall now mention another proof that woodcocks breed in England.

The Reverend Mr. White of Selborn, who is not only a well-read naturaliſt, but an active ſportſman, informs me, that he

[n] Brit. Zool, p. 309.

[o] Elenchus Animalium per Auſtriam, p. 261. Viennæ, 1756.

[p] Brit. Zool, p. 312.

[q] This elegant little bird is very common in Hudſon's Bay, where it feeds chiefly on the birch trees; which being more common in the northern than ſouthern parts of Great Britain, may account for the bird's being more often ſeen northward.

hath frequently killed woodcocks in March, which, upon being opened, had the rudiments of eggs in them, and that it is usual at that time to flush them in pairs; Willughby also observes the same[r].

This bird, therefore, certainly pairs before its supposed migration; and can it be conceived that this strict union (which birds in a wild state so faithfully adhere to[s]) should take place before they traverse oceans, and when they cannot as yet have pitched upon a proper place for concealing their nest and nestlings?

Let us examine if this intercourse before migration takes place in other birds, which are supposed to cross wide extents of sea: and a quail affords such proof.

I have been present when these birds have been caught in the spring, which always turn out to be males, and are enticed to the nets by the call of the hen; quails therefore pair after they appear in England.

But I shall now consider the other two instances of birds which are seen with us in the winter, and are not observed in the summer; I mean the fieldfare and redwing.

And, first, let us examine, where these birds are actually known to breed: the northern naturalists say, in Sweden; Klein, in the neighbourhood of Dantzick, which is only in lat. 54° 30′[t]; and Willughby, in Bohemia.

As

[r] B. III. c. 1.

[s] It is believed that no mule-bird was ever seen in a wild state, notwithstanding M. de Buffon suspects many an intrigue in the recesses of the woods (Hist. Nat. des Oiseaux, tom. I.) Such irregular intercourse is only observed in cages and aviaries, where birds are not only confined, but pampered with food.

[t] See Klein, de Avibus Erraticis, p. 178. Klein, however, cites Zornius, who lived in the same part of Germany, and who asserts that the

I turdus

As they therefore build their nests in more Southern parts of Europe, there is certainly no natural impossibility of their doing so with us; though I must own I never yet heard of but one instance, which was a fieldfare's nest found near Paddington [u].

I cannot, however, but think it is only from want of observation, that more of such nests have not been discovered, which are only looked after by very young children; and the chief object is the eggs, or nestlings, not the bird which lays them [x].

The plumage therefore and flight of the fieldfare or redwing being neither of them very remarkable, it is not at all improbable they may remain in summer, without being attended to; and particularly the redwing, which scarcely differs at all in appearance from thrushes. It is not also improbable, that the young fieldfares, before they have moulted, may much resemble the common thrush. Thus the chough is by no means peculiar to Cornwall, as is commonly supposed, but is mistaken for the jackdaw or rook.

turdus Iliacus (or redwing) leaves those parts in the spring. The circumstance therefore of the redwing's breeding in numbers (*per multitudines*) had escaped the notice of Zornius, though he hath written a dissertation on this question.

Is it at all surprizing, after this, that such discoveries, if made at all, should not be commonly heard of?

I have not before referred to Klein, who hath written a very able treatise, in which he argues against the possibility of migration in birds; because, though I should be very happy to support my poor opinion by his authority, yet I thought it right neither to repeat his facts, or arguments.

[u] See also Harl. Misc. Vol II p. 561.

[x] Many birds also build in places of such difficult access that boys cannot climb to; birds-nesting is confined almost entirely to hedges and low shrubs.

But it may be ſaid, that theſe birds fly in flocks during the winter, and if they remain here during the ſummer, we ſhould ſee them equally congregate.

This circumſtance, however, is by no means peculiar to the fieldfare and redwing; moſt of the hard-billed ſinging birds do the ſame in winter, but ſeparate in ſummer, as it is indeed neceſſary all birds ſhould during the time of breeding.

I ſhall now conſider another argument in favour of migration, which I do not know hath been ever inſiſted upon by thoſe writers who have contended for it, and which at firſt appearance ſeems to carry great weight with it.

There are certain birds which are ſuppoſed to viſit this iſland only at diſtant intervals of years; the Bohemian chatterer and croſs-bill [y] (for example) once perhaps in twenty.

The fact is not diſputed, that ſuch birds are not commonly obſerved in particular ſpots from year to year; but this may ariſe from two cauſes, either a partial migration within the verge of our iſland, or perhaps more frequently from want of a ready knowledge of birds on the wing, when they happen to be ſeen indeed, but cannot be examined.

I never have diſputed ſuch a partial migration; and indeed I have received a moſt irrefragable proof of ſuch a flitting, from Mr. White, whoſe accurate obſervations I have before had occaſion to argue from.

[y] This bird varies much in the colour of its plumage, and is ſometimes red.

The firſt account we have of their being ſeen, is in the Ph. Tr. abr. Vol. V. p. 33. where Mr. Edward Lhwyd ſuſpects them to be Virginia nightingales, from their feathers being red, and had no difficulty of at once ſuppoſing that they had croſſed the Atlantic.

The

The rock (or ring-ouzel) hath always hitherto been confidered as frequenting only the more mountainous parts of this ifland: Mr. White, however, informs me that there is a regular migration of thefe birds, which flock in numbers, and regularly vifit the neighbourhood of Selborn, in Hampfhire [z].

I therefore have little doubt but that they equally appear in others of our Southern counties; though it efcapes common obfervation, as they bear a fort of general refemblance to the black-bird, at leaft to the hen of that fpecies.

I own alfo, that I always conceived the Bohemian chatterer was not obferved in Great Britain but at very diftant intervals of years, and then perhaps only a fingle bird, whereas Dr. Ramfey (profeffor of natural hiftory at Edinburgh) informs Mr. Pennant, that flocks of thefe birds appear conftantly every year in the neighbourhood of that city [a].

As for crofs-bills, they are feen more and more in different parts of England, fince there have been fo many plantations of firs. this bird is remarkably fond of the feeds of thefe trees, and therefore changes its place to thofe parts where it can procure the greateft plenty of fuch food [b].

This

[z] See alfo Br. Zool. III. p. 56.

[a] Thefe birds are faid to be particularly fond of the berries of the mountain-afh, which is an uncommon tree in the Southern parts of Great Britain, but by no means fo in the North.

[b] This bird fhould alfo, for the fame reafon, be found from year to year in the cyder counties, if it was true (as is commonly fuppofed) that he is particularly fond of the kernels of apples, which it is conceived he can inftantly extract with his very fingular bill.

Mr. Tunftall, F.R.S. however, at my defire, once placed an apple in the cage of a crofs-bill, which he had kept for fome time in his very valuable and capital collection of live birds. Upon examining the apple a fortnight afterwards, it remained untouched. The notion of this bird, however, feeding on apple-kernels, is very antient. A. D. 1251, quædam aves mirabiles quæ nunquam in Angliâ antea vifæ erant, in pomeriis maxime

This flitting therefore by no means amounts to a total and periodical migration over ſeas; but is no more than what is experienced with regard to ſeveral birds.

For example, the Britiſh Zoology informs us [c], that, at an average 40,000 dozen of larks are ſent up from the neighbourhood of Dunſtable to ſupply the London-markets; nor do I hear, upon inquiry, that there is any complaint of the numbers decreaſing from year to year, notwithſtanding this great conſumption.

I ſhould not ſuppoſe that 500 dozen of ſkylarks are caught in any other county of England; and it ſhould therefore ſeem that the larks from the more adjacent parts croud in to ſupply the vacuum occaſioned by the London epicures, which may be the cauſe poſſibly of a partial migration throughout the whole iſland.

I begin now to approach to ſomething like a concluſion of this (I fear) tedious diſſertation: I think, however, that I ſhould not omit what appears to me at leaſt as a demonſtration, that one bird, which is commonly ſuppoſed to migrate acroſs ſeas, cannot poſſibly do ſo.

A landrail [d], when put up by the ſhooter, never flies 100 yards; its motion is exceſſively ſlow, whilſt the legs hang down like thoſe of the water-fowls which have not web feet, and which are known never to take longer flights.

This bird is not very common with us in England, but is exceſſively ſo in Ireland, where they are called corn-creaks.

Now thoſe who contend that the landrail, becauſe it happens to diſappear in winter, muſt migrate acroſs oceans, are reduced to the following dilemma.

maxime apparuerunt, pomorum grana & non aliud de eiſdem pomis comedentes. Habebant autem partes roſtric ancellatas, per quas poma quaſi forcipe dividerunt. Matthew Paris, p. 825. & additamenta, p. 263.

[c] P. 235.

[d] Br. Zool. p. 387.

They

They muſt firſt either ſuppoſe that it reaches Ireland periodically from America; which is impoſſible, not only becauſe the paſſage of the Atlantic includes ſo many degrees of longitude, but becauſe there is no ſuch bird in that part of the globe.

If the landrail therefore migrates from the continent of Europe to Ireland, which it muſt otherwiſe do, the neceſſary conſequence is, that many muſt paſs over England in their way Weſtward to Ireland; and why do not more of theſe birds continue with us; but, on the contrary, immediately proceed acroſs the St. George's channel?

Whence ſhould it ariſe alſo, if they paſs over this iſland periodically in the ſpring and autumn, that they are never obſerved in ſuch paſſage, as I have already ſtated their rate in flying to be exceſſively ſlow? To which I may add, that I never ſaw them riſe to the height of twenty yards from the ground, nor exceed the pitch of a quail.

I have now ſubmitted the beſt anſwers that have occurred, not only to the general arguments for the migration of birds acroſs oceans, but alſo to the particular facts, which are relied upon as actual proofs of ſuch a regular and periodical paſſage.

Though I may be poſſibly miſtaken in many of the conjectures I have made, yet I think I cannot be confuted but by new facts, and to ſuch freſh evidence, properly authenticated, I ſhall moſt readily give up every point, which I have from preſent conviction been contending for.

I may then perhaps alſo flatter myſelf, that the having expreſſed my doubts with regard to the proofs hitherto relied upon, in ſupport of migration, may have contributed to ſuch new and more accurate obſervations.

It is to be wiſhed, however, that theſe more convincing and deciſive facts may be received from iſlanders (the more diſtant

from

from any land the better[e]) and not from the inhabitants of a continent; as it does not ſeem to be a fair inference, becauſe certain birds leave certain ſpots at particular times, that they therefore migrate acroſs a wide extent of ſea.

For example, ſtorks diſappear in Holland during the winter, and they have not a very wide tract of ſea between them and England; and yet this bird never frequents our coaſts[f].

The ſtork, however, may be truly conſidered as a bird of paſſage by the inhabitants of thoſe parts of Europe (wherever ſituated) to which it may be ſuppoſed to reſort during the winter, and where it is not ſeen during the ſummer.

I am, &c.

[e] I would particularly propoſe the iſlands of Madera and St. Helena; to theſe, I would alſo add the iſland of Aſcenſion (had it any inhabitants), as likewiſe Juan Fernandez, for the Pacifick ocean.

[f] Kempfer however mentions that ſtorks continue throughout the whole year at Japan, vol. I. p. 129.

ESSAY

ESSAY V.

ON THE TORPIDITY OF THE SWALLOW TRIBE, WHEN THEY DISAPPEAR.

IN the foregoing treatiſe upon the migration of birds, the appearance and diſappearance of the ſwallow-tribe hath neceſſarily been touched upon; but I think it better to reſerve, for a ſeparate diſſertation, what more particularly relates to their being during the winter in a ſtate of torpidity.

I have for many years attended carefully to the motions of theſe birds from the latter end of March to the latter end of April, at which time I have travelled into, or returned from, North Wales.

For the laſt twelve years the ſpring ſeaſons in that part of Great Britain have been generally dry, the eaſt winds prevailing during the month of April.

The conſequence hath been, that on my journey towards Wales, or upon my arrival in the principality, I have perhaps ſeen a ſtraggling ſwallow or ſwallows [a]; but upon the weather growing

[a] As often martins. I ſhall here ſubjoin a letter which I received from that ingenious and obſervant naturaliſt the Rev. Mr. White, of Selborne in Hampſhire.

"Dear Sir, *Selborne, Nov.* 22, 1777.

You cannot but remember that the 26th and 27th of laſt March were very hot days; ſo ſultry that every body complained, and were reſtleſs unde

growing more ſevere; they have diſappeared perhaps for a fortnight or more, ſo that I never have been able to procure any, though

under thoſe ſenſations to which they had not been reconciled by gradual approaches.

This ſudden ſummer-like heat was attended by ſummer coincidences; for on thoſe two days the thermometer roſe to 66 in the ſhade; many ſpecies of inſects revived and came forth, ſome bees ſwarmed in this neighbourhood; the old tortoiſe near Lewes in Suſſex awakened and came forth out of his dormitory; and, what is moſt to my preſent purpoſe, many houſe-ſwallows appeared, and were very alert in many places, and particularly at Cobham in Surry.

But as that ſhort warm period was ſucceeded, as well as preceded, by harſh ſevere weather with frequent froſts and ice, and cutting winds, the inſects withdrew, the tortoiſe retired again into the ground, and the ſwallows were ſeen no more until the 10th of April, when the rigour of the ſpring abated, and a ſofter ſeaſon began to obtain.

Again: it appears by my journals for many years paſt, that houſe-martins retire, to a bird, about the beginning of October; ſo that a perſon not very obſervant of ſuch matters would conclude, that they had taken their laſt farewell; but then it may be ſeen in my diaries alſo that conſiderable flocks diſcover themſelves again in the firſt week of November, and often on the 4th day of that month, *only for one day*; and that not as if in actual migration, but playing about at their leiſure, and feeding calmly as if no enterprize of moment at all agitated their ſpirits: and this was the caſe in the beginning of this very month; for on November the 4th more than twenty houſe-martins, which in appearance had all departed about the 7th of October, were ſeen again for that *one morning only* ſporting in my fields, and feaſting on inſects which ſwarmed in that ſheltered diſtrict. The preceding day was wet and bluſtering; but the fourth was dark and mild and ſoft, the wind at S. W. and the thermometer at 58½, a pitch not common at that ſeaſon of the year. Moreover, it may not be amiſs to add in this place, that whenever the thermometer is above 50 the Bat comes flitting out in every autumn and winter-month.

From all theſe circumſtances laid together it is obvious, that torpid inſects, reptiles, and quadrupeds, are awakened from their profoundeſt ſlumbers by a little untimely warmth: and therefore, that nothing ſo much promotes this death-like ſtupor as a defect of heat. And farther it is reaſonable to ſuppoſe, that two whole ſpecies, or at leaſt many individuals

though I have ſent people out with guns to ſhoot them. My inducement was to examine them upon their firſt appearance, and to ſee in what plight they might be, both as to caſe and plumage [b]; as alſo what they might feed upon before many winged inſects are to be found.

Upon my return towards London I have commonly ſeen five or ſix ſkimming over the river Clwyd [c], near the gate of the town of Ruthin, which is called Porthydwr.

After this, it hath commonly happened, that I have not obſerved any of this tribe of birds but at the diſtance of 20, 30, or 40 miles, and this always depending upon the approach to rivers or ponds, ſo that I could be tolerably certain where I might expect to obſerve them.

Theſe circumſtances ſeem to me very deciſive, that ſwallows are concealed near the place where they begin to appear; and on firſt conſideration of theſe facts it may be perhaps inferred, that theſe birds are all to be found under the water; it muſt however

dividuals of thoſe two ſpecies of Britiſh hirundines, do never leave this iſland at all, but partake of the ſame benumbed ſtate; for we cannot ſuppoſe that, after a month's abſence, houſe-martins can return from ſouthern regions to appear for *one morning in November*, or that houſe-ſwallows ſhould leave the diſtricts of Africa to enjoy in *March* the tranſient ſummer of a *couple of days*.

I am, with great eſteem,

Your obliged and humble ſervant,

G. L. WHITE.

[b] I have been informed however by Mr. Corniſh, an ingenious naturaliſt and ſurgeon at Totneſs, that he hath been more fortunate, and that the plumage of the birds look as uſual, but that their bodies are much emaciated.

[c] I need ſcarcely remind the reader of the old Greek proverb, tranſlated into ſo many languages, "that one ſwallow does not make the *ſpring*,"

 be

be recollected, that they probably procure more food in such situations when on the wing, whatever may have been their winter residence. By the latter end of April the swallow-tribe appears in numbers.

I shall now state such facts as I have myself observed, or received from ingenious correspondents, in relation to each species of swallow, and without hesitation make my own inferences, leaving them to be corrected by those who may be more fortunate in collecting more decisive instances.

I shall begin with the *Swallow*, as Mr. Pennant does in his British Zoology [d]; and premise that I mean the species whose tail is most fork'd, and which is mark'd with a red spot on the forehead and chin[e].

This bird appears the first of its tribe, and (as I conceive at least) hides itself under water during the winter, because, in the few instances where the relator hath been able to particularize the species thus found, it hath happened to be a swallow.

There is scarcely a treatise on ornithology, written in the Northern parts of Europe, which does not allude to the submersion of swallows during the winter, as a fact almost as well known as their peopling the air during the summer; and because the name of Linnæus is respected by most of the incredulous on this head, I copy from him the following words in the description of the bird.

"Hirundo [*Rustica*], habitat in Europæ domibus intra tectum, "unaque cum *urbica* demergitur, vereque emergit [f]."

[d] Vol. II. p. 282.

[e] This distinguishes the bird at once to every reader; but, if I was to call it the Hirundo Rustica of Linnæus, few would comprehend what bird I meant, as the continuing in the country is much more applicable to the sand martin.

[f] Systema Naturæ, 1766. This authority indeed extends also to Martins.

It is alſo clear from the expreſſion of *demergitur* (though perhaps not claſſical) that this naturaliſt conceived theſe birds hid themſelves under water during the winter; and it is to be obſerved, that he ſeems to have ſtated it after a proper examination, becauſe in the Fauna Suecica, publiſhed five years before, he omits the mention of this circumſtance [g].

As the inſtances of finding ſwallows under water are moſt common in the Northern parts of Europe, I ſhall begin with the teſtimony of the inhabitants of that part of the globe.

Mr. Peter Brown, a Norwegian and ingenious painter [h], informs me, that from the age of 6 to 17, whilſt he was at ſchool near Sheen [i], he with his companions hath conſtantly found ſwallows in numbers torpid under the ice, which covered bogs, and that they have often revived upon being brought into a warm room [k].

Baron Rudbeck, a Swediſh gentleman, who was not long ſince in England, hath aſſured me that this fact was ſo well known in Sweden as to leave no doubt with any one.

[g] Iſaac Biberg, in his Diſſertation on the Oeconomy of Nature, read before the Academy of Upſal, ſtates the ſubmerſion of ſwallows as a known fact in that part of the world.

Mr. Boyle took notice that ſwallows live under frozen water in the Baltic. Birch's Hiſt. R. S. Vol. I. p. 180.

The ſwallows, before they ſink under water, ſing their *ſwallow-ſong*, as it is called, *and every one knows*. Pontoppidan, part II. p. 98.

See many well atteſted inſtances of ſwallows being ſo found in the Northern Parts of Germany. Klein.

[h] Author of the New Zoology. He lives at Nº 85. Queen Ann Street, Eaſt.

[i] N. Lat. 59.

[k] The beſt way, however, of awakening them from their torpid ſtate is, to put them into one's boſom, or hold them in one's hand, as Mr. Corniſh, an ingenious ſurgeon of Totneſs, in Devonſhire, hath informed me, who hath made many curious experiments upon bats in that ſtate.

Mr.

Mr. Stephens, A. S. S. informs me, that when he was 14 years of age, a pond of his father's (who was vicar of Shrivenham in Berkshire) was cleaned during the month of February, that he picked up himself a cluster of three or four swallows (or martins) which were caked together in the mud, that the birds were carried into the kitchen, on which they soon afterwards flew about the room, in the presence of his father, mother, and others, particularly the Rev. Dr. Pye. Mr. Stephens also told me that his father observed at the time, he had read of similar instances in the Northern writers. Though I have stated these birds to have been either swallows (or martins) I rather suppose them to have been the former, from their being found under water.

The compilers of the Encyclopedie (art. Mort.) have inserted the following observation and fact in relation to swallows discovered in the same situation.

" Plusieurs oiseaux passent aussi tout l'hyver sous les eaux, telles " sont les *hirondelles*, qui loin d'aller suivant *l'erreur populaire fort* " *accreditée*, dans les climats plus chauds, se precipitent au fond " de la mer, des lacs, & des rivieres, &c."

It is there also stated, that Mr. Falconet, a physician, living at Paris, had seen in one of the provinces, " une masse de terre que " les pecheurs avoient tirée de l'eaue; apres avoir lavée & debro- " nillée, il appercut que ce n'etoit autre chose qu'un amas d'hi- " rondelles," which, on being brought to the fire, revived, the fishers declaring that this was not uncommon.

The late ingenious Mr. Stillingfleet informs us, that one swallow's being found at the bottom of a pond in winter, and brought to life by warmth, was attested to him by a gentleman of character[1].

Some years ago the moat of Aix-la-Chapelle was cleaned during the month of October, and the water let out for that purpose,

[1] Misc. Tr. p. 106.

when

when on the ſides of the moat, and much below the parts which had been covered with water, a great number of ſwallows were ſeen to all appearance dead, but their plumage not impaired.

Du Tertre mentions, that a Ruſſian of credit had told him, that, a piece of ice in a village of Muſcovy having been brought into a houſe with ſwallows in it, they all revived [m].

There are ſeveral reaſons why ſwallows ſhould not be frequently thus found; ponds are ſeldom cleaned in the winter, as it is ſuch cold work for the labourers, and the ſame inſtinct which prompts the bird thus to conceal itſelf, inſtructs it to chooſe ſuch a place of ſecurity, that common accidents will not diſcover it.

But the ſtrongeſt reaſon for ſuch accounts not being more numerous, is, that facts of this ſort are ſo little attended to; for though I was born within half a mile of the pond near Shrivenham, and have always had much curioſity with regard to the natural hiſtory of animals, yet I never heard a ſyllable about this very material and intereſting intelligence till very lately.

To theſe inſtances I muſt alſo add, that ſwallows may be conſtantly taken in the month of October, during the dark nights, whilſt they ſit on the willows in the Thames; and that one may almoſt inſtantaneouſly fill a large ſack with them, becauſe at this time they will not ſtir from the twigs, when you lay your hands upon them. This looks very much like their beginning to be torpid before they hide themſelves under the water.

A man near Brentford ſays, that he hath caught them in this ſtate in the eyt oppoſite to that town, even ſo late as November.

I ſhall conclude the proofs on this firſt head by the dignified teſtimony of Sigiſmond King of Poland, who affirmed, on his

[m] Vol. II. p. 260. Paris, 1667.

oath, to Cardinal Commendon[n], that he had frequently ſeen ſwallows which were found at the bottom of Lakes.

I ſhall now proceed to the ſecond ſpecies of the ſwallow-tribe, called a *martin*, which hath no colours but black and white, hath a ſhorter tail than the preceding, and builds commonly under the eaves of houſes.

I may be miſtaken, but I ſhall here again hazard a conjecture that this ſpecies does not hide itſelf under water during the winter, but rather in the crevices of rocks or other proper lurking places above ground, as moſt of thoſe which have been diſcovered in ſuch ſituations have been martins.

The inſtances of this ſort are ſo numerous from all parts, that to bring them within a moderate compaſs I muſt only ſelect a few of them; promiſing thoſe who are incredulous, that I can moſt readily furniſh many more than I ſhall now produce.

I ſhall begin with a letter dated at Towyn in Merionethſhire, dated March 22, 1773.

EXTRACT from a Letter relative to torpid MARTINS.

"SIR, *Towyn, Merionethſhire, March* 22, 1773,

I received yours; and according to your deſire I made as much enquiry as I could concerning the ſwallows. Richard Hugh, a boatman at Aberdyſyny, tells me, that he lived with Mr. Anwil about twenty years ago, when they were found by Mr. Anwil himſelf, who ordered him, with ſome others of his ſervants, to go along with him to ſee them; and the ſaid Richard Hugh really believes that there were ſome thouſands of them; and Mr. Anwil, with his own hand, put ſome of them into a part of the

[n] See the Life of that Cardinal, p. 211. Paris, 1671, 4to.

clift

cliff which remained in the rock, they could at firſt ſcarcely perceive life in them, but ſoon they began to crawl a little, then they carried ſome into the houſe, and held them near the fire, when they became pretty lively. Richard Hugh cannot recollect who was the perſon that ſaw them beſide himſelf and Mr. Anwil, neither can he remember exactly what month it was, but he is ready to make oath, that it was a very uncommon time of year to ſee ſwallows, and to the beſt of his memory it was either the latter end of January or the beginning of February. I went to Mr. Griffith Evans at Tymaur, to aſk whether he had heard any thing of them; and he told me, that he now well remembers to have heard Mr. Anwill telling a deal about them, how remarkable it was to ſee them at ſuch time of the year, and he believes it was about twenty years ago; and Mr. Griffith Evans ſays he is poſitive that it is true. Alſo one Hugh Richard, a very credible old man in this town, ſays, that he really heard Mr. Anwil mentioning them."

I have another account of the ſame ſort with regard to ſwallows (or martins) being diſcovered, about 16 years ago, at Yew-Law Caſtle, near Hawarden, in Flintſhire.

I have received alſo the ſame kind of information relative to torpid ſwallows, in Carnarvonſhire, and Caſtleton in Derbyſhire.

Sir William Bellers told the late Dr. Chauncey that he happened to ſtop at a Fiſherman's houſe in Cornwall, whoſe net had been much torn by a large clod of earth, which, upon being examined, was very full of ſwallows, that awaked from their torpidity upon being brought near the fire. I ſhould rather ſuppoſe however that they were martins, from the circumſtance of their being found in a large clod of earth, which had probably dropt from the bank a little while before

 By

By a letter from Dr. Finley, Provoſt of the college of New Jerſey, dated May 1, 1765, to the late Dr. Chandler, and ſoon afterwards communicated to the Royal Society, it appears that the ſame notion prevails in America, with regard at leaſt to ſome ſpecies of their ſwallows. Kalm alſo mentions their being found torpid in holes and clefts of rocks near Albany [o].

Dr. Pallas gives an account that on the 18th of March a ſwallow (perhaps martin) was brought to him, near Uſa, which had been found in a field, to all appearance lifeleſs, but having remained a quarter of an hour in a warm room, it flew about, and lived ſome days, till killed by accident [p].

Mr. Corniſh, an ingenious ſurgeon, who reſides at Totneſs in Devonſhire, was fiſhing in the river Dart, at the beginning of November, 1774, and on a very warm day obſerved ſeveral martins iſſuing from ſome large rocks, overgrown with ivy and thicket. On this appearance, at ſuch a time of the year, he deſiſted from his amuſement, that he might more attend to the motions of theſe birds, which had been brought out of their winter-quarters by the fineneſs of the weather, the ſun at that time ſhining ſtrong on the rocks. They continued to flit backwards and forwards for almoſt half an hour, keeping very near together, and never flying in a direct line, nor when at the fartheſt above a hundred yards diſtant from the rocks, cloſer to which they now (as the ſun lowered) began to gather very faſt. Their numbers were then leſſened conſiderably, and in a very ſhort time they all returned to the fiſſures of the rocks, from whence they had been induced to venture out by the warmth of the evening. Mr. Corniſh concludes this account by aſſerting very poſitively, that there was not one ſwallow amongſt theſe martins [q].

[o] Vol II. p. 146.

[p] Pallas's Travels through the Ruſſian Territories, part II. book I. p 13 Peterſburg, 1773.

[q] Phil. Tranſ. vol. LXV. part I. p. 343.

The

The ſame ingenious naturaliſt afterwards mentions, that he hath ſeen martins at Totneſs in the months of December [r] and January, though he never obſerved a ſwallow at that ſeaſon; in which fact he is confirmed by a perſon whoſe name is Didham, and who ſaw two martins on the 26th of December at a place called Syfferton [s].

I ſhall here ſubjoin other facts of the ſame kind, which I have received from the ſame good authority.

Mr. Manning, a ſurgeon of reputation in Kingſbridge, when a boy, and in ſearch of ſparrows neſts, on a headland called the Hope, pulled out from under the thatch of an uninhabited houſe great numbers of ſwallows (or martins) which he conſidered as dead, but they afterwards revived; and their number amounted to more than 40. Mr. Manning recollects the fact at preſent as if it had been more recent, and likewiſe remembers, that the plumage was in perfect order, which was the caſe alſo with ſome martins, which I received myſelf during the winter, from Camerton in Somerſetſhire, in which there was not the leaſt mark of putrefaction.

Another perſon drew out a great number of martins from the wall of an old caſtle in Wales during winter, and the heat of his hands recovered ſome of them ſo as to fly.

Again, a plumber in Mr. Corniſh's neighbourhood hath made a ſolemn depoſition, that being at work on the leads of Foraby-houſe (ſituated on the ſea-coaſt in Torbay) early in the ſpring, he found in ſome of the ciſterns ſeveral martins: that he at firſt believed them to be dead; but as they looked not at all decayed, he began to ſuppoſe they might be only aſleep, and that in conſequence of this idea, curioſity tempting him to hold one of them

[r] He obſerved ſome ſo recently as the 7th of December, 1778.
[s] Phil. Tranſ. vol. LXV. part I. p 346 and 349.

in his hand for a few minutes, the bird became ſtrong enough to fly two or three yards.

Kyrcher ſpeaks of a deep cavern high up the Teverone, which the mountaineers told him was never left by the ſwallows in winter [t].

The Rev. Dr. Boſworth obſerved five ſwallows (or martins) creep out of the wall of Merton College, Oxford, during the month of January, which returned again to their dormitories on the weather becoming colder.

Mr. Hooper, F. R. S. hath informed me, that martins were ſeen at Chriſtchurch in Hampſhire ſo late as Chriſtmas, in 1772, when the flies alſo began to be troubleſome. I ſhall here ſubjoin the words of a letter on this ſubject from an eye-witneſs, "As my "neighbours and ſelf were ſtanding in the churchyard [u], we told "fourteen on the wing at one time, near the Eaſt end of the "church, and could ſee others flying about over my houſe, and "different parts of the town." Mr. Rickman went home, and immediately wrote the following memorandum in his almanack: "Dec. 9, 1772. This day a conſiderable number of martins or "ſwallows were ſeen round the church. They were in indefinite "numbers (as during the ſummer), and flew with as much ve-"locity as at that time of the year. They decreaſed daily till "the 23d of December, after which I have not heard of one being "ſeen."

I have alſo received an account of two ſwallows or martins appearing on the 21ſt of December, in this ſame year, *viz.* 1772, at or near the town of Pool, in Dorſetſhire.

I am laſtly informed, by an intelligent ſervant of the Right Hon. Mr. Mackenzie, that being with his maſter at Lord Strafford's

[t] Latium Vetus.

[u] Sc. of Chriſtchurch.

in

in Yorkshire, seven or eight years ago, the latter end of October, a conversation began with the game-keeper about swallows crossing the seas; which the game-keeper disbelieved, because he said he could then carry any one to some neighbouring coalworks, where he was sure of finding them by that time. On this many of the servants attended him to the coalpits, where several martins were observed in a torpid state, but shewed motions of life upon their being brought near to the fire.

Most of these instances are so well attested, that I conceive it cannot be disputed by any one, that martins at least appear occasionally throughout the winter, whenever the weather is remarkably mild, and which agrees with what Sir William Hamilton hath informed me, in relation to his scarcely ever passing between Naples and Pozzuoli without seeing some of these birds, when the season at that time of the year was temperate.

With regard to the third species of swallows, the sand martin, I have never been able to collect a decisive instance of their being observed at all during the winter, though possibly sometimes not distinguished from the more common martin; I will not therefore pretend to conjecture what may be their peculiar lurking places, though I conceive that they undoubtedly have such. I have however been negatively informed that they are not found in the holes where they make their nests. This bird is commonly so distant from the habitation of man, and is so much in the dark, that its habits are not easily attended to.

As for the fourth species, called the *Swift* [x], which is well known by its superior size, and being almost entirely black, Linnæus asserts, that it winters in the holes of churches [y].

[x] Hirundo Apus.

[y] Templorum foraminibus.

I have

I have however the following instance of their sometimes choosing other places of concealment.

The Rev. Mr. Williams of Bishop's Waltham in Hampshire found three Swifts in the battlements of an old flint tower belonging to that town during the winter, which being brought into a warm room shewed signs of life, but afterwards hanging them up in a paper bag close to the kitchen fire they were either stifled by the closeness of the bag, or killed by the too great heat. See also an instance of three Swifts being found in an old oak during the winter, which, on being laid before the fire, soon recovered strength enough to fly about the room, though they died soon after[z]. Aristotle indeed asserts, that in Greece the Swift never disappears, φαινεται δ᾽ο μεν απους πασαν ωραν[a].

I shall now endeavour to corroborate these facts with regard to most of the species of swallows being observed during the winter either in a torpid state, or on the wing, by some other proofs, which seem to make strongly against the periodical migration of such birds across oceans.

They who maintain this opinion, always suppose that these birds pass to the northward upon the approach of spring, in great flocks; of which however I have not been able to find any instance in what hath been printed on this subject, except what is stated in the Philosophical Transactions, of a number having lighted upon the sails of Sir Charles Wager's fleet in the Channel. I flatter myself also, that I have (in a previous essay) fully answered any inferences to be drawn from this relation in support of migration; and must likewise repeat, that such instances must happen as regularly as the return of the seasons, did swallows then pass to the northward.

[z] Phil. Transf. Vol. LXV. p. 347. and another instance, p. 349.
[a] Arist. de Hist. Anim. L. I. c. 1.

But

But this is not all, as if I can depend upon my own obſervations, as well as thoſe of others, ſwallows ſhould, according to this ſuppoſition, always firſt appear in flocks on the Southern coaſt of this iſland; whereas they are ſeen but in ſmall numbers, diſperſed almoſt equally over all parts of it, and if any cold weather happens they then immediately diſappear, being obſerved in the ſame numbers again when the mild weather is more confirmed, and are afterwards joined by myriads from every lurking place and retreat.

All animals are endowed with a providential inſtinct to avoid what may be prejudicial to them, and therefore it ſhould ſeem that the ſwallow tribe would never leave the coaſt of Africa in their ſpring migration to the Northward till a month later than they generally appear, as then there would be no occaſion for a ſudden retreat on the froſts, which are ſo frequently experienced in the early parts of our ſpring. Lying however in their torpid ſtate they cannot reſiſt the mild influence of the firſt genial weather, but know where to ſecure themſelves when it becomes ſevere.

That the ſwallow-tribe are concealed during the winter, not far from the place where they have been hatched, may be inferred from the following facts.

Mr. Stephens, F. S. A. hath informed me that martins continued to have a neſt for 16 years together in the hall of an old houſe which belongs to him at Camerton in Somerſetſhire, though the door was conſtantly ſhut during the night, and ſometimes for a few hours during day-light, when the parent birds muſt have been not a little impatient to feed their neſtlings.

The ſame fact hath been atteſted to me by Mr. Sanxay, with regard to the porch of a gentleman's houſe in Derbyſhire[b], though

[b] John Burrows, Eſq. of Overſtone, near Derby.

the

the birds did not continue to build for ſo many years as in the preceding inſtance.

The following fact relates to a ſwallow which built for two years together on the handles of a pair of garden ſheers, that were ſtuck up againſt the boards in an outhouſe; and, what is ſtranger ſtill, another bird of the ſame ſpecies made its neſt on the wings and body of an owl that happened by accident to hang dead, and dry, from the rafter of a barn. This owl, with the neſt on its wings and eggs, was brought to Sir Aſhton Lever, who deſired the perſon that furniſhed him with this curioſity to fix a large ſhell where the body of the owl had hung. The perſon did as he was ordered, and the following year a neſt was made and eggs laid in the ſhell by a pair of ſwallows [c].

Now it is clear, from theſe well-atteſted inſtances, that both martins and ſwallows chooſe to build, for a ſucceſſion of years, in the ſame place [d], though an inconvenient one, and is it to be ſup-

[c] The neſt, eggs, and ſhell, are now alſo to be ſeen in Sir Aſhton Lever's Muſeum.

[d] Kalm, in his account of N America, informs us, that Dr. Franklin's father lived near two rivers, in the one of which herrings conſtantly were obſerved, but not in the other. Mr. Franklin therefore made an experiment, by removing ſome of the ſpawn, which occaſioning a breed in the ſecond river, herrings were afterwards obſerved at the proper ſeaſon, as frequently as in the other, the grown herrings depoſiting their ſpawn where they had been hatched themſelves. Kalm, vol. I p. 294. This fact ſeems to prove that fiſh, as well as birds, always breed in the ſame places, and it may be therefore aſked why a bird ever builds a new neſt. To this I anſwer, that the materials of ſome are deſtroyed by the winter, but where they are not thus rendered uſeleſs, and are out of the reach of man, it is commonly obſerved that the ſame neſt, with ſome trifling repairs, ſerves for ſeveral years. Witneſs thoſe of herons, kites, and rooks, all of which I have ſeen in the ſame field at Sir Nicholas Baily's, in the iſland of Angleſey, and which were conſtantly upon the ſame trees.

poſed

posed that they constantly return to the same spot from the coast of Africa, rather than they should be torpid during the winter, in no very distant place of concealment.

But they who maintain that swallows periodically leave Europe and proceed to Africa, rely much upon their being seen to congregate not long before they disappear, which happens however with regard to many other birds, and the assemblage consists of the first brood, who are left by their parents to shift for themselves, swallows and martins uniting.

This therefore seems to arise from such birds considering themselves as rather in a defenceless state, unless

Defendit numerus.

That this is the fact, particularly with the swallow tribe, appears by the repeated observations of that attentive and ingenious naturalist the Rev. Mr. White[e].

It is well known that the swallow and martin have two broods every year, and consequently that their first nestlings must be abandoned by the parents: how therefore are the produce of the first nest to be conducted over the Atlantic from Great Britain and Ireland, to Africa?

How also can it be expected, that the second brood, which I have known myself to be hatched in October, should be equal to such a passage, in which they have no insects to feed upon, and in which they never seem to have been observed by any ship at a considerable distance from land, or by any person on shore, who can properly assert that they were bent on such periodical migration?

I will here add an observation which relates to the Swift only. This bird, by the length of its wings, is certainly better calculated

[e] Of Selborne, in Hampshire. See Phil. Trans. vol. LXV. p. 261.

for a long flight than any of the ſwallow-tribe, and yet it is the lateſt comer, and diſappears the earlieſt of this whole genus [f], long before the inſects on which it feeds are wanting.

But this is not all. When this bird is firſt ſeen in the ſpring it is all over of a gloſſy dark ſoot colour (except their chins, which are white); but by being for a conſiderable time in the ſun and air, they become weather-beaten and bleached before they diſappear [g]?

Now would not this alteration in the colour be occaſioned by their paſſage over the Atlantic, and do we not know that the quicker the motion is, and the longer continued without intermiſſion, the more our own ſkins and hair are changed; and are we not to ſuppoſe that the ſame effects will be produced on the feathersa nd hairs of other animals?

I will now beg leave to ſtate another objection to the migration of ſwallows from Europe to Africa, which is, that if this conjecture is true, the ſame thing muſt hold with regard to the Northern and Southern parts of Aſia. On the contrary, I am informed, that ſwallows hide themſelves in the banks of the Ganges during what are called the winter months in that part of the world. Du Tertre likewiſe mentions, that the few ſwallows ſeen in the Caribbee Iſlands are only obſerved in the ſummer, as in France.

Now we are aſſured, by Dr. Pallas, that they have not only ſwallows in Ruſſia and Siberia, but that on the banks of the Okka, which empties itſelf into the Wolga, in N. Lat. 57, on froſt taking place about the 4th of Auguſt, they diſappeared for that year [h].

[f] Viz. At the latter end of April and Auguſt, Phil. Tranſ. vol. LXV. p. 264, et ſeq.

[g] Phil. Tranſ. vol. LXV. p. 269.

[h] Pallas's Account of his Travels through Ruſſia.

Theſe birds therefore ſhould, according to the hypotheſis of migration, have been paſſing to the more Southern parts of Aſia, but I do not find it obſerved by any Aſiatic traveller that they have the ſame ſpecies of hirundines with us, or that they are only ſeen in thoſe parts during our winter.

Between what hath been advanced in the preceding and preſent diſſertations, the arguments againſt the periodical migration of ſwallows have filled many pages, and it may be right to bring them to a concluſion, by anſwering an objection which is much relied upon by thoſe who maintain the contrary opinion.

It is frequently aſked by theſe, where and when the ſwallow moults, if this does not happen in parts of the globe to the Southward of Europe.

To this I do not pretend to anſwer by informing them where or when theſe birds change their feathers; but I may equally aſk the queſtion with regard to nine of the birds out of ten which have been deſcribed by naturaliſts, becauſe we are entirely uninformed about this matter, except in relation to thoſe which we uſually eat, or keep in cages.

It is true, that moſt, if not all of theſe, commonly moult with great regularity, but it is alſo known that there are often exceptions to every general obſervation or rule; nor do I ſee why it is more neceſſary that every bird ſhould moult, than that every fiſh ſhould not have wings, which would have been moſt confidently maintained by the old naturaliſts who were unacquainted with the flying fiſh.

Again, it is part of the known definition of a bird to be an animal covered with feathers, and yet thoſe of the Caſſowary and the Silky fowl of the Eaſt Indies rather reſemble hairs than plumage; and this is the caſe ſo ſtrongly with the latter, that it hath given occaſion to the impoſition at Bruſſels, where they are ſhewn as the mix'd breed of a fowl and rabbit.

I therefore do not conceive it to be abſolutely neceſſary that this tribe of birds ſhould change their feathers at all, or perhaps they may do ſo only the ſecond or third year, and at a time different from that in which other birds moult.

But I will now aſk the direct queſtion of the partiſans of migration, whether the feathers are renewed whilſt the ſwallow tribe are in Africa during the winter?

Now in all the birds which we are well acquainted with, moulting begins in the autumn; and therefore if ſwallows drop their plumage in Africa during the winter, it is nearly as much contrary to what happens in relation to the change of feathers in other birds, as the not being liable to any change at all.

It is not alſo abſolutely impoſſible that theſe birds may moult during the time of their concealment, to which the fact already mentioned of the Swift's plumage being moſt bright and gloſſy, when it firſt appears in the ſpring, ſeems to give ſome countenance, and Ariſtotle aſſerts, that this happens to the τρυγων (commonly rendered the turtle-dove) whilſt it is hid [1].

How little do we know, with accuracy, in relation to the renewal of our own hair; which I rather believe to be brought about by ſuch degrees as to be almoſt imperceptible, nor are the hair-cutters, or friſeurs, perhaps capable of giving us any material information on this head.

Whatever weight, however, theſe anſwers may be thought to carry with them, it is as much incumbent upon thoſe who maintain the migration of ſwallows from Europe to Africa, to inform us where and when they moult, as it is upon thoſe who deny that they paſs from one continent to another.

[1] φωλει. Ariſt. Nat. Hiſt. L. viii. c. 16.

ESSAY VI.

ON THE PREVAILING NOTIONS WITH REGARD TO THE CUCKOW.

THOUGH it hath been ſo implicitly believed for centuries, that the cuckow neither hatches nor rears its young, I hope to be permitted to expreſs my doubts, with regard to this moſt unnatural neglect in the parent bird being general.

I find that this moſt prevailing opinion takes its riſe from what is ſaid by Ariſtotle, in the ninth book, and twenty-ninth chapter, of his Natural Hiſtory, who there aſſerts, thas the cuckow does not build a neſt itſelf, but makes uſe moſt commonly of thoſe of the wood-pigeon, hedge-ſparrow, lark, (which he adds are on the ground) as well as that of the χλωρις [a], which is in trees.

Now if we take the whole of this account together, it is certainly not to be depended upon ; for the wood-pigeon [b] and hedge-ſparrow

[a] The χλωρις is rendered *luteola*; but, as there is no deſcription, it is difficult to ſay what bird Ariſtotle here alludes to, Zinanni ſuppoſes it to be the greenfinch.

[b] The wood-pigeon, from its ſize, ſeems to be the only bird which is capable of hatching, or feeding, the young cuckow; yet, if it is recollected that this bird lives on ſeeds, it is probable that the cuckow, whoſe nouriſhment is inſects, would either be ſoon ſtarvtd, or incapable of digeſting what was brought by the foſter-parent. This objection is equally applicable to the χλωρις, if it is our greenfinch.

ſparrow do not build upon the ground, and it is believed that no one ever pretended to have found a cuckow's egg in the neſt of a lark, which, indeed, is ſo placed. It is likewiſe to be obſerved, that the witneſſes often vary with regard to the bird in whoſe neſt the cuckow's egg is depoſited [c]; and Ariſtotle himſelf, in the ſeventh chapter of his ſixth book, confines the foſter-parents to the wood-pigeon and hedge-ſparrow, but chiefly the former.

In the age [d] of Ariſtotle is conſidered, when he began to collect the materials for his Natural Hiſtory, by the encouragement of Alexander after his conqueſts in India [e], it is highly improbable he ſhould have written from his own obſervations. He therefore ſeems to have haſtily put down the accounts of the perſons who brought him the different ſpecimens from moſt parts of the then known world.

Inaccurate, however, and contradictory as theſe reports often turn out, it was the beſt compilation which the ancients could have recourſe to; and Pliny therefore profeſſes only to abridge him, in which he often does not do juſtice to the original.

Whatever was aſſerted by Ariſtotle, is well known to have been moſt implicitly believed, till the laſt century; and I am convinced

[c] Thus Linnæus ſuppoſes it (in the Fauna Suecica) to be the white wagtail, which bird builds in the banks of rivers, or roofs of houſes, (See Zinanni, p. 51.) where it is believed no young cuckow was ever found.

[d] He did not leave the ſchool of Plato till the age of thirty-eight (or, as ſome ſay, forty), after which, ſome years paſſed before he became Alexander's preceptor, who was then but fourteen: nor could he have written his Natural Hiſtory, probably, till twelve years after this, as Pliny ſtates that ſpecimens were ſent to him by Alexander, from his conqueſts in India. Ariſtotle therefore muſt have been nearly ſixty when he began this great work, and conſequently muſt have deſcribed from the obſervations of others.

[e] Pliny, L. viii. c. 16.

that

that many of the learned in Europe would, before that time, not have credited their own eyesight against what he had delivered.

There cannot be a stronger proof that the general notion about the cuckow arises from what is laid down by Aristotle, than the chapter which immediately follows, as it relates to the goatsucker, and states that this bird sucks the teats of that quadruped.

From this circumstance, the goatsucker hath obtained a similar name in most languages, though it is believed no one (who thinks at all about matters of this sort) continues to believe that this bird sucks the goat [f], any more than the hedgehog does the cow.

I beg leave, however, to explain myself, that I give these reasons only for my doubting with regard to this most prevailing opinion in relation to the cuckow; because I am truly sensible that many things happen in nature, which contradict all arguments from analogy, and I am persuaded, therefore, that the first person who gave an account of the flying fish, was not credited by any one, though the existence of this animal is not now to be disputed. All that I mean to contend for is, that the instances of such extraordinary peculiarities in animals, should be proportionably well attested, in all the necessary circumstances.

I must own, for example, that nothing short of the following particulars will thoroughly satisfy me on this head.

[f] See Zinanni, p. 95. who took great pains to detect this vulgar error. Though it now is agreed both by Ray Buffon and Pennant, that the porcupine does not shoot its quills, yet this notion will continue to be believed perhaps for centuries, and Linnæus hath stated in the 12th edit. of his Systema Naturæ, "quod spinas in hostem jaculare valet non extrahendas." Bosman also in his voyage to Guinea asserts, that the animal really does so. We are always ready to suppose that we see what we have no doubt with regard to. How long was the poisonous effect of the Tarantula, and Ants hoarding for winter, credited?

The

The hedge-ſparrow's neſt muſt be found with the proper eggs in it, which ſhould be deſtroyed by the cuckow, at the time ſhe introduces her ſingle egg [g]. Ariſtotle aſſerts this to be the fact; but Pliny ſays, all the eggs are hatched.

The neſt ſhould then be examined, at a proper diſtance, from day to day, during the hedge-ſparrow's incubation, as alſo the motions of the foſter-parent attended to, particularly in feeding the young cuckow, till it is able to ſhift for itſelf [h].

As I have little doubt that the laſt-mentioned circumſtance will appear deciſive to many, without the others which I have required, it may be proper to ſtate my reaſons, why I cannot conſider it alone as ſufficient; though Willoughby gives it as his chief argument for believing the popular notion.

There is ſomething in the cry of a neſtling for food, which affects all kinds of birds, almoſt as much as that of an infant, for the ſame purpoſe, excites the compaſſion of every human hearer.

I have taken four young ones from a hen ſkylark, and placed in their room five neſtling nightingales, as well as five wrens, the greater part of which were reared by the foſter parent [i].

[g] I could alſo wiſh that the following experiment was tried. When a hedge-ſparrow hath laid all her eggs, a ſingle one of any other bird, as large as a cuckow, might be introduced, after which if either the neſt was deſerted, or the egg too large to be hatched, it would afford a ſtrong preſumption againſt this general opinion: and would alſo ſhew whether the cuckow throws out the five eggs of the hedge-ſparrow, and whether the ſingle cuckow egg is depoſited upon removing the firſt or all of them?

[h] A notion prevails in many parts, that the hedge-ſparrow is at laſt ſwallowed by the cuckow.

[i] I am perſuaded that a cuckow is oftener an orphan than any other neſtling, becauſe, from the curioſity which prevails with regard to this bird, the parents are eternally ſhot.

It

It can hardly in this experiment be contended, that the ſkylark miſtook them for her own neſtlings, becauſe they differed greatly, not only in number and ſize, but in their habits, for nightingales and wrens perch, which a ſkylark is almoſt incapable of, though, by great aſſiduity, ſhe at laſt taught herſelf the proper equilibre of the body. If ducks are turned over to a hen turkey ſhe will generally take as much care of them as of her own brood, and I have been moſt credibly informed, that a rabbit hath been rear'd by a cat. Lucretius is therefore miſtaken when he aſſigns the following reaſon for each ſpecies of birds not varying from the prototype:

> Nec ratione aliâ proles cognoſcere matrem,
> Nec mater poſſet prolem.

I have likewiſe been witneſs of the following experiment: two robins hatched five young ones in a breeding cage, to which five others were added; and the old birds brought up the whole number, making no diſtinction between them.

The Aedologie alſo mentions (which is a very ſenſible treatiſe on the nightingale [k]) that neſtlings of all ſorts may be reared in the ſame manner, by introducing them to a caged bird, which is ſupplied with the proper food. In the ſame manner the ducklings hatch'd by artificial heat in China, are immediately put under old ones, who nurture them [l].

Not only grown birds, however, attend to this cry of diſtreſs from neſtlings, but young ones alſo which are able to ſhift for themſelves.

I have ſeen a chicken, not above two months old, take as much care of younger chickens as the parent would have ſhewn to them which they had loſt, not only by ſcratching to procure them food,

[k] Paris, 1771.
[l] Mandeſlo's Travels, p. 225.

but by covering them with her wings; and I have little doubt but that ſhe would have done the ſame by young ducks.

I have likewiſe been witneſs of neſtling thruſhes of a later brood being fed by a young bird which was hatched earlier, and which indeed rather over-crammed the orphans intruſted to her care; if the bird however erred in judgement, ſhe was certainly not deficient in tenderneſs, which I am perſuaded ſhe would have equally extended to a neſtling cuckow.

An inſtance moreover is recorded by Dr. Birch of two pigeons (not more than ſeven weeks old) ſitting on ſuppoſititious eggs, and not only hatching, but rearing them [m].

If it is conſidered, that with regard to the nurture of young birds there can be no difficulty but on the part of the dam, half the wonder of many of the foregoing inſtances muſt immediately ceaſe, when it is recollected, that if neſtlings perfectly fledged are taken, they are as ready to receive their food from man as from the parent bird, and are as clamorous for it. As theſe advances are therefore conſtantly made on the part of the infant brood, there can be but one reaſon for withholding the food that is implored, which is the foſter-bird's being a hen, with a large brood of her own, under which circumſtances even it hath been proved that ſhe is willing to rear them, for there ſeems to be a pleaſure and perhaps pride in other animals, as well as man, to have their dependents. Nor is aſſiduity wanting on the part of the neſtlings to preſerve the continuance of this protection by every coaxing endearment on their part, which, if man becomes the foſter parent, is equally ſhewn to him. Nor is this merely diſſimulation, in order to procure food and nurture, for they are enlivened by his preſence after a hearty meal, and

[m] See a letter from Dr. Wallis, Hiſtory R.S. vol. I. p. 313.

pine during his abſence. A French gentleman, whoſe name is Moriſette, hath ſhewn me frequent proofs of this in his young chickens, which were hatched in ovens. Theſe of courſe were fed by his ſervant till they were of an age to be turned into a little garden, when they would not run about, and feed kindly, unleſs the old woman was preſent who had reared them, and who therefore had a particular ſeat, in which ſhe continued the greateſt part of the day, whilſt the chickens played round her, and endeavoured to jump into her lap.

The young cuckow therefore being fed by a hedge-ſparrow or other bird ſeems to afford no irrefragable proof of having hatched the cuckow's egg, becauſe, if ſhe hath young ones of her own, it appears from ſome of the preceding facts, ſhe will probably take to this large foundling, and much more ſo if ſhe hath loſt her own brood, or perhaps they have forſaken her, on being completely fledged.

A cuckow is certainly a gigantic orphan to be nouriſhed and protected by a hedge-ſparrow, but all animals love ſociety, let the diſparity in ſize be what it may.

I ſhall here, on this head, ſubjoin part of a letter which I have received from my often-mentioned correſpondent the Rev. Mr. White, of Selborn, in Hampſhire.

" There is a wonderful ſpirit of ſociality in the brute creation independent of ſexual attachment. The congregating of gregarious birds in the winter is a remarkable inſtance. Many horſes, though quiet with company, will not ſtay one minute in a field by themſelves; the ſtrongeſt fences cannot reſtrain them. My neighbour's horſe will not only not ſtay by himſelf abroad, but he will not bear to be left alone in a ſtrange ſtable, without diſcovering the utmoſt impatience, and endeavouring to break the rack and manger with his fore-feet: he has been known to leap

out

out at a ſtable-window after company; and yet, in other reſpects, is remarkably quiet. Oxen and cows will not become fat by themſelves, but will neglect the fineſt paſture that is not recommended by ſociety. It would be needleſs to inſtance in ſheep, which conſtantly flock together.

But this propenſity ſeems not to be confined to animals of the ſame ſpecies; for we know a doe, ſtill alive, that has lived ever ſince it was a little fawn, with a dairy of cows; with them it goes a-field, and with them it returns to the yard. The dogs of the houſe take no notice of this deer, being uſed to her; but if ſtrange dogs come by, a chace enſues; while the maſter ſmiles to ſee his favourite ſecurely leading her purſuers over hedge, gate, or ſtile, till ſhe returns to the cows, who with fierce lowings and menacing horns drive the aſſailants quite out of the paſture.

Even great diſparity of kind and ſize does not always prevent ſocial advances, and mutual fellowſhip; for a very intelligent perſon aſſured me, that in the former part of his life keeping but one horſe, he happened alſo on a time to have but one ſolitary hen: theſe two incongruous animals ſpent much of their time together in a lonely orchard, where they ſaw no creature but each other. By degrees apparent regard began to take place between theſe two ſequeſtered individuals. The fowl would approach the quadruped with notes of complacency, rubbing herſelf gently againſt his legs; while the horſe would look down with ſatisfaction, and move with the greateſt caution and circumſpection, leſt he ſhould trample on his diminutive companion. Thus by mutual good offices each ſeemed to conſole the vacant hours of the other. So that Milton, when he puts the following ſentiment in the mouth of Adam, ſeems to be ſomewhat miſtaken:

"Much leſs can bird with beaſt, or fiſh with fowl,
"So well converſe; nor with the ox the ape."

The

The bare fact therefore that a hedge-ſparrow, or other ſmall bird, being obſerved to feed a young cuckow, is by no means ſatisfactory proof that the cuckow's egg was hatched by ſuch a dam, eſpecially as ſhe muſt have continued to ſit after her own five eggs had been removed; nor can we ſuppoſe that the cuckow could have depoſited her ſingle egg, without having perceived the intruſion of ſo large a ſtranger.

Can we preſume again, that hedge-ſparrows are not like other birds created to propagate their own ſpecies; but, on the contrary, chiefly for the purpoſe of hatching and feeding young cuckows?

That diſtinguiſhed anatomiſt Mr. Hunter hath diſſected ſeveral hen cuckows [n], and found that they are as well formed for incubation as other birds [o]; but ſuppoſing that they were not ſo, why does not the cuckow pitch upon the neſt of a thruſh or blackbird, rather than that of a hedge-ſparrow, as both neſt and dam of the former are ſo much nearer to the proper ſize, and the young cuckow therefore muſt have an infinitely better chance of being reared?

But other objections remain to the popular opinion, as, till all the proper circumſtances are proved to eſtabliſh the fact, we muſt reaſon from analogy.

If the hedge-ſparrow (or other ſmall bird) is a complete mother to the young cuckow, ſhe muſt not only diſregard the removal of her own five eggs, but the colour of them, for the

[n] Which were ſhot in the iſland of Belliſle during the winter.

[o] This is not the caſe with the oſtrich, which leaves her eggs in the ſand, the legs of that bird being ſo long as not to be diſpoſed of under her body, which would be ſcorched by the burning ſoil, as likewiſe the excluſion of the young too much accelerated by the united warmth of the ſands and the dam. It need ſcarcely be obſerved, that an oſtrich's neſt muſt be on the ground.

cuckow's,

cuckow's egg is not only much larger, but is of a dirty yellow ſpotted with black, whereas her own are of a fine pale blue.

Again, all other neſtlings, whilſt callow, want to be covered by the plumage of the dam; but how can this gigantic orphan receive ſuch warmth from a hedge-ſparrow?

The time, moreover, of the egg being hatched, is commonly in proportion to its ſize, the hedge-ſparrow therefore would probably adandon it, ſuppoſing it to be addled. I muſt alſo aſk what is to become of the hen cuckow during the time that the hedge-ſparrow is performing its parental functions; is ſhe employed from day to day in dropping her ſingle egg into other neſts, in which circumſtance likewiſe ſhe differs from almoſt every other bird, as I do not recollect an inſtance of leſs than two, and the greater part lay five?

It will undoubtedly be urged, however, that all reaſons from analogy are of little weight againſt poſitive facts, to which I moſt readily aſſent; but though I have made many inquiries about this extraordinary notion, I never could hear evidence of any other circumſtance to ſupport it, except that the young cuckow had been fed by a ſmall bird; which I hope to have ſhewn is by no means ſufficient to prove that it was alſo hatched by the hedge-ſparrow. Of this latter circumſtance nothing leſs than the hedge-ſparrow's eggs being removed by the cuckow, her own ſingle egg ſubſtituted in the place, and afterwards hatched, will convince me, as the proof of what contradicts the general laws of nature muſt be proportionally ſtrong.

On the contrary, I have received ſeveral well-atteſted inſtances of cuckows hatching and feeding their own neſtlings, which I ſhall here ſtate.

I have been favoured by that eminent naturaliſt Mr. Pennant with the following, from a MS diſſertation of Dr. Derham's:

"The

"The Rev. Mr. Stafford was walking in Bloſſop-dale[p], and "ſaw a cuckow riſe from its neſt, which was on the ſtump of "a tree that had been ſome time felled, ſo as to reſemble the "colour of the bird. In this neſt were two young cuckows; "one of which he faſtened to the ground by means of a peg and "line; and very frequently, for many days, beheld the old "cuckow feed theſe her young ones."

I have been alſo furniſhed with two other inſtances of cuckow's neſts, and the proper parents feeding their young, within four miles of London, and likewiſe on the S. Weſtern coaſt of Merionethſhire.

I remember myſelf having been in Herefordſhire, not many years ago, when a girl brought a young cuckow to the houſe where I happened to be; and on my aſking what ſort of bird it was fed by, the girl anſwered, by ſuch another, only ſomewhat larger

From theſe facts it muſt be allowed, that all cuckows at leaſt are not the unnatural parents they are commonly ſuppoſed to be.

I muſt however here repeat, that though I cannot but diſtruſt the commonly received opinion from the time of Ariſtotle to the preſent, that I by no means take upon myſelf peremptorily to deny it, as I do not want to be convinced, that the general rules and inſtinct by which animals are actuated, may ſometimes be broken through, notwithſtanding the reaſon for ſuch exception may not be very obvious.

I muſt however deſire thoſe who may perhaps be rather aſtoniſhed that any one ſhould preſume to doubt what is ſo generally credited, to recollect what hath happened with regard to the

[p] Derbyſhire.

goat-

goat-ſucker's ſuppoſed ſucking the teats of quadrupeds, the bite of the Calabrian tarantula, the porcupine ſhooting its quills, or the effects of the moon upon madmen, though they are called lunatics.

The true philoſophical temper is neither to credit nor diſbelieve extraordinary facts too haſtily:

> Nîl ſpernat auris, nec tamen credat ſtatim.
>
> PHÆDRUS.

Another notion with regard to the cuckow prevails, that during the winter it conceals itſelf in the ſtumps of trees, and which perhaps is as well atteſted, as the young cuckow's being hatched by the hedge-ſparrow.

"Certum eſt cuculum hyeme latere in concavis arborum et "lapidum [q]."

"Cuculus hyeme in terræ lapidum et arborum cavis ſe abdit, "in iiſque per totam hyemem latet [r]."

"Cuculus hyeme occultatur [s]."

"Cuculus hyeme in cavernis arborum latet, muta procedit "vere, &c. [t].

Willoughby relates, from Jo. Faber, a cuckow's being found in the winter which lived the two following years. He alſo cites Aldrovandus for the ſame notion; as likewiſe accounts he had heard from his countrymen, though upon the whole he rather ſuppoſes this bird to migrate during the winter.

Though many of theſe citations are from men of learning, and poſitively aſſert cuckows being thus found, I ſhall leave them to

[q] Geſner citing Albert.
[r] Johnſon's Nat Hiſt. Amſterdam, 1659, fol.
[s] Raczynſky Nat. Hiſt. of Poland, p. 277. Sandomiriæ, 1721.
Schwenfeld's Hiſtoria Avium Sileſiæ. Lipſiæ, 1600.

the

3

the reader's judgement, the fact is as credible as that the young is hatched and reared by the hedge-ſparrow, and perhaps better atteſted.

Another notion is very prevalent, that a young cuckow never lives long enough to make its call in the ſucceeding ſpring.

I have inquired much with regard to the truth of this opinion, and never could hear of but one inſtance [u], in addition to that before cited from Geſner, which was from a ſhopkeeper in Holborn, who informed me, that he had known this bird to have lived more than two years in a cage. I have myſelf indeed ſeen two cuckows, which having been reared by hand, did not die till the latter end of March, and appeared a few days before to be in perfect health.

There ſeems to be little doubt therefore, that cuckows having lived ten or eleven months may ſtill ſurvive this critical period of the ſucceeding ſpring, and I ſhould conceive that the occaſion of their uſually dying about that time is the following.

Willoughby informs us, that he diſſected the ſtomach of a cuckow, and found in it caterpillars, with other inſects; when a young bird of this kind therefore happens to be caught, the ſuccedaneum is commonly raw meat, cut into ſmall pieces,

[u] I have moſt recently indeed been furniſhed with another inſtance:

A very creditable old woman, who ſupplied Newgate-market with live poultry, hath frequently informed her cuſtomers, that having reared a young cuckow, it diſappeared during the whole winter, and was concluded to have been killed; but in the ſpring it crept out of its lurking place, and was afterwards very lively. This old woman died about 10 years ago, aged 90, and was known by the name of Mother Bentham.

which equally anſwers for other neſtlings who live on the ſame food [x].

All animals throughout the creation eat as long as they can ſwallow, if they have plenty of food before them; and man only forbears what is equally pleaſant to his palate, from the conſideration of the bad conſequences to his health, as alſo from the convenience and good ſociety which attends ſtated meals.

Thoſe animals which are granivorous ſeem to thus ſatiate themſelves with impunity; ſome of theſe however chew the cud afterwards; and in thoſe which do not, graſs is certainly a food of very light digeſtion.

Carnivorous animals, on the other hand, have not their prey always lying before them, and are on that account calculated for long faſts. If you conſtantly ſupply them therefore with what they are at all times ready to devour, nature is counteracted, and the animal is ſhort-liv'd.

Now I conſider birds which live on inſects as carnivorous, and Linnæus indeed aſſerts, that cuckows devour ſmall birds in the autumn [y]; I am for this reaſon perſuaded, that the neſtlings reared in a cage die by over cramming themſelves, when the bad effects of repletion are more likely to be experienced, as the ſpring approaches.

It is much to be wiſhed indeed, for the illuſtration of Zoology, that many birds were not only reared, but kept for years in cages; nor is this ſo difficult a feat to accompliſh as many may ſuppoſe.

[x] Robins, for example; but as they grow up it is commonly changed for vegetable, or at leaſt great part of their food.

[y] I have ſome doubts with regard to the truth of this obſervation, as alſo what the ſame naturaliſt aſſerts about its devouring the foſter water-wagtail.

I have

I have before obſerved, that raw meat cut into ſlices proportionable to the ſize of the neſtling is a good ſuccedaneum for inſects, as is the common ſubſtitute given to young canary birds, for thoſe neſtlings which live on the produce of vegetables.

When the young ones are properly fledg'd the dam ſhould be taken with them [z]; after which ſhe will immediately feed them, at leaſt I have ſeen frequent inſtances of this in robins and ſky-larks; nor can I conceive that the parental στοργη can be confined merely to theſe birds only. If the dam however cannot be caught, they who mean to rear the neſtlings by hand ſhould imitate her, in not cramming them too much, for ſhe does not feed her young oftner than in five minutes, and then with a very ſmall portion. If the neſtlings alſo are hung in a cage near the ſpot where the neſt was found, the dam will generally feed them; but ſuch young birds are often deſtroyed by vermin, and are ſeldom very tame, though they may indeed be rendered ſo with no great trouble [a].

I once prevailed upon a bird-catcher to try whether he could not rear ſome young martins by the promiſe of a guinea, if any one of them lived till Chriſtmas; he did not catch the dam, however, as I wiſhed him to do; and having fed the neſtlings

[z] By birdlime, properly diſpoſed near the neſt, or in ſome ſituations by a net being put over her. The cock bird will alſo feed the young but is not ſo much to be depended upon as the hen.

[a] The beſt means for effecting this is, to ſhew the animal that it is abſolutely in your power, and that you mean notwithſtanding to uſe it kindly. Take therefore a bird which hath been juſt caught, and carry it into a dark place, letting it perch upon your finger. The bird, in this ſituation, does not ſtir, and ſhould be ſtroaked with the other hand, whilſt occaſionally it is permitted to perch upon another finger, placed under its breaſt. In nine or ten minutes introduce ſome light by degrees, and many ſmall birds will inſtantaneouſly feed out of your hand.

for ten days, when they could fly, the whole brood died, by which he was ſo diſcouraged as never to have repeated the experiment, though it ſhould ſeem, that having lived ten days they might have ſurvived as many months, and perhaps years.

As theſe birds were martins, it perhaps might have been expected that they ſhould have been torpid during the winter; but this ſleeping ſtate does not take place with ſome other animals of the ſame habits, when they are ſupplied with food and warmth, witneſs the bear, the viper, and the common fly, which under theſe circumſtances are not only awake, but chearful and alert.

It is ſcarely neceſſary to refute another vulgar error, which ſeems to have taken its riſe from what is mentioned by Pliny, as he ſuppoſes the cuckow to become a hawk at the approach of autumn [b], and which poſſibly is alſo the occaſion of the notion that it preys upon ſmall birds at the ſame time of the year; this aſſertion being likewiſe advanced by the ſame authority.

Beſides other material diſtinctions, the cuckow hath two claws before and two behind, whereas every hawk hath three before and only one behind. It is indeed rather ſurpriſing that this difference ſhould have eſcaped Linnæus, when he gravely aſſerts, that this metamorphoſis does not take place; but it is remarkable that the Swediſh ornithologiſt conſiders the touraco [c] as a cuckow, which hath three claws before, and only one behind.

Another notion prevails, that the froth ſeen on many plants is occaſioned by this bird, and it is therefore termed *cuckow ſpit*;

[b] There is likewiſe a prevailing notion, equally ill founded, that a land rail becomes a water-rail, which is at once refuted by the great difference between the bills of theſe two birds.

[c] A moſt beautiful bird of Africa, of which there are two ſpecimens in Sir Aſhton Lever's Muſeum.

this

this however is now known to be the receptacle for the eggs of grasshoppers; nor does the cuckow ever scarcely light upon the ground; it therefore can as little deposit this froth, as feed upon the plant *arum*, which with us is called *cuckow pint*. Perhaps it is more probable both the one and the other may have obtained this name from their being seen at the same time that the cuckow appears, than that the bird occasions the former, or feeds upon the latter [d], which is an early plant of the spring.

[d] Arum is too acrid to be eaten by a cuckow, or probably any other animal; nor did I ever see the least appearance of its having been touched.

ESSAY VII.

ON THE LINNÆAN SYSTEM.

AFTER the death of our illuſtrious countryman Ray, the ſtudy of Natural Hiſtory ſeems to have ſlept, not only in England, but in moſt parts of Europe; which may perhaps be attributed to the Newtonian Philoſophy's affording a more intereſting ſubject of diſcuſſion, till by the force of truth it was thoroughly eſtabliſhed.

In the Northern part of Sweden, however, a man of very uncommon abilities, and great penetration in examining ſpecimens, aroſe, who publiſhed his firſt edition of a Syſtema Naturæ in 1735; I need ſcarcely ſay that I mean the celebrated Linnæus.

The firſt perſon who introduced the knowledge of this comprehenſive work to the Engliſh reader is believed to have been Sir John Hill; and it was afterwards much commended by the late Mr. Stillingfleet, who tranſlated ſome eſſays of the Univerſity of Upſal, written under the inſpection of their preſident Linnæus.

I am truly ſenſible of his merit in claſſing the different kingdoms of nature; and moſt readily allow, that it is perhaps the beſt dictionary and grammar which the naturaliſt can uſe, when he goes into a muſeum, or means to travel into diſtant regions.

I am

I am ſenſible alſo of the great convenience in conforming to any general nomenclature, and that much confuſion is thereby avoided, from the ſame reaſon that it ſignifies little to geographers whence the firſt meridian is taken, if any particular one is but univerſally adopted.

Theſe advantages, however, ſhould not make us blind to Linnæus's defects, and the bad conſequences which perhaps are to be apprehended from his ſyſtem prevailing to the excluſion of others, to whom the naturaliſt muſt for ever be ſo much indebted.

I have ſeen ſeveral letters written by Linnæus, the latinity of which a young ſchool boy with us would be aſhamed of, and indeed in many periods the common rules of grammar were broken[a].

Lord Kaims therefore expreſſes himſelf moſt juſtly on this head, " a language as barbarous as the German Metaphyſics of " Leibnitz, or the Swediſh Natural Hiſtory of Linnæus, which " are not even intelligible, except to thoſe who have made a par- " ticular ſtudy of their lingo's[b]."

This is really a moſt material defect in any one who treats on ſubjects of Natural Hiſtory; for the deſcription ſhould be couched in terms that can leave no doubt about the author's meaning, and by ſuch accuracy make the expence of engraving unneceſſary.

It may, however, be now expected, that I ſhould furniſh ſome inſtances of deſcriptions which cannot be eaſily comprehended

[a] I ſhould almoſt ſuſpect likewiſe that he did not underſtand French or Engliſh, as in the 12th edition of his Syſtema Naturæ, he refers only to Geſner, Aldrovandus, Johnſtone, Ray, Briſſon *, and Houtinus, without any mention of Buffon, or Pennant.

[b] Preface to Lord Kaims's 3d vol. on language.

* Briſſon's deſcriptions are both in Latin and French.

by the reader, on account of the terms employed; whilſt I premiſe that I do not require elegance, but only that the expreſſions ſhould be clear, and not liable to be miſunderſtood. But though I do not inſiſt upon claſſical latinity, yet every reader hath a right to expect, that in a dead language no new words ſhould be introduced, or eſtabliſhed terms uſed, in a manner for which proper authority cannot be produced.

I ſhall not have much trouble in citing ſuch inſtances from the Syſtema Naturæ, and Fauna Suecica, as every page almoſt where there are two lines of deſcription, affords them.

Linnæus thus ſpeaks of the woodcock:

" Scolopax [*ruſticola*] habitat in *appropriatis* locis, volitans per " noctes quaſi viam *ſtrictiſſimam* in ipſo aëre, &c."

The ſpecific difference aſſigned to this bird is *ruſticolà*, which can only mean, that it frequents the country; but is not this applicable to ninety-nine birds out of a hundred? Linnæus therefore intends to convey ſome other idea to his reader; but what that may be I muſt own I cannot comprehend.

Geſner indeed conceives the woodcock to be the Perdix ruſtica of the antients; but very erroneouſly, his authority being probably the following lines from Martial.

Ruſtica ſim, an perdix, quid refert, *ſi ſapor idem eſt?*
Carior eſt perdix, ſic ſapit illa magis.

Now by another epigram of Martial's it appears that the perdix was a very ſcarce bird in Italy:

Ponitur Auſoniis avis hæc [c] rariſſima menſis,
Hanc in lautorum mandere, ſæpe ſoles.

But without entering into a critical diſcuſſion what birds were termed by the antients *perdix*, and *ruſtica*, it is plain by this

[c] Sc. the perdix.

citation,

citation, that a woodcock was not alluded to by the latter name; for can any one say that the flavour of the two birds[d] hath the least resemblance:

"Quid refert, *si sapor idem est?*"

The truth of the matter is, that as the woodcock hath been called *scolopax* from the time of Aristotle, and as Linnæus hath made it a distinct genus by that name, the *woodcock* should have taken the lead, and the others of the same genus be distinguished by specific appellations.

The next expression in this short citation from Linnæus, that I shall take notice of, is "*in appropriatis locis*;" which I conceive to be no word of classical Latinity; but supposing it to be so, what is the reader to understand by it? Can the ornithologist mean that it frequents peculiar places? or if he does mean so, is not this applicable to almost every other bird?

But the citation proceeds, "volitans per noctes quasi viam "*strictissimam* in ipso aëre." What is again to be inferred from these expressions, and more particularly *viam strictissimam*? if a *strait road* is intended, was the term *stricta* ever used in that sense? and do not many other birds fly in a direct line from point to point?

For another example of the same sort I shall here subjoin part of what Linnæus observes with regard to the horse, "animal "generosum, superbum, aptissimum equitando, cursu furens, "sylvis delectatur, *posteriora* curat, caudâ conopes tabanosque abi-"git, *alterum scalpit*, pullum injuriæ obnoxium *reponit*, &c."

[d] The reading, in some editions of Martial.

"Rustica *sum* perdix,"

is clearly erroneous.

 Though

Though there is a wide field of objection to the matter of this defcription, I fhall confine myfelf to the latinity and obfcurity of it.

And firft what is intended by *pofteriora curat?* for though perhaps a meaning may fuggeft itfelf to fome readers, yet it is not true in fact that the horfe is more cleanly than many other quadrupeds in that circumftance, by any care or trouble which he takes himfelf.

What is the reader to underftand again by *alterum fcalpit?* does this fignify that one horfe rubs itfelf againft another? and, if it does, is this circumftance peculiar to this quadruped?

The next unintelligible expreffion is, "pullum injuriæ ob-"noxium *reponit*;" to which, for a confiderable time, I could affix no fenfe whatfoever, but have a diftant guefs that it means, "*when the foal is in danger, the dam places it behind her*;" but is this circumftance again peculiar to the horfe?

Having produced thefe proofs of defcriptions unintelligible, or at leaft obfcure, by the ufe of improper terms; I fhall not dwell upon the difagreeable (but moft eafy) tafk of ftating multitudes of other paffages equally objectionable; and may truly fay, that I fcarcely ever examined, with attention, an article in the Syftema Naturæ, with regard to the terms of which I have not continued to have my difficulties, though I have confulted fome of Linnæus's moft zealous admirers.

There is fcarcely any naturalift who hath publifhed fince the Linnæan fyftem began to have a vogue, who hath not condemned many parts of it; fo that I am not fingular in fuppofing that it hath its defects.

But I conceive, that there is not only foundation for many of thefe objections; but that it hath, in many inftances, been pre-

judicial

judicial to the knowledge of that very ſubject which it is intended chiefly to inculcate.

Linnæus hath compriſed the animal kingdom of the whole globe, except inſects, (viz. Beaſts, Birds, Reptiles, and Fiſh,) in 532 pages, octavo: and what can this poſſibly amount to more than a vocabulary, grammar, or dictionary, be it as excellent as it may?

But it may poſſibly be ſaid, that the cheapneſs of ſo much inſtruction, as well as its being ſo portable, are great recommendations of this uſeful publication, which I am very ready to allow: ſo are Cole's Latin Dictionary and Hedericus's Lexicon deſervedly in great requeſt; but though theſe will anſwer my purpoſe very well whilſt I am at ſchool, I ſhall want better aſſiſtance when I have left it.

Again, it will be urged, that they who ſtudy the Linnæan Syſtem are not debarred from peruſing the works of other naturaliſts; but I appeal to experience, whether thoſe who are zealous admirers of the Swediſh profeſſor often go beyond the elementary knowledge of their inſtructor, or contribute any uſeful additions to any article of natural hiſtory.

In other words, ſo much time is taken up in maſtering the Linnæan elements, that we grow old before we can apply to any particular branch of this comprehenſive ſtudy.

I may therefore perhaps, in ſome meaſure, compare this to a perſon's peruſing with great care treatiſes on huſbandry in every latitude and quarter of the globe, whilſt no particular attention is paid to the culture of his own eſtate, where alone he can make any improvement either in knowledge or profit.

I have already admitted, that ſo uſeful a repertory cannot be carried into any muſeum, or upon an extenſive voyage, as Linnæus's Syſtema Naturæ, but after all, when we have found ſome account of the unknown animal in this celebrated work, what further instruction do we really procure, but that Linnæus hath either seen or heard of it? Surely this amounts to very little, whilst the habits of the animal, the uses for which its limbs are peculiarly adapted, with other such circumstances, deserve only the name of natural history, or can be really interesting.

The celebrated Mr. Gray therefore thus speaks of the Linnæan system, "not much to my edification; for though he is "pretty well acquainted with their persons, he is not so with "their manners [e]."

What Mr. Gray thus requires from the naturalist, is only to be attained by attending to the animals of our own country, or rather district. And to give an idea of what I conceive at least to be the proper articles of observation, I will beg leave to refer to four letters of the Rev. Mr. White on the four species of British swallows [f]. But perhaps the admirers of Linnæus may suggest, that such an account of the animals of Sweden is to be found in his Fauna Suecica, and it is true that the descriptions in this his later work are rather more full, but they by no means answer what one should expect from a zoologist of so distinguished pre-eminence, and smell of the lamp, rather than the country excursion.

The great use in publications like those of Linnæus, is to find out the animal or plant which one happens to see to the right or left, for how few museums can be resorted to in most parts, even of this scientific country? I will suppose therefore, that the common brown linnet is what I have seen either on the wing, or lies dead before me.

[e] Gray's Letters, who had employed the latter part of his life chiefly in the study of natural history.

[f] Phil. Transf.

The

The firſt circumſtance I want to know is its ſex, with regard to which Linnæus is ſilent in the 12th edition of his Syſtema Naturæ, though publiſhed five years after his Fauna Suecica, where the difference is indeed noticed. But my ſpecimen hath a red head and breaſt, and by having heard it ſing, I rather ſuppoſe it to be a cock; and how can I reconcile this to the plumage of a male bird kept for ſome years in a cage, which hath no red on either of theſe parts? Here again Linnæus fails me, who did not know, that the common linnet, when he moults in captivity, never reaſſumes his red plumage.

In my walks I happen to find a deſerted neſt of this bird, as to the component parts of which Linnæus gives me no information; as alſo with regard to the eggs, either in colour or number, nor how long the hen ſits upon them.

I hear again the moſt pleaſing and mellow notes of this bird, which being unnoticed by Linnæus, my diſtruſt is again raiſed whether I may ſuppoſe the bird to be a linnet.

I ſee theſe birds alſo during the autumn and ſpring flying in large flocks, whilſt ſome of them have a different motion from the reſt, as likewiſe have a peculiar call: Linnæus however is ſilent as to this flock, conſiſting of linnets and *twites*, which at thoſe ſeaſons often aſſemble together, as fieldfares and redwings accompany each other during the winter.

In fact, the only circumſtance which he adds to the dry deſcription ſeems rather to miſlead the reader, becauſe he mentions that the linnet chiefly lives on alder-ſeeds, which it is believed this bird never touches in England, or certainly does not make its principal ſubſiſtence.

After all, therefore, what inſtruction have I reaped by conſulting Linnæus, but that the common linnet is one ſpecies of fringilla noticed by him, which is about as much knowledge as

is

is picked up from a common dictionary, with regard to the import of a word, when I want to find whether it hath not been used in a different signification.

I admit, indeed, that the name alone, together with its classifaction, nearly compleats the natural history of a fossil, but surely the circumstances omitted by Linnæus are the most interesting parts of zoology.

If I was to refer again to Linnæus's description and account of another well-known bird (the goldfinch) I should not find any more material circumstances, whilst, as I conceive, he would mislead me by saying, that the tips of the wings and tail-feathers are white in the autumn, and black in the spring, which with us continue of the same colour throughout the year. To this I must add, that the goldfinch in England does not particularly frequent junipers, nor do I understand what part of this shrub this bird is to feed upon during the summer; the fact being, that all the finch tribe live during that season upon groundsel, chickweed, and other plants, both the stalks, flowers, and leaves of which afford them plentiful nourishment

It may be however asked, if Linnæus is not to be consulted, to whom I would refer the naturalist for information? to which my answer is, that he should have recourse to the ornithologist who hath lived in, and observed the animals of, the country where the bird may be found in its wild state, and if that country be England, he will find satisfaction as to many of these particulars from Willoughby and Pennant. Doing otherwise may be compared to the looking into a Polyglot dictionary for the signification of a word in a particular language, instead of a capital compilation confined to the terms of that single country.

I have hitherto confined myself to Linnæus's zoology, but have also my apprehensions with regard to the use of the botanical part

of

of his ſyſtem, which in general are nearly the ſame with the ſuppoſed defects in his Zoology.

As this ſyſtem, however, comprehends the plants of the whole globe, it is a moſt uſeful repertory for a large botanical garden, provided the plants are in flower, and the botaniſt hath the proper apparatus for diſſecting and examining them. If the collection on the other-hand conſiſts of dried plants, the ſyſtem is almoſt entirely uſeleſs, as thoſe minute parts (the chives [g] and pointals) are commonly deranged or loſt in ſuch ſpecimens. The ſame holds with regard to all engravings of plants before this ſyſtem was introduced, where the ſame minute parts are not attended to.

But as the chief amuſement in botany is the finding a plant in its wild ſtate (for the ſeeing it in a conſervatory is like ſhooting in a farm yard, or fiſhing in a ſtew) I will ſuppoſe the *wild-carot* to be ſtumbled upon; of which the botaniſt is ignorant, till he can conſult his Linnæus.

For what the ſtudent is to wade through before he can procure this information I ſhall refer to Dr. Withering's arrangement of the vegetables of Great Britain [h].

If the botaniſt therefore hath recourſe to Linnæus he muſt turn to the ſecond order [Digynia] of his claſs [Pentandria] and to the ſecond ſubdiviſion, which conſiſts of thirty plants, where he will at length find the Daucus Carota of the Swediſh botaniſt, if the plant happens fortunately to be in flower, and is nicely examined with the proper apparatus.

I will now ſuppoſe this plant to be viſited a month afterwards, when the flowers have fallen, and when ſuch a metamorphoſis hath taken place, that it cannot be ſuppoſed to be the ſame; for the flowering part, which was before horizontal, is now become

[g] Theſe likewiſe often vary in number.

[h] Introd. p xxv.

deeply concave, and the ſides approach each other ſo nearly as to form a ſtrong reſemblance to a bird's neſt.

Should therefore ſuch a remarkable change in the appearance of a plant be omitted in the deſcription of it by any botaniſt? and if it is omitted, will not the ſtudent be often miſled?

I will now ſuppoſe the ſame botaniſt to be furniſhed only with Ray's Synopſis of Britiſh plants, and to conſult it on the ſame occaſion.

Ray divides the *perfect* plants of our iſland (and ſuch is the *wild carot*) into twenty-three genera, the 11th of which conſiſts of the *herbæ umbelliferæ* [1], to which, if I am not blind, I muſt immediately know, at almoſt any ſeaſon, that this plant muſt belong, though I am at ſome diſtance from it. This claſs (or genus) again contains but 25 principal plants, which are alſo divided into ſeven clear and diſtinct ſubdiviſions, and which reduces my trouble probably to the examination of not more than five ſpecies, whereas if I conſult Linnæus, I muſt pore over thirty; nor then can receive any information, except when the plant is in full flower. Notwithſtanding this ſuperior facility of procuring the more perſpicuous and intereſting account from Ray, many an Engliſh botaniſt hath been deterred from proſecuting this branch of ſtudy by the difficulties of the Linnæan ſyſtem, which he is told perhaps is the only one that deſerves to be conſulted.

After this compariſon can there be a doubt whether the Engliſh botaniſt ſhould conſult Ray or Linnæus for an Engliſh plant, the former not only being the more compendious guide, but pointing out the road at moſt ſeaſons, whilſt the other only gives rather obſcure directions for a ſingle month of the year? I have before allowed, that there is a great advantage in adopting any

[1] Having a rundle ſupported by fruit-ſtalks or ſpokes.

ſyſtem whatſoever, ſo that confuſion may not be created by referring to different ſynonyms ; but till this becomes the univerſal practice amongſt naturaliſts, the new ſyſtem occaſions the greateſt confuſion, and muſt do ſo for perhaps half a century.

Is it to be expected, for example, that an Engliſh botaniſt, who is well acquainted with the plants of his own country, by the aſſiſtance of Ray, ſhall immediately drop the name of a plant, now become familiar to him, in order to new-chriſten it by the Linnæan appellation ?

One of the great pleaſures in botany is, to produce a rather uncommon plant to thoſe who know it to be curious ; but the Engliſh botaniſt will not have much ſatisfaction in ſhewing it to a ſimpler, who is not acquainted with it under the name given by Gerard or Ray.

I remember to have once met an elderly gentleman, near Tenterden, who had in his hand a very fine ſpecimen of the *Touch-menot*, or *Balſamine lutea* of Ray ; and when I had congratulated him upon having found this rare plant, he immediately told me, that he would not but have met me for five pounds, as it ſignifed little to have made the diſcovery in his neighbourhood, where no one had the leaſt tincture of botany.

If I had upon accoſting him, however, referred this Rayian botaniſt to the Syngeneſia Monogamia of Linnæus, there would have been an end of our conference, and he would have only ſtared, conſidering me as either ignorant, or an affecter of unintelligible terms. I muſt add, that I think he had a good right ſo to do ; for in England the ſynonyms of Gerard and Ray ſhould be referred to, with which moſt Linnæans are entirely unacquainted, whilſt by this confuſion of names the diſciples of Ray and Linnæus are perpetually at croſs purpoſes. If I mention the plant alſo by Gerard's Engliſh ſynonym, I may poſſibly by inquiries either confirm or refute the popular notions with regard to the virtues and uſes of the plant, which is certainly the moſt material part of botany.

And here I will take the liberty to ſay that plants may be diſtinguiſhed by ſome circumſtances which none of the writers on that part of natural hiſtory have attended to.

If the taſte or ſmell indeed is very remarkable, it is often noticed; but the leaves, flowers, ſeeds, and roots, often differ in theſe particulars.

The form of the root is again totally neglected if it is not bulbous, whereas the ſuperficies above ground does not vary more than what is under ground. The colour alſo of the leaves, when they fade in the autumn, is a material circumſtance in the natural hiſtory of the plant.

Their medicinal uſe indeed is generally mentioned; but the culinary too much neglected, as in the inſtance of water-creſſes, which, when boiled, are an excellent ſuccedaneum for ſpinnage, and are of a more beautiful green when ſerved on table than any of the products of the kitchen-garden.

Some botaniſts have, in a few inſtances, taken notice of the inſect which feeds upon particular plants; this however ſhould be general, as well as mention made of the bird, or other animal, which chiefly ſubſiſts upon them.

Having thus preſumed to recommend ſome particulars to the attention of the writers on botany, I ſhall conclude by repeating, that I do not deny the great merit of Linnæus's Syſtema Naturæ, as a general repertory, though it ſeems to me that the naturaliſt who deſcribes the production of the country which he inhabits ſhould always be preferred, as affording more complete and more

intereſting

interesting information. In other words, let the Systema Naturæ be reserved for the Museum, or botanical garden, rather than be the Naturalist's companion, on excursions within his own neighbourhood.

The chief merit of the Linnæan system consists undoubtedly in the having paid greater attention to the parts of fructification in plants than was shewn by preceding writers on the same subject; but it must never be forgotten, that the chives and pointals are too minute, too uncertain in their number, and too seldom in a state proper to be examined, to afford very interesting criteria in distinguishing plants.

I will conclude with an extract from the late Sir John Hill: "Such is the system of Linnæus: *novelty* made it please, and its "obscurity rendered it admired; but it cannot be lasting[k]."

[k] British Herbal; in the introduction to his second class. Sir John Hill was himself captured with the novelty, and had much commended this new system; this opinion therefore was given as to the merits, after thorough examination, with the strongest prejudice in its favour.

Jan. 28, 1780.

AS it appears from ſome of the foregoing eſſays that I have paid attention to ſome particular articles of Natural Hiſtory, I take this opportunity of laying before the public my poor endeavours, as an unworthy member of the Royal Society, for the promotion of knowledge in this branch of ſcience, as it chiefly relates to an agreement with the preſent King of Spain for that purpoſe; which is ſtill unaccompliſhed on the part of his Catholic Majeſty.

The Royal Society hath almoſt from its firſt inſtitution collected ſpecimens for a muſeum; which, ſo far back as the year 1681, had become ſo conſiderable, that Dr. Grew publiſhed a handſome catalogue, in folio, of the ſeveral articles, together with engravings; and that great architect Sir Chriſtopher Wren gave a well-conſidered plan for the building a repoſitory to receive theſe natural productions, which was not only approved of by the ſociety, but carried into execution,

This elegant room, together with the ſpecimens, were almoſt totally neglected; and I had the good fortune to prevail upon the council of the ſociety (about nine years ago) to lay out ſome money in neceſſary repairs and alterations.

Having been the occaſion of this expence, I then thought it was incumbent upon me to do what lay in my power to add to the collection of ſpecimens; when it occurred, that our forts in Hudſon's Bay would probably ſupply thoſe which were moſt rare, as this is the moſt Northern part of America inhabited by Europeans, and was never viſited by any naturaliſt.

I accordingly applied to Mr. Wegg, V Pr. and Treaſurer of the Royal Society; who, in concert with the other directors of the Hudſon's Bay Company, moſt obligingly gave orders, that many of the animals near their forts ſhould be ſent over by the

the enſuing autumn; and this being repeated for three ſucceſſive years produced a great many duplicates[a].

The collection being by this means much enlarged[b], it occurred, that we might ſtill augment it by a judicious barter of theſe duplicates; and more particularly ſo with Spain, as the animals of Hudſon's Bay could not be procured by his Catholic Majeſty but from England; whilſt Peru, Chili, Buenos Ayres, and the Philippines, would furniſh what we only could obtain from the Spaniards.

The late Prince Maſſarano, who was ambaſſador from his Catholic Majeſty to our court, was not only a fellow of the Royal Society, but ſometimes attended their meetings; and this plan of exchange between the two countries having been propoſed to his excellency, he undertook to lay it before his Royal Maſter.

The King of Spain at that time happened to be forming a cabinet of natural hiſtory, and therefore ſignified that he would ſend orders to his governors to collect for him, and would make the Royal Society a proper return for any preſents they might deſtine for him from Hudſon's Bay.

The Royal Society accordingly tranſmitted a conſiderable number of ſpecimens from that part of the world to his Catholic Majeſty in 1773 (through M. Eſcarano, then reſident at our court); but we have never received any natural productions from South America, or the Philippines, though I have ſeen the printed

[a] Lord Dartmouth, then Secretary of State, and F. R. S. was likewiſe ſo obliging as to write to the governors of ſome of our Southern colonies for procuring natural productions; but whether from the rebellion which the mother country hath lately experienced, or from what other cauſe I will not determine, the Royal Society hath never received any ſpecimens, in conſequence of theſe orders.

[b] I underſtand that the old collection is now preſented by the Royal Society to the Britiſh Muſeum, together with theſe additions.

orders alluded to by his Catholic Majeſty, which iſſued immediately after this naturaliſt-treaty was concluded.

It is to be hoped indeed, that, notwithſtanding the preſent war between the two countries, this undertaking on the part of the King of Spain (in a matter of mere ſcience, and for which his Majeſty hath received a valuable conſideration) will not be forgotten; but, leaſt it ſhould, I leave this poor teſtimony of what hath been done on our ſide, and what is incumbent upon the court of Spain in return. And I do this the rather, becauſe this promiſed exchange is the only method of obtaining ſpecimens from the Spaniſh part of South America, or the Philippines.

ACCOUNT

Η σοι γ'εκ γενεης τα δαμ' εσπετο θαυματα εργα,
Ηε τις αθανατων, ηε θνητων ανθρωπων
Δωρον αγαυον εδωκε, και εφρασε θεσφιν αοιδην,

HOMER's Hymn on Mercury

ACCOUNT OF A VERY REMARKABLE YOUNG MUSICIAN.

In a LETTER to MATHEW MATY, M. D. Sec. R. S[a].

SIR,

IF I was to ſend you a well-atteſted acccunt of a boy who meaſured ſeven feet in height, when he was not more than eight years of age, it might be conſidered as not undeſerving the notice of the Royal Society.

The inſtance which I now deſire you will communicate to that learned body, of as early an exertion of moſt extraordinary muſical talents, ſeems perhaps equally to claim their attention.

Joannes Chryſoſtomus Wolfgangus Theophilus Mozart was born at Saltzbourg, in Bavaria, on the 17th of January, 1756[b].

[a] This is re-printed from the LXth volume of the Philoſophical Tranſactions, for the year 1770.

[b] I here ſubjoin a copy of the tranſlation from the regiſter at Saltzbourg, as it was procured from his excellency Count Haſlang, envoy extraordinary and miniſter plenipotentiary of the electors of Bavaria and Palatine:

"I, the under-written, certify, that in the year 1756, the 17th of "January, at eight o'clock in the evening, was born Joannes Chryſoſtomus Wolfgangus Theophilus, ſon of Mr. Leopold Mozart, organiſt of "his highneſs the prince of Saltzbourg, and of Maria Ann his lawful "wife (whoſe maiden name was Peitlin), and chriſtened the day following, at ten o'clock in the morning, at the prince's cathedral church "here; his godfather being Gotthel Pergmayr, merchant in this city. "In truth whereof, I have taken this certificate from the parochial regiſter of chriſtenings, and under the uſual ſeal, ſigned the ſame with "my own hand.

Saltzbourg, Jan 3, 1769.

"Leopald Comprecht,
"Chaplain to his Highneſs in this city."

I have

I have been informed, by a moſt able muſician and compoſer, that he frequently ſaw the boy at Vienna, when he was little more than four years old.

By this time he not only was capable of executing leſſons on his favourite inſtrument the harpſichord, but compoſed ſome in an eaſy ſtile and taſte, which were much approved of. His extraordinary muſical talents ſoon reached the ears of the preſent empreſs dowager, who uſed to place him upon her knees whilſt he played on the harpſichord. This notice taken of him by ſo great a perſonage, together with certain conſciouſneſs of his moſt ſingular abilities, had much emboldened the little muſician. Being therefore the next year at one of the German courts, where the elector encouraged him, by ſaying, that he had nothing to fear from his auguſt preſence; little Mozart immediately ſat down with great confidence to his harpſichord, informing his highneſs, that he had played before the empreſs.

At ſeven years of age his father carried him to Paris, where he ſo diſtinguiſhed himſelf by his compoſitions that an engraving was made of him. The father and ſiſter who are introduced in this print are exceſſively like their portraits; as is alſo little Mozart, who is ſtiled, "Compoſiteur et Maitre de Muſique, agé de ſept "ans[c]" After the name of the engraver follows the date, which is in 1764; Mozart was therefore at this time in the eighth year of his age.

Upon leaving Paris, he came over to England, where he continued more than a year. As during this time I was witneſs of his moſt extraordinary abilities as a muſician, both at ſome public concerts, and likewiſe by having been alone with him for a conſiderable time at his father's houſe; I ſend you the following account, amazing and incredible almoſt as it may appear.

[c] An engraving of the boy himſelf is annexed.

I carried

I carried to him a manuſcript duet, which was compoſed by an Engliſh gentleman to ſome favourite words in Metaſtaſio's opera of Demofoonte. The whole ſcore was in five parts, viz. accompanyments for a firſt and ſecond violin, the two vocal parts, and a baſe. I ſhall here likewiſe mention, that the parts for the firſt and ſecond voice were written in the counter-tenor cleff; the reaſon for taking notice of which particular will appear hereafter.

My intention in carrying with me this manuſcript compoſition, was to have an irrefragable proof of his abilities as a player at ſight, it being abſolutely impoſſible that he could have ever ſeen the muſic before.

The ſcore was no ſooner put upon his deſk, than he began to play the ſymphony in a moſt maſterly manner, as well as in the time and ſtile which correſponded with the intention of the compoſer. I mention this circumſtance, becauſe the greateſt maſters often fail in theſe particulars on the firſt trial. The ſymphony ended, he took the upper part, leaving the under one to his father.

His voice, in the tone of it, was thin and infantine, but nothing could exceed the maſterly manner in which he ſung.

His father, who performed the under part in this duet, was once or twice out, though the paſſages were not more difficult than thoſe in the upper one; on which occaſions the ſon looked back with ſome anger, pointing out to him ſome miſtakes, and ſetting him right.

He not only however did complete juſtice to the duet, by ſinging his own part in the trueſt taſte, and with the greateſt preciſion: he alſo threw in the accompanyments of the two violins, wherever they were moſt neceſſary, and produced the beſt effects. It is well known that none but the moſt capital muſicians are capable of accompanying in this ſuperior ſtile.

As many of thoſe who may be preſent when this letter may have the honour of being read before the ſociety, may not poſſibly be acquainted with the difficulty of playing thus at ſight from a muſical ſcore, I will endeavour to explain it by the moſt ſimilar compariſon I can think of.

I muſt, at the ſame time, admit, that the illuſtration will fail in one particular, as the voice in reading cannot comprehend more than what is contained in a ſingle line. I muſt ſuppoſe, however, that the reader's eye, by habit and quickneſs, may take in other lines, though the voice cannot articulate them as the muſician accompanies the words of an air by his harpſichord.

Let it be imagined, therefore, that a child of eight years old was directed to read five lines [a] at once, in four [b] of which the letters of the alphabet were to have different powers.

For example, in the firſt line A, to have its common powers.

In the ſecond that of B.

In the third of C.

In the fourth of D.

Let it be conceived alſo, that the lines ſo compoſed of characters, with different powers, are not ranged ſo as to be read at

[a] By this I mean,
The two parts for the violins.
The upper part for the voice.
The words ſet to muſic.
And laſtly, the baſe.

[b] By this I mean,
The violin parts in the common treble cleff.
The upper part for the voice in the counter-tenor cleff, as before-mentioned.
The words in common characters.
And the baſe in its common cleff.

all

all times one exactly under the other, but often in a desultory manner.

Suppose, then, a capital speech in Shakespeare [c] never seen before, and yet read by a child of eight years old, with all the pathetic energy of a Garrick.

Let it be conceived likewise, that the same child is reading, with a glance of his eye, three different comments on this speech, tending to its illustration; and that one comment is written in Greek, the second in Hebrew, and the third in Arabic characters.

Let it be also supposed, that by different signs he could point out which comment is most material upon every word; and sometimes that perhaps all three are so, at others only two of them.

When all this is conceived, it will convey some idea of what this boy was capable of, in singing such a duet at sight in a masterly manner from the score, throwing in at the same time all its proper accompanyments.

When he had finished the duet, he expressed himself highly in its approbation, asking, with some eagerness, whether I had brought any more such music.

Having been informed, however, that he was often visited with musical ideas, to which, even in the midst of the night, he would give utterance on his harpsichord; I told his father that I should be glad to hear some of his extemporary flights.

The father shook his head at this, saying, that it depended entirely upon his being as it were musically inspired, but that I might ask him whether he was in humour for such a composition.

[c] The words in Metastasio's duet, which little Mozart sung, are very pathetic.

Happening to know that little Mozart was much taken notice of by Manzoli, the famous ſinger, who came over to England in 1764, I ſaid to the boy, that I ſhould be glad to hear an extemporary *Love Song*, ſuch as his friend Manzoli might chooſe in an opera.

The boy on this (who continued to ſit at his harpſichord) looked back with much archneſs, and immediately began five or ſix lines of a jargon recitative proper to introduce a love ſong.

He then played a ſymphony which might correſpond with an air compoſed to the ſingle word, *Affetto*.

It had a firſt and ſecond part, which, together with the ſymphonies, was of the length that opera ſongs generally laſt: if this extemporary compoſition was not amazingly capital, yet it was really above mediocrity, and ſhewed moſt extraordinary readineſs of invention.

Finding that he was in humour, and as it were inſpired, I then deſired him to compoſe a *Song of Rage*, ſuch as might be proper for the opera ſtage.

The boy again looked back with much archneſs, and began five or ſix lines of a jargon recitative proper to precede a *Song of Anger*. This laſted alſo about the ſame time with the *Song of Love*; and in the middle of it he had worked himſelf up to ſuch a pitch, that he beat his harpſichord like a perſon poſſeſſed, riſing ſometimes in his chair. The word he pitched upon for this ſecond extemporary compoſition was, *Perfido*.

After this he played a difficult leſſon, which he had finiſhed a day or two before[d]; his execution was amazing, conſidering that

[d] He publiſhed ſix ſonatas for the harpſichord, with an accompanyment for the violin, or German flute, which are ſold by R. Bremner, in the Strand, and are intituled, Oeuvre Troiſme.

that his little fingers could ſcarcely reach a ſixth on the harpſichord.

His aſtoniſhing readineſs, however, did not ariſe merely from great practice; he had a thorough knowledge of the fundamental principles of compoſition, as, upon producing a treble, he immediately wrote a baſe under it, which, when tried, had a very good effect.

He was alſo a great maſter of modulation, and his tranſitions from one key to another were exceſſively natural and judicious; he practiſed in this manner for a conſiderable time with an handkerchief over the keys of the harpſichord.

The facts which I have been mentioning I was myſelf an eye-witneſs of; to which I muſt add, that I have been informed by two or three able muſicians, when Bach the celebrated compoſer had begun a fugue and left off abruptly, that little Mozart hath immediately taken it up, and worked it after a moſt maſterly manner.

Witneſs as I was myſelf of moſt of theſe extraordinary facts, I muſt own that I could not help ſuſpecting his father impoſed with regard to the real age of the boy, though he had not only a moſt childiſh appearance, but likewiſe had all the actions of that ſtage of life.

For example, whilſt he was playing to me, a favourite cat came in, upon which he immediately left his harpſichord, nor could we bring him back for a conſiderable time.

He is ſaid in the title page to have been only eight years of age when he compoſed theſe ſonatas.

The dedication is to the Queen, and is dated at London, January 8, 1765.

He ſubſcribes himſelf, " tres humble, et tres obeiſſant *petit* ſerviteur."

Theſe leſſons are compoſed in a very original ſtile, and ſome of them are maſterly.

He

He would alſo ſometimes run about the room with a ſtick between his legs by way of horſe.

I found likewiſe that moſt of the London muſicians were of the ſame opinion with regard to his age, not believing it poſſible that a child of ſo tender years could ſurpaſs moſt of the maſters in that ſcience

I have therefore for a conſiderable time made the beſt inquiries I was able from ſome of the German muſicians reſident in London, but could never receive any further information than that he was born near Saltzbourg, till I was ſo fortunate as to procure an extract from the regiſter of that place, through his excellency Count Haſlang.

It appears from this extract, that Mozart's father did not impoſe with regard to his age when he was in England, for it was in June, 1765, that I was witneſs to what I have above related, when the boy was only eight years and five months old.

I have made frequent inquiries with regard to this very extraordinary genius ſince he left England; and was told laſt ſummer, that he was then at Saltzbourg, where he had compoſed ſeveral oratorios, which were much admired.

I am alſo informed, that the prince biſhop of Saltzbourg, not crediting that ſuch maſterly compoſitions were really thoſe of a child, ſhut him up for a week, during which he was not permitted to ſee any one, and was left only with muſic-paper, and the words of an oratorio. During this ſhort time he compoſed a very capital oratorio, which was moſt highly approved of upon being performed.

Having ſtated the above mentioned proofs of Mozart's genius, when of almoſt an infantine age, it may not be improper perhaps to compare them with what hath been well atteſted with regard to other inſtances of the ſame ſort.

Amongſt

Amongſt theſe, John Barratier hath been moſt particularly diſtinguiſhed, who is ſaid to have underſtood Latin when he was but four years old, Hebrew when ſix, and three other languages at the age of nine.

This ſame prodigy of philological learning alſo tranſlated the travels of Rabbi Benjamin when eleven years old, accompanying his verſion with notes and diſſertations. Before his death, which happened under the age of twenty, Barratier ſeems to have aſtoniſhed Germany with his amazing extent of learning; and it need not be ſaid, that its increaſe in ſuch a ſoil, from year to year, is commonly amazing.

Mozart, however, is not much more than thirteen years of age; and it is not therefore neceſſary to carry my compariſon further.

The Rev Mr Manwaring (in his *Memoirs of Handel)* hath given us a ſtill more appoſite inſtance, and in the ſame ſcience.

This great muſician began to play on the clavichord when he was but ſeven years of age; and is ſaid to have compoſed ſome church-ſervices when he was only nine years old, as alſo the opera of Almeria when he did not exceed fourteen.

Mr. Manwaring likewiſe mentions that Handel, when very young, was ſtruck ſometimes whilſt in bed with muſical ideas; and that, like Mozart, he uſed to try their effect immediately on a ſpinnet, which was in his bedchamber.

I am the more glad to ſtate this ſhort compariſon between theſe two early prodigies in muſic, as it may be hoped that little Mozart may poſſibly attain to the ſame advanced years as Handel, contrary to the common obſervation, that ſuch *ingenia præcocia* are generally ſhort-lived.

I think I may ſay without prejudice to the memory of this great compoſer, that the ſcale moſt clearly preponderates on the ſide of

Mozart

Mozart in this comparison, as I have already stated that he was a composer when he did not much exceed the age of four.

His extemporary compositions also, of which I was a witness, prove his genius and invention to have been most astonishing; least however I should insensibly become too strongly his panegyrist, permit me to subscribe myself, SIR,

Your most faithful humble servant,

DAINES BARRINGTON.

Jan. 21, 1780.

ON this republication of what appeared in the LXth volume of the Philosophical Transactions, it may be right to add, that Mozart (though a German) hath been honoured by the pope with an order of merit called the Golden Spur, and hath composed operas in several parts of Italy. I have also been favoured by D. Burney with the following account of one of his latest compositions.

"Mozart being at Paris, in 1778, composed for Tenducci a "scene in 14 parts, chiefly obligati; viz. two violins, two te- "nors, one chromatic horn, one oboe, two clarinets, a Piano "forte, a Soprano voice part, with two horns, and a base di "rinforza.

"It is a very elaborate and masterly composition, discovering "a great practice and facility of writing in many parts. The "modulation is likewise learned and recherchée; however, though "it is a composition which none but a great master of harmony, "and possessed of a consummate knowledge of the genius of dif- "ferent instruments, could produce; yet neither the melody of "the voice part, nor of any one of the instruments, discovers "much invention, though the effects of the whole, if well exe- "cuted, would, doubtless, be masterly and pleasing."

ACCOUNT OF MR. CHARLES WESLEY.

CHARLES[a] was born at Briſtol, Dec. 11, 1757. He was two years and three quarters old when I firſt obſerved his ſtrong inclination to muſic. He then ſurprized me by playing a tune on the harpſichord, readily and in juſt time. Soon after he played ſeveral, whatever his mother ſung, or whatever he heard in the ſtreets.

From his birth ſhe uſed to quiet and amuſe him with the harpſichord; but he would not ſuffer her to play with one hand only, taking the other, and putting it on thé keys, before he could ſpeak. When he played himſelf ſhe uſed to tie him up by his backſtring to the chair, for fear of his falling. Whatever tune it was he always put a true baſs to it. From the beginning he played without ſtudy or heſitation; and, as the maſters told me, perfectly well.

Mr. Broadrip[b] heard him in petticoats, and foretold he would one day make a great player.

Whenever he was called to play to a ſtranger, he would aſk, in a word of his own, "Is he a muſicker?" and if anſwered, "Yes," he played with the greateſt readineſs.

He always played *con ſpirito*. There was ſomething in his manner above a child, which ſtruck the hearers, learned or unlearned.

[a] I was favoured with this account of his eldeſt ſon by the Rev. Mr. Charles Weſley.

[b] Organiſt at Briſtol.

At four years old I carried him with me to London. Mr. Beard was the first that confirmed Mr. Broadrip's judgment of him, and kindly offered his interest with Dr. Boyce, to get him admitted among the King's boys. But I had then no thoughts of bringing him up a musician.

A gentleman carried him next to Mr. Stanley, who expressed much pleasure and surprize at hearing him, and declared he had never met one of his age with so strong a propensity to music. The gentleman told us, he never before believed what Handel used to tell him of himself, and his own love of music, in his childhood.

Mr. Madan presented my son to Mr. Worgan, who was extremely kind; and, as I then thought, partial to him. He told us, he would prove an eminent master, if he was not taken off by other studies. Mr. Worgan frequently entertained him with the harpsichord. Charles was greatly taken with his bold full manner of playing, and seemed even then to catch a spark of his fire.

At our return to Bristol we left him to ramble on till he was near six; then we gave him Mr. Rooke for a master; a man of no name, but very good-natured, who let him run on *ad libitum*, whilst he sat by, more to observe than to control him.

Mr. Rogers, the oldest organist in Bristol, was one of his first friends. He often sat him on his knee, and made him play to him, declaring he was more delighted in hearing him than himself."

What follows contains the strongest and fullest approbation of Mr. Charles Wesley's manner of playing on the organ by the most eminent professors; to which commendation they who have the pleasure of hearing him at present will give the most ample credit.

I re-

I received the following account of his ſon SAMUEL from the Rev. Mr. CHARLES WESLEY.

Samuel was born on St. Matthias's Day, Feb. 24, 1766, (the ſame day which gave birth to Handel 82 years before). The ſeeds of harmony did not ſpring up in him quite ſo early as in his brother; for he was three years old before he aimed at a tune[c]: his firſt were "GOD ſave great George our King," Fiſcher's minuet, and ſuch like; moſtly picked up from the ſtreet organs. He did not put a true baſs to them, till he had learnt his notes.

While his brother was playing he uſed to ſtand by, with his childiſh fiddle, ſcraping and beating time. One obſerving him, aſked me, "And what ſhall this boy do?" I anſwered, "Mend "his brother's pens." He did not reſent the affront as deeply as Marcello; ſo it was not indignation which made him a muſician[d].

Mr. Arnold was the firſt, who, hearing him at the harpſichord, ſaid, "I ſet down Sam for one of my family." But we did not much regard him, coming after Charles. The firſt thing which drew our attention was, the great delight he took in hearing his

[c] His mother, Mrs. Weſley, however, hath given me the following moſt convincing proof that he played a tune when he was but two years eleven months old, by producing a quarter guinea, which was given to him by Mr. Addy, for this extraordinary feat, wrapped in a piece of paper, containing the day and year of the gift, as well as the occaſion of it. Mrs. Weſley had alſo an elder ſon, who died in his infancy, and who both ſung a tune, and beat time, when he was but twelve months old.

[d] This alludes to a well-known ſtory in the muſical world. Marcello, the celebrated compoſer, had an elder brother, who had greatly diſtinguiſhed himſelf in this ſcience, and being aſked what ſhould be done with little Marcello, he anſwered, let him *mend my pens*; which piqued the boy ſo much, that he determined to exceed his elder brother.

brother play. Whenever Mr. Kelway came to teach him, Sam constantly attended, and accompanied Charles *on the chair*. Undaunted by Mr. Kelway's frown, he went on; and when he did not *see the harpsichord* * he crossed his hands on the chair, as the other on the instrument, without ever missing a time.

He was so excessive fond of Scarlatti, that if Charles ever began playing his lesson before Sam was called, he would cry and roar as if he had been beat. Mr. Madan, his Godfather, finding him one day so belabouring the chair, told him, "He should have a "better instrument by and by."

I have since recollected Mr. Kelway's words. "It is of the ut- "most importance to a learner *to hear the best music*." And, "If "any man would learn to play well, let him hear Charles." Sam had this double advantage from his birth. As his brother employed the evenings in Handel's Oratorios, Sam was always at his elbow, listening and joining with his voice. Nay, he would sometimes presume to find fault with his playing when we thought he could know nothing of the matter.

He was between four and five years old when he got hold of the oratorio of Samson, and by that alone taught himself to read words, soon after he taught himself to write. From this time he sprung up like a mushroom, and when turned of five could read

* Incredible as this may appear, it is attested by the whole family; and that he generally turned his back to his brother whilst he was playing. I think however that this extraordinary fact may be thus accounted for. There are some passages in Scarlatti's lessons which require the crossing of hands (or playing the treble with the left, and the base with the right) but as what calls for this unusual fingering produces a very singular effect, the child must have felt, that these parts of the composition could not be executed in any other way. It is possible indeed that he might have observed his brother crossing hands at these passages, and imitated him by recollecting that they were thus fingered.

perfectly

perfectly well; and had all the airs, recitatives, and choruſes of Samſon and the Meſſiah, both words and notes, by heart.

Whenever he heard his brother begin to play, he would tell us whoſe muſic it was, (whether Handel, Corelli, Scarlatti, or any other) and what part of what leſſon, ſonata, or overture.

Before he could write he compoſed much muſic. His cuſtom was, to lay the words of an oratorio before him, and ſing them all over. Thus he ſet (extempore for the moſt part) Ruth, Gideon, Manaſſes, and the Death of Abel. We obſerved, when he repeated the ſame words, it was always to the ſame tunes. The airs of Ruth in particular he made before he was ſix years old, laid them up in his memory till he was eight, and then wrote them down.

I have ſeen him open his prayer-book, and ſing the Te Deum, or an anthem from ſome Pſalm, to his own muſic, accompanying it with the harpſichord. This he often did, after he had learnt to play by note, which Mr. Williams, a young organiſt of Briſtol, taught him between ſix and ſeven.

How and when he learnt counter-point I can hardly tell; but without being ever taught it, he ſoon wrote in parts.

He was full eight years old when Dr. Boyce came to ſee us; and accoſted me with, "Sir, I hear you have got an Engliſh "Mozart in your houſe: young Linley tells me wonderful things "of him" I called Sam to anſwer for himſelf. He had by this time ſcrawled down his Oratorio of Ruth. The doctor looked over it very carefully, and ſeemed highly pleaſed with the performance. Some of his words were, "Theſe airs are ſome of the pretticſt I "have ſeen: this boy writes by nature as true a baſe as I can by "rule and ſtudy. There is no man in England has two ſuch "ſons, &c." He bad us let him run on *ad libitum*, without any check of rules or maſters.

After this, whenever the Doctor visited us, Sam ran to him, with his Song, Sonata, or Anthem; and the Doctor examined them with astonishing patience and delight.

As soon as Sam had quite finished his Oratorio he sent it as a present to the Doctor, who immediately honoured him with the following note:

"To Mr Samuel Wesley.

"Dr. Boyce's compliments and thanks to his very ingenious "brother-composer Mr S W ; and is very much pleased and "obliged by the possession of the Oratorio of Ruth, which he "shall preserve with the utmost care, as the most curious product "of his musical library."

For the year that Sam continued under Mr. Williams, it was hard to say which was the master and which the scholar. Sam chose what music he would learn, and often broke out into extemporary playing, his master wisely letting him do as he pleased.

During this time he taught himself the violin ; a soldier assisted him about six weeks ; and some time after Mr. Kinsbury gave him twenty lessons. His favourite instrument was the organ.

He spent a month at Bath, while we were in Wales ; served the abbey on Sundays, gave them several voluntaries, and played the first fiddle in many private concerts.

He returned with us to London greatly improved in his playing. There I allowed him a month for learning all Handel's Overtures. He played them over to me in three days Handel's Concertos he learnt with equal ease ; and some of his Lessons, and Scarlatti's. Like Charles, he mastered the hardest music without any pains or difficulty.

He borrowed his Ruth to tranfcribe for Mr Madan. Parts of it he played at Lord D's, who rewarded him with fome of Handel's Oratorios.

Mr. Madan now began carrying him about to his mufical friends. He played feveral times at Mr. W's, to many of the nobility, and fome eminent mafters and judges of mufic. They gave him fubjects and mufic which he had never feen. Mr. Burton, Mr. Bates, &c. expreffed their approbation in the ftrongeft terms. His extemporary fugues, they faid, were juft and regular, but could not believe that he knew nothing of the rules of compofition.

Several companies he entertained for hours together with his own mufic. The learned were quite aftonifhed. Sir J H cried out, " Infpiration ! Infpiration !" Dr. C. candidly acknowledged, " He has got that which we are fearching after," although at firft, out of pure good-nature, he refufed to give him a fubject. An old mufical gentleman, hearing him, could not refrain from tears.

Dr. B. was greatly pleafed with his extemporary play, and his purfuing the fubjects and fugues which he gave him ; but infifted, like the reft that he muft have been taught the rules.

Mr. S. and Mr. B. expreffed the fame furprize and fatisfaction. An organift gave him a fonata he had juft written, not eafy, nor very legible. Sam played it with great readinefs and propriety, and better (as the compofer owned to Mr. Madan) than he could himfelf.

Lord B. Lord A. Lord D. Sir W W. and other lovers of Handel, were highly delighted with him, and encouraged him to hold faft his veneration for Handel, and the old mufic. But old or new was all one to Sam, fo it was but good. Whatever was prefented he played at fight, and made variations on any tune :

and

and as often as he played it again made new variations. He imitated every author's ſtile, whether Bach, Handel, Schobert, or Scarlatti himſelf.

One ſhewed him ſome of Mozart's muſic, and aſked him how he liked it. He played it over, and ſaid, "It was very well for "one of his years."

He played to Mr. Kelway, whom I afterwards aſked what he thought of him. He would not allow him to be comparable to Charles; yet commended him greatly, and told his mother, "It was a gift from heaven to both her ſons; and as for "Sam, he never in his life ſaw ſo free and degagé a gentleman." Mr. Madan had often ſaid the ſame, "that Sam was every where "as much admired for his behaviour as for his play."

Between eight and nine he was brought through the ſmall-pox by Mr. Br—'s aſſiſtance; whom he therefore promiſed to reward with his next Oratorio.

If he loved any thing better than muſic, it was regularity. He took to it himſelf. Nothing could exceed his punctuality. No company, no perſuaſion, could keep him up beyond his time. He never could be prevailed on to hear any opera or concert by night. The moment the clock gave warning for eight, away ran Sam, in the midſt of his moſt favourite muſic. Once in the playhouſe he roſe up after the firſt part of the Meſſiah, with, "Come, Mamma, "let us go home, or I ſhan't be in bed by eight."

When ſome talked of carrying him to the Queen, and I aſked him if he was willing to go? "Yes, with all my heart (he an-"ſwered), but I won't ſtay beyond eight."

The praiſes beſtowed ſo laviſhly upon him did not ſeem to affect, much leſs to hurt him; and whenever he went into the company of his betters, he would much rather have ſtayed at home; yet when among them, he was free and eaſy; ſo that ſome remarked,

remarked, "be behaved as one bred up at court, yet without a "courtier's ſervility."

On our coming to town this laſt time, he ſent Dr. Boyce the laſt anthem he had made. The Doctor thought, from its correctneſs, that Charles muſt have helped him in it; but Charles aſſured him that he never aſſiſted him, otherwiſe than by telling him, if he aſked, whether ſuch or ſuch a paſſage were good harmony; and the Doctor was ſo ſcrupulous, that when Charles ſhewed him an improper note he would not ſuffer it to be altered.

Mr. Madan now carried him to more of the firſt maſters. Mr. Abel wrote him a ſubject, and declared, "Not three maſters in "town could have anſwered it ſo well."

Mr. Cramer took a great liking to him, offered to teach him the violin, and played ſome Trios with Charles and him. He ſent a man to take meaſure of him for a fiddle; and is confident a very few leſſons would ſet him up for a violiniſt.

Sam often played the ſecond, and ſometimes the firſt, fiddle, with Mr. Treadway, who declared "Giardini himſelf could not "play with greater exactneſs."

Mr. Madan brought Dr. N. to my houſe, who could not believe that a boy could write an oratorio, play at ſight, and purſue any given ſubject. He brought two of the King's boys, who ſang over ſeveral ſongs and choruſes in Ruth. Then he produced two bars of a fugue. Sam worked this fugue very readily and well, adding a movement of his own; and then a voluntary on the organ, which quite removed the Doctor's incredulity.

At the Rehearſal at St. Paul's Dr. Boyce met *his brother* Sam; and ſhewing him to Dr. H. told him: "This boy will ſoon ſur"paſs you all" Shortly after he came to ſee us, took up a Jubilate which Sam had lately wrote, and commended it as one of Charles's; when we told him whoſe it was, he declared he

 could

could find no fault in it; adding, "There was not another boy "upon earth who could have composed this;" and concluding with, "I never yet met with that person who owes so much to "nature as Sam. He is come among us dropt down from "heaven."

Ore puer, puerique habitu, sed corde sagaci,
Æquabat senium.

SILIUS ITALICUS, L. VIII.

I first had an opportunity of being witness of Master Samuel Wesley's great musical talents at the latter end of 1775, when he was nearly ten years old.

To speak of him first as a performer on the harpsichord, he was then able to execute the most difficult lessons for the instrument at sight, for his fingers never wanted the guidance of the eye in the most rapid and desultory passages. But he not only did ample justice to the composition in neatness and precision, but entered into its true taste, which may be easily believed by the numbers who have heard him play extemporary lessons in the stile of most of the eminent masters.

He not only executed crabbed compositions thus at sight, but was equally ready to transpose into any keys, even a fourth [f]; and if it was a Sonata for two trebles and a base, the part of the

[f] Most musicians, when they transpose, conceive the succession of notes to be written in a cleff in which they have been used to practice, as the base cleff, tenor cleff, &c. but the transposition of a 4th belongs to no cleff, except that which the Italians term the *Mezzo Soprano*, or an intermediate cleff, between the treble and counter tenor, and which, not being ever marked in our compositions, cannot be fancied by an English performer when he is obliged to transpose a fourth.

first

first treble being set before him, he would immediately add an extemporary base and second treble to it.

Having happened to mention this readiness in the boy to Bremner (the Printer of music in the Strand), he told me that he had some lessons which were supposed to have been composed for Queen Elizabeth; but which none of the harpsichord masters could execute, and would consequently gravel the young performer. I however desired that he would let me carry one of these compositions to him by way of trial, which I accordingly did, when the boy immediately placed it upon his desk, and was sitting down to play it; but I stopped him, by mentioning the difficuties he would soon encounter, and that therefore he must cast his eye over the music before he made the attempt.

Having done this very rapidly (for he is a devourer of a score, and conceives at once the effect of the different parts), he said that Bremner was in the right, for that there were two or three passages which he could not play at sight, as they were so queer and aukward, but that he had no notion of not trying; and though he boggled at these parts of the lesson, he executed them cleanly at the second practice[g].

I then asked him how he approved of the composition? to which he answered, "*not at all*, though he might differ from a "queen; and that attention had not been paid to some of the "established rules." He then pointed out the particular passages to which he objected, and I stated them to Bremner, who allowed that the boy was right; but that some of the great composers had occasionally taken the same liberties.

[g] Possibly though he succeeded in this attempt, some of the other lessons might have been too difficult, but I had only this single one to lay before him.

The next time I ſaw Maſter Weſley, I mentioned Bremner's defence to what he had blamed; on which he immediately anſwered, "*that when ſuch excellent rules were broken, the compoſer* "*ſhould take care that theſe licenſes produced a good effect*; *whereas* "*theſe paſſages had a very bad one.*" I need not dwell on the great penetration, acuteneſs, and judgement of this anſwer. Lord Mornington, indeed, (who hath ſo deep a knowledge of muſic) hath frequently told me, that he always wiſhed to conſult Maſter Weſley upon any difficulty in compoſition; as he knew no one who gave ſo immediate and ſatisfactory information.

Though he was always willing to play the compoſitions of others, yet for the moſt part he amuſed himſelf with extemporary effuſions of his own moſt extraordinary muſical inſpiration, which unfortunately were totally forgotten in a few minutes; whereas his memory was moſt tenacious of what had been publiſhed by others.

His invention in varying paſſages was inexhauſtible; and I have myſelf heard him give more than fifty variations on a known pleaſing melody, all of which were not only different from each other, but ſhewed excellent taſte and judgement.

This infinite variety probably aroſe from his having played ſo much extempore, in which he gave full ſcope to every flight of his imagination, and produced paſſages which I never heard from any other performer on the harpſichord.

The readineſs of his fingering what was moſt difficult to be executed on the inſtrument, and in the only proper manner, was equal to his muſical fancy; of which I will mention the following proof.

Since the comic Italian operas have been performed in England, there is frequently a paſſage in the baſe, which conſiſts of a ſingle note,

note, to be perhaps repeated for two or three bars, at quick and equal intervals, and which cannot be effected on the harpſichord by one finger, as any common muſician would attempt to do, but requires a change of two.

I laid an opera ſong before Maſter Weſley with ſuch a paſſage, and happening to be at the other end of the room when he came to this part of the compoſition, I knew from the execution, that he muſt haue made uſe of ſuch a change of two fingers, the neceſſity of which that eminent profeſſor of muſic Dr. Burney had ſhewn me. On this I aſked him from whom he had learnt this method of fingering; to which his anſwer was, "*from no-*" *one; but that it was impoſſible to play the paſſage with the proper*" *effect in any other manner.*"

In his extemporary compoſitions he frequently hazarded bold and uncommon modulations; ſo that I have ſeen that moſt excellent muſician Mr. Charles Weſley (his elder brother [h]) tremble for him Sam however always extricated himſelf from the difficulties in which he appeared to be involved, in the moſt maſterly manner, being always poſſeſſed of that ſerene confidence which a thorough knowledge inſpires, though ſurrounded by muſical profeſſors, who could not deem it arrogance.

And here I will give a proof of the goodneſs of his heart, and delicacy of his feelings:

I had deſired him to compoſe an eaſy melody in the minor third,

[h] Mr. Charles Weſley hath compoſed ſome ſingular peices for two organs, which would have great merit if performed by others, but have ſtill more ſo when executed by the two brothers, as they are ſo well acquainted with each other's manner of playing, and are ſo amazingly accurate in the preciſion of their time. Such as have heard the two *Pla's* in duets for the hautbois may well conceive the effect of theſe compoſitions from the Weſley's.

for

for an experiment on little Crotch [1], and that he would go with me to hear what that very extraordinary child was capable of. Crotch was not in good humour, and Master Wesley submitted, amongst other things, to play upon a crack'd violin, in order to please him; the company however having found out who he was, pressed him very much to play upon the organ, which Sam constantly declined. As this was contrary to his usual readiness in obliging any person who had curiosity to hear him, I asked him afterwards what might be the occasion of his refusal; when he told me, "*that he thought it would look like wishing to shine at little* "*Crotch's expence.*"

Every one knows, that any material alteration in the construction of an organ, which varies the position of certain notes, must, at first, embarrass the player, though a most expert one. I carried Sam, however, to the Temple organ, which hath quarter notes, with the management of which he was as ready, as if he had made use of such an instrument all his life. I need scarcely say how much more difficult it must be to play passages which must be executed, not by the fingers, but the feet. Now the organ at the Savoy hath a compleat octave of *pedals*, with the half-notes; on which part Sam appeared as little a novice as if he had been accustomed to it for years. Nay, he made a very good and regular shake on the pedals, *by way of experiment*, for he had too much taste and judgement to suppose that it would have a good effect

He was able to sing at sight (which commonly requires so much instruction with those even who are of a musical disposition) from the time of first knowing his notes; his voice was by no means strong, and it cannot yet be pronounced how it may turn

[1] An account of the success of this experiment will be given in what I shall hereafter say about that other musical prodigy.

I out;

out; his more favourite ſongs were thoſe of Handel, compoſed for a baſe voice, as "*Honour and Arms*[k]," &c.

He hath lately practiſed much upon the violin, on which he bids fair for being a moſt capital performer. Happening one day to find him thus employed, I aſked him how long he had played that morning; his anſwer was, "Three or four hours; which "Giardini had found neceſſary."

The delicacy of his ear is likewiſe very remarkable, of which I ſhall give an inſtance or two:

Having been at Bach's concert, he was much ſatisfied both with the compoſitions and performers; but ſaid, "*The muſical* "*pieces were ill arranged*[l], *as four had been played ſucceſſively* "*which were all in the ſame key.*"

He was deſired to compoſe a march for one of the regiments of guards; which he did to the approbation of all who ever heard it, and a diſtinguiſhed officer of the royal navy declared, that it was a movement which would probably inſpire ſteady and ſerene courage, when the enemy was approaching.

As I thought the boy would like to hear this march performed, I carried him to the parade at the proper time, when it had the honour of beginning the military concert. The piece being finiſhed, I aſked him whether it was executed to his ſatisfaction? to which he replied, "*by no means*;" and I then immediately introduced him to the band (which conſiſted of very tall and ſtout muſicians), that he might ſet them right. On this Sam immediately told them, "*That they had not done juſtice to his com-* "*poſition.*" To which they anſwered the urchin with both aſtoniſhment and contempt, by "*Your compoſition!*" Sam, how-

k Having heard him ſing, "Return, O God of Hoſts!" and an Italian air, ſince this ſheet was in the preſs, I can now venture to pronounce, that his voice is a pleaſing counter-tenor, and that his manner is excellent. Without any practice alſo he hath acquired an even and brilliant ſhake.

l It is ſuppoſed that this was a mere accident in the perſon who made out the muſical bill of fare.

ever,

ever, replied, with great ſerenity, "*Yes, my compoſition!*" which I confirmed. They then ſtared, and ſeverally made their excuſes, by proteſting, that they had copied accurately from the manuſcript which had been put into their hands. This he moſt readily allowed to the hautbois and baſoons, but ſaid it was the French Horns who were in fault; who making the ſame defence, he inſiſted upon the original ſcore being produced, and ſhewing them their miſtake, ordered the march to be play'd again, which they ſubmitted to with as much deference as they would have ſhewn to Handel.

This concert of wind inſtruments begins on the parade at about five minutes after nine, and ends at five minutes after ten, when the guard proceeds to St. James's.

I ſtayed with him till this time; and aſked him what he thought of the concluding movement, which he ſaid deſerved commendation; but that it was very injudicious to make it the finiſhing piece, becauſe, as it muſt neceſſarily continue till the clock of the Horſe-guards had ſtruck ten, it ſhould have been recollected that the tone of the clock did not correſpond with the key note of the march.

I ſhall now attempt to give ſome account of this moſt extraordinary boy conſidered as a compoſer, and firſt of his extemporary flights.

If left to himſelf when he played on the organ, there were oftener traces of Handel's ſtile than any other maſter, and if on the harpſichord, of Scarlatti; at other times however his voluntaries were original and ſingular.

After he had ſeen or heard a few pieces [m] of any compoſer, he was fully poſſeſſed of his peculiarities, which, if at all ſtriking,

[m] I aſked him once to imitate Lord Kelly's ſtile, which he declined, as he had never heard any compoſition of his Lordſhip's, except the Overture to the Maid of the Mill, which he highly approved of, however, for its brilliancy and boldneſs.

he

he could inſtantly imitate at the word of command, as well as the general flow and turn of the compoſition. Thus I have heard him frequently play extemporary leſſons, which, without prejudice to their muſical names, might have been ſuppoſed to have been thoſe of Abel, Vento, Schobert, and Bach [1].

But he not only entered into the ſtile of the harpſichord-maſters, but that of ſolo players on other inſtruments.

I once happened to ſee ſome muſic wet upon his deſk, which he told me was a ſolo for a trumpet. I then aſked him if he had heard Fiſcher on the hautboy, and would compoſe an extemporary ſolo, proper for him to execute. To this Sam readily aſſented, but found his little legs too ſhort for reaching the ſwell of the organ, without which the imitation could not have its effect. I then propoſed to touch the ſwell myſelf, on his giving me the proper ſignals; but to this he anſwered, "*That I could neither do "this ſo inſtantaneouſly as was requiſite, nor ſhould I give the greater "or leſs force of the ſwell (if a note was dwelt upon) which "would correſpond with his feelings.*" Having ſtarted this difficulty, however, he ſoon ſuggeſted the remedy, which was the following:

He ſtood upon the ground with his left foot, whilſt his right reſted upon the ſwell, and thus literally played an extemporary ſolo,

"Stans pede in uno;"

the three movements of which muſt have laſted not leſs than ten minutes; and every bar of which Fiſcher might have acknowledged as his own. Every one who hath heard that capital muſician muſt have obſerved a great ſingularity in his cadences, in the imitation of which Sam ſucceeded as perfectly as in the

[1] He would as readily compoſe a ſong proper for the ſerious or comic opera the inſtant it was requeſted, particularly the airs of Handel for a baſe voice.

other parts of the compofition. After this I have been prefent when he hath executed thirty or forty different folo's for the fame inftrument, totally almoft varied the one from the other, to the aftonifhment of feveral audiences, and particularly fo to that eminent performer on the hautboy Mr. Simpfon.

Having found that the greater part of thofe who heard him would not believe but that his voluntaries had been practifed before, I always endeavoured that fome perfon prefent (and more particularly fo if he was a profeffor) fhould give him the fubject upon which he was to work, which always afforded the convincing and irrefragable proof, as he then compofed upon the ideas fuggefted by others, to which ordeal it is believed few muficians in Europe would fubmit. The more difficult the fubject (as if it was two or three bars of the beginning of a fugue), the more chearfully he undertook it, as he always knew he was equal to the attempt, be it never fo arduous

I once carried that able compofer Mr. Chriftopher Smith to the boy, defiring that he would fuggeft the fubject; which Sam not only purfued in a moft mafterly manner, but fell into a movement of the minor third, which might be naturally introduced. When we left Mr. Wefley's houfe, Mr. Smith, after expreffing his amazement, faid that what he had juft heard fhould be a caution to thofe who are apt to tax compofers as plagiaries; for though he had wrote on the fame fubject, and the mufic had never been feen by any one, this wonderful boy had almoft followed him note by note Baumgarten found the fame, upon a like trial, of what he had never communicated to any one.

I can refer only to one printed proof of his abilities as a compofer, which is a fet of eight leffons for the harpfichord, and which appeared in 1777, about the fame time that he became fo

known

known to the muſical world that his portrait was engraved, which is a very ſtrong reſemblance. Some of theſe leſſons have paſſages which are rather too difficult for common performers, and therefore they are not calculated for a general vogue.

His father, the Rev. Mr. Weſley, will permit any one to ſee the ſcore of his Oratorio of Ruth, which he really compoſed at ſix years of age, but did not *write* till he was eight; his quickneſs in thus giving utterance to his muſical ideas is amazingly great; and, notwithſtanding the rapidity, he ſeldom makes a blot or a miſtake.

Numbers of his other compoſitions, and almoſt of all kinds, may be likewiſe examined; particularly an anthem to the following words, which I ſelected for him [m], and which hath been performed at the Chapel Royal, and St. Paul's:

"1 O LORD GOD of Hoſts, how long wilt thou be angry
"at the prayer of thy people?
"2. Turn thee again, O LORD, and we ſhall be ſaved!
"3. For thou art a great GOD, and a great King above all
"gods."

The firſt part of this anthem was compoſed for a ſingle tenor; the ſecond a duet for two boys; and the third a chorus. With regard to the merits, I ſhall refer to that moſt diſtinguiſhed ſinger of cathedral muſic the Rev. Mr. Mence, who hath frequently done it moſt ample juſtice.

[m] In pitching upon theſe words, I attended to a circumſtance which perhaps deſerves ſome conſideration in compoſitions for the voice. The third perſon ſingular in the Engliſh verbs as written, when our tranſlation of the Bible was made, ends with *th*, which cannot be pronounced by many foreigners, nor ſounds well even in the mouth of an Engliſhman. Words with ſuch a termination are not to be found in theſe paſſages, nor is it eaſy to ſelect many ſuch from our verſion of the Pſalms.

As I happen to have by me a little ballad of his compoſition, I ſhall here ſubjoin it, and deprecate the ſeverity of critics with regard to the words, by mentioning that it was written by a child of nine years old [n]. Little Weſley had ſcarcely caſt his eyes over it but he ſat down to his harpſichord, and ſung the following air, which I conceive to have the true melody and ſimplicity proper for a ballad. In this compliance he ſhewed his readineſs to oblige; and I may add, his condeſcenſion, as he would have rather choſen a harder taſk ſhould have been impoſed upon him, if any thing could be difficult to his ſurpriſing verſatility of invention, adapting itſelf inſtantaneouſly to every ſpecies of compoſition.

[n] Maſter Thomas Percy (a nephew of the preſent dean of Carliſle and born Sept. 13th, 1768) who hath written the firſt canto of an Epic Poem, conſiſting of more than 600 lines, the ſubject being the Invaſion of Britain by Julius Cæſar; as alſo the firſt act of a tragedy, founded upon a Peruvian ſtory. In both of theſe there are ſtrong marks of a moſt early genius for poetry, which he likewiſe recites admirably well upon the firſt ſtool you may place him. I aſked this wonderful boy how many books he intended to divide his Epic Poem into; when he anſwered, that he could not well bring all his matter into leſs than twenty-four.

He was carried to the Muſeum at Leiceſter-houſe (being himſelf a virtuoſo) ſoon after which he expreſſed his admiration of what he had ſeen in ſome verſes addreſſed to Sir *Aſhton Lever*, in which he noticed moſt kind of the natural productions in that moſt capital collection. I happen to recollect one of the lines, which may give ſome idea of the other parts of the poem:

" Here crocodiles extend their ſcaly length."

I ſhould rather ſuppoſe, that no other verſes are to be found upon the ſame ſubject; and therefore Maſter Percy, on this occaſion, could not have been aſſiſted by imitation. If it is wiſhed to ſee the whole poem, the Gentleman's Magazine for June, 1779, p. 319, may be conſulted; as alſo the ſame compilation for a paſtoral, written by him, at a ſtill earlier age. See that for April, 1778, p. 183. Both the ſong here inſerted, and the verſes addreſſed to Sir Aſhton Lever, are printed as they were haſtily written. The paſtoral indeed was corrected by Maſter Percy himſelf, before it was publiſhed in the Magazine; for this early genius hath, in ſome inſtances, given a patient reviſal of his little labours.

SONG,

SONG, (written by Master PERCY) Composed by Master WESLEY.

The

II.

The youths with ſickles ſeek the fields,
To gather all that Ceres yields;
The farmer's barns are ſtor'd:
They toſs about the jovial bowl,
While joy enlivens ev'ry ſoul;
The pudding ſmoaks the board.

III.

Each chuſes out his nut-brown fair,
A Lucy or a Lydia there,
To dance away the hours:
Some tune the flute, ſome ſound the reed,
Like ſhepherds on the graſſy mead,
And dreſs 'em up with flowers.

IV.

O may the golden age return,
And men with gen'rous ardour burn,
For ſweet retirement's lot!
O may the Muſes all conſpire,
To light my breaſt with genuine fire,
And fix me in a cot!

SOME

SOME ACCOUNT OF LITTLE CROTCH.

Et mentem ſua non capit ætas.

STATIUS, V. 14.

ANOTHER muſical prodigy hath lately appeared, whoſe name is William Crotch, born at Norwich, on the 5th of July, 1775, of whom Dr. Burney hath given a very full and informing account in the Philoſophical Tranſactions [*], which ſuperſedes the neceſſity of my mentioning many particulars relative to the proofs of early genius, in this moſt remarkable child.

I firſt heard him play on the 10th of December, 1778, when he was nearly three years and a half old; and find that I made the following memorandum on returning home:

"Plays, "*God ſave great George our King*," and "*Minuet de la* "*Cour,*" almoſt throughout with chords, reaches a ſixth with his "little fingers; cries *no*, when I purpoſely introduced a wrong "note; delights in chords and running notes for the baſe; plays for "ten minutes extemporary paſſages, which have a tolerable con"nection with each other; ſeldom looks at the harpſichord, and "yet generally hits the right intervals, though often diſtant from "each other. His organ rather of a hard touch, many of his "paſſages hazarded and ſingular, ſome of which he executes by "his knuckles, tumbling his hands over the keys."

[*] Vol. LXIX. part I. for the year 1779.

At

At the ſame time, I received the following account from the mother, of the firſt appearance of a muſical diſpoſition in the child.

His father is an ingenious carpenter of Norwich, and had made an organ, on which he was capable of playing two or three eaſy tunes, and which had not been uſed for ſome time. When little Crotch was two years and three weeks old, he heard, "God ſave "great George our King," on this inſtrument, after which he was exceſſively fractious, whilſt they were putting him to bed; his mother then conceived, that he wanted to get at the organ, and placing him ſo as to command the keys, the boy immediately ſtruck them, though ſhe did not then diſtinguiſh that he played any particular tune. The next morning however there was no doubt but that he ſucceſsfully attempted, "God ſave great George "our King." After this, the child's muſical fame ſpread quickly through the city of Norwich [b].

The accuracy of this child's ear is ſuch, that he not only pronounces immediately what note is ſtruck, but in what key the muſic is compoſed [c]. I was witneſs of an extraordinary inſtance of

[b] This account differs, in ſome particulars of no great moment, from that given by Dr. Burney in the Philoſophical Tranſactions, which I conceive, however, to be more minutely accurate, as the information which he received depends upon the authority of others, as well as that of the mother. I have not the moſt diſtant ſuſpicion indeed that ſhe wilfully miſſtated a ſingle circumſtance, but all memories are fallible, when we are queſtioned on a ſudden about tranſactions that have happened at ſome diſtance of time.

[c] I have the ſatisfaction of being confirmed by Dr. Burney, with regard to both theſe extraordinary facts; who adds, that the child diſtinguiſhed any particular note, when he was but two years and half old, by laying his finger upon that key of the organ.

As to the latter proof of his moſt exquiſite ear, impoſſible almoſt as it ſeems, yet it muſt neceſſarily follow, that from two or three bars of the comof his being able to name the note touched [d], at Dr. Burney's, who hath a Piano Forte, with ſeveral keys both in the baſe and treble beyond the ſcale in the common inſtruments of the ſame ſort [e].

Upon any of theſe very low or high notes being ſtruck, he diſtinguiſhed them as readily as the intermediate notes of the inſtrument. Now it is well known that the harpſichord tuners do not ſo eaſily manage theſe extremes, as their ears are not uſed to ſuch tones, and more particularly the loweſt notes.

A ſtill more convincing proof perhaps of the ſame kind hath been mentioned to me by maſter Weſley, who takes little Crotch much under his protection. The child hath lately taught himſelf to play on the violin, which he holds as a violincello, and touches only with two of his fingers [f]. Maſter Weſley hath ſometimes miſtuned the inſtrument on purpoſe to excite his anger, which he never fails to expreſs; adding, at the ſame time, whether it ſhould be *higher* or *lower* [g]. He likewiſe

compoſition, he either knows what muſt be the concluding note of the baſe; or otherwiſe he muſt retain in his memory every ſucceſſive note of the three bars, and from thence determine the key. In this experiment, (which I have tried myſelf), I ſuppoſe the three bars not to enter into extraneous modulation; for if they were ſuch, the boy would then name the proper key, though not that of the principal compoſition.

[d] If a chord of four notes is ſtruck, he names them all in ſucceſſion.

[e] Theſe notes are added to give ſufficient room for two performers to ſit down to the ſame inſtrument, and execute duets.

[f] Maſter Weſley heard him when he had taken to the violin for about a fortnight, but I happened to be preſent a few days afterwards, when he had found out the neceſſity of uſing more fingers, as he improved in his execution. Crotch can alſo play on the common flute and *ſticcado Paſtorello*, and deals much in the *rapid runs* which are uſually introduced by thoſe who can amuſe themſelves with that poor inſtrument.

[g] He does not ſay *ſharper* or *flatter*.

judges moſt accurately of what are called *extremes* [h] on the violin, which ſeems to be ſtill more aſtoniſhing, as the child hath ſcarcely ever heard any other inſtrument but the organ, which is defective in theſe quarter-tones. In other words, it ſeems to prove, that Crotch's ear is ſo very exquiſite as to diſtinguiſh quarter tones, whilſt the notes of the organ are only ſubdivided into half-tones; all of which are to a certain degree imperfect, and the ability of the tuner is ſhewn by diſtributing this defect, as equally as poſſible, amongſt them all. Surely therefore this great refinement may be pronounced to have been almoſt innate in the child; for though perhaps he might have heard a Norwich fiddler, yet it is highly improbable that ſuch performer ſhould have ſtopped with this great preciſion.

Dr. Burney indeed mentions, that Crotch was preſent at a concert in London where Pachierotti ſung, and where undoubtedly there might be ſome able muſicians.

I once happened to be preſent when he was playing a well-known air, called *Minuet de la Cour*, in the greater third and key of A, which he afterwards repeated in that of B. Obſerving this readineſs in the child to tranſpoſe, I deſired him to try it in C; which he not only complied with, but proceeded regularly through the whole octave, whilſt he ſometimes looked back with great archneſs upon me, inquiring whether I knew in what key he was then playing; and having anſwered him once or twice wrong on purpoſe, he triumphed much in ſetting me right.

[h] Theſe notes are marked in ſome compoſitions for violins with a double ſharp; and to exemplify, when F ſharp occurs, in the greater third and key of E, it ſhould be ſtopped by the performer perhaps nearly a quarter of a note more ſharp than it is upon the harpſichord, or approaching to an intermediate quarter tone between F ſharp and G natural. Fiſcher executes ſuch quarter tones with great preciſion on the hautbois.

I muſt

I muſt acknowledge alſo, that at laſt he really puzzled me, for he concluded by a tranſpoſition into the key of F ſharp, which is never uſed by Engliſh compoſers, and which I was not able to name on his word of command, not having attended to the laſt note of his baſe.

I need ſcarely ſay, that I left the room after this in great aſtoniſhment; and it then occurred, that it might be right to make an experiment, whether he would be equally ready to tranſpoſe in the minor third, in which probably the child had never heard any compoſition whatſoever, it being ſo ſeldom uſed in the preſent times[1].

I then communicated what I had been witneſs of to Maſter Weſley, deſiring that he would write down a ſimple melody of a few bars in the minor third; which he imediately complied with, and went with me to little Crotch, in order to aſſiſt in the experiment.

I was in great hopes that the child would catch this little air, after Maſter Weſley had repeated it five or ſix times; but in this I was diſappointed; for little Crotch happened not to be in humour, though we endeavoured much to coax him to the organ. Having obſerved however that he would ſometimes play from pique, when intreaties had no effect, I deſired Maſter Weſley to give the treble only, and told Crotch that he could not add the baſe to it. On this the urchin ſat down by Maſter Weſley, accompanying with the proper baſe this ſame tune, tranſpoſed in the minor third through the whole octave.

[1] This probably ariſes from the greater brilliancy occaſioned by the open notes on the violin, which occur more frequently in the major than minor third.

When he had finiſhed, Maſter Weſley had a curioſity to try um in tranſpoſing through the octave in the major third; which Crotch inſtantly did, and in a manner too peculiar not to be fully ſtated.

The tune pitched upon for trying this experiment a ſecond time was, as before, *the Minuet de la Cour*; but Crotch conceiving at once what Maſter Weſley wiſhed to be a witneſs of, only played three or four bars of the firſt part, and then inſtantly changed the key throughout the octave.

I ſhall here inſert one of Crotch's *Voluntaries*, which was taken down whilſt he was playing it. I told the child that it ſhould be publiſhed as *Crotch's* compoſition; on which he wiſhed to be ſtiled *Doctor*, which title it ſeems Dr. Randal of Cambridge, and muſical profeſſor there, had given the boy. The exact notes of this extemporary flight are here given, though the third bar may be deemed contrary to the eſtabliſhed rules of muſical compoſition.

The

The child both looks[k] and is very intelligent in other matters, which do not relate to mufic, and draws in a bold mafterly way with chalk on the floor. One of his moft favourite objects to reprefent is a violin, which he forms inftantaneoufly with a few ftrokes; I need fcarcely mention the difficulty of reverfing the two fides, and S's, which muft be very obvious to penmen, as well as painters. The boy likewife fucceeds very well in the hafty outline of a fhip. He is generally good humoured, though fo often teazed to play, which he readily complies with for the moft part, if a child of the fame age is not in the room, whofe company he is not pleafed with, perhaps apprehending that he will be fet down to his organ, a property of which he feems to be extremely jealous[l].

The prefent Earl of Mornington[m] furnifhes an inftance of a ftill earlier attention to mufical inftruments.

His father played well (for a gentleman) on the violin, which always delighted the child whilft in his nurfe's arms, and long

[k] Crotch had now been vifited by moft of the mufical people in London, and his portrait was engraved; but the refemblance is by no means a good one.

[l] As I have mentioned fo many other proofs of early genius in children, I here cannot pafs unnoticed Mafter Lawrence, fon of an inn-keeper at the Devifes in Wiltfhire.

This boy is now [viz February, 1780] nearly ten years and a half old; but at the age of nine, without the moft diftant inftruction from any one, he was capable of copying hiftorical pictures in a mafterly ftile, and alfo fucceeded amazingly in compofitions of his own, particularly that of Peter denying CHRIST. In about feven minutes he fcarcely ever failed of drawing a ftrong likenefs of any perfon prefent, which had generally much freedom and grace, if the fubject permitted. He is likewife an excellent reader of blank verfe, and will immediately convince any one, that he both underftands and feels the ftriking paffages of Milton or Shakefpeare.

[m] Well known to the mufical world, for his great abilities as a compofer.

before he could ſpeak. Nor did this proceed merely from a love, common to other children, of a ſprightly noiſe; as may appear by the following proof. Dubourg, who was thirty years ago a diſtinguiſhed performer on that inſtrument[n], happened to be at the family ſeat[o]; but the child would not permit him to take the violin from his father till his little hands were held; after having heard Dubourg however the caſe was altered, and there was then much more difficulty to perſuade him to let Dubourg give the inſtrument back to his father. Nor would the infant ever afterwards permit the father to play, whilſt Dubourg was in the houſe.

At the ſame period he beat time to all meaſures of muſic, however difficult; nor was it poſſible to force him to do otherwiſe, the moſt rapid changes producing as rapid an alteration in the child's hands.

Though paſſionately fond of muſic, from indolence he never attempted to play on any inſtrument till he was nine years old. At that time an old portrait painter came to the family ſeat, who was a very indifferent performer on the violin, but perſuaded the child that if he tried to play on that inſtrument, he would ſoon be able to bear a part in a concert.

With this inducement he ſoon learned the two old catches of the *Chriſt Church Bells*, and *Sing one, two, three, come follow me*; after which his father and the painter accompanying him with the two other parts, he experienced the pleaſing effects of a harmony to which he himſelf contributed.

Soon after this he was able to play the ſecond violin in Corelli's Sonatas, which gave him a ſteadineſs in time that

[n] He was alſo a diſtinguiſhed muſician when very young, and played a ſolo, on a joint-ſtool, at the famous concert of Tom Briton the ſmall-coal man. Sir John Hawkins's Hiſtory of Muſic, vol. V. p. 76.

[o] Dangan, in the county of Meath.

never deſerted him. For the next muſical ſtage he commenced compoſer, from emulation of the applauſe given to a country-dance made by a neighbouring clergyman. He accordingly ſet to work, and by playing the treble on the violin, whilſt he ſung a baſe to it, he formed a minuet, the baſe of which he wrote in the treble cleff [p], and was very profuſe of his fifths and octaves, being totally ignorant of the eſtabliſhed rules of compoſition [q].

This minuet was followed by a duet for two French horns, whilſt the piece concluded by an *Andante* movement, thus conſiſting of three parts, all of which being tacked together, he ſtiled a ſerenata. At this time he had never heard any muſic, but from his father, ſiſters, and the old painter.

He ſtuck to the violin till he was fourteen; but had always a ſtrong inclination to the harpſichord; from which his ſiſters drove him continually, ſaying that he ſpoiled the inſtrument, notwithſtanding which he ſometimes ſtole intervals of practice.

About this time the late Lord Mornington declared his intention of having an organ for his chapel, telling his ſon, that he ſhould have been the organiſt, had he been able to play on the inſtrument. On this the ſon undertook to be ready as ſoon as the organ could be finiſhed; which being accompliſhed in leſs than a year and a half, he ſat down at the maker's, played an extemporary fugue, to the aſtoniſhment of the father, as well as others, who did not conceive that he could have executed a ſingle bar of any tune.

It is well known that this inſtrument is more likely to form a compoſer than any other, and his lordſhip, in proceſs of time,

[p] Having only played in this cleff on the violin.

[q] Which forbid two fifths or two octaves to follow each other in the ſame direction, the ear being glutted with ſuch perfect conſonances in ſucceſſion.

both read and ſtudied muſic, whilſt he at the ſame time committed his ideas to writing. As he had however never received the leaſt inſtruction in this abſtruſe, though pleaſing ſcience, he wiſhed to conſult both Roſengrave and Geminiani, who, on examining his compoſitions, told him they could not be of the leaſt ſervice to him, as he had himſelf inveſtigated all the eſtabliſhed rules, with their proper exceptions

Though ſimple melodies commonly pleaſe moſt in the earlier ſtages of life, he had always a ſtrong predilection for church muſic, and full harmony, as alſo for the minor third, in which for that reaſon he made his firſt compoſition.

In proceſs of time his lordſhip was ſo diſtinguiſhed for his muſical abilities, that the univerſity of Dublin conferred upon him the degree of Doctor and Profeſſor of muſic.

I have happened to ſtumble upon two other inſtances of children, ſhewing a moſt early diſpoſition to muſic.

In Dodſley's Regiſter for the year 1763 there is an account from Brookefield in North America, of a boy, who, at the age of twenty-two months, ſung the treble to one of Dr. Watts's hymns, whilſt accompanied by a baſe voice; and at three years and a half the ſame child would ſing twenty different tunes, by rules commonly uſed for teaching [r]. The compiler alſo mentions a clergyman's ſon in London, who, at five years of age, could execute difficult leſſons on the harpſichord, after they had been once played over to him.

Many have wiſhed that theſe early geniuſes might be left to themſelves, in order perhaps to produce a better ſtile of muſic than we are poſſeſſed of at preſent; a conceit which Dr. Burney hath moſt ably refuted. I could almoſt wiſh however, that little

[r] He was the ſon of Thomas Banniſter of that place.

Crotch, who hath not only heard, but can execute, ſeveral tunes, ſhould be brought up in a village, where there was neither muſician nor ring of bells. For though probably his muſic would not be abſolutely wild; he might perhaps hazard ſome moſt ſingular paſſages, which might have an amazing effect, when properly introduced by an able compoſer.

It may now perhaps not be improper to make ſome compariſon between the impreſſions made upon us by muſical notes, and words, during our infancy.

And here it will firſt appear, that the muſical connexion is much the ſtronger; for no child can at once repeat a ſhort ſtory, or even ſentence; but we find that a tune is immediately executed by them, both by their own voices, and on inſtruments.

At firſt it may be ſuppoſed, that this ariſes from the nurſe ſinging to the child; but this cannot be the cauſe, for they generally give over their *lullabies* when the infant is ſix months old, nor is one nurſe in twenty capable of ſinging a tune throughout. How few children alſo are able to do this, even after they are grown up, and have had ſo many better ſubjects to imitate!

But perhaps it may be urged, that though the nurſe is not muſical, the parents may be ſo. To which I anſwer, that I have known ſeveral inſtances where both the father and mother have been bleſſed with a love of muſic, yet many of the children have not ſhewn the leaſt diſpoſition of the ſame kind.

I know very well, that many conceive they have a taſte or ear for muſic; but whether they have or not is inſtantly diſcovered, if they attempt to hum an air. I would not by this intimate, that it is incumbent upon every perſon to have a good voice; but they who have a muſical ear will never ſing conſiderably out of tune, though their tone, or organs of voice, may be never ſo indifferent.

Another criterion, (though perhaps not so irrefragable as the preceding) is the being able to beat time, which the greater part of grown people cannot do even to a minuet, where it is more marked than in any other measure, and therefore perhaps is more generally applauded than any other musical movement. We find that Lord Mornington was capable of this, before he could speak, though perhaps no grown person can explain, whence, without either *beating* or *counting*, he is always sensible when the musical bar commences.

I will not apologize for stating these criteria of a musical ear, because, if the pupil is not capable of both, I should conceive, that the time and expence of his being instructed are thrown away, and that the supposed fondness for music may be rather considered as a love of noise.

I do not pretend however to assert, that there never hath been an instance of a musical taste being acquired by those who are advanced in life; though I rather believe that the examples are rare.

But the connexions of musical sounds not only seem to make an earlier, but a more lasting impression on us than what we hear by the medium of words, as we retain the melody when every verse and line of the ballad is lost, which hath been learnt in our nurseries. I have found this to be the case with most persons whom I have interrogated on this subject, provided they had ever been masters of the tune throughout, when a bar or two, in any part, would immediately recall the whole to their memory.

The late Lord Bathurst mentioned to me once a very strong proof of this.

As his Lordship had much frequented the opera in the time of Queen Anne, Frederick prince of Wales wanted him to

4 sing

sing a favourite air of Nicolini [s], which he could not at that instant recollect, as it had been performed not less than 40 years before.

Some time afterwards his Lordship dreamed that Nicolini sung part of the air to him, and when he awoke he remembered the whole song, repeating it from hour to hour till he had waited on his royal highness, before it had escaped his memory.

In another opera of the same reign Nicolini performed the part of Theseus. His lordship told me, that this famous singer had a particular pleasure in beating the minotaur very soundly, and that the man who represented the monster might submit more chearfully to this drubbing, Nicolini always gave him a crown. As the singer chose however to have his pennyworth out of the minotaur, he generally thrashed him so heartily as to lose his own breath, which was often inconvenient, as a song of triumph was to ensue over the prostrate foe.

I took the liberty to desire his Lordship to give me an idea of this air, when he immediately sung it throughout, and imitated at the same time the catches of breath in Nicolini, from these extraordinary exertions. Lord Bathurst was at this time eighty-seven, to the best of my recollection, and therefore affords a strong instance of the musical memory being very perfect, even in that late stage of life. It need scarcely be observed also, that he could not probably have heard this song for more than three-score years [t].

[s] The music of operas was not then published from season to season, as it hath been of late years.

[t] It might indeed have occasionally occurred to him, though he certainly had not heard it performed.

A third proof of the greater connexion between musical sounds and any ideas obtained by the communication of words may be perhaps evidenced by repeating a tune and story of the same length to a child who can both sing and read, when I am confident that a note either omitted or mis-arranged would be more noticed, than the either dropping or misplacing a word in the short narrative.

Strong however and early as the love of music is in many children, yet it must be admitted that this most capital pleasure falls not to the lot of the greater part of mankind, even in any stage of their life.

This may be occasioned in many by a defect in their organs of hearing; but may be in others attributed to the discouragement of parents when the child first attempts to be a musician, and particularly if a boy. I should conceive however that this strong prejudice against musicians arises from observing, that itinerant fidlers are commonly of abandoned morals, whence it is supposed, that those who are stationary, and have had a regular education, deserve perhaps no better a character. This prejudice in many hath taken so deep a root, that the contempt is transferred from the professors to the science itself, whilst they do not recollect that it is honoured with degrees in both our universities, that it constitutes a part of our cathedral service [u], and that it

[u] If it was not for this establishment of choirs in most parts of England, a concert could scarcely be perfo med any where but in the metropolis. I might add perhaps, that music would be almost annihilated in the country, for the harpsichords there are mostly tuned by the organist or singers of the cathedral. Even with this assistance most of these instruments are commonly out of order, from the expence, if the city is at any distance; it is therefore to be wished, that the tuners would attend regularly, at particular towns, upon certain days, from whence the instruments of the neighbourhood might be put in order at no ruinous a price.

 affords

affords a most rational relaxation to those who happen to have a musical disposition.

I am ready to allow however that the greater part of the inhabitants of this country should get their livelihood by more laborious means, with which the practising upon instruments should not too much interfere; but I have frequently been astonished that those who intend to leave ample fortunes to their children, without destining them to any profession, should check this strong impulse of nature, while the fingers are supple, and brilliancy of execution may be acquired. We begin too late if we are to stay till we are own masters.

I have before ventured to call music a rational amusement, but I may almost pronounce it a necessary one in the decline of life, for most eyes begin to fail at 50, whereas the ear commonly continues perfect to a much later period. As all parents therefore wish that their children may attain a good old age, they should not withold from them the

miseris—viatica canis,

which will probably be the consequence of preventing their playing on instruments at an age when alone they can become practical musicians, and thence acquire a taste for the striking effects of harmony.

ON

ON THE DELUGE IN THE TIME OF NOAH.

THERE seem to be the strongest objections to the supposition of an universal deluge; some of which, without mentioning others, may be thus shortly stated.

He must be a more ingenious architect than even Bishop Wilkins[a], who can contrive a single vessel large enough for Noah and his family, the beasts, fowls, reptiles, and insects, of the whole globe, together with provisions for their sustenance, during the space of a twelvemonth[b]; whilst the lives of each animal, in this confined state, must also have continued for that time, otherwise some genus or species must have been intirely destroyed, without a new creation.

If we are to understand likewise the expression literally of ALL, the extirpation of the web-footed fowls would not have followed; nor of the water reptiles and insects.

On the other hand, there must have been a new creation of either the salt or fresh water fish, supposing the fluid which covered the face of the globe to have been either salt or fresh, as the former could not have lived a twelvemonth in water so much freshened, or the latter in an element become so much salter.

[a] See his Works.

[b] No mention is here made of fuel, as well as many other bulky but necessary articles.

How

How could the animals, almoſt peculiar to the arctic circle (a rein-deer for example), or thoſe only found in America at preſent, have been procured for the ark, or inſects in their different metamorphoſes? How was the proper food alſo to be ſupplied for the animals of the whole globe, for a year, when many of them, particularly inſects, only feed upon peculiar plants, which therefore muſt have continued to vegetate in part of the ark deſtined for a conſervatory. The animals again are directed to be male and female; many of which, within the twelvemonth, would have procreated; and from what ſtores on board the ark was this numerous offspring to be ſupported?

The deluge, if univerſal, likewiſe continuing for a twelvemonth, all the annual plants of the globe muſt have been deſtroyed, not to mention both ſhrubs and trees, many of which would have loſt all vegetative power, after they had been covered ſo long by water, either freſh or ſalt.

Having thus briefly ſtated ſome of the principal objections to a general deluge, it may be right to ſuggeſt the beſt anſwer I am able to the only ſuppoſed proof of ſuch an inundation, which confeſſedly carries with it much plauſibility, after which I ſhall endeavour to explain the chapters of the book of Geneſis, which relate to this great event.

It is frequently urged, that ſhells of marine animals are found on the tops of mountains, which could not be conveyed thither by any other method.

The firſt anſwer to this is, that ſuppoſing the whole globe to be covered with water, what could have been the inducement to the ſhell-fiſh (many of which perhaps cannot move) to deſert their proper habitation in the bed of the ſea, in order to tranſport themſelves to the top of an inland mountain, where they muſt immediately ſtarve, for want of their uſual nouriſhment.

The

The next anſwer is, that ſuch foſſils in the cabinets of virtuoſi are often reported by the ſeller to have been found in ſuch places, contrary to the real fact, as the ſpecimen, with many collectors, is, on that account, more valued.

M. le Roy therefore, who was employed to procure timber in the Pyrenees, ſpeaks thus of his fruitleſs ſearches for ſuch foſſils, "Je n'ai appercu aucun coquillage dans les Pyrenees, ſeule- "ment qulques empreintes ſur les pierres, que j'ai toujours crus "formées par des *filtrations*[c]."

"Neither in the Apennines, Alps, Pyrenees, or Grampian "Mountains, nor in thoſe of Aſia, Africa, or America, are ſhells "or marine bodies of any kind to be found[d]."

Moſt foſſiliſts again agree, that the ſhells thus diſcovered do not belong to the ſea fiſh of the neighbouring coaſt, whilſt, for the greater part, no known animal can be pointed out as the inhabitant[e]. The argument is therefore reduced to this, the ſhell bears a general reſemblance to that of ſome cruſtaceous or other fiſh, and conſequently muſt have originally been depoſited at the bottom of the ſea.

Much is in like manner ſaid about impreſſions of ſubterraneous plants, which are frequently attributed to the ſame cauſe of a general deluge; and which commonly bear a ſtrong, but not exact reſemblance, to fern, polypody, and box.

Now it is firſt to be obſerved, that theſe ſuppoſed plants are ſeldom, if ever, doubled, or the foliage diſplaced, which muſt continually happen if they were the exuviæ of real plants. At certain times of the year likewiſe the backs of fern leaves are

[c] Londres, 1776. 4to p. 4.
[d] Weſley's Nat. Hiſt vol. III. p. 139.
[e] See Hiſt. Acad. Sc. for 1743. p. 111.

covered

covered with the feed, and the box both flowers and feeds, yet I have never happened to fee any, of thefe foffil plants with either the one or the other. Many fuch fpecimens alfo have no ftalk or root. They are more commonly feen in coal-flates (or the ftratum above the coal), than perhaps in any other foil. Whence can it arife likewife that the leaves or branches of other plants and trees are not found as frequently? I have alfo feen foffils which have borne fome refemblance to the barks of trees, and chiefly fir; but they were flat, and not convex, as muft happen when they vegetate.

Petrified and foffil bones of animals, quadrupeds, and fifh, are likewife fuppofed to be frequently difcovered; but I never heard of more than fragments being thus found; when, if thefe were really the bones of animals, the perfect fkeleton muft often be met with in a foffil ftate.

Strata of thefe, and of a confiderable length, are met with, both in Dalmatia and the rock of Gibraltar, which feem to be compofed of human bones; but thefe are chiefly thofe of the leg; nor is it fcarcely poffible that they fhould have been any part of a human creature, notwithftanding the very ftrong refemblance.

We will fuppofe thefe however to have been thus depofited, after a great flaughter in battle, or the fudden ravage of a peftilential diforder.

Upon thefe occafions the numerous corpfes muft neceffarily be buried in one general pit, and confequently the fkulls and other bones would be at the fame time dug up, and within a very fmall compafs; whereas thofe in Dalmatia lie for furlongs in narrow ftrata along the fea-coaft, and the fame is believed with regard to the fpecimens from Gibraltar. At all events, in fuch only poffible cafes, the complete human fkeleton would be difcovered.

But it will be urged, that we are to believe our own eyes, when the resemblance is so strong; to which I am ready to answer, Yes; if you will compare the fossil plant or animal with candour and accuracy.

For example, I will suppose the instance of a fossil prawn to be examined, which not one in ten thousand will distinguish from a large shrimp; yet if it is contended that this must be a shrimp from the strong resemblance, the assertion is not true.

The same holds with regard to the specimen of a large fossil crawfish, which differs specifically from a small lobster, though naturalists only will discern the proper criteria.

Many learned writers, and amongst these some distinguished fossilists, have denied the inferences often drawn from these subterraneous specimens in support of an universal deluge.

Dr. Grew (in his Catalogue of the Museum of the Royal Society) expresses himself thus on this head.

"Although nature cannot be said to imitate art, yet it may "fall out, that the effects of both may have some likeness. Those "white concretions which the Italians (from the place where "they are found) call, *confetti di Tivoli*, are sometimes so like "round confects, and the rough kind of sugared almonds, that "by the eye they cannot be distinguished. To call these *petrified* "*sugar plumbs* were senseless. Doth not Sal Ammoniac often "shoot into millions of little ones? If we find in other stones "the resemblance of plants, why not naturally there, as well as in "frosty weather upon glass windows; or as salts sometimes "figure themselves into some likeness to the plants whereof they "are made? Nay, why not to a face, or other animal form? "Since we see that there are diverse palm-nuts which have the "same [f]."

[f] P. 254.

Again,

Again, the ſame writer in deſcribing a foſſil, "in ſhape ſo like a "ſhark's tooth that one tooth cannot be liker to another; yet if it "be ſuch, then by comparing thoſe in the head of a ſhark, that to "which this belonged muſt have been about 36 feet in length[g]."

Lhuyd, in his additions to Camden's Britannia[h], ſpeaks in the ſame manner with regard to the ſuppoſed impreſſions of plants found in coal and other pits. Impreſſions of moſſes, and to the full as ſtrong a reſemblance as the foſſil plants, are allowed by many of the virtuoſi to be *luſuſes*; but I cannot conceive why it is not as difficult to effect an imitation of the one as of the other.

As we cannot account exactly how every pebble we tread upon is formed, it may by many be thought preſumptuous to make this endeavour, with regard to foſſil bodies; though ſuch as attribute them to a general deluge, certainly fall under this blame (if it is deſerved) as much as thoſe who aſſign them to other cauſes.

I do not pretend to produce my own hypotheſis in regard to the formation of many of theſe ſubterraneous bodies, with any degree of confidence; but I have at leaſt perſuaded myſelf that it may deſerve ſome attention.

I ſhall therefore venture to ſubmit, that ſubterraneous inſects may have occaſioned many of theſe ſtrong reſemblances (or *luſuſes*) either by their claws or *antennæ*, or perhaps by emitting a liquor which may both excavate and diſcolour the ſtone, or other body, on which they may happen to work.

The firſt objection to this conjecture will probably be, that proof is wanting of the exiſtence of ſuch inſects, and which I

[g] Ibid. p. 257.

[h] Art. Flintſhire.

admit must rest upon what at most will amount to a probability.

We know with certainty, that a quadruped, so large as a mole, not only exists, but finds its proper nourishment under ground, as also a considerable number of insects. We likewise know that the toad hath been frequently found at a considerable depth under the soil, inclosed with stone almost in contact with its body. This fact indeed hath been much ridiculed by some, and chiefly because it was supposed that the animal could not have continued to exist, both for want of air and food, whilst in such a situation. We are not however to reject well-attested accounts of facts in Natural History, merely because they happen to contradict what we generally observe to be necessary for the preservation of animal life; and that able anatomist Mr. John Hunter, F. R. S. having inclosed a toad between two stone flower pots for more than 14 months, found it as lively as when first confined.

But insects, tender as their bodies are, frequently penetrate into the hardest surfaces[i]; which labour they would not throw away, did it not answer to them either for food or depositing their eggs, or young.

Geoffroy informs us, that some of the Teignes [tineæ] excavate stones to lay their larvæ in[k], and our own naturalist poet Thomson says,

> secure
> Within its winding citadel, the stone
> Holds multitudes.
> [sc. of Insects.]

[i] There is a species of ant in the Mauritius which will eat through a trunk in a night. See a Voyage to that Island, in 1758.

[k] Account of Insects in the environs of Paris, vol. II. p. 178.

Turnefort again mentions that, "Rocks are peopled and "eaten by ſmall worms covered with ſhells of a green or aſh-"colour [l]."

Another argument of moſt conſiderable weight for the exiſtence of ſuch inſects, at almoſt any depth, ariſes from ſuch a vaſt maſs of matter as our globe conſiſts of, under the ſurface, or even the deepeſt of our mines, not contributing to the life or conveniences of any animal whatſoever, which can ſcarcely be ſuppoſed, without the ſtrongeſt and moſt irrefragable proof.

Particular foſſils again are commonly found in the ſame particular ſtrata; and does not this afford a proof that the inſects which inhabit ſuch ſtrata are the occaſion of the ſingular bodies which we there diſcover? A general deluge, on the other hand, muſt diſperſe theſe bodies indiſcriminately in every kind of ſtrata [m].

Some animals moreover form their ſhells by emitting a juice, which faſhions the layers of their habitation. "So the ſhells of "ſnails and oyſters are formed, their reſpective animals throwing "out periodically the oſſeous juice, or teſtaceous matter, which "adheres to the former ſhell, and concretes, and thus the ſuc-"ceſſive layers are produced [n]."

As

[l] This circumſtance may account for many of the foſſil ſhells, the living inhabitant of which hath never been diſcovered by any naturaliſt

[m] There are two ſtone quarries near Swindon in Wiltſhire; and in that which is at the leaſt diſtance from the town there are ſcarcely any foſſils which bear the moſt diſtant reſemblance to thoſe of marine ſhells, whereas they are found in conſiderable numbers in a quarry at no greater diſtance than a quarter of a mile. This fact ſeems to prove, that the ſtrata of the ſecond quarry are more convenient to certain inſects than thoſe of the firſt, whilſt it cannot be ſuppoſed that this difference is to be attributed to a general deluge.

[n] Ellis, Ph. Tranſ. vol. LXVI. p 8.

I do

As we know therefore, that certain animals which we are well acquainted with, form their habitations in this manner, why is this to be denied to ſubterraneous inſects, the exiſtence of which may be fairly inferred from what hath been ſtated, nor can we go further in the proof, except our deepeſt mines are more attended to than they have yet been by any naturaliſt. The ſearch indeed into theſe deep caverns, commonly ariſes from other motives than that of promoting ſcience.

It is unneceſſary to mention inſtances of the regularity and ingenuity with which inſects conſtruct their habitations, or prepare the proper receptacle for their eggs and young. I have myſelf however frequently obſerved, under the bark of a decayed bough, marks made by their punctures, exactly in the form of leaves, and with as ſtrong a reſemblance to a plant as any foſſil of the ſame kind. If inſects therefore above ground produce ſuch imitations, why may not the ſame happen under the ſurface of the earth, or at leaſt is the impoſſibility of this ſo great, that it is neceſſary to have recourſe to a general deluge?

But I ſhall now perhaps be told, that all theſe objections to the whole globe being covered with water in the time of Noah, cannot weigh an inſtant againſt the poſitive words of the book of Geneſis, which therefore it will be now right to examine, in the ſame manner that expreſſions in every other author ſhould be underſtood.

No apology for this need be made in a proteſtant country, as otherwiſe we muſt give up the Copernican ſyſtem, and literally believe that Joſhua not only ordered, but obliged, the ſun (and

I do not by this mean to contend, that no foſſil ſhell was ever found, but there cannot be a ſtronger proof that ſuch inſtances are rare at any diſtance from the coaſt, than that extravagant prices are given for ſpecimens which have the pearly coat.

4 not

not the earth) to ſtand ſtill for a whole day; and in countries of the Roman Catholic perſuaſion, excuſes are made for entertaining this opinion in every publication where it is alluded to.

The whole of this much controverted point depends principally upon the ſignification of the word *earth*, which in Engliſh more commonly includes the whole globe, unleſs confined by the context to a diſtrict, or more circumſcribed ſpot.

And firſt, let us conſider the occaſion of the deluge; which is ſtated to be,

"That God ſaw the wickedneſs of man was great upon *the* "*earth*," Gen. vi. 5.

"And the Lord ſaid, I will deſtroy man whom I have created, "from *the face of the earth*, both man and beaſt, and the creeping "thing, and the fowls of the air," ver. 7.

"*But* Noah found grace in the eyes of the Lord," ver. 8.

The exception here ſtated, "But Noah found grace, &c." ſeems moſt ſtrongly to prove, that the wickedneſs complained of related to the diſtrict in which he lived; for in the then uninhabited part of the globe there could have been none to offend, and involve with their own deſtruction the whole race of animals. This however was neceſſary in that portion of Aſia where Noah dwelt, as the animals not included in the ark might have contributed to the ſupport of ſome of the guilty.

I ſhould conceive therefore, that the term *Earth* is to be confined in theſe chapters of Geneſis to that portion of the globe where the calamity happened, the ſynonyms in moſt languages being equally reſtrained by the context, or at leaſt often ſo [o].

[o] "*The earth*," in this and other paſſages of the three chapters of Geneſis which relate to the deluge, is always anxiouſly repeated, as "and "every thing which is *in the earth* ſhall die," Gen. vi. 17. where, if the whole globe was intended, it would have been ſaid only, "*every thing* "*ſhall die*." The ſame may be obſerved with regard to the two former citations from Gen. vi. 7, and 8.

Thus

Thus in the 12th book of the Odyſſey γαια only means an iſland[p].

—— ουδε τις αλλη

Φαινετο γαιαων, αλλ' ουρανος, ηδε θαλασσα. Od. M. 403.

It ſometimes is ſtill more circumſcribed, and relates to the ſoil immediately under our feet, as in the firſt book of the Iliad.

Ποτι δε σκηπτρον βαλε γαιη, as alſo,

—— ρεε δ' αιματι γαια.

Iliad. Δ. 451.

The ſenſe of the word *(terra)* equally depends upon the context, and does not always import the whole ſurface of the globe, as in the following line of Virgil:

Poſtquam altum tenuere artes, nec jam amplius ullae
Apparent terrae——

Sometimes no more than a very ſmall portion of ſoil, as

—— haud paravero,
Quod aut avarus ut Chremes terra premam;
Diſcinctus aut perdam ut nepos.

Horat. Epod. i.

I ſhall now ſhew that *the earth* is neceſſarily uſed in a confined ſenſe in ſome of the chapters of Geneſis which relate to the flood.

"There were giants in the *earth* in thoſe days," Gen. xi. 4. where it muſt mean the adjacent country, for I believe it never was contended, that there were at this time giants over the whole ſurface of the globe. The ſenſe of the word being thus aſcertained

[p] What thus follows is printed chiefly from vol. IV. of the Archaeologia, p. 323, & ſeq.

when

when it is first introduced in these chapters of Genesis, it seems to follow, that it must continue to be used in the same signification, when it occurs afterwards in the account of the flood.

Thus again, "and the flood was forty days upon the earth, and "the waters increased and bare up the ark, and it was lift up "*above the earth*"

When the *earth* is thus introduced a second time, it must mean only the space of ground which was under the ark[q]; whilst it is also expository of the same word used in the preceding part of the verse, which cannot therefore reasonably be extended beyond the district.

The next term which hath occasioned the misunderstanding the scripture account is that of *Heaven*, the sense of which again, and its synonyms, in most languages, depends upon the context, as it often signifies no more than the atmosphere over a particular district, or scarcely more sometimes than the vertical point over our heads.

Thus in the 12th book of the Odyssey ουρανος means only the atmosphere above a high rock.

———ουρανον ευρυν ἱκανει
Οξειη κορυφη——— Od. M. 74.

And again in the last book of the Iliad,

——— λειβε δε οινον,
Ουρανον εισανιδων, ——— Il. Ω. 306.

where it is confined to the clouds above the person who is to make the libation.

The Latin term *Coelum* is often likewise not applied to more than the atmosphere of a district, or a still smaller portion; thus in the often cited line of Horace,

Coelum non animum mutant, qui trans mare currunt;

[q] Gen. vii. 16.

whilſt Virgil confines it to the void ſpace above a tree ;

Exiit ad coelum ramis felicibus arbos.

Thus Jacob's ladder reaches from the earth to *heaven*, Gen. xxviii. 12, in which paſſage nothing more than a very ſmall point can be implied.

As again, "A tower whoſe top may reach to heaven," Gen. xi. 4.

There is a third expreſſion uſed in theſe three chapters of Geneſis which it may be right to explain, viz. *the fountains of the deep*, as it is much relied upon by the partiſans of an univerſal deluge, and ſuppoſed to account for the extraordinary height of the inundation ; whilſt ſome conceive it to ſignify the ſea, and others ſubterraneous waters incloſed within the ſurface of our globe. I underſtand, however, by this expreſſion, nothing more than the fountains of the atmoſphere, the word *deep*, in ſome languages, relating to what is over our heads, as well as under our feet.

The term, therefore, by which *the deep* is rendered in the Septuagint, is αβυσσος [r], which ſignifies indeed *without bottom*, but for the ſame reaſon *without top*.

[r] This term occurs in Pſ. xlii. 7. "*Deep* calleth unto *deep* at the noiſe "of thy water-ſpouts," which in the Septuagint runs αβυσσος αβυσσον επικαλειται εις φωνην των καταρακτων σου. It is impoſſible that the Pſalmiſt can here allude to either waters under the ſurface of our globe, or to the ſea which is at ſuch a diſtance from Judea ; but, on the contrary, it muſt relate to what is above him, from καταρακται being mentioned, which always ſignify the precipitate deſcent of a river. Thus alſo αβυσσος is joined to the καταρακται του ουρανου, Gen. vii. 11. as again Gen. viii. 2. which being ſtopped, the rain from heaven is reſtrained.

This term (viz. αβυσσος) is twice uſed likewiſe in the revelations, viz. ix. 11. and xx 3. in both which verſes it muſt mean, probably, ſome inferior part of the heavens, and neither the bottom of the ſea, or waters within the central parts of our earth.

This word is more properly αβυθος, but Suidas informs us, Ιωνες δε τον βυθον βυσσον φασιν.

Thus

Thus *profundus* is applied by Virgil to Heaven,

Terraſque tractuſque maris, coelumque profundum,

Ecl. iv.

Altus likewiſe ſignifies either *high* or *deep*, as in the line of Virgil,

Poſtquam *altum* tenuere rates.

Having thus endeavoured to fix the ſenſe in which the 6th, 7th, and 8th chapters of Geneſis have introduced theſe expreſſions, I will beg any candid reader to peruſe them, ſubſtituting my acceptation of theſe words, inſtead of the terms in which theſe chapters are rendered either into Greek, Latin, or Engliſh.

It is proper, however, that I ſhould here ſtate the only text[c], which may ſeem to require being underſtood to extend to a general deluge.

"And the waters prevailed exceedingly upon the earth, and all "the high hills that were under the *whole heaven* were covered.

"Fifteen cubits upwards did the waters prevail, and the moun- "tains were covered." Gen. vii. 19 and 20.

That the *whole* heaven can here only imply the atmoſphere above the country in which the deluge happened, ſeems evident from the following reaſons:

The hiſtory of this flood is commonly ſuppoſed to have been written by Moſes, and if he received the tradition from Noah with the utmoſt accuracy, yet the Patriarch could only give an account of what he was able to obſerve himſelf; therefore theſe words muſt be confined to the diſtrict in which the ark

[c] All fleſh is likewiſe uſed, Gen. ix. 15, and occurs alſo twice more in the ſame chapter; but I ſhould conceive, that theſe general expreſſions muſt be confined in their ſignification for the reaſons which I ſhall give in relation to Gen. vii 19, 20.

floated. It must be added to this, that it is stated, the mountains were covered with water to the depth of fifteen cubits; this cannot, however, relate to every mountain on our globe, but to those only which Noah might be acquainted with the height of; even mount Ararat, on which the ark is supposed to have rested, is by no means the highest mountain of our earth.

Besides this, such general words (as *all*) must frequently be confined in their signification.

Thus when it said by St. Luke, that there went out a decree from Cæsar Augustus that *all the world* should be taxed, Luke ii. 1 [t], this can only refer to that part of it which was under the Roman government; for Parthia (not far from Judea) was so far from being subjected to the Roman yoke, that they had not more than half a century before this, totally defeated Crassus's army.

Thus

[t] The expression in the Greek is πασαν την οικεμενην, but this is equally inaccurate, if the words are translated in their more literal sense, and confined to the inhabited part of the globe. Thus also three of the Evangelists inform us (Matthew xxvii 45. επι πασαν την γην. Mark xv. 33. and Luke xxiii. 44. εφ' ολην την γην) that darkness prevailed over the whole earth for three hours after the crucifixion, this, however, must relate only to Judea, for such a most remarkable event is not mentioned by any other writer who lived at the time or later The elder Pliny must have probably remembered this darkness, if it had extended to Italy; and he would certainly have introduced it into his Natural History, as he hath a chapter, entitled, Dierum lux nocte, l. ii. c. 33. which would have been followed by "Nocturni tenebrae die."

"The Lord God of heaven hath given me *all* the kingdoms of the "*earth*," Ezra speaking in the name of Cyrus, 1st and 2d.

"And there stood up one of them, named Agabus, and signified by the spirit, that there should be a great dearth *throughout all the world* [εφ' ολην την οικεμενην] which came to pass in the days of Claudius Cæsar," Acts xi 28. Which expression Bishop Lowth, in his lately published commentary on Isaiah, confines to the Roman empire, or Judea, p. 91. *notes*.

After

Thus alſo, when Petronius ſays,

> *Orbem jam totum* victor Romanus habebat,
> Qua mare, qua tellus, qua ſidus currit utrumque,

it is well known, that there were many parts even then unſubdued; as there were in the time of Antoninus, whom Oppian addreſſes as,

> Κοιρανε γαιης.

It ſhould ſeem therefore, from the common rules and obſervations by which a paſſage or words uſed by any other writer would be explained, that the general terms of the three chapters of Geneſis which relate to the deluge, are to be confined to the country in which Noah lived; and to contend otherwiſe ſeems moſt unneceſſarily to multiply unanſwerable difficulties and objections. As the univerſality of the deluge is no article of faith, it may be freely diſcuſſed; and I have already ſhewn, that a living and diſtinguiſhed prelate of our church hath explained the expreſſion of *all the world*, in Acts xi. 28. to be confined to the Roman empire, or *perhaps Judea*, when the Jews had greater intercourſe with other nations, than in the time when the Old Teſtament was written. The Jews indeed, before the Roman

After a few generations from Noah the attempt was made to build the tower of Babel, and the firſt verſe of the chapter which relates to this intention begins, "and the *whole earth* was of one language and of one ſpeech." Can this paſſage poſſibly relate but to the immediate deſcendants of Noah, and the diſtrict which they inhabited? And does it not moſt ſtrongly prove, that the expreſſion of *all the earth* continues to be uſed in the book of Geneſis, according to its original import, with regard to the flood?

In theſe early times indeed the deſtruction of the neighbouring inhabitants ſeems to have been ſuppoſed to include thoſe of the whole globe, for Lot's daughter, after the deſtruction of Sodom, conceive that their father is the only ſurviving male *upon the earth*, Gen. xix. 31.

conqueſt,

conqueſt, had ſcarcely any communication but with the Aſſyrians or Egyptians, and certainly in the time of Noah could not have been acquainted with any but the inhabitants in their own diſtrict, of which particular tract they therefore can be only preſumed to have ſpoken. All general terms muſt, in like manner, be reſtrained by the context, or ſubject they allude to; and when the ambitious views of Lewis the 14th, for *univerſal empire*, were moſt exclaimed againſt; no one ever ſuppoſed they extended to the dominion of the globe.

Oxford, May 12, 1746[a].

Mr. DODSLEY,

NOTHING which hath lately appeared in print, hath given me greater ſatisfaction than the ſuperior merit of our Engliſh authors to the French, which hath been ſo ingeniouſly ſupported in one or two of your Muſeums. After the peruſal of them, the agreeable reflexion ſo naturally reſulting to an Engliſhman produced in me the following dream. Methought I was conveyed into a large library, in which I heard a confuſion of French voices, which, by the frequent repetition of the word *Muſeum* with anger, I imagined to proceed from diſcontent at your late criticiſms. Seeing however no perſon in the library, I was examining, with no ſmall aſtoniſhment, from whence this uproar aroſe; and was not a little ſurprized, you may imagine, to find that each book had the faculty of expreſſing itſelf for its author. After I had tolerably reconciled myſelf to this unuſual manner of intercourſe, I found that I was not miſtaken in my

[a] The above letter was written at the time it bears date, and was addreſſed to the Editor of a periodical paper, intituled, *The Muſeum*, which was printed for Dodſley. I did then intend it ſhould have followed two diſſertations in that work, which aſſerted the ſuperiority of our Engliſh to the French authors, but from ſome circumſtance, which I do not now remember, it never reached the Editor. I need not inform the Reader that the idea of this engagement between the writers of the two nations, is taken from, *The Battle of the Books*.

first conjecture; for Descartes, desiring that he might be heard, after having with difficulty obtained silence, spoke in the following words; "I need not mention to you the indignities offered to the whole French nation, and to me in particular, by the author of the Museum: shall my ingenious hypotheses be destroyed by Newton, whose low genius was obliged to depend entirely on experiment for his reputation? This tedious circumspect manner of philosophising may suit well with the phlegmatic temper of an Englishman, but let the French vivacity and genius never be reproached with having had recourse to such low and mechanical means of discovering truth. I would dwell longer on this, but resentment will not suffer me; my advice however is, that we immediately take signal vengeance on the author of our disgrace. The English, as they are so deeply concerned, will undoubtedly support him with all their force; therefore let us immediately make choice of a general, and dispose of our strength in such a manner as to execute our design in spite of opposition. Believe me, we cannot fail of success, for I will engage that our engineers shall play such quantities of *materia subtilis* upon them, that they shall dread us as much, as Nature does a *vacuum*." When he had ended, the French by their shouts approved of his proposal; but then, every one thinking that he had the justest pretensions to the command, there arose a second confusion of voices, each author proclaiming his own deserts to the assembly. This continued for a considerable time: many at last finding that there would be no end of this dissension, unless they agreed to fix upon some person of distinguished merit, Racine, with the consent of the major part of the assembly, proposed Boileau. What induced them to make choice of him for this important charge was, that he had composed some excellent rules for military discipline, which, if they strictly adhered to, they could not well fail of defeating their enemies. Every one now waving their particular pretenſions, Boileau was upon the point of being declared Generaliſſimo, when Deſcartes, with great indignation, reproached them for not making a proper diſtinction between a rhymer and a philoſopher. You cannot but be ſenſible, added he, that the Engliſh will pitch upon Newton for their Commander: and who is capable of oppoſing him but myſelf? I have already prepared one of my largeſt vortexes to receive his attack with, in which I will make him ſo giddy, that he ſhall for ever repent denying the exiſtence of them. He concluded with ſaying, that any one who oppoſed his juſt pretenſions, muſt expect a more dreadful fate than that which he had juſt threatened to Newton. The French, who moſt of them thought that he was able, and would not fail to execute his menaces, inſiſted no longer on their former choice, and Boileau himſelf, who was rather more proper for celebrating the actions of his Monarch, than performing any himſelf, ſneaked away, and left his adverſary in quiet poſſeſſion of the command. Deſcartes no ſooner found himſelf maſter of the authority he aſpired to, than he diſpoſed of his troops in the following manner. He reſolved himſelf to lead on the centre of the army: Corneille had the command of the right, and Boileau of the left wing; the former of which had in his diviſion Racine, Malherbe, the Conteſſe de la Suz, Racan, and many others: the latter had Moliere, Rabelais, Scaron, and Voiture. Deſcartes himſelf placed on one ſide of him Voltaire's Henriade and Chapelain; on the other Ronſard and Marot; and being deſirous of having ſome intelligence concerning the ſtrength and diſpoſition of the Engliſh, he pitched upon Voltaire as the propereſt perſon for that purpoſe, who engaged to acquit himſelf in this truſt to the General's ſatisfaction. It was not long before he returned, and informed him in what part, and by what means, the enemy might be attacked with the greateſt probability of ſucceſs. There is Shakſpeare, ſaid he, who hath the command of the Engliſh right wing: now there are ſome parts of his troops, which, if they were not mingled with bad ones, it would be impoſſible for the whole French army to ſuſtain the ſhock of. I ſhould adviſe therefore that you give orders to your engineers to charge the artillery which is to be pointed againſt him with the unities of time and place, which cannot fail of producing its proper effect. This advice had its weight with Deſcartes, who began to enquire further how formidable he thought his antagoniſt Newton. Voltaire ſeemed very unwilling to make any reply to this queſtion; but being much preſſed, anſwered him in the following manner: "I have often with attention conſidered the ſurpriſing greatneſs of that man, and you muſt pardon my freedom when I tell you, that if you was to join to your aſſiſtance all the philoſophers that ever exiſted, they would not be able to withſtand even a ſmall degree of the force he is capable of exerting. It is impoſſible to expreſs the indignation of Deſcartes at this reply; he turned from him without vouchſafing an anſwer, and joined the other generals who were waiting his orders. He there accuſed Voltaire of an inclination to deſert, ſaid he could not put ſufficient confidence in him to entruſt him with any command, and deſired their advice in what manner he ſhould be treated. Racine, who was ſenſible of their want of an Epic Poet to make ſome ſmall ſtand againſt Milton, gave it as his opinion that the Henriade, being the beſt poem of that kind in their language, ſhould be allowed to remain in the place where Deſcartes had firſt placed it; which as it was very near himſelf, he might have a watchful eye over it during the engagement. This was approved of, and now every thing being thus ſettled, orders were given to charge. The Engliſh, in the

mean

mean time, did not want intelligence of the attack designed by the French : there were no factions or cabals raised about the person to be fixed upon as General ; for every one, with a kind of reverential awe, intreated Newton to accept the post ; he modestly complied with their request, and begged that Milton might be joined with him in command. Milton did not decline this honour, and, on account of his loss of sight, desired that Addison might be appointed to assist him, for he found that he was infinitely stronger when that able critic was near. The whole army was led on in the following manner : Newton and Milton took their post in the centre, in which were likewise Bacon, Locke, and Spenser. Shakspeare commanded the right wing, and had in his division, Rowe, Otway, Dryden, Waller, Cowley, and Gay. Pope had under his command, in the left wing, Congreve, Swift, Butler, Jonson, and many more. I have forgot, I believe, as yet mentioning one very particular circumstance, which was, that after Descartes first spoke, each book had occasionally taken upon itself the shape of its author. The engagement had now begun. Descartes advanced with great intrepidity, but his troops, every step he took towards Newton, visibly decreased, and his Vortexes, which he had so much relied on, immediately disappeared. I was a good deal surprised at this sudden change ; but looking towards Newton, I saw that he had a shield of adamant presented to him on that occasion by Natural Philosophy, which the moment any thing false, though never so ingenious, struck against, it was immediately reduced to its proper state of *nothing*. Newton, being content with having humbled Descartes's arrogance, took pity on his condition ; and no enemy in the field being of consequence enough for him to honour with a defeat, he chose, like Edward the Third, to be only spectator of the fight, and view with pleasure the valour of his countrymen.

Locke,

Locke, who was behind Newton before, now being the firſt in the line, attacked Malbranche, and drove him preſently from the field; then, together with Bacon, finding no more enemies remaining, he retired towards Newton, where it was eaſy to perceive in their converſation, the reciprocal eſteem theſe great men had for each other. Milton, the moment he was informed by Addiſon that Voltaire was preparing to attack him in front, while Brebeuf and Chapelain flanked him, could not help laughing at their inſignificancy, and ſaid that he ſhould do right in ſending Sir Richard Blackmore's Prince Arthur to engage them; but as the enemy had the preſumption by this time to begin the attack, he deſired Addiſon only to play the deſcription of the artillery of Satan upon them, which immediately occaſioned a rout. Spenſer met with as great ſucceſs againſt Marot and Ronſard. Many of the Italian allegorical poets were ſeen hovering round him, and preventing any prejudice that might have otherwiſe been done to him by his antagoniſts; particularly Arioſto, who deſcended from an upper ſhelf upon an unruly Ippogrif, and preſented him with an enchanted dart, which nothing could withſtand, whilſt he at the ſame time proclaimed him the chief of allegorical poets. Thus every thing in the centre was obliged to give way to the ſuperior merit of the Engliſh. The engagement in the two wings, during this time, was extremely obſtinate. The right wing of the French, as before mentioned, was commanded by Corneille, as that of the Engliſh was by Shakſpeare; Shakſpeare, immediately upon the ſound of the trumpet, advanced to attack his adverſary, but notwithſtanding he behaved himſelf with the greateſt reſolution, yet he did not meet with all the ſucceſs he had promiſed himſelf; for the artillery charged with the unity of time and place, made a terrible havock among his troops. Addiſon, obſerving this, deſired leave of Milton that he might aſſiſt him,

him, which being granted, he charged the Engliſh artillery with an eſſay againſt bombaſt declamation in tragedy. This had as terrible an effect upon Corneille as the other had on Shakſpeare; upon this the battle was renewed with ſtill greater obſtinacy, but neither being able to obtain a decided advantage over the other, though Shakſpeare had the ſuperiority, Corneille propoſed a ceſſation, and preſented Shakſpeare with his Cid, who in return gave him his Othello, and both retired to their different parties, fully convinced of each other's abilities. Racine all this while maintained his poſt againſt the united forces of Otway and Rowe; his were all ſelect troops, which were headed by the Athalia, and formed all together a kind of Macedonian phalanx that could not be broke through. Dryden, ſeeing this, was advancing at the head of ſix battalions to the aſſiſtance of his countrymen; but, upon his coming pretty near to the enemy, being haſty levies, they immediately went off, and left him diſconſolate to maintain the attack alone. Newton, in the mean time, perceiving that there was no impreſſion made upon the enemy, ſent Sir William Temple to inſtruct the Engliſh writers of tragedy how to attack Racine in the moſt advantageous manner. Temple, with an eager zeal for the honour of his country, gave Otway a ſword, round the blade of which was engraved ſome ſhort but excellent objections againſt repreſenting Turks and Romans with the manners of a Frenchman. This was of ſignal ſervice to Otway, for Racine could not prevent its driving ſome of his greateſt heroes from the field; but notwithſtanding this, with his remaining force, it was impoſſible to put him in diſorder, ſo excellent diſcipline and regularity had he kept up among his troops. Homer, who had all this while been ſpectator of the fight, thinking that the ſtruggle had already laſted too long, ſent Talthybius and Idæus, in order to put a ſtop to the conteſt, which, by their mediation,

ation, was effected, to the satisfaction of both parties. And now the Countess de la Suz, Malherbe, and Sarrazin, advanced against Waller, Cowley, and Gay; the tender Waller however could not be prevailed upon to engage any of the fair sex with weapons that did not suit their delicacy, and answered all the Countess's attacks with passionate and melting couplets, which made such an impression on the lady, that a mutual passion presently banished all national resentments. The dispute between Malherbe and Cowley was infinitely more warm. Cowley's Pindaricks attacked with great briskness, but their fire however was not by any means regular, which indeed is agreed on by most masters of military discipline to be the properest method for those kind of troops to charge. Malherbe however stood the shock tolerably well, when Pindar presented Cowley with a horse that had won a prize at the Olympic games; this Cowley immediately mounted, and at the same time crying out,

—— I'll cut through all,
And march the Muse's Hannibal.
(Cowley's 1st Ode.)

He rushed into the thickest of the enemy, and bore down every thing before him. Pope and Boileau were by this time engaged in the left wing, in which every one on both sides seemed to have forgot all animosities, while they were attending to the contest of these two great men. The Rape of the Lock, and Essay on Criticism, immediately singled out the Lutrin, and Art of Poetry; and notwithstanding the address of each general, it was difficult to determine on which side the victory would incline. The Satires of the French Poet at the same time attacked those of the English, which, being assisted by the Essay on Man, began to to make their adversaries think of retreating, when Homer, who had ſuch infinite obligations to his excellent tranſlator, appeared at the head of 48 battalions, and ſaid that he ſhould look upon all thoſe as his enemies, who oppoſed a poet who had made him ſpeak Engliſh with the ſame ſpirit and force, that he himſelf ſhould have done, had he wrote in that language. Boileau, who had the greateſt reverence for Homer, was now upon the point of retiring, when Pope advancing, ſaid that he had long before been ſenſible of the excellencies of his poems, was now more than ever convinced of them by the late trial, and at the ſame time begged he would honour him with his friendſhip. Boileau anſwered his compliments with great politeneſs; and added, with a ſmile, that ſatiriſts, above all other kind of writers, ought to live in the ſtricteſt amity with each other, as they generally had a great number of enemies, who would rejoice at their diſſenſions. I am much miſtaken, continued he, if this engagement hath not already given great ſatisfaction to Cibber and Cotin. Fontaine, who was poſted ready to aſſiſt Boileau, ſeeing Chaucer and Prior, who attended upon Pope, advanced with reverence towards Chaucer, and ſaid that if ſuch a genius as his had appeared in the moſt elegant and learned age, it could not have been ſufficiently admired; but as he had lived in a time when the Muſes were ſo little regarded, he could ſcarce refrain from adoring. Chaucer embraced Fontaine, called him his ſon, and ſaid he was the only writer ſince himſelf that had told a ſtory with a beautiful ſimplicity. Rabelais had now the preſumption to attack Swift; but he only expoſed his weakneſs, for Swift with his Tale of a Tub (which dilated to a vaſt ſize) immediately covered nine parts out of ten of his forces; the few remaining, rallied by Pantagruel, made ſome reſiſtance; but Swift producing one of his Brobdingnag heroes preſently put him to flight. Scarron, who was juſt

 by

by Rabelais, ſeeing Swift and Butler advance towards him, and knowing that to oppoſe would be in vain, laughed at Rabelais as he was ſneaking off, and had even the impudence to cut a joke upon Pantagruel. He then began being witty upon his own perſon; and ſaid he was ſurprized that Deſcartes could think of taking him for a ſoldier, as he was ſome feet below the ſtandard of any nation; he at the ſame time made ſuch a droll compliment to Swift and Butler, that they could not help beginning a converſation with him, in which they were infinitely delighted with his wit. Nothing now remained to be decided but the diſpute between the Comic Poets, which was juſt going to begin with great warmth on each ſide, when Plautus interpoſing preſented Moliere with a crown. Congreve and Jonſon, notwithſtanding their merit, acquieſced in this determination, and were advancing to pay their reſpects to the French Poet, when the *Laureat*, thinking that proper regard was not paid to his deſerts, ſtepped abruptly in with an intention to diſpute the authority of Plautus; but unluckily for him ſome enemy of his repeating the firſt ſtanza of his laſt Ode, there followed ſo univerſal a laugh, that it prevented the continuation of my dream.

THE

THE following Dialogue was written at Oxford, during the year 1746, having been preceded by ſome obſervations upon Homer; which perhaps fortunately for the reader I have now miſlaid. I had at that time peruſed moſt of the ancient Greek and Roman writers, and conceived, that amongſt their numerous beauties, there were ſome few defects, which the moderns had been more happy in avoiding.

The elegant writers of antiquity become our earlieſt models, nor can we have better; but as our taſte is formed from theſe excellent examples, ſhould not their miſtakes be pointed out to the young ſcholar, as well as their perfections? Yet every commentator becomes ſo zealous a partiſan for the Latin or Greek author which he is to explain or illuſtrate, that we never hear of a blemiſh, or, if there be a palpable one, it is often defended by ſuch reaſons, as the annotator muſt himſelf be ſenſible are very inſufficient.

I could therefore wiſh, that when any new edition of a claſſic was publiſhed, the commentator would rather dwell upon the imperfections than perfections of the writer; our preſent claſſical charts always repreſenting a clear coaſt, and never pointing out the rocks or ſhallows which lie contiguous.

Sophron.] We ſeem to have ſufficiently conſidered both the beauties and failings of Homer: ſuppoſe we were now to examine into the merit of the ancient dramatic writers? Whether the Chorus is an advantage or not to the drama, when properly made uſe of, will in a great meaſure determine the diſpute between us to which the preference is due, and therefore I do not think it will be improper to begin with examining a little into the nature of this part of the ancient tragedy. The peculiar office of the Chorus cannot be better explained than by the lines in Horace's Art of Poetry, which comprehend almoſt every circum- that it ever interferes with.

Actoris partes Chorus officumque virile
Defendat, neu quid medios intercinat actus
Quod non propoſito conducat, & hæreat apte.
Ille bonis faveatque & concilietur amicis
Et regat iratos, & amet peccare timentes, &c.

The exact manner in which the Chorus performed its part ſeems to have puzzled the moſt diligent enquirers into antiquity; and to enter into a diſcuſſion of this nature would not at all ſuit our preſent deſign. I ſhall only ſay in general what hath occurred to me upon reading the ancient tragedies, with regard to its having been originally introduced. Theſpis, the firſt writer for the ſtage that we have any account of, acting his tragedies from town to town [a]; and that ſpecies of poetry being by no means carried by him to any great perfection, his audiences probably conſiſted of the lower kind of people, who I believe in all coun-

[a] Ignotum tragicæ genus inveniſſe Camœnæ
Dicitur, & plauſtris vexiſſe poemata Theſpis.

tries

tries have been much pleaſed with a ſong or muſic of any kind.[b]. Theſpis, finding this part of his tragedies moſt attended to, thought, and perhaps very judiciouſly, that no kind of ſong or muſic would be ſo proper as that which in general might have ſome connexion with the drama, though poſſibly he did not inviolably adhere to the rule,

> —— Neu quid medios intercinat actus
> Quod non propoſito conducat, & hareat aptè.

which indeed was generally obſerved by the later writers of tragedy. Æſchylus then, and the other poets that followed him, finding the Chorus already eſtabliſhed, had by no means the courage to baniſh it, though at the ſame time they muſt have been ſenſible that it was not eſſential to the drama; and indeed I am not at all ſorry that they preſerved it, for theſe Choruſes often are the moſt elevated and touching pieces of poetry that we have any where extant. In theſe the poet gave his genius the free ſcope, which he indulged with the greateſt fire and happineſs; and if they are ſtill conſidered as excreſcences, they are ſuch which for my own part I could not conſent to lop off.

Horace lays it down as a rule, that the Chorus ſhould keep inviolably ſecret every thing intruſted to them; this indeed is a moſt neceſſary injunction, and which I believe hath always

[b] It is not contended by this that what the Chorus ſaid was always ſet to muſic, it oftentimes is to be conſidered as a ſingle perſon concerned in the play, which part of its office was probably performed by the Coryphæus only.

been obſerved by the ancients; but this fidelity however in the Chorus doth not take from the abſurdity of the principal characters, in truſting thoſe (who ſometimes have not the leaſt connection with them) with their moſt important ſchemes and deſigns. There is a moſt flagrant inſtance of this in the Medea of Euripides. Medea is repreſented by the poet, according to her juſt character, crafty, diſſembling, and at the ſame time of implacable revenge; this deſigning woman, who in other parts of the tragedy ſhews herſelf a perfect miſtreſs of diſſimulation, diſcovers to the Chorus her reſolution of murdering her own children and Jaſon's ſecond wife, by ſending her a preſent of an envenomed garment [*]. The Chorus, though they are bound by no oath of ſecrecy, make their uſual reflections upon this deſign, and though Jaſon comes in immediately afterwards, whilſt they continue upon the ſtage, conceal it from him, when they muſt be induced by all kinds of conſiderations to reveal it. There is in the Hippolytus of Euripides another inſtance, to the full as ſtrong as this: Phædra, who is repreſented in the greateſt depth of diſtreſs, through a paſſion which ſhe cannot gratify, is earneſtly preſſed by her nurſe to let her know the cauſe of the alteration in her health. Phædra

[*] Who could ſuppoſe however that this Chorus, in which ſhe puts ſo entire a confidence, are Corinthian women to whom ſhe is an utter ſtranger, and who, as being Corinthians, muſt be ſuppoſed to be attached to the intereſt of the perſon ſhe intends to deſtroy? When ſhe hath alſo diſcovered to them theſe horrid intentions, ſhe at laſt intreats their ſecreſy by no better reaſons than if "*they wiſh her well, and are women.*"
I ſhould rather ſuppoſe, that this abſurdity alſo aroſe from what was uſual in the time of Theſpis, when there was only a ſtage of boards, probably for the actors to perform upon, without any retiring room for the Chorus, who were therefore neceſſarily preſent. Poſſibly the whole play was performed from the cart, without any ſtage at all, when the chorus would have ſtill leſs opportunity to withdraw.

how-

however is obſtinate, for a conſiderable time, in concealing the ſource of her affliction; and when doth ſhe diſcloſe it at laſt? Not while her nurſe, whoſe fidelity ſhe can abſolutely depend upon, is *only* preſent, but when the Chorus (a number of Træzenian women, with whom ſhe doth not appear to have had any great intimacy) have intruded themſelves into her preſence. How infinitely better is this conducted in Racine! where the confidant is the ſole perſon attending, whoſe affection for her Phædra cannot doubt. I promiſed you I would not dwell long on the imperfections of the Chorus, and I have been, I hope, as good as my word; however, I cannot help taking a little notice here of the ancient prologues, which ſometimes are made by a Deity (as by Venus in the Hippolytus); and ſometimes by a ghoſt (as that of Polydorus in the Hecuba). My objection however to theſe prologues is not their being ſpoken by deities[d], but that they generally chooſe to diſcover and anticipate all the principal events in the play, particularly the cataſtrophe. This I take to be exceſſively improper, and very prudently avoided by the moderns in their prologues, for when the audience is acquainted with the event, the ſtory becomes leſs intereſting, and prevents all the agreeable ſurprize that might ariſe from well choſen and unforeſeen incidents. Deities too are ſometimes introduced into the ancient tragedies, when there is by no means any *dignus vindice nodus*, as in the Αιας μαστιγοφορος[f], where Minerva appears in

[d] Not but that perhaps it would be as well if they were ſpoken by mortals But as a prologue is by no means a part of the tragedy (as it certainly is not leſs a tragedy without it), I ſhould imagine that the poet may by the ſevereſt critic be allowed this liberty, particularly as it hath the ſanction of Taſſo and Guarini, the firſt of which poets makes the God of Love ſpeak the prologue to his Aminta, and the latter the river Alpheus to his Paſtor Fido.

[f] Of Sophocles.

the firſt ſcene, and holds a converſation with Ulyſſes, without any abſolute neceſſity for the preſence of a Goddeſs.

Muſeodorus.] I admit in general of your objections; but while the ancient tragedies have that ſimplicity of ſubject which is almoſt peculiar to them, (for few indeed of our moderns ſeem to have followed them in this point), ſome trifling improprieties will never prevent the preference that is due to them upon the whole.

Soph.] I moſt readily own that ſimplicity in the ſubject of the drama cannot be too much commended, and that the ancients have in general attended more to it, than the moderns, but I believe I may venture to aſſert, that many of their ſubjects are ſo *ſimple* indeed that they are almoſt entirely unintereſting [e]. I beg you would for example conſider a little the Rheſus of Euripides, which I will allow you is perhaps as ſimple as a ſubject can well be; but I do not recollect a ſingle circumſtance, or incident in the whole, that can be ſaid to be affecting. The play opens with a ſcene between Hector and the Chorus, who inform him, that the Græcians are lighting fires in their camp; Hector imagines from this that they are going to retire: the Chorus, however, who do not appear to be of any great diſtinction in the army, but only common centinels, doubt much of this: he is after-

[e] It is not pretended by this that the ſubject's being unintereſting proceeds from its ſimplicity, but only that by a too ſcrupulous attention to the latter, the play often becomes ſo, and this is generally the caſe when a writer pitches upon a ſimple ſtory, when at the ſame time he hath not genius and imagination ſufficient to render it affecting, for the greater the ſimplicity is, the greater is the difficulty in this point. This is therefore not a charge upon the ancients for their adherence to this ſimplicity; but only for chooſing ſuch ſubjects as they wanted genius ſometimes to make intereſting, or perhaps that were incapable of becoming ſo, which I take to be the caſe of Euripides's Rheſus.

wards

wards overruled by Æneas in his ſcheme for attacking the enemy, and it is agreed that a ſpy ſhould be ſent into the Grecian army. Upon this Dolon offers himſelf, bargains with Hector for his reward, and is promiſed by him the chariot of Achilles. A meſſenger then makes his appearance, and gives an account of the arrival of Rheſus at the Trojan Camp: Rheſus himſelf follows immediately after, where he is very coldly received by Hector, for having ſo long delayed his march; and this ſcene, which is a pretty long one, and in which the expectation of the audience is reaſonably raiſed, while theſe two principal characters are preſent, is as dull and tireſome a one I believe as was ever penned. Diomede and Ulyſſes, in the mean time, favoured by the night, come with an intention to ſurprize Hector in his tent; but are diverted from this by Minerva, who adviſes them to fall upon the quarters of Rheſus, which they accordingly do, and ſucceed in killing him while aſleep. This is not done on the ſtage, but the audience hath very properly an account of the diſaſter from a ſervant of Rheſus's, who taxes Hector with the murder. After this the Muſe Terpſichore laments the loſs of her ſon, and I think, really, that from a Muſe, one might have expected ſomething more pathetic and touching upon the occaſion. Now I appeal to you whether in this whole play there is any ſingle intereſting circumſtance; and if I was to aſk you what the moral was, I am afraid you could not eaſily find it out.

Phil.] I recollect having read, ſome time ago, this tragedy of Euripides (as it is generally called) and remember that it appeared to me almoſt below criticiſm; but I muſt own, that for my own part, I cannot heſitate a moment to declare that the play is not written by that author. There always have been diſputes, I believe, who this tragedy is to be attributed to, and if I was acquainted with the name of the worſt

 writer

writer in that age, I ſhould make no ſcruple of giving the honour of that performance to him.

Muſ.] Well, this is one way of getting rid of the charge; and I will not inſiſt upon many arguments that might be produced againſt this liberty of diſowning whatever makes for our own diſcredit Father Hardouin, you know, will carry this farther, and prove that none of the tragedies aſcribed to Euripides were written by him. I will not ſay of the Alceſtis that the ſubject is uninteresting; but I believe I may ſay, that it is a very improper one for a tragedy; at leaſt as Euripides hath managed it. A wiſe that reſolves to ſave her huſband by her own death, will certainly always prejudice the audience in her favour; but I believe no woman, under thoſe circumſtances ever occaſioned ſo little pity as Alceſtis, which proceeds entirely from the improbability and abſurdity of the whole ſtory; ſuch a one I think as a judicious writer would never have pitched upon. The rule of Horace,

Ficta voluptatis cauſâ, ſint proxima veris.

can never be too much attended to; Euripides however ſeems in this play not to have the leaſt conſidered it. The piece throughout is conſiſtent (if I may be allowed[f] the expreſſion) in impropriety; for I do not recollect a ſingle incident in the whole which doth not ſhock, as being improbable. The evening advances; but as we return to the houſe I ſhall ſtate, for your conſideration another objection to parts of the dialogue in

[f] So great an anachroniſm is not by this incurred, as to ſuppoſe that Euripides could really have attended to this rule, as laid down by the Roman poet, but as the maxim is founded on common ſenſe, whether it was at that time or no an axiom, every writer of tragedy ſhould not have neglected it.

most

moſt of the ancient tragedies, when the characters anſwer each other for a conſiderable time by a ſingle line, and often the ſame number of words. This ſhort and abrupt intercourſe might now and then be attended with propriety, by expreſſing anger, but this obſcure dialogue generally happens when the perſons ſpeaking are in their uſual temper, and about the moſt indifferent circumſtances. I cannot expect, however, that you ſhould be able to defend the ancient writers on tragedy upon this head till you have examined the parts I refer to in your library; when, out of many others, I can, from a memorandum in my pocket, point out Euripides's Medea, l. 663, *et ſeq.* as alſo his Hippolytus, l. 80. *et ſeq.*

I have already preſumed to mention ſome uninteresting tragedies of the ancients, and conceive that I may alſo venture to ſay, that there are few ſcenes even that command the involuntary tear from the reader, which circumſtance I ſhall always conſider as the true teſt of the merits of a tragedy; as the involuntary laugh ſeems to be that of a comedy. Critics may write ingenious diſſertations; but if the reader is not affected till he is taught to be ſo, I ſhall always diſtruſt the abilities of the author.

IN the year 1773 I tranſlated and publiſhed King Ælfred's Anglo-Saxon Verſion of Oroſius, in which the Royal Author hath made ſome inſertions, which are not borrowed from the Latin Hiſtorian.

Amongſt others an account is introduced of Othere's navigation to the Northern Seas, which I have endeavoured to illuſtrate by a geographical map, containing the then ſtate of the globe, with the Anglo-Saxon names and orthography of the countries, and in which alſo the ſuppoſed tracts of Othere are particularly marked.

As I conceive this map to be intereſting for explaining the geography of the 9th century, and may cite no leſs an opinion than that of Monſ. d'Anville, for its being ſo conſidered, I have directed a proper number of copies to be rolled off from the plate, for the preſent miſcellaneous publication, as alſo great part of the firſt chapter from the Anglo-Saxon verſion to be reprinted.

My principal reaſon for doing this is, that the number of copies which I publiſhed from King Ælfred's tranſlation was very ſmall, and conſequently cannot have fallen into the hands of many readers.

OUR *elders* have divided all the circuit of the earth into three parts (quoth Oroſius) comprehending what is ſurrounded by *Oceanus, which men call* GARSECG[a]; and they named theſe three parts Aſia, Europe, and Africa, though ſome have ſaid that there are only two diviſions, Aſia and Europe. Aſia is bounded to the ſouthward, northward, and eaſtward, by the Ocean,

[a] This word ſignifies a vaſt tract of Sea or Ocean, and when narrower is is always termed ſea or *ſea*, as Ƿendel-ſea, the Mediterranean, &c. I take an early opportunity of ſaying, that I am not anſwerable for the

Ocean, and thus divides all this earth from the eastern parts. All to the northward is Asia, and to the southward Europe and Asia are separated by the Tanais; then south of this same river (along the Mediterranean, and west of Alexandria) Europe and Asia join.

Europe begins (as I said before) at the river Tanais, which takes its source from the northern parts of the Riphæan mountains, which are near the Ocean that men call *Sarmondisc* [b]; and this river runs directly south, on the west side of Alexander's temples, to the nation of the Rhocovasci [c]. Here rises that *fen* [d] (*which men call* Mæotis;) and thence it issues with a great *flood* near the town called Theodosia [e], from whence it empties itself to the eastward into the Euxine Sea, and then becoming narrow for a considerable tract, it passes by Constantinople, and thence into the Mediterranean. The south-west [f] end of Europe is in Spain bounded by the Ocean; but the Mediterranean almost entirely closes at the islands called Gades, where Hercules's pillars

accuracy of either Ælfred or Orosius in this geographical description; and where such a number of places are mentioned, one after another, it is something difficult to discover to which of them the context relates; it is therefore very probable that I have myself made some mistakes also in the punctuation, upon which much depends.

[b] Sarmatico Oceano in Orosius. where the Saxon however plainly refers to a known name of a place or sea, I generally shall translate the Saxon corruption, by what is the real, and commonly accepted name.

[c] Roxolani, in Orosius, and those who desire to know where this nation was situated, may consult Havercamp's edition

[d] I have translated this literally, by using the Saxon term ꝼen, as I shall in every instance where the modern English is clearly derived from that language, and shall commonly print such word in Italics.

[e] Literally, which *men* call Theodosia, but as I have given two instances before of this Saxonism, I shall nos repeat it.

[f] West-south, in the Saxon, which we never say, though so many of our nautical expressions are borrowed from the Saxon, as *Starboard*, &c.

ſtand. In this ſame Mediterranean, to the weſtward, is *Scotland* [g].

Aſia and Africa are divided by Alexandria (a city of Egypt); and that country is bounded to the ſouth by the river Nile, and then by Ethiopia to the weſtward, quite to the ſouthern Ocean. The north-weſtern boundary of Africa is the Mediterranean ſea, where it is divided from the Ocean, near Hercules's pillars; the true weſtern boundaries are the mountains called Atlas, and the iſlands *Fortunatus*.

Thus have I ſhortly mentioned the three diviſions of this earth; and I will now (as I before intimated) ſtate how theſe are bounded by land and water.

Oppoſite to the middle of the eaſtern part of Aſia the river Ganges empties itſelf into the Sea, whilſt the Indian Ocean is to the ſouthward, in which is the port Caligardamana. To the ſouth-eaſt of that port is the iſland Taprobane, and to the north of this port are mouths of the river called Corogoire, in the Ocean named Sericus.

Now theſe are the boundaries of India. Mount Caucaſus is to the north, the river Indus to the weſt, the Red Sea to the ſouth, and the Ocean to the eaſt. In this land of India are four and forty nations, beſides the iſland of Taprobane, which hath ten *boroughs* in it, as alſo many others which are ſituated on the banks of the Indus, and lie all to the weſtward of India. Betwixt this river of Indus, and another river to the weſt, called the Tigris (both which empty themſelves into the Red Sea), are the

[g] This is a ſtrong additional proof, that ſome of the Scoti came from Spain, as is aſſerted by Lhuyd, in his Welch Preface to the Archæologia, where he argues both from this colony being called, in the old Iriſh MSS. *Kin-Skuit*, (or the Scottiſh nation) as alſo from the great affinity between the Iriſh language and the old Cantabrian. See the tranſlation of this Preface, in Biſhop Nicolſon's Hiſt. Library.

countries of Oracaſſia, Parthia, Aſilia, Paſitha, and Media (though writers call all this land both Media and Aſſiria); the country is much parched by the ſun [h], and the roads very hard and ſtony. The northern boundary of this land is Mount Caucaſus, and to the ſouthward the Red Sea; in this country are two great rivers, the Hyſtaſpes, and the Arbis; in this land alſo are two and twenty nations, though it is all called by the general name of Parthia. To the weſtward from hence, all that lies between the Tigris and Euphrates is either Babylonia, Chaldæa, or Meſopotamia. Within this country are eight and twenty nations, the northern boundaries of which are mount Caucaſus, and Taurus, and to the ſouth the Red Sea. Along the Red Sea, and at the north angle of it, lies Arabia, Sabæa, and Eudomane. Beyond the river Euphrates, quite weſtward to the Mediterranean, and northward to mount Taurus, even unto Armenia, and ſouthward, near Egypt, are many countries, namely, Comagena, Phœnicia, Damaſcus, Coelle, Moab, Ammon, Idumæa, Judæa, Paleſtine, and Sarracene, though all theſe nations are comprehended under the name of Syria. To the north of Syria are the hills called Taurus, and to the north of theſe is Cappadocia and Armenia (the latter being weſt of the former), and to the weſt of Cappadocia is the country called the Leſſer Aſia, and to the north of Cappadocia is the plain called Temiſcre, and betwixt Cappadocia and the Leſſer Aſia is Cilicia and Iſaurio.

Aſia is entirely ſurrounded with ſalt water, except to the eaſtward; to the north is the Euxine Sea, but to the weſt the Propontis, and the Helleſpont; whilſt the Mediterranean is to the ſouth. In this ſame Aſia is the high mountain of Olympus.

[h] The Saxon word is beorhte, or bright, which I have ventured to tranſlate *parched by the ſun*, as this ſignification agrees well with the context.

To

To the northward of *hither* Egypt is Palestine, to the eastward the land of Saracene, to the west Libya, and to the south the mountain called Climax. The head of the Nile is near the *cliffs* of the Red Sea, though some say it is in the western part of Africa, near mount Atlas, whence it flows over a large tract of sand till it sinks; it then proceeds in its course till it becomes a great sea; and the spot where the river takes its rise, is called by some Nuchul, and by others Dara. Hence, at some distance from the wider part, before it rises from the sand, it runs westward to Ethiopia, where the river is called Ion, till it reaches the eastern parts, where it becomes wider [1], and then it sinks again into the earth; after which it appears opposite to the cliffs of the Red Sea (as I mentioned before), and from this place (where it rises again) is the river called Nilus. Then running from thence westward, the Nile divides its stream round an island called Meroë, and taking a turn to the northward, it empties itself into the Mediterranean, where (in the winter season) the current at the mouth is opposed by the northern winds, so that the river is spread all over Egypt, and by the rich earth which it carries along with it, fertilizes all that country. The *further* Egypt lies along the southern part of the Red Sea, and to the east lies the Ocean, and to the west is the nearer Egypt, and in the two Egypts are four and twenty nations.

As we have given a description of the north part of Asia, now will we speak of the south part. We have before informed you that mount Caucasus is to the north of India, which begins first eastward of the Ocean, and lies due west of the Armenian mountains, which the inhabitants of the country call Parcoadræ, from which mountains the river Euphrates takes its rise, and from

[1] Literally *a great sea*.

the Parcoadrian ridge, mount Taurus continues due west quite to Cilicia. To the north of these mountains, along the Ocean (quite to the north-east end of the earth) the river *Bore* empties itself into the Ocean, and from hence westward along the Ocean, to the Caspian Sea (which extends to mount Caucasus); all this land is called *Old Scythia*, and Ircania. In this country are three and forty nations, situated at great distances from each other, on account of the barrenness of the soil. Then to the west of the Caspian Sea, unto the river Tanais, and to the *fen* Mæotis, thence south to the Mediterranean and mount Taurus, and north to the Ocean, is all Scythia; though it is divided by two and thirty nations, and the land on the eastern bank of the Tanais. The country is inhabited by a nation called the *Albaori*, in the Latin tongue, and which we now name *Liobene*. Thus have I shortly stated the boundaries of Asia.

Now will I also state those of Europe, as much as we are informed concerning them. From the river Tanais, westward to the river Rhine (which takes its rise in the Alps, whence it runs northward to the *arm of* the Ocean, that surrounds Bryttania, and south to the river Danube, whose source is near that of the Nile, and runs northward of Greece till it empties itself into the Mediterranean) and north even unto the Ocean (which men call *Cwen* sea) are many nations, and the whole of this tract of country is called Germany.

Hence to the north of the source of the Danube, and to the east of the Rhine, are the East Francan, and to the south of them are the Suevæ; on the opposite bank of the Danube, and to the south and east are the Beath-ware in that part which is called Regnesburgh. Due east from hence are the Beme, and to the

the north-east [k] the Thyringæ, to the north of these are the *Seaxan*, to the north-west are the Fryſæ, and to the west of *Old Saxony* is the mouth of the Elbe, as alſo Frifeland. Hence to the north-weſt [l] is that land which is called *Angle*, Sillende, and ſome part of Dena; to the north is Apdrede, and to the north-eaſt the wolds [m] which are called Æfeldan. From hence eaſt-ward is Wineda-land, which men call Syſyle, and great part of the country to the ſouth-weſt Maroaro, and theſe Maroaro have to the weſt the Thyringæ and Behemæ, as alſo half of the Beathware, and to the ſouth, on the other ſide of the Danube, is the country called Carendre. Southward, towards the Alps, lie the boundaries of Beathwara, as alſo Swæfa; and then to the eaſtward of the Carendre country, and beyond the weſt part, is Bulgaria. To the eaſt is Greece, to the eaſt of Maroara is Wiſleland, and to the eaſt of that is Datia, though it formerly belonged to the Goths. To the north-eaſt of Maroaro are the Dalamenſæ; eaſt of Dalamenſæ are the Honithi, and north of the Dalamenſæ are the Sarpe, to the weſt alſo are the Syſle. To the north of the Honithi is Mægthaland, and north of Mægthaland is Sermende, quite to the Riphæan mountains. To the ſouth-weſt of the Dene is that *arm* of the Ocean that ſurrounds Brytannia, and to the north is that arm of the Sea *which is Oſt Sea*, to the eaſt and to the north are the North Dene, either on the continent or on the iſland, to the

[k] Eaſt-north, in the Saxon, as I have before obſerved, with regard to the ſouth-weſt, which in the Saxon is weſt-ſouth, a ſingle inſtance follows, however, where the point ſouth-weſt is mentioned, and not weſt-ſouth.

[l] This ſhould be north-eaſt.

[m] Fylte.

east are the Afdrede, to the south is the mouth of the Elb, and some part of Old Saxony. The North Dene have, to the northward, that same arm of the sea which *is called Ost*, to the east is the nation of the Osti, and Afdrede to the south. The Osti have, to the north of them, that same arm of the Sea, as well as the Winedæ and the Burgundæ, and to the south is Hæfeldan. The Burgundæ have this same arm of the Sea to the west, and the Sueon to the north; to the east are the Sermende, to the north, over the wastes, is *Cwenland*, to the north-west are the Scride Finnas [p], and to the west the Northmen.

" Ohthere told his Lord (King Ælfred) that he lived to the
" north of all the Northmen. He *quoth* that he dwelt in that
" land to the northward, opposite the west *Sea*; he said, how-
" ever, that the land of the Northmen *is due north* from that Sea,
" and it is all a waste, except in a few places, where the Finnas
" for the most part dwell, for hunting in the winter, and in
" the summer for fishing in that Sea. He said, that he was
" determined to find out, once on a time, how far this country
" extended due north, or whether any one lived to the north of
" the wastes before-mentioned. With this intent he proceeded
" due north *from this country* [q], leaving all the way the *waste*

[p] Hakluyt terms the country Scrick-finnia; and Richard Johnson, in his account of Nova Zembla, says, " That south-east of the castle of " Wardhus, are the Scrick-finnes, who are a wild people, who neither " know God nor good order; and these people live in tents made of " deer skins, and they have no certain habitations, but continue in herds " and companies, by one hundred and two hundreds." Hakluyt, vol. 1 p. 283.

[q] þa ꝼoꞃ he noꞃðꞃiꞇe be ðæm lanðe, which is not fully translated; " atque ea propter se recta versus septentrionem esse profectam." See the Oxford edition, by the scholars of University College.

" *land*

" *land* on the ſtarboard, and the whole ſea on the Bæcbord[r].
" He was within three days as far north as the Whale-*hunters*
" ever go, and then proceeded in his courſe due north, as far as
" he could ſail within another three days, whilſt the land lay
" from thence due eaſt, even unto the *inland Sea*, he knows not
" how far [in that direction][s]. He remembers, however, that
" he ſtayed there waiting for a weſtern wind, or a point to the
" north, and ſailed near that land, as far as he could in four
" days, where he waited for a due north wind, becauſe the land
" there lies due *ſouth, quite to the inland Sea, he knows not how*
" *far*[t]: from whence he ſailed along the coaſt due ſouth, as far
" as he could in five days. A great river lies up this land, and
" *when they had gone ſome way up this river, they returned*[u], be-
" becauſe they could not proceed far, on account of the inha-
" bitants being hoſtile, and all that country was inhabited on
" one ſide of this river, nor had Ohthere met with before any
" land that was inhabited ſince he came from his own home.
" All the land to his right, during his whole voyage, was a de-
" ſert, and without inhabitants (except fiſhermen, fowlers, and
" hunters)[w], all of which were Finnas, and he had a wide ſea
" to his left. The Beormas, indeed, had well-peopled their

[r] Or to the left.

[s] The words in the original are, oþþe ȝio ſea in on þæt land he nyſte hwæþer, which, in the Latin tranſlation, runs, " Neſcire autem ſe num " infra terram illam *ſit* mare," but the objection to this tranſlation is, that there is no word in the Saxon to be rendered *ſit*.

[t] By this the land and inland Sea before-mentioned is plainly alluded to.

[u] I muſt here object again to the Latin tranſlation of the following words þa cyrdon hy up on þa ea, viz. " ad ejus oſtia ſe ſubſtitiſſe," which is by no means the ſenſe of the paſſage.

[w] Ohthere hath explained before this reſort to have only been occaſional.

" country,

" country, for which reaſon *Ohthere* did not dare enter upon it; " and the Terfenna [x] land was all a deſert, except when it was " inhabited by fiſhers and fowlers.

" The Beormas told him many particulars about their " land [y], as well as of the other countries near them; but " Ohthere could not rely upon their accounts, becauſe he had " not an opportunity of ſeeing with his own eyes; it ſeemed " however to him, that the Beormas and the Finnas ſpoke the " ſame language. He went the rather, and *ſhaped* his courſe to " each of theſe countries [z], on account of the *horſe*-whales, be- " cauſe they have very good bone in their teeth [a], ſome of which " he brought to the King [b], and their hides are good for ſhip- " ropes. This ſort of whale is much leſs than the other kinds, " it being not longer commonly than ſeven ells; but [Ohthere " ſays] that in his own country is the beſt whale-*hunting*, be- " cauſe the whales are eight and forty ells long, and the *largeſt* [c] " fifty; that he had killed *ſome* ſix; and ſixty [d] in two days.

[x] Mr Lye, in his Saxon Dictionary, refers to this word in this chapter of Oroſius, and renders it *Tartary*.

[y] It muſt be owned that this rather contradicts what is mentioned in the preceding period.

[z] Sc. of the Finnas and the Beormas.

[a] It is ſaid that one of theſe teeth, in the 16th century, ſold for a ruble. Hakluyt, vol. 1 p 280.

[b] Sc. Ælfred. From this circumſtance it hath been inferred, that Ohthere was ſent by this king on this diſcovery, which however is by no means concluſive, for every traveller, in relating his voyage, ſhews the product of the countries he hath viſited. Richard Chancellor, ſpeaking of the commodities of Ruſſia, ſays, " There are alſo a fiſh's teeth, which " fiſh is called a Morſe." Hakluyt, vol 1. p. 237

[c] Mæſtan, very improperly rendered in the Latin tranſlation *nonnullæ*.

[d] I conceive that ſyxa ſhould be a ſecond time repeated here inſtead of ſyxtig, or ſixty, it would then only be aſſerted that *ſix* had been taken in two days, which is much more probable than ſixty.

" Ohthere

" Ohthere was a very rich man in ſuch goods as are valuable in thoſe countries (namely, in wild deer), and had, at the time he came to the king [e], ſix hundred tame deer, none of which he had purchaſed; beſides this, he had ſix decoy [f] rhein-deer, which are very valuable amongſt the Finnas, becauſe they catch the wild ones with them.

" Ohthere himſelf was one of the moſt conſiderable men in thoſe parts, and yet he had not more than twenty horned cattle, twenty ſheep, and twenty ſwine, and what little he ploughed was with horſes. The rents in this country conſiſt chiefly of what is paid by the Finnas, in deer-ſkins, feathers, and whale-bone, ſhip-ropes, made of whales hides, or thoſe of ſeals. Every one pays according to his ſubſtance; the wealthieſt pay the ſkins of fifteen martins, five rhein-deer, one bear's ſkin, ten buſhels of feathers, a cloak of bear's or otter's-ſkin, two ſhip-ropes, (each ſixty ells long,) one made of whale's and the other of ſeal's-ſkin.

" Ohthere moreover ſaid, that Northmanna land was very long and narrow, and that all of the country which is fit either for paſture or plowing is on the ſea coaſt, which however is in ſome parts very rocky; to the eaſt-ward are wild moors, parallel to the cultivated land. The Finnas inhabit theſe moors, and the cultivated land is broadeſt to the eaſtward, and grows narrower to the northward. To the eaſt it is ſixty miles

[e] This ſhews, that Ohthere was a man of conſiderable ſubſtance when he left his own country to come to England, and there is not the leaſt alluſion to his having been ſent to the northward by Ælfred, as his voyage ſeems to have happened long before he was known to that king.

[f] The Saxon word is ſtæl-hranaſ; and we apply, even to this day, the word *ſtale* to a dead bird, which is placed on a tree in a living attitude, ſurrounded with lime-twigs, in order to entice the wild ones.

" broad,

" broad, in ſome places broader, about the middle it is perhaps " thirty miles broad, or ſomewhat more, to the northward " (where it is narroweſt) it may be only three miles [from the " Sea] to the moors, which are in ſome parts ſo wide, that a " man could ſcarcely paſs over them in a fortnight, and in " other parts perhaps in a week[g]. Oppoſite this land, to the " ſouth, is Sweoland, on the other ſide of the moors, quite *to* " *that northern land*[h], and oppoſite to that again, to the north, " is Cwenaland[i]. The Cwenas ſometimes make incurſions " againſt the *Northmen* over theſe moors, and ſometimes the " Northmen on them; there are very large freſh *meres* amongſt " the moors, and the Cwenas carry their *ſhips*[i] over land into " the meres, whence they make depredations on the Northmen; " their *ſhips* are ſmall and very light.

" Ohthere ſaid alſo, that the *ſhire* which he inhabited is called " Halgoland[k], and that no one dwelt to the north of him[l]; " there is likewiſe a port to the ſouth of this land, which " is called Sciringes-heal, which no one could reach in a " month, if *he watched in the night*[m], and every day had a fair " wind;

[g] Theſe very minute particulars ſeem plainly to be taken down by Ælfred, from Ohthere's own mouth, as he corrects himſelf moſt ſcrupulouſly, in order to inform the king with accuracy.

[h] i. e. Normanna land, Ohthere's own country.

[i] Theſe *ſhips* were probably the ſame with the ſmall boats to this day called coracles, which are uſed both on the Towy and the Wye. They make them near Monmouth, not to weigh above 45 lb. and they are eaſily therefore carried on a fiſherman's back over ſhallows

[k] "The land was full of little iſlands, called Ægeland and *Halgeland*, in lat 66. deg. N" Hakluyt, vol. 1. p 235 where the following note is inſerted in the margin, "In this land dwelt Ochther, as it ſeemeth"

[l] It ſhould ſeem that this is to be underſtood as confined to Halgeland, as the port to the ſouth, which follows plainly, relates to the ſame province.

[m] The word in the original is ƿicode, which is rendered curſum ſiſ-"tens;" but it properly ſignifies *to go back*, and not ſtop. I cannot, therefore,

" wind; during this voyage he would sail near land, on his " right hand would be Iraland, and then the islands which are " between Iraland and this land. This country continues quite " to Sciringes heal, and all the way on the left, as you proceed " northward to the south of Sciringes heal, a great sea makes " a vast bay, and is so wide, that no one can see across " it. Gotland is opposite on the other side, and afterwards " the Sea of Sillende lies many miles up in that country. " Ohthere further says, that he sailed in five days from Sciringes " heal, to that port which men call Æt-Hæthum, which is be- " tween the Winedum, Seaxum, and Angle, and makes part of " Dene.

" When Ohthere sailed to this place from *Sciringes heal*, Den- " mark was on his *left*, and on the right a wide sea for three " days, as also two days before he came to Hæthum, Gotland, " Sillende, and many islands [these lands were inhabited by the " Angle before they came hither[n]]; for two days the islands " which belong to Dene were on the left."

" Wulfstan said, that he went from Heathum to Truso in " seven days and nights (the ship being under sail all the time) " that Weonothland was on his right, but Langoland, Læland,

therefore, but think that it should be ꞃacoꝺe, and the meaning would then be, that this port was distant a month's sail, if the vessel continued it's course both by day and night. As for this port called Sciꞃinᵹeꞅ-heal in order to find out what place is hereby intended, we should suppose it to be pronounced *Shiringes*-heal, for *sc*, followed by the vowels *i* and *e* (and sometimes by others) seems always to have been pronounced by the Saxons, as it is by the Italians in the word *Sciolto* pronounced *Shiolto*. Thus we pronounce ꞅcip *ship*, ꞅciell *shell*, ꞅcilꝺ *shield*, ꞅcina *shin*, ꞅciꞃe *shire*, ꝼiꞅcaꞅ *fish*, &c.

[n] This clears up most decisively the doubts in Camden's preface, p. clviii. with regard to the situation of the Angles.

" Falster, and Scoley on his left, all which belong to Denemarca, *we*° had also Burgenda-land on our left, which hath a king of its own. After having left Burgendaland, the islands of Becinga, Meroe, Eouland, and Gotland, were on our left, which country belongs to Sweon; and Weonodland was all the way on our right, to the mouth of the Wesel. This river is a very large one, and near it lies Willand and Weonodland, the former of which belongs to Estum, and the Wesel does not run through Weonodland, but through Estmere, which lake is fifteen miles broad. Then runs the Ilsing, from the eastward into Estmere; on the bank of which stands Truso, and the Ilsing flows from Eastland into the Estmere, and the Wesel from Weonodland to the south; the Ilsing, having joined the Wesel takes its name, and runs to the west of Estmere, and northward into the Sea, when it is called the Wesel's mouth. Eastland is a large tract of country, and there are in it many towns, and in every town is a king; there is also a great quantity of honey and fish, and the king and the richest men drink nothing but milk, whilst the poor and the slaves use mead. They have many contests

° It seems very clear, from this expression of *we*, that when king Ælfred came to this part of Orosius's geography, he consulted Ohthere and Wulfstan, who had lived in the northern parts of Europe, which the ancients were so little acquainted with, and that he took down this account from their own mouths. For the same reason it is not improbable that there may be some mistakes in the King's relation, as though these northern travellers spoke a language bearing an affinity to the Anglo Saxon, yet it was certainly a dialect with material variations. For proof of this let a chapter of the *Speculum Regale*, written in the old Icelandic, or Norwegian, be compared with the Anglo-Saxon. This very curious work was published at Soroe, in 1768.

" amongst

" amongſt themſelves, and the people of Eſtum brew no ale, " though they have mead in profuſion [q].

" There is alſo a particular cuſtom amongſt this nation, that " when any one dies, the corpſe continues unburnt with the re- " lations and friends for a month or two, and the bodies of " kings and nobles [r] (according to their reſpective wealth) lye " for half a year before the corpſe is thus deſtroyed, and it " continues above ground in the houſe, during which time drink- " ing and ſports laſt till the day on which the body is conſumed. " Then, when it is carried to the funeral pile, the ſubſtance of " the deceaſed (which remains after theſe drinking bouts and " ſports) is divided into five or ſix heaps (ſometimes into more) " according to what he happens to be worth. Theſe heaps are " diſpoſed at a mile's diſtance from each other, the largeſt heap " at the greateſt diſtance from the town, and ſo gradually the " ſmaller at leſſer intervals, till all the wealth is divided, ſo that " the leaſt heap ſhall be neareſt the town where the corpſe lies.

" Then all thoſe are to be ſummoned who have the fleeteſt " horſes in that country, within the diſtance of five or ſix miles " from theſe heaps, and they all ſtrive for the ſubſtance of the " deceaſed; he who hath the ſwifteſt horſe obtains the moſt diſ- " tant and largeſt heap, and ſo the others, in proportion, till the " whole is ſeized upon. He procures, however, the leaſt heap, " who takes that which is neareſt the town, and then every one " rides away with his ſhare, and keeps the whole of it; on ac- " count of this cuſtom, fleet horſes are extremely dear. When " the wealth of the deceaſed hath been thus exhauſted, then they " carry the corpſe from the houſe, to burn it, together with the

[q] Here Wulfſtan's voyage ends in Hakluyt.
[r] *High men* in the Saxon.

"dead man's weapons and cloaths; and generally they ſpend "the whole wealth of the deceaſed, by the body's continuing ſo "long in the houſe before it is buried [s]; what, however, remains, "and is thus diſpoſed in heaps on the road, is taken away by "theſe foreign competitors.

"It is alſo a cuſtom with the Eſtum, that the bodies of all the "inhabitants ſhall be burned; and if any one can find a ſingle "bone unconſumed, it is a cauſe of anger. Theſe people alſo "have the means of producing very ſevere cold, by which the "dead body continues ſo long above ground without putrefying [t]; "and if any one ſets a veſſel full of ale or water, they contrive "that the liquors ſhall be frozen, be it ſummer [u] or be it winter."

[s] That is, by the conſequential expences.

[t] Phineas Fletcher, who was ambaſſador from Queen Elizabeth to Ruſſia, gives an account of the ſame practice continuing in ſome parts of Muſcovy. "In winter time, when all is covered with ſnow, ſo many "as die are piled up in a hovel in the ſuburbs, like billets on a wood-"ſtack; they are as hard with the froſt as a very ſtone, till the ſpring-"tide come and reſolve the froſt, what time every man taketh his dead "friend, and committeth him to the ground." See a note to one of Fletcher's eclogues, p. 10, printed at Edinburgh, in 1771, 12mo. See alſo a poem written at Moſcow, by G. Tuberville, in the firſt volume of Hakluyt, p. 386, where the ſame circumſtance is dwelt upon, and the reaſon given, that the ground cannot be dug. Bodies, however, are now buried at Moſcow during the winter.

[u] This muſt have been effected by ſome ſort of an ice houſe; and it appears by the Amœnitates Academicæ, that they have now ice-houſes in Sweden and Lapland, which they build with moſs.

JOURNAL

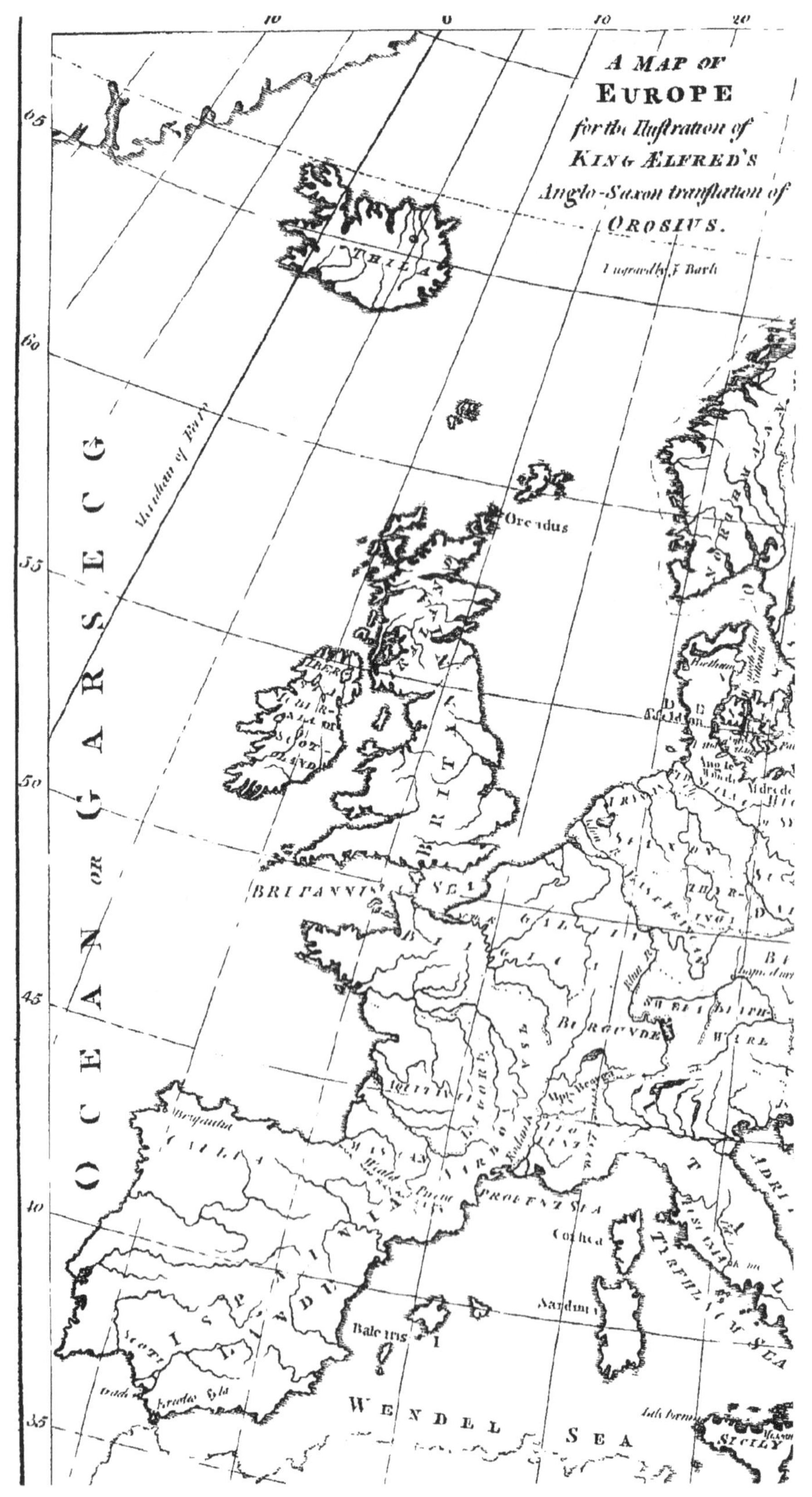
A MAP OF
EUROPE
for the Illustration of
KING ÆLFRED'S
Anglo-Saxon translation of
OROSIUS.
OCEAN OR GARSECG
Orcadus
THILA
BRITANNIS SEA
WENDEL SEA
SICILY
Corsica
Sardinia
Baleeris I
PROVENTSEA
BURGUNDE
AQUITANIA
TIRRHENUM SEA
ADRIATIC
Ocean

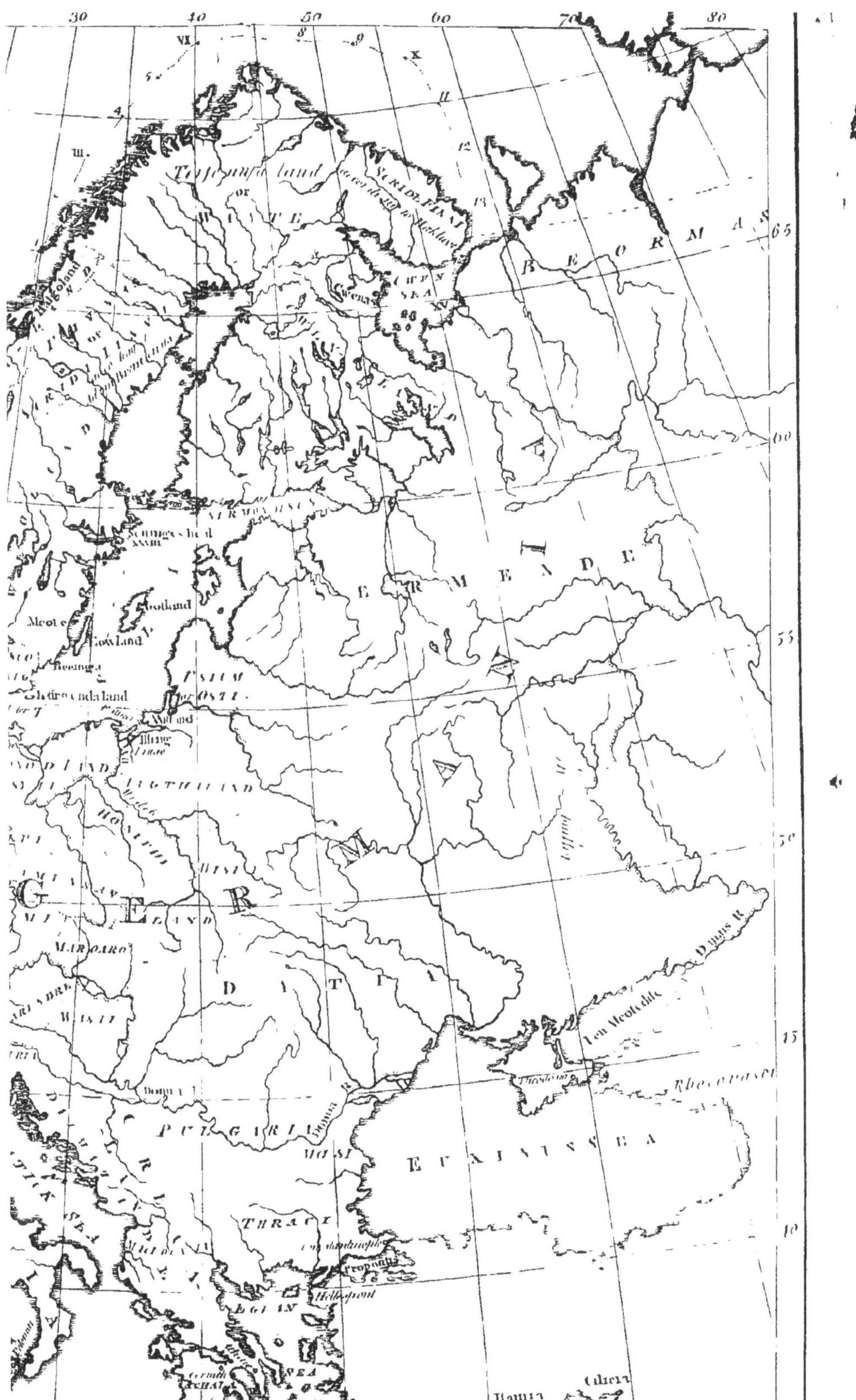

30
40
50
60
70
80
65
60
55
50
45
40
Terfenna land
or
SCRIDEFINNI
CWEN SEA
Cwenas
Helgoland
N O R M A S
SERMONICUS
Gotland
Meore
Gowland
Beemga
Wit land
Illing
Witland
Eastland
ESTUM
OSTI
HOREFTHI
R E D M E N D E
A
M
G E R
A
D A T I A
DACIA
WISLE
MAROARO
PULGARIA
Donua R.
Donua R.
MOSI
EUXINUS SEA
THRACI
Constantinople
Propontis
Hellespont
EGIAN
SEA
Dunus R.
Theodosia
Corinth
ACHAI

JOURNAL

OF

A VOYAGE IN 1775.

To explore the coaſt of America, Northward of California,

By the ſecond Pilot of the Fleet, Don FRANCISCO ANTONIO MAURELLE, in the King's Schooner, called the Sonora, and commanded by Don JUAN FRANCISCO DE LA BODEGA.

PREFACE.

THE following journal having been placed in my hands for perusal, I conceived it to be so interesting for the improvement of Geography, that I desired permission to translate and publish it.

I was principally induced to take this trouble, because I supposed, that the Spaniards, from their most peculiar jealousy with regard to their American dominions[a], would never permit that navigators of other countries (particularly the English) should know the excellent ports of the Western part of America in high Northern Latitudes, which are here laid down with such accuracy and precision, together with the abundant supply of masts, fire wood, and water which may be procured in most of them.

[a] That most able Historian Dr. Robertson, after having mentioned, that most of the American papers are deposited in the Archivo of Simanca, near Valladolid, thus proceeds:

"The prospect of such a treasure excited my most ardent curiosity; "but the prospect of it only is all that I have enjoyed. Spain, with "an excess of caution, hath uniformly thrown a veil over her trans-"actions in America: from strangers they are concealed with peculiar "solicitude." Preface to the History of America, p. ix.

It appears, by Venegas's Hiſtory of California, publiſhed in 1747[b], that great jealouſy was then entertained of our diſcovering a N. W. paſſage[c], becauſe they apprehended we ſhould annoy the coaſts of Mexico and Peru.

Nothing however can be more groundleſs than theſe ſuſpicions, for whenever a N. W. or any other Northern communication is found between the Atlantic and Pacific Oceans, it may be boldly pronounced that ſuch paſſage will be ſo very precarious, as never to anſwer the purpoſe of expeditions in time of war, or commerce during peace.

The Spaniards ſhould, after our late voyages of diſcovery (which reflect ſo much honour upon his Majeſty's reign), be convinced that the Engliſh Nation is actuated merely by deſiring to know as much as poſſible with regard to the planet which we inhabit, and to which our geographical inquiries are neceſſarily bounded.

This diſtruſt on the part of Spain would more wiſely be directed againſt the Ruſſians, who from Camſkatſka might eaſily eſtabliſh themſelves on the W. coaſt of America, and from thence perhaps in time ſhake their unwieldy, and already tottering empire[d].

From theſe ill-founded apprehenſions of what the Engliſh may meditate againſt their American Dominions on the Weſtern coaſt of that vaſt continent, they will not permit an individual,

[b] Madrid, 3 vol. Quarto.

[c] Igualmente notorias ſon las *ruidoſas*, y *porfiadas* tentativas de los *Ingleſes*, para hallar un paſſage al mar del *Sur*, por *el Norte de America*. Ibid. T. III. p. 225.

[d] I am accordingly informed, that the Empreſs means to fit out four veſſels on the coaſt of Camſkatſka, which are to be employed in diſcoveries, during the proper ſeaſon of 1781.

even of our nation, to ſet his foot in their part of America, even for ſcientific purpoſes [e].

Notwithſtanding this perpetual diſtruſt of this country in the Spaniards, and our preſent war with them, I will venture to ſay, that an attack upon the city or province of Mexico, would not be adviſable on our part. If the Spaniards indeed acted wiſely, they ſhould themſelves abandon it, for the mines

[e] The tranſaction I here allude to is the following. Lord Morton, as Preſident of the Royal Society, applied to the then Spaniſh ambaſſador at our Court in 1766, for leave that an Engliſh Aſtronomer might obſerve the Tranſit of Venus (expected in 1769) on ſome part of California. This was however refuſed, when his Lordſhip requeſted, that Father Boſcowich, a *foreigner* and *good Catholick*, might have the ſame permiſſion; in which he was at firſt more ſucceſsful, but the favour was even then granted with many clogs, and the permiſſion at laſt recalled, on account of his being a Jeſuit, who were at that time baniſhed from Old and New Spain.

At the ſame time Chappe Dauteroche obtained this permiſſion, and for the ſame purpoſe; the conſequence of which hath been, that a draft of the city of Mexico, in its preſent ſtate, was found amongſt his papers, and publiſhed by his Catholic Majeſty's good allies, the French, for the information of his enemies.

I once applied myſelf to the late Prince Maſſerano (ſo deſervedly eſteemed whilſt reſident as Miniſter of Spain in England) that an ingenious German, named Kukahn [*], might be permitted, under any reſtrictions, to go from La Vera Cruz, to any part of the province of Mexico, merely to collect ſpecimens of Natural Hiſtory I was alſo reſponſible that he never would attend to any thing, during his journies, but the animals he might meet with. Though I made this application by a channel which his excellency would have been deſirous to oblige, yet he excuſed himſelf, from its being a fundamental rule with the Court of Spain, that no foreigner be permitted to paſs through any part of their dominions on the continent of America.

[*] See an account of his method of preſerving animals, and placing them in their proper attitudes (Ph. Tranſ.) He is now eſtabliſhed in Jamaica, and hath ſucceeded in raiſing many European fruits, as alſo products of our kitchen-gardens in ſome ground which he hath purchaſed, about half way up a mountain.

within any convenient distance are nearly exhausted, whilst the charge of bringing quicksilver from La Vera Cruz is thereby greatly augmented. Venegas therefore informs us, that it is not worth while to work the more abundant mines of Sonora to the Northward, from this increase of expence. The silver indeed, at so distant a period as 150 years ago, was chiefly brought from St. Lewis de Sacateeas, which is nearly 100 leagues N of Mexico[f]. This objection does not hold with regard to the continuing to work the silver mines of Peru, as the famous one of quicksilver, called *Guanacabelica*, is situated in the same province. It is believed also, that the *gold mines* in America, as they are improperly called, answer as little to the Spaniards. At least I have been informed, by a person who resided two or three years in Brasil, which furnishes the greatest quantity of this precious metal, that those who go in search of it are not paid above a shilling per day for their labours. Gold is never found in the state of ore, or by digging deep into the bowels of the earth; the adventurers therefore go in companies of five or six to explore those parts where they conceive themselves to have the best chance of finding it near the surface, but often return after being out months, with a very small portion, by which the fatigues and dangers they have incurred are poorly compensated.

As little would it answer to take possession of Acapulco, for the sake of an annual ship which would presently change its rendesvouz for another port, or of Panama, in order to inter-

[f] To this it may be added, that the situation of Mexico is very unhealthy, *Gage* comparing the many canals to those of Venice, which are often highly offensive. [See Gage's Survey of the W. Indies.] It is also subject to great inundations; and Don Alzate informs the Academy of Sciences at Paris, that during the years 1736 and 1768 more than one-third of the inhabitants died of the black vomit.

cept

cept the flotilla, which by late regulations is never to touch there [g].

The Spaniards moreover should learn from what England hath suffered by conquering Canada for our ungrateful colonies, that the settlement of a rival nation to the Northward of Mexico, would possibly operate in favour of the mother country.

We have experienced this most unnatural rebellion within a few years after we had removed the dread of the French in Canada from them, and after every fostering indulgence on our part. What may the Spaniards therefore have occasion to dread from their vast American Empire, the inhabitants of which they are perpetually oppressing with their enormous duties and taxes?

Thus much have I ventured to say in hopes that the court of Spain will rather promote, than obstruct, any future voyage of discovery, in the Northern parts of the Pacific Ocean.

I am sorry that I have not an opportunity of engraving with this journal the nine charts which should accompany it; but as the Latitudes and Longitudes of the new Discoveries on the coast of America are so accurately stated, I should hope that the publication will at least convince the Spaniards how little it will answer the purpose of mystery to withhold them.

It appears by this journal that the Viceroy of Mexico sent some other ships on discovery to the Northward in a preceding year, and

[g] The silver from Peru and Chili is either now sent over part of the Andes to Buenos Ayres, or otherwise transmitted in single register ships round Cape Horn. The establishment of Galeons sailing in a fleet from Cadiz being now also abolished, Carthagena, Porto Bello, and Panama, are become more than useless to the Spaniards, as the climates are bad, whilst the civil and military establishment at each is very expensive.

that

that they proceded to N. Lat. 55. Don Juan Peres, who was *enſign*[h] on board the Frigate in the preſent voyage, had ſome ſtation in the former, and carried with him a chart of the coaſt, in many of the parts which were then explored.

I am ſorry not to be able to ſtate any further particulars, but think it right to mention thus much, in hopes that it may produce ſome account of this former voyage.

I ſhould conceive, that both the one and the other were produced by our attempts to diſcover a N. W. Paſſage; becauſe it will be found, that wherever the Spaniards landed they were inſtructed to take poſſeſſion (though not to keep it) with every poſſible formality, which undoubtedly was to be ſet up as a complete title againſt future claimants, by right of diſcovery.

The compiler of the preſent journal, D. Antonio Maurelle, ſerved on board the ſchooner employed on this voyage (together with a frigate) under the title of Second Pilot of the Fleet[i].

In one of the written opinions which he gave whilſt thus employed, he ſtates, that he had ſerved ten years in the Bay of Biſcay[k], and ſeems to have been a moſt diligent navigator; whilſt, to his honour, he always adviſes the proceeding to as high a Northern Latitude as poſſible, though ſome of his brother officers almoſt deſpair.

At the cloſe of the journal a very accurate table is given of the ſhip's courſe for each day, with no leſs than nine columns.

Having however conſulted ſome moſt experienced and able ſea-officers on this occaſion, they have adviſed me only to print

[h] *Alferez.*

[i] I underſtand that we have no rank in our marine ſervice which anſwers at all to this.

[k] The expreſſion in the original is *Golfo de las Yeguas*, or the *Gulf of Mares*. The Spaniards alſo call the gulf of Mexico *Golfo de las Cieruas*, or Gulf *of Does*.

5 a few

a few of theſe heads [l], as ſome of them would not be eaſily underſtood by any navigator, who is not a Spaniard.

Upon the whole, it is hoped, that this account of an eight months navigation on the unfrequented coaſt of America, will prove a valuable addition to geography; eſpecially as our immortal Captain Cook had ſo few opportunities of examining moſt parts of the ſame continent to the Weſtward [m], though his diſcoveries to the Northward will prove ſo intereſting.

[l] It is right alſo to obſerve, that (though I give the column which ſtates the Variation of the Needle) it is not ſpecified whether the Variation is Weſt or Eaſt; I ſhould rather indeed ſuppoſe it to be the latter, on the authority of Dr. Halley, though perhaps the direction may have altered ſince the laſt century. This doubt however will be ſettled when Capt. Cook's laſt voyage is publiſhed.

[m] This is ſaid to have been occaſioned by unſavourable winds.

A

PREFACE OF DON ANTONIO MAURELLE.

FOR the better underſtanding this Journal, it will be proper to premiſe the following particulars.

The charts which we uſed during the voyage were thoſe of Monſ. Bellin, the one publiſhed in 1766, and the other in 17—; the firſt of which places the port of St. Blas, 110 degrees W. Long. from Paris, and the ſecond 114, differing conſequently 4 degrees. For this reaſon I have always reckoned the Weſtern Longitude from St. Blas[a], and not from Paris.

At the end there is an accurate table, every page of which includes a month, with an account of the Ship's courſe each day, together with the number of leagues ſailed, the longitude, latitude, variation of the needle (which laſt, when attended to, is marked with an aſteriſk), and the diſtance from the neareſt land.

[a] San Blas is a very ſmall hamlet, on the W. coaſt of the province of Mexico, at the mouth of the River S. Pedro It is but within theſe few years that the Spaniards have made a ſettlement there, for the conveniency of tranſporting the troops and proviſions they ſend to California. Dr. Robertſon's map places it about the 22d degree of N. Lat. and 88th W Long from Fero. See alſo Chappe D'Auteroche's account of his journey from La Vera Cruz to S Blas in 1769. The Latitude of this port is not ſettled by this Journal, nor Longitude except by reference.

The plans of the ports which have been discovered, follow these tables, as also a chart of the whole coast, drawn with the greatest accuracy, as we always marked the most distinguishable points. In order also that we might be more exact, we compared the ship's course with that of the coast, and repeated our observations, both in sailing Northwards, and returning to the South.

We likewise have omitted every longitude, in which we conceived there had been mistakes, by accidents that had happened, and when we only doubted in distances of no great moment, we have laid them down, making the proper allowances.

The latitudes of the charts [b] are marked with the greatest precision, in those situations where it may be of the most use, having had sufficient time to make the proper observations, whilst the allowances for refraction were attended to.

[b] These charts unfortunately did not accompany the Journal.

January, 1775.

BEING on board the King's ſtoreſhip [c] the *Santa Rica*, which then lay in the port of Vera Cruz, I received on the 10th of that month an order from his Excellency the Viceroy [d] Don Antonio Maria de Bucarely and Orſua, to undertake the function of firſt pilot in the expedition, which was then fitting out at the port of St. Blas for diſcoveries on the Northern coaſt of California [e].

As I have always had the ſtrongeſt deſire to ſerve his Majeſty (be the riſque what it may) I readily accepted this commiſſion, and ſetting out from La Vera Cruz on the 12th of January, I reached Mexico on the 18th in order to receive his Excellency's further commands. I left Mexico again on the 16th of February, and arrived at the Port of St. Blas [f], putting myſelf under the orders of the officer, who was to fit out the expedition, Don Bruno Heceta. The ſhips prepared for this purpoſe were a frigate and ſchooner [g], the latter being 36 feet long [h], 12 feet wide, and 8 deep, commanded by the Lieutenant Don Juan de Ayala, aſſiſted by Don Juan Francisco de la Bodega, of the ſame

[c] Urca.

[d] Sc. of Mexico.

[e] It ſhould ſeem from this journal, that the Spaniards deem all the N. W. coaſt of America beyond California to be part of that province.

[f] The journey from La Vera Cruz to Port S. Blas is ſuppoſed to be 300 leagues, thus divided: from La Vera Cruz to Mexico 110 leagues; and from the latter to S. Blas 190.

[g] Goleta.

[h] 18 codos, each codo being two feet.

rank, and I embarked in the ſchooner. It ſo happened that the pacquet-boat S. Carlos was at this time in the port of S. Blas, commanded by the Lieutenant D. Miguel Maurrique, who was to proceed to the eſtabliſhment at Monterey[i].

Whilſt we continued here, we laid in proviſions for a year's voyage; all of which were procured from the neighbourhood.

On the 16th of March we had taken on board all ſuch neceſſaries; and at 10 o'clock at night the three veſſels ſet ſail, ſteering N. W. with a gentle land-breeze at N. N. E. but though we did every thing in our power during the night to keep company with the other ſhips, we were not able, which we conceived to ariſe from the cargoe not being properly ſtowed, becauſe the ſchooner's reputed rate of ſailing, by thoſe who were well-acquainted with her, left us ſcarcely any doubt with regard to this being the real cauſe.

As ſoon as day appeared on the 17th it grew calm, and continued ſo till three in the afternoon; when a breeze from the N. W. ariſing, we ſteered N. N. E. and towards the coaſt, till ſun-ſet, when the wind fell. At this time we caſt anchor, and found ourſelves 4 leagues N. N. E. of S. Blas, and in this manner we proſecuted our voyage, making uſe of the ſea-breeze during the day, and the land-breeze during the night, gaining very little to windward[k], and caſting anchor when the wind fell, in order not to loſe ground by the currents[l], after ſo little progreſs, and with ſuch trouble.

[i] The latitude of Monterey is ſettled afterwards by this journal to be in 36 44 N. Lat. and 17 0 W. Long. from St. Blas. It is ſituated on the Weſtern coaſt of California, and a miſſion of Jeſuits is there eſtabliſhed.

[k] Barlovento.

[l] The currents are ſo ſtrong in this ſea that a promontory S. of S. Blas is called Corrientes.

On

On the 13th at three in the evening the S. Carlos Pacquet-boat made a fignal for help, on which our captain fent a boat, in which Don Mignel Maurique (who commanded the Pacquet) was brought to our fhip, when we plainly difcovered, by his actions, that he was out of his fenfes. On this our principal officers accompanied him on board the frigate, that the captain might give the proper orders on this occafion, when a council being held, and the furgeons examined, as well as ocular proofs appearing of D. Maurique's madnefs, it was determined to fet him on fhore, as alfo to give the command of the pacquet-boat to Don Juan d'Ayla, lieutenant of the frigate, and that of the fchooner to Don Juan Francifco de la Bodega and Quadra, who had the fame rank.

On the 20th, the breeze being moderate, it was difcovered that the foretopfail [m] was rent in feveral places, which defect it was neceffary to repair immediately.

Whilft the wind thus continued, the commander of the fchooner tried many experiments, to make her fail better, one of which indeed rather improved her rate; but the frigate, notwithftanding, was ftill obliged to fhorten fail, in order to keep us company, and indeed to take us in towe [n].

On the 24th at noon we had fight of the Southernmoft of the Marias [o], lying to the N. E. at the diftance of three leagues, which makes the then fituation of our fhip exactly a degree W. of S. Blas, according to M. Belin's map of 1756, and in N. Lat. 21. 4. m. Now this differs from my obfervations, being 26 minutes too far Northwards.

[m] El maftelero de velacho.

[n] In the original another experiment is ftated, which I have not tranflated, as I conceive it would be uninterefting to the reader.

[o] There are three iflands thus called.

Whilſt we were in this ſituation we loſt ſight of the pacquet-boat, but we continued our courſe ſteering S. W.[p] when we obſerved many birds, ſome of which were black, with a white ſpot on their breaſt, the wings long, beak rather large, belly prominent, and tail like a pair of ſciſſars[q], others again were entirely white; whilſt ſome were grey, with a ſingle large feather. We likewiſe ſaw other birds, which dived often under the water, named bobos.

During great part of March the wind freſhened in the day, and fell at night, particularly a little before the new moon[r], (which happened on the 29th,) after which we had often calms, the wind having before blown from the N. W. to the N. on this ſame day (viz. the 29th) we ſaw an iſland at ſunſet, which is ſaid to be called Socorro[s], by which name it is not to be found in the French maps, nor in the Hiſtory of California[t]. We had a view of it whilſt it lay to the Eaſtward at the diſtance of 9 or 10 leagues, which with difficulty we gained to windward[u], wiſhing to ſail as nearly as poſſible upon the meridian of that iſland.

On the 30th we endeavoured to approach nearer to Socorro, when it lay W. N. W.[x] at the diſtance of four leagues, but

[p] Sudoeſte quarta al oeſte.

[q] Tixera.

[r] Great attention to the moon, and its ſuppoſed effects on the weather, is to be obſerved in other parts of this journal.

[s] This iſland, in Dr. Robertſon's map, is placed in 19 N. Lat. and 94 W. Long. from Fero.

[t] This is probably the hiſtory of that country publiſhed by Miguel Venegas (a Mexican Jeſuit) at Madrid, in 1758, which was tranſlated into Engliſh, and printed at London in 1759. It is not at all extraordinary however that this iſland ſhould not be mentioned in that account, as Venegas chiefly deſcribes the E. coaſt of California. Socorro is conſiderably to the South of that Peninſula.

[u] Orzando.

[x] Quarta al oeſte.

we

we could not effect this on account of the currents to the S. which carried us to Leeward [y].

From the 31ſt of March till the 4th of April we had either calms or light breezes, on which account we could not ſail further from this iſland than we loſt by the currents. For this reaſon alſo we tried by towing the ſchooner, and uſing of our oars, whether we might not make ſome part of the iſland, where we might procure water; but in this we could not ſucceed on account of the violent currents.

This iſland, which, as was ſaid before, is not named Socorro in any maps, is undoubtedly that which was diſcovered by Hernando Triabba, who commanded a ſhip diſpatched from Guantepeque, by Hernan Cortes, to explore the coaſt of California. This veſſel ſailed 300 leagues ——— [z] and fell in with an iſland named St. Thomas, which is ſo called in the French maps, though erroneouſly placed, becauſe its real latitude is 18° 53′ N. Lat. and W. Long. from S. Blas 5° 18′.

On the 4th of April we loſt ſight of Socorro to the E N E. and proſecuted our voyage to windward as much as poſſible, without any other accident but the frigate's bowſprit being damaged, which we ſoon repaired.

At this time we found that the ſky was not ſo clear as before, we approached Socorro, that the ſun did not appear ſo frequently, that the miſts were not ſo thick, that the wind was much more cold, and in ſhort we experienced a very different temperature.

Till the 14th, when the full moon happened, the breezes were ſlight, and the currents always to the South, after this

[y] Sotovento.

[z] There is a chaſm in the MS with regard to the direction in which ſhe ſailed.

however

however the wind freſhened to the N. N. E. ſometimes flitting to the N. E. and blowng more ſtrongly from that point. By theſe means we had an opportunity of trying the ſailing capacity of the ſchooner, for the rougher the ſea the more ſail was ſet, ſo that the deck was conſtantly two planks [a] under water to leeward; which thoroughly convinced thoſe on board the frigate of our determined reſolution to proſecute our voyage.

The crews of both ſhips, who obſerved what a preſs of ſail was carried by the ſchooner, from the determined reſolution of the officers to proceed as far Northward as poſſible, ſaw plainly that they were in ſome degree miſtaken, by conceiving at our firſt departure that the ſchooner would be obliged to return to S. Blas in a fortnight. They however ſtill ſhewed their apprehenſions if ſhe purſued her voyage, whilſt ſome of the ſchooner's company began to ſicken, and wiſh themſelves on board the frigate, where there were medicines and a ſurgeon. The ſurgeon however declared, that if ſuch ſeamen were removed to the frigate, they would be probably ſeized with a fever, on which the Captain thought it right that this opinion ſhould be made known to the ſchooner's crew, as he ſuppoſed it would have a greater effect than the threats of any puniſhment. To ſay the truth, we could not but be ſorry to obſerve the horror that the crew conceived of the bad condition of the ſchooner, which afforded miſerable quarters for the ſick, as the ſeamen could not do the buſineſs without being thoroughly wet, except when it was calm.

Theſe diſtreſſes would have become inſufferable, had not the commander behaved with the greateſt kindneſs to the crew, he encouraged them to perſiſt alſo, by giving them frequently ſmall

[a] Tablas.

presents, and reminded them of the glory they would obtain on their return, if they reached the proper latitude [b]. He added also, that the risque was nearly equal [c] to both vessels, and that as each ship's company valued their lives, they might be sure that it would not be attempted to proceed further than was consistent with their mutual safety. This interposition of the commander had at length the proper effect, and we agreed to live and dye together.

On the 11th of May the wind began to veer about, and on every point to the Eastward, but ended to the E. & S. E. with many squalls [d] and mists. The strong currents which we had before experienced to the S. were now scarcely to be perceived.

On the 21st our commander held a council, in which it was to be determined whether we should continue our voyage, or put into the establishment at Monterey, and that the resolutions we should come to might be the more deliberate, our opinions, with the reasons on which they were founded, were reduced to writing. As the wind however was very violent, there could be no personal communication between the officers of the two ships, and our opinions were therefore transmitted by means of a cask.

[These opinions follow, in the journal at length, but as they would not be very interesting even to the navigator, I shall only state that they all agree in advising that they should proceed as far N. as 43. rather than put into Monterey. The principal

[b] It appears afterwards that they were instructed to proceed as far N. as 65 if practicable.

[c] It must be recollected that at this time the frigate towed the schooner.

[d] Chuvascos, which is supposed to be a term used in the Mexican Seas.

reason

reaſon for this advice is, that Martin de Aguilar had diſcovered a river in this latitude, where they hoped conſequently to water, and repair their veſſels [e].]

We proceeded on our voyage therefore with briſk winds from the N. & N. N. E. the ſea running high till the 30th, when the new moon happened during which interval we made many tacks, and did not accurately obſerve our longitude or latitude.

On this ſame day we had gentle breezes between N. W. & S. W. varying thus for the three following days, after which the wind was ſteady in the W. N W. and blew freſher as the moon increaſed.

On the firſt of June one of our ſeamen was ſo drunk with ſpirits that we thought it right to remove him to the frigate [f], where he afterwards died in leſs than ſix hours. On the ſame day we obſerved ſome ſea-weeds, the top of which much reſembled an orange [g], from the upper part of which hung large and broad leaves.

At the extremity of this plant is a very long tube, which fixes to the rocks on the coaſt till it is looſened by the ſea, when it often floats to the diſtance of 100 leagues. We named this plant the *Orange-Lead*.

The next day we ſaw another plant, with long and narrow leaves like a ribband, which is called *Zacate del Mar*; we alſo ſaw many ſea-wolves, ducks, and fiſh.

[e] In the account of this voyage in 1601, added to Venegas's Hiſtory of California, this river is ſaid to have been diſcovered by the pilot Lopes, and not by Martin de Aguilar. In ſome maps it is placed in 45 N. Lat.

[f] Becauſe there was a ſurgeon on board that ſhip, probably.

[g] Una naranja.

On

On the 5th our towing rope[h] was broke; which indeed had happened ſeveral times before, notwithſtanding the greateſt care of both ſhip's companies, on which accident we reſolved to proceed, as well as we could, without this very inconvenient appendage.

On the 7th, from the colour of the ſea, we judged ourſelves to be in ſoundings, and we ſuppoſed ourſelves to be about thirty leagues from the coaſt.

By noon on the ſame day we diſtinguiſhed a large tract of the coaſt (though at a conſiderable diſtance) lying from the S. W. to the N E. but we were not able to get nearer to it, by the winds falling calm during the night and the following day.

On the 8th we ſaw the coaſt much clearer at the diſtance of about 9 leagues, and the next 24 hours the currents to the S. increaſed ſtrongly, ſo that there was a difference in the latitude by obſervation and our reckoning of 29 minutes.

The ſame day the wind freſhening, the commander made ſignal for the ſchooner to reconnoitre the coaſt, which direction we complied with to our utmoſt, ſteering to the N. N. E. and hoping to do this before the night. In effect, by ſix in the evenning, we diſtinguiſhed many headlands, bays, plains, and mountains, with trees and green fields.

By eight at night we were not more than two leagues diſtant from the land, nor the frigate more than three; we then ſailed towards her, and thus paſſed the night.

On the 9th at break of day the frigate made us a ſignal to join them, and by 10 in the morning we followed their courſe till we came to another part of the coaſt, where we ſaw, with the greateſt clearneſs, the plains, rocks, bays, headlands, breakers,

[h] El remorque.

 and

and trees : here we ſounded in 30 fathoms, the bottom being a black ſand. At the ſame time we ſailed along the coaſt, and endeavoured to find out a port, being at the diſtance only of a mile, and approaching to a high cape, which ſeemed to promiſe ſhelter, though we were obliged to proceed cautiouſly, as many ſmall iſlands concealed from us ſome rocks, which ſcarcely appeared above the ſurface of the ſea.

As we now perceived a land-locked harbour to the S. W. we determined to enter it, making at the ſame time a ſignal to the frigate to lend us an anchor, which however they were not able to do, from their diſtance, as well as that the wind blew freſh. For theſe reaſons the ſchooner entered the port alone, ſounding all the way, with the greateſt care, and the frigate followed in our wake.

Whilſt we were thus entering the port, we obſerved two canoes from the N. which came cloſe to the frigate, and exchanged their ſkins for bugles, and other trifles, with our ſeamen, whilſt in the mean time the ſchooner caſt anchor oppoſite to a little village [k], which was ſituated at the bottom of a mountain: the inhabitants however did not ſend out any canoes to us.

After this we ſounded the interior parts of the port, and we found ſufficient depth of water to anchor at a bow's ſhot from the land, we ſaw likewiſe the frigate at the bottom of the port, and faſtened our cables to ſome rocks which nature ſeemed to have fixed there for this purpoſe. We took however the precaution to let fall two anchors on the oppoſite ſide; (viz. to the S. and S. W.) on which the frigate followed our example.

[k] Rancheria.

As

As ſoon as we had anchored, ſome Indians in canoes came on board, who, without the leaſt ſhyneſs, trucked ſome ſkins for bugles.

And here it may be right to obſerve the inaccuracies of the French map [l], both with regard to the capes, and the lying of the coaſt. It ſhould ſeem indeed that the abſolute want of authentic materials hath been the occaſion of laying down at random ſome large bays, which we neither found to the N. or to the S. as we muſt certainly have fallen in with them above Cape Fortuna, which is placed 18 leagues to the S. of Cape Mendocino [m], whereas we were twenty leagues to the N. which makes an error of two degrees of latitude [n].

On the 11th we had fixed every thing with regard to our anchorage, and we determined to take poſſeſſion of the country, upon the top of a high mountain, which lyes at the entrance of the port. For this purpoſe our crews divided into different parties, which were properly poſted, ſo that the reſt might proceed without any danger of an attack. We moreover placed centinels at a conſiderable diſtance, to reconnoitre the paths uſed by the Indians, who poſſeſſed themſelves of thoſe parts from which we had moſt to fear. With theſe precautions the crews marched in two bodies, who adored the holy croſs upon diſembarking, and when at the top of the mountain formed a ſquare, the centre of which became a chapel. Here the holy croſs was again raiſed, maſs celebrated, with a ſermon, and poſſeſſion taken, with all the requiſites enjoined by our inſtructions. We alſo fired both

[l] Of Monſ. Bellin.

[m] So called from Mendoza, a Viceroy of Mexico, who ſent ſome ſhips on diſcovery. Moſt maps place this on the N. W. point of California

[n] De ocho cavos.

our mufquetry and cannon, which naturally made the Indians fuppofe we were irrefiftible. After they had recovered their fright however, and found that we had done them no harm, they vifited us again, and probably to examine more nearly what had occafioned the tremendous noife which they had never heard before. As we thus took poffeffion on the day when holy mother church celebrates the feftival of the moft holy Trinity, we named the port accordingly [o].

The following days were taken up in procuring wood and water, whilft the fchooner was careened. We likewife cut fome mafts for her.

We could not but particularly attend to all the actions of the Indians, their manner of living, habitations, garments, food, government, laws, language, and arms, as alfo their [p] hunting and fifheries. The diftruft indeed which we naturally entertained of thefe barbarians, made us endeavour to get as great an infight into all thefe as poffible, yet we never obferved any thing contrary to the moft perfect friendfhip and confidence which they feemed to repofe in us. I may add, that their intercourfe with us was not only kind, but affectionate.

There houfes were fquare, and built with large beams, the roofs being no higher than the furface of the ground, for the

[o] There is certainly fome ufe to geographers in this cuftom of the Spaniards naming places from the Saint's, day in which they take poffeffion, or make the difcovery, as it points out to pofterity the time of the year when the event happened.

[p] Sus *cazas*, which like the French word *chaffe* and Italian *caccia*, comprehends alfo fowling. In Sir Afhton Lever's moft capital mufeum may be feen what contrivances are ufed by the Indians of St. George's Sound N. Lat 50. on this fame coaft and for thefe purpofes. There is alfo in the fame noble repofitory fome birdlime from the newly difcovered Sandwich iflands.

doors

3

doors to which they make ufe of a circular hole, juft large enough for their bodies to pafs through. The floors of thefe huts are perfectly fmooth and clean, with a fquare hole[q] two feet deep in the centre, in which they make their fire, and round which they are continually warming themfelves, on account of the great cold. Such habitations alfo fecure them, when not employed out of doors, from the wind and noxious animals.

The men however do not wear any covering, except the cold is intenfe, when indeed they put upon their fhoulders the fkins of fea-wolves, otters, deer, or other animals: many of them alfo have round their heads[r] fweet-fmelling herbs. They likewife wear their hair either difhevelled over their fhoulders, or otherwife *en caftanna*[s].

In the flaps of their ears they have rings like thofe at the end of a mufquet[t].

They bind their loins and legs quite down to the ancles, very clofely, with ftrips of hide or thread.

They paint their face, and greater part of their body, regularly either with a black or blue[u] colour.

Their arms are covered with circles of fmall points in the fame manner that common people in Spain often paint fhips and anchors.

[q] Oyo or eye literally.

[r] Una rueda, literally a garland in the form of a wheel

[s] The Spaniards apply caftanna to a particular method of dreffing the hair—*peinado en caftanna*, literally fignifies, hair dreffed to refemble a chefnut tree.

[t] I am informed by a gentleman long refident in Spain, that it is not unufual to have rings fo placed, and that they are of ufe to prevent the knapfack from falling off.

[u] Azarcoir.

The

The women cover the tops of their heads with an ornament like the creſt of a helmet[x], and wear their hair in two treſſes[y], in which they ſtick many ſweet-ſmelling herbs. They alſo uſe the ſame rings in their caps (which are of bone) as the men are before deſcribed to do, and cover their bodies with the ſame ſkins, beſides which they more decently wear an apron of the ſame kind, about a foot wide, with ſome threads formed into a fringe. They likewiſe bind their legs in the ſame manner with the men.

The underlip of theſe women is ſwelled out into three *faſcias*, or riſings, two of which iſſue from the corners of the mouth to the loweſt part of the beard[z], and the third from the higheſt point, and middle of that point to the lower, like the others[a], leaving between each a ſpace of clear fleſh, which is much larger in the young than in the older women, whoſe faces are generally covered with punctures[b], ſo as to be totally diſfigured.

On their necks they wear various fruits[c], inſtead of beads; ſome of theſe ornaments alſo conſiſt of the bones of animals, or ſhells from the ſea-coaſt.

This tribe of Indians is governed by a ruler, who directs where they ſhall go both to hunt and fiſh for what the community ſtands in need of. We alſo obſerved that one of theſe Indians always examined carefully the ſea-ſhoar, when we went

[x] Copa de timbras.

[y] Colgadas par las meſillas.

[z] That is, I ſuppoſe, what would be beard in men.

[a] I muſt own, that I do not thoroughly comprehend this deſcription, though I think I cannot have mis-tranſlated it.

[b] *Picadura*, ſo that I conclude theſe ſwellings on the face, in ſuch forms as deſcribed, muſt be occaſioned by a ſort of *tattooing*.

[c] Rather ſeeds perhaps.

to our ſhips on the cloſe of twilight[d], the occaſion of which probably was to take care that all their people ſhould return ſafe to their habitations about that time.

It ſhould ſeem that the authority of this ruler is confined to a particular village of theſe habitations, together with ſuch a diſtrict of country as may be ſuppoſed to belong to the inhabitants of ſuch a community, who ſometimes are at war with other villages, againſt whom they appeared to aſk our aſſiſtance, making us ſigns[e] for that purpoſe. There are however many other villages which are friendly to each other, if not to theſe Indians; for on our firſt arrival more than 300 came down in different parties, with their women and children, who were not indeed permitted to enter the village of our Indians.

Whilſt this ſort of intercourſe continued between us, we obſerved an infant who could ſcarcely be a year old, ſhooting arrows from a bow proportioned to his ſize and ſtrength, and who hit one's hand at two or three yards diſtance, if it was held up for a mark

We never obſerved that theſe Indians had any idols, or made ſacrifices: but as we found out that they had a plurality of wives, or women, at leaſt, we inferred, *with good reaſon, that they were perfect atheiſts.*

Upon the death of one of theſe Indians they raiſed a ſort of funeral cry, and afterwards burned the body within the houſe of their ruler; but from this we could not pronounce they were idolaters, becauſe the cry of lamentation might proceed from affliction, and the body might have been burnt, that the corpſe

[d] *A la oracion*, in the original, at which time the Spaniards uſually make a ſhort prayer.

[e] What theſe were is not ſtated.

ſhould

ſhould not be expoſed to wild beaſts ; or perhaps this might have been done to avoid the ſtench of the deceaſed, when putrefaction might commence.

We were not able to underſtand one of their regulations, as they permitted our people to enter all their houſes, except that of their ruler; and yet when we had broken through this etiquette, we could not obſerve any thing different between the *palace*, and the other huts.

It was impoſſible for us to underſtand their language, for which reaſon we had no intercourſe but by ſigns, and therefore both parties often continued in a total ignorance of each other's meaning: we obſerved however that they pronounced our words with great eaſe [f].

Their arms are chiefly arrows pointed with flint, and ſome of them with copper or iron [g], which we underſtood were procured from the N. and one of theſe was thus marked C///. Theſe arrows are carried in quivers of wood or bone, and hang from their wriſt or neck.

[f] From hence it may be inferred, that theſe Indians pronounce gutturally, as all the nations of Europe indeed do, except the Engliſh, French, and great part of Italy.

[g] Such are to be ſeen at Sir Aſhton Lever's Muſeum from K. George's ſound N. Lat. 50. which confirms the journal in their being brought from the North. I ſhould conceive that the copper and iron here mentioned muſt have originally been bartered at our forts in Hudſon's Bay, with the travelling hordes of Indians who reſort there at ſtated times. Some of our own people are alſo very enterprizing in their excurſions, as one of them within theſe few years hath been as far as N. Lat. 72. W Long from Fort Churchill 24. where he ſaw an open ſea.—In the ſame noble Muſeum is a moſt particular bow from the W. coaſt of America N. Lat. 50. which exactly reſembles one from the Labradore Coaſt.

But

But what they chiefly value is iron, and particularly knives or hoops of old barrels; they also readily barter for bugles, whilst they rejected both provisions or any article of dress. They pretended however that they sometimes approved the former, in order to procure our esteem; but soon after they had accepted any sort of meat, we observed that they set it aside, as of no value. At last indeed they took kindly to our biscuits, and really eat them.

Amongst these Indians there was one who had more familiar intercourse with us than all the rest, sitting down with us in sight of his countrymen.

They used tobacco, which they smoaked in small wooden pipes, in form of a trumpet, and procured from little gardens where they had planted it [h].

They chiefly hunt deer, cibulos, sea-wolves, and otters, nor did we observe that they pursued any others. The only birds we met with on this part of the coast were daws, hawks, very small paroquets, ducks, and gulls; there were also some parrots with red feet, bills, and breasts, like lories both in their heads and flight.

The fish on that coast are chiefly sardines, pejerey [i], and cod; of which they only bring home as much as will satisfy the wants of the day.

We tried to find if they had ever seen other strangers, or ships than our own, but though we took great pains to inform ourselves on this head, we never could perfectly comprehend what they said; upon the whole we conceived that we were the only foreigners who had ever visited that part of the coast.

[h] It need scarcely be observed that tobacco is an indigenous plant in N. America, as it is also of Asia.

[i] In this and other instances where I do not know the animal alluded to, I shall give the Journalist's name

We likewiſe endeavoured to know from them whether they had any mines or precious ſtones; but in this we were likewiſe diſappointed.

What we ſaw of the country leaves us no doubt of its fertility, and that it is capable of producing all the plants of Europe. In moſt of the gullies of the hills there are rills of clear and cool water, the ſides of which are covered with herbs (as in the meadows of Europe) of both agreeable verdure and ſmell[i]. Amongſt theſe were Caſtilian roſes, ſmallage, lilies, plantain, thiſtles, camomile, and many others. We likewiſe found ſtrawberries, raſberries, blackberries, ſweet onions, and potatoes, all which grew in conſiderable abundance, and particularly near the rills. Amongſt other plants we obſerved one which much reſembled percely (though not in its ſmell), which the Indians bruiſed and eat, after mixing it with onions.

The hills were covered with very large, high, and ſtrait pines, amongſt which I obſerved ſome of 120 feet[k] high, and 4 in diameter towards the bottom.

All theſe pines are proper for maſts and ſhip-building.

The outline of the port is repreſented in Chart the 6th[l], which was drawn by D. Bruno Heceta, D. Juan Fr. de la Bodega, and myſelf. Though the port is there repreſented as open, yet it is to be underſtood that the harbour is well ſheltered from the S.W.W. & N.W. as alſo from the N.N.E. & E.

[This diſcovery was made by the ſchooner on the 9th of June.]

[i] Perhaps the accounts given by navigators of the beauty of a country or its productions after a long voyage may be not entirely relied upon, as they are commonly exagerated.

[k] Seſanta varas.

[l] Theſe Charts, which amount to nine, have never been tranſmitted to England.

In the W. part there is a hill 50 fathoms[m] high, joining to the continent on the N. ſide, where there is another riſing of 20, both of which afford protection not only from the winds, but the attack of an enemy.

At the entrance of the port is a ſmall iſland of conſiderable height, without a ſingle plant upon it; and on the ſides of the coaſt are high rocks, which are very convenient for diſembarking[n]; goods alſo may be ſhipped ſo near the hill[o], that a ladder may be uſed from the land to the veſſel; and near the ſand are many ſmall rocks, which ſecure the ſhip at anchor from the S.E. and S. W.

We compleated our watering very early from the number of rills which emptied themſelves into the harbour; we were likewiſe as ſoon ſupplied with wood.

We paid great attention to the tides, and found them to be as regular as in Europe.

We made repeated obſervations with regard to the latitude of this harbour, and found it was exactly 41 degrees and 7 minutes N. whilſt we ſuppoſed the Longitude to be 19 degrees and 4 minutes W. of S. Blas.

We had thus thoroughly inveſtigated every thing which relates to this harbour, except the courſe of a river which came from the S. W. and which appeared whilſt we were at the top of the hill[p]. We took therefore the boat on the 18th, and found that the mouth was wider than is neceſſary for the diſcharge of the water, which is loſt in the ſands on each ſide, ſo that we

[m] Tueſſas.
[n] By the water being deep cloſe to theſe rocks.
[o] Sc. That of 50 fathoms in height.
[p] The going thither hath been before mentioned.

 could

could not even enter it except at full tide. However we left our boat, and proceded a league into the country, whilſt the river continued of the ſame width; viz. 20 feet, and about five deep.

On the banks of this river were larger timber trees than we had before ſeen, and we conceived that in land-floods the whole plain (which was more than a quarter of a league broad) muſt be frequently covered with water, as there were many places where it continued to ſtagnate.

We gave this river the name of *Pigeons*, becauſe at our firſt landing we ſaw large flocks of theſe, and other birds, ſome of which had pleaſing notes.

On the ſides of the mountains we found the ſame plants and fruits, as in the more immediate neighbourhood of Trinity-Harbour.

On the 19th of June, at 8 in the morning, we took up our anchors, and ſailed with a gentle breeze from N W. which had continued in the ſame direction all the time we were in port. It fell calm however at ten, on which we caſt anchor about a cannon's ſhot from the little iſland, where we had ten fathom water, and a muddy bottom.

On the 20th in the evening the wind blew again from the N. W. and we ſailed to the E S W. & S. E. the wind continuing N. W. which made the ſea run high.

On the 21ſt was new moon, and the wind veered about to the W. with ſmall rains and miſts, which ſeparated the two ſhips for ſix or eight hours, during which we made our ſignals by lights, and firing guns.

In order to get into the courſe we were to ſteer, if the wind proved favourable, I mentioned to our commander what I had read

read in D. Juan Perez's journal [q], which had been delivered to him, where it was obſerved that this navigator had the winds from the S. & S E. with which it was eaſy to run along the coaſt, to a high Northern latitude, and for that reaſon Perez was of opinion that the coaſt ſhould not be approached till 49, in which I agreed with him. Our commanders indeed kept as much to windward as poſſible in order to take advantage of the wind, when it ſhould become fair; but it ſoon changed to the W. & N. W. which drove us on that part of the coaſt which we wanted to avoid.

On this ſame day we repaired ſeveral damages which our ſhip had ſuffered, with the greateſt alacrity, in hopes of proſecuting our diſcoveries, and found that ſhe ſailed better comparatively with the frigate than ſhe had done before [r].

On the 2d of July ſome other damages were repaired.

Although we laid great ſtreſs upon getting to the Weſtward, in order that we might afterwards proceed N. as alſo diſcover ſome port in a lower latitude than 65, yet we were not able to effect this, as the wind from being W. turned to the N. W. and drove us upon the coaſt [too early].

On the 9th of July I conceived myſelf to be in the latitude of the mouth of a river [s], diſcovered by John de Fuca (according to the French map) which we therefore endeavoured to make for, whilſt at the ſame time we obſerved that the ſea was coloured, as in ſoundings; many fiſh [t], reeds 20 feet long, and the *Orange-*

[q] It appears afterwards that this D Juan Perez was *enſign* on board the frigate, and that he had ſailed in a former voyage of diſcovery to a conſiderable N. Latitude on the W. coaſt of America.

[r] The particulars of theſe repairs, as alſo in what reſpect ſhe ſailed better, are omitted as unintereſting.

[s] Perhaps *gulf* [boca].

[t] *Tonnas*, ſuppoſed to be porpeſſes.

heads

heads[a] likewiſe appeared; all of which circumſtances ſhewed that we were not far diſtant from the coaſt.

The ſame day both wind and ſea increaſed ſo much that our deck was thoroughly wetted, and our ciſtern of water alſo was much damaged, on which account it became neceſſary to ſteer S.W. from five in the evening till day-break, when the ſea became more calm, and wind more fair; ſo that we ſailed N. and a point to the E. hoping to diſcover the land.

At ſun-ſet the horizon was more clear, and the ſigns of approaching the coaſt greatly increaſed; as we could not diſtinguiſh it however we kept in the wake of the frigate, by very clear moonlight.

On the 11th at day break the ſky was very bright, there was an appearance of ſoundings, much ſea-weed, many birds, and the greateſt ſigns of being near land. In effect at 11 the ſun ſhone, and we diſtinguiſhed the coaſt to the N. W. when we were about 12 leagues from it.

In the evening both wind and ſea roſe ſo much that the frigate thought it right to keep us in ſight, and we were much fatigued by the violence of the weather.

On the 12th we had got five or ſix leagues to the N. of the frigate, whilſt we were but three leagues from the land, with a more favourable wind and calmer ſea, ſo that we joined her by eleven. At ſix in the evening the coaſt was not more diſtant than a league, when we diſtinguiſhed various headlands, many ſmall iſlands, as alſo mountains covered with ſnow.

We likewiſe found a barren iſland about half a league in circumference, which we called *de Dolores*.

[a] A ſea-plant before deſcribed.

We

We now carried all the ſail we could to follow the frigate, but we could not do ſo at the proper diſtance, in ſo much that at ſun-ſet we loſt ſight of her, and although during the whole night we hung out lights, fired our guns, as alſo rockets, ſhe never anſwered our ſignals, from which we concluded that they could not be diſtinguiſhed by our companion.

On the 13th however the frigate appeared at a great diſtance, and ſeemed to be making for the coaſt.

We now ſounded, and found 30 fathoms of water, caſting anchor two leagues and half from the land. At twelve on the ſame day we ſaw the frigate ſtill at a greater diſtance to leeward, though ſhe endeavoured to approach the coaſt. On this we ſet ſail to join her, keeping at the ſame time as near to the land as we could, and being not farther diſtant than a mile, we plainly diſtinguiſhed, as we paſſed to the S. W. the plains, ſmall detached rocks, and low headlands, till ſix in the evening. As we could not however find any port, and could not bear to loſe the Northing we had gained with ſo much trouble, we determined to caſt anchor near a point, where we thought we ſhould be able to procure wood and water, as well as maſts.

The frigate was now not more than half a league diſtant, and we therefore made a ſignal to her to caſt anchor, having eight fathoms of water upon ſounding.

After this I ſoon went on board the frigate, the Captain of which told me that the Commander of the ſchooner ſhould come to him, in order to hold a council, whether the ſchooner ſhould proceed or not to a higher latitude, as every minute we ſtayed longer on the coaſt, would ſubject us to greater riſques, both from the winds and ſea. This was alſo the more to be dreaded, as the whole crew of the frigate had been ſick for the two laſt days, whilſt the commander himſelf was far from well. The

captain

captain of the ſchooner therefore was to keep near, and jointly take poſſeſſion of this part of the coaſt. I accordingly carried theſe orders to the ſchooner, whoſe captain directed that the next day we ſhould join the frigate.

In the mean while nine canoes of tall and ſtout Indians appeared, who invited the crew of the ſchooner with great cordiality to eat, drink, and ſleep with them.

Our commander took care to regale them in the beſt manner he could, and particularly their chieftains, as well as thoſe who came the moſt readily on board, giving them whatever they ſeemed moſt to deſire.

The Indians, being obliged by theſe civilities, rowed near to our ſhip, making friendly ſigns, and as we anſwered by the ſame civilities, they left us at nine, and ſoon returned with fiſh of many ſorts, *pagro*, whale, and ſalmon, as alſo fleſh of ſeveral animals, well cured under ground. Theſe preſents, in ſufficient abundance, were offered to our commander, after which they returned to their villages, leaving us in high admiration of their noble proceedings.

On the 14th in the morning the ſea ebbed ſo low, that the ridges of rocks appeared along the coaſt, which prevented us from then ſailing, and obliged us to wait for the full of the tide, which was to happen at 12 at noon. During this interval the Indians trafficked with us for various ſkins of animals, for which they expected ſome peices of iron in exchange, which they manifeſted by putting their hands upon the rudder-irons*; our people therefore procured them ſuch, from old cheſts, after which they returned to their village, making the ſame ſigns as they had done the day before.

* Los Machos del timon.

On

On the 1ſt of July we were to go on ſhore by order of our commander; and as we were ſtill to continue our voyage for ſome time, it was neceſſary we ſhould procure a ſufficient quantity of water (ſo much being uſed ſince we failed from Port Trinity) though hitherto we had not been able to effect this from want of a proper tide, which at the ſame time prevented us from getting wood and a maſt. For this reaſon ſuch part of the crew was pitched upon who were likely to be moſt active in the ſervice, each of them taking a gun and piſtol, and ſome of them a cutlaſs[y] and cartridge-box, the whole party being put under the command of Pedro Santa-Ana[z], who always diſtinguiſhed himſelf upon ſuch occaſions. They alſo took with them hatchets, and were directed to ſend us back the boat, that we might fill it with caſks, after which they were to carry them to that part of the coaſt where they could ſooneſt compleat their watering.

Our detachment therefore contrived to land where there was the deepeſt water, and the neareſt poſſible to a river. They had ſcarcely done this, however, when the Indians ruſhed out from the mountains to the number of 300, and ſurrounding our ſeamen immediately, we concluded that the whole detachment would have been cut off, as we only perceived a ſingle fire from our people, and that two of them running to the ſhore threw themſelves into the ſea, whoſe fate we could not know on account of the ſhallows of the coaſt.

As we therefore could not help our comrades, by not having ſufficient depth of ſea for our veſſel, we fired our great guns and

[y] Sabre.

[z] He is ſtated to have been contro-maeſtre, or perhaps maſter's mate.

muſkets; but as our ſhot did not reach the Indians, nor could they know what damage we might do them at a leſs diſtance, they did not move at all, or deſiſt from their treacherous attack. On this, not being able to ſuccour our comrades, we hoiſted a ſignal of diſtreſs, which the frigate being ſo far off could not diſtinguiſh. The Indians however at eleven returned to their villages, whilſt we neither could ſee our ſeamen or their boats.

By twelve at noon it was full ſea, and we endeavoured to reach the frigate, every one exerting themſelves to the utmoſt; our whole crew, indeed, now conſiſted of but five men and a boy, who were in health, with four that were ſick.

As ſoon as we had ſet ſail, nine canoes of Indians, with an increaſed number of men on board, placed themſelves at a fixed diſtance from us, whilſt one of them, with only nine chieftains[a] on board, rowed pretty near to the ſide of our veſſel, offering us, whilſt their bows were unbent, ſome handſome jackets, and practiſing their former arts of deceit, by tempting us with the proviſions they had before ſupplied.

But we were now upon our guard, and preparing for our defence, though we ſtill thought it right on our part to entice them nearer, by ſhewing bugles and other trifles, which had as little effect upon our enemies, who contrived however to make ſigns that we ſhould go on ſhore. At laſt they were tired of theſe overtures, and knowing the ſmall number of our crew, they made a ſhew of ſurrounding our veſſel; holding their bows bent againſt us.

On the other hand, though we had but three on board able to handle a muſquet (viz. our Captain, his ſervant, and myſelf)

[a] So the original; and I conclude the meaning to be, that in this canoe there were none but chieftains.

yet

yet we ſoon killed ſix of the Indians, as alſo damaged their canoe. They now experienced how much we were able to annoy them, and ſeemed to be aſtoniſhed. They afterwards covered their dead with their jackets, and at laſt returned to ſuch a diſtance that we could not reach them with our ſhot; in which retreat they were aſſiſted by the other canoes, who had not before ſupported them. They then held a council, which ended in their going back to their village.

Our commander, in the mean time, hearing the diſcharge of our muſquets, thought we ſhould want ammunition, and ſent us ſome in the launch, in which we caſt anchor along ſide of the frigate. We then went on board, hoping that we ſhould be permitted to uſe the launch, land with an armed force, deſtroy the villages of the Indians, and try to recover thoſe of our own people, who perhaps had hid themſelves in the woods, or had ſaved themſelves by ſwimming.

On this point we held a council, at which the commander ſtated our dangerous ſituation, the difficulties in landing we were to expect, both from ſea and weather, and the diſtance of the village; he alſo added, that the deſtruction of our people was almoſt diſtinctly ſeen, and therefore that there could be little probability of any one's having eſcaped.

D. Criſtoval de Revilla and D. Juan Perez were of opinion we ſhould directly ſail, although the commander [b] and myſelf preſſed taking ſome revenge for the butchery of our comrades, as likewiſe waiting to know the fate of thoſe who might have ſurvived by ſwimming, and who muſt neceſſarily ſurrender themſelves to the Barbarians. We alſo dwelt upon the ſtrong preſumption, that it would be agreeable to his majeſty that the Indians

[b] The commander ſeems to have given different advice before.

dians ſhould feel the ſuperior force of his arms, who would otherwiſe treat future diſcoverers in the ſame manner; we added, that though the village was not near, yet if we waited till next day we might reach it, whilſt it might be expected that the winds would not blow with violence at the new moon.

The reaſons on both ſides having been thus urged, the commander readily conſented to follow the advice and wiſhes of the majority.

When this point was decided, our commander took our opinions with regard to the ſchooner's proceeding, as ſhe was in ſo bad plight; when (except D. Criſtoval de Revilla) we all agreed that ſhe ſhould continue to proſecute her voyage. Theſe our opinions were reduced into writing on the 16th.

[Theſe are again omitted, as probably unintereſting to the reader: but both the captain of the ſchooner, and the journaliſt agreeing to proceed;]

On the 14th of July we ſailed, at five in the evening, from this road, which lies in 47. 21 N. Lat[c]. the wind being N. W. and N. N. W. by which we left the coaſt, ſteering S. W.

On the 19th our captain received ſome letters from Don Juan Perez (enſign[d] of the frigate) as likewiſe the ſurgeon, in which they ſtated the then health of their crew, and deſiring our opinion thereon.

[Here follow the anſwers of the captain of the ſchooner and Maurelle the journaliſt, who, to their great credit, perſiſt in their voyage of diſcovery.]

[c] The longitude is not ſtated, but by the ſhip's reckoning I find that the W. Longitude from St Blas was 21 19.

[d] Alferez.

Till the 24th the wind continued N. W. & N. when the ſchooner received ſrom the frigate a cannon, with a box of powder and ball.

From the 24th to the 30th we ſteered N. W. when at ſunſet there were great threatenings of a ſtorm, and the weather becoming dark, the ſea ran ſo high, that we could not diſtinguiſh the lights of the frigate, and were obliged to make our ſignals by guns and rockets.

On the 31ſt it continued to be ſo dark that even during the day we could not ſee the frigate.

On the 1ſt of Auguſt at day-break we had the ſame dark weather, ſo that we could not diſtinguiſh at half a league's diſtance, nor had we ſight of the frigate we kept on however (the wind abating) with a Weſterly courſe, till the 4th, when we ſuppoſed ourſelves to be 17 leagues W. of the continent.

On the 5th the wind began to be favourable from the S. W. and the frigate ſtill not appearing, our captain conſulted us whether we ſhould proſecute our diſcoveries. We had indeed for the laſt two months been reduced to ſhort allowance of provisions, and a quart of water each day, ſince we left the laſt land; our bread alſo was almoſt ſpoiled by the ſea getting into the bread-room, and the ſeaſon for ſailing to the Northward began almoſt to end. Yet notwithſtanding theſe, and other objections, we continued unanimouſly of opinion to execute our orders; as, if we did otherwiſe, his majeſty muſt have incurred the expence of a freſh expedition. Our crew likewiſe was now animated, and every one agreed to contribute proportionably for a ſolemn maſs to our Lady of Bethlem, intreating her that we might be able to reach the Latitude enjoined by our inſtructions. This propoſal of the crew being communicated to the captain, he applauded much their ardour and devotion, which was rewarded before evening, by the winds blowing from a favourable quarter.

On the 10th there was a full moon, and the wind blew fresh from the S. W.

On the 13th we conceived ourselves to be in soundings from the colour of the sea; at the same time appeared *Orange heads*, many flags, many birds, with red feet, breast, and beak, as also many whales; all which were certain signs of our nearer approach to land.

During the 14th and 15th these signs increased, when we found ourselves in N. Lat. 56, 8. & 154 leagues W. of the continent, and 69 leagues from an island to be found in our chart[e], which likewise pointed out an archipelago in the same parallel. This search however was attended with great difficulty, as the wind blew with great violence, whilst the mists did not permit us to distinguish any distant object.

At noon on the 16th we saw land to the N. W. at the distance of six leagues, and it soon afterwards opened to the N. E. presenting considerable headlands and mountains, one of which was of an immense height, being situated upon a projecting cape, and of the most regular and beautiful form I had ever seen. It was also quite detached from the great ridge of mountains. Its top was covered with snow, under which appeared some wide gullies, which continue till about the middle of the mountain, and from thence to the bottom are trees of the same kind as those at Trinity[f].

We named this moutain *St. Jacinthus*[g] and the cape *del Enganno*[h], both of which are situated in N. Lat. 57. 2. and by two

[e] I should rather suppose that this was the chart of D. Juan Perez, who was on board, and had been on a former voyage of discovery.

[f] Before described to be pines.

[g] There is a monastery of *St. Jacinthus*, at a small distance from Mexico. Gage's Survey of the W. Indies.

[h] Or of deceit.]

repeated

repeated obſervations at a mile's diſtance we found the W. Long. from St. Blas to be 34. 12.

From this cape we fixed the principal points on the coaſt, as will appear by our chart.

On the 17th the wind blew moderate from the S. by means of which we entered a bay that was three leagues wide at its mouth, and which was protected from the N. by cape *del Engano*; on the oppoſite ſide to this cape we diſcovered a port more than a league wide at the entrance, perfectly ſecure from all winds but the S. We nearly approached the ſides of this bay, and never found leſs than fifty fathoms in depth; but we could not perceive any kind of flat or plain, as the mountains come quite down to the ſhore. Notwithſtanding this we diſtinguiſhed a ſmall river, which (it being night) we did not further attend to, but caſt anchor in 66 fathoms, the bottom being a clay, as we found upon drawing up our anchors.

This port is ſituated in 57. 11 N Lat. and 34. 12. W. Long. from S. Blas; which, together with the headland, we named Guadelupe.

On the 18th we ſailed again, with little wind; when two canoes, with four Indians in each, appeared (viz. two men and two women) who, however, did not ſeem to wiſh to come on board us, but only made ſigns that we ſhould go on ſhore.

We continued our courſe however (the wind being N W) till nine in the morning, when we entered another port, not ſo large indeed, but the adjacent country much more deſirable to navigators, as a river empties itſelf here of eight or ten feet wide, whilſt the harbour is protected from almoſt every wind, by means of a long ridge of high iſlands, almoſt joining each other, with anchorage of 18 fathoms, the bottom being a ſand. Here we caſt anchor at a piſtol's ſhot from the land, where we ſaw, on the

the bank of the river, a high houſe, and a parapet[i] of timber ſupported by ſtakes drove into the ground, where we obſerved ten Indian men, beſides women and children.

We named this port *de los Remedios*, and found that it was ſituated in 57. 18 N Lat. and 34. 12 W. Long. from St. Blas.

The ſame day, having prepared ourſelves for defence againſt the Indians, five of us landed about noon, when, having poſted ourſelves in the ſafeſt place we could fix upon, we planted the croſs with all proper devotion, cutting another on a rock[k], and diſplaying the Spaniſh colours, according *to our inſtructions* on that head.

When we had thus taken poſſeſſion of the country we advanced quite to the bank of the river, in order to fix upon the moſt convenient place for water, which we were in great want of, as well as ſtill greater of wood; ſo that we were under an abſolute neceſſity of providing ourſelves with both. Having fixed upon the proper ſpot, we now returned to the ſhip, the Indians having not come forth from their parapet.

We ſoon however perceived them approach the place where we had fixed the croſs, which they took away, and fixed it on the front of their houſe, in the proper direction, whilſt at the ſame time they made us ſigns with their open arms, that they had thus taken poſſeſſion of our croſs.

On the 19th we landed at a point ſomewhat diſtant, to procure wood and a maſt, whilſt we ſecured our retreat by a proper diſpoſition of ſwivels and muſquetry.

Afterwards we returned to the mouth of the river, to fill our barrels with water, when the Indians hung out a white leaf[l] from

[i] Probably this was a ſtage for curing fiſh, of which theſe Indians ſoon offered a preſent to the Spaniards.

[k] Penna.

[l] Ora.

we

a pole, fixed very near to their houſe, and advancing to the oppoſite bank without any arms, they made ſeveral ſigns, which we did not comprehend. We however ſignified to them in the beſt manner we could that we came only for water [m]; on which the chieftain of the Indians, conceiving that we were very dry, brought with him a cup of it, with ſome cured fiſh, as far as the middle of the river, where it was received by one of our ſeamen, who directed the Indian to preſent the water and fiſh to our captain, who immediately returned him in exchange bugles and ſmall pieces of cloth. The Indians however were not to be ſo ſatisfied, but inſiſted on other barter for the water, which we refuſing on our part, they threatened us with long and large lances pointed with flint, which we paid no other attention to but that of ſecuring our poſt. Our aſſailants at laſt finding that we

[m] The behaviour of theſe Indians in their intercourſe with the Spaniards ſeems to prove a rather ſuperior degree of civilization, than is generally experienced from Barbarians.

We find by this account, that the Spaniards, having fixed a croſs upon their ground, the Indians reſent this mark of ownerſhip, and (as a Spaniard would have done in his own country if his neighbour thus endeavoured to make good a claim) immediately remove the croſs, in which the laws of Europe would certainly have ſupported them. The leaving any ſymbol of poſſeſſion upon an uninhabited and uncultivated diſtrict may indeed give a right againſt poſterior claimants who cannot ſet up a better, but this part of the American continent was not only peopled, but we are informed a houſe and fiſhing-ſtage had been built upon it.

We find by this journal, that the Viceroy of Mexico moſt particularly enjoined by his inſtructions that poſſeſſion ſhould be thus taken, conceiving probably that the converting Indians to the Chriſtian faith, entitles the converter to every thing which may belong to the converts. This flimſy right however could not be maintained an inſtant even upon this ground, in any Court of common ſenſe, for the Spaniards neither intended then, or hereafter, to make a ſettlement in this Northern Latitude, without which it is impoſſible that ſuch pious intentions could be accompliſhed.

The

we did not wish to surround them, but held them in contempt, went back to their houses, as we did to our ship, having procured the wood and single mast which we wanted, though not so much water as would have been convenient; but we did not think it right to carry away more, that we might not further irritate the inhabitants.

At the mouth of the river there was abundance of fish, of which our people caught many whilst we were on shoar, and we could have procured a sufficient quantity to have lasted us a great while, had we been prepared with proper tackle. They were well tasted, and in vast numbers.

The mountains were covered with the same sort of pines as at *Trinity*: the inhabitants also use the same dress, only rather longer; they likewise wear a cap over their hair, which covers their whole head.

The Spaniards, after this, inform the Indians, by signs, that they want water, on which one of the Americans brings a cup thus filled, with some cured fish, half way across the river, and stops there till a Spaniard advances the other half to receive it, whilst bugles and other trifles are offered in exchange by the Spaniards, and refused by the Indians, who insist on a better sort of payment.

It is evident, by the presents of the cup of water * and cured fish, that the Indians wished to supply all the wants of these strangers as far as they were able, notwithstanding they had thus endeavoured to gain a wrongful possession of their country; they seem therefore to have had a right to that species of barter which they stood most in need of.

This contempt for bugles, and other trifles, offered by the Spaniards, is a further proof of the civilization of these Indians, whose progenitors, it should seem, must be rather looked for on the Asiatic, than Labradore coast, as I am informed that they have beards, which the Indians of the central and Eastern coast of N America have not. It is said indeed by some, that these Indians eradicate their beard from its earliest appearance; but I can as little believe that this can be effected by any industry, as that they could by any art or pains make hair grow upon the palms of their hands.

* I am informed, that the inhabitants of K. George's Sound, on this same coast, insisted upon Capt. Cook's paying for the grass he had cut.

We found the weather exceſſively cold, with much rain and fogs, nor did we ſee the ſun for the three days we continued here. At the ſame time we had only faint land-breezes; from all which circumſtances, as well as the great fatigue of our ſeamen, little cover from the bad weather, and great want of proper cloaks to keep them warm, our ſhip's company ſo ſickened, that we could only muſter two men for every watch.

On the 21ſt we ſteered N. W. the wind being at S. E. in order to diſcover whether there was any land to the E. when we might reach two degrees of higher latitude to the N. or whether it did not lie to the W. which we conceived to be more probable.

On the 22d we knew, by our reckoning, that we muſt be near the Eaſtern part of the coaſt [m], as we found ourſelves by an obſervation at noon to be in 57. 18 N. Lat.

At two in the evening the wind blew freſh at N. W. when we wanted to gain ſo much Weſting as to permit the reaching a higher Northern Latitude, in which attempt we muſt have therefore loſt many days, whilſt the ſeaſon for proſecuting our diſcoveries drew ſo near to an end. To this it muſt be added, that the ſickneſs of our crew increaſed every day, by their great fatigues, on which account we deſiſted from our Northern courſe, and ſteered S. E. approaching the coaſt at a leſs diſtance than a mile, and endeavouring to obſerve every projection of it.

Though we now therefore determined to return to S. Blas, yet we comforted ourſelves in having reached ſo high a latitude as 58 [n], beyond what any other Navigators had been able to effect in thoſe ſeas, though our veſſel ſailed ſo indifferently that we often had thoughts of quitting her.

[m] Sc. as laid down by Bellin.

[n] By the table only 57. 57. Capt. Cook however is ſaid to have traced the W. coaſt of America beyond 60 N. Lat. when it runs for ſome degrees nearly E.

In ſailing along the coaſt we took indefatigable pains to obſerve with preciſion how it lay, from which innumerable objections offered themſelves to M. Bellin's Charts.

This engineer hath chiefly founded himſelf upon the tracks of two Ruſſian Navigators, Beering and Tſchirikow, who were ſent upon diſcoveries in 1741. It is evident however that the Ruſſian maps are not to be depended upon, for if they had been tolerably accurate we ſhould have fallen in with the land to the Weſtward, more eaſily than to the Eaſt [o].

Bellin is not leſs erroneous in laying down the American coaſt, and indeed it is not at all extraordinary that his errors ſhould be ſo numerous, as he had no materials for his charts, but his own fruitful imagination; no navigator having viſited many parts of the American continent in theſe high latitudes but ourſelves.

We now attempted to find out the ſtraits [p] of Admiral Fonte, though as yet we had not diſcovered the Archipelago of S. Lazarus, through which he is ſaid to have ſailed.

With this intent we ſearched every bay and receſs of the coaſt, and ſailed round every headland, lying to during the night, that we might not loſe ſight of this entrance; after theſe pains taken, and being favoured by a N. W. wind [q], it may be pronounced that no ſuch ſtraits are to be found.

On the 24th at 2 in the evening, and being in 55. 17 N. Lat. we doubled a cape, and entered into a large bay, diſcovering to

[o] The journaliſt ſeems to ſpeak here with regard to the then ſituation of the ſchooner Other objections follow to Bellin s map, which cannot be comprehended without having the chart before one

[p] Entrada, or entrance into them rather In a map which I have procured, this entrance is laid down in N. Lat. 48. and ſaid to have been diſcovered by Juan de Fuca in 1592.

[q] It muſt now be recollected that the ſchooner is returning to S. Blas.

the N. an arm of the ſea, where the temperature was very unpleaſant [r], but the ſea perfectly calm, being ſheltered from the wind. This *arm* alſo affords excellent water from rills and pools, whilſt the anchorage is good, with a vaſt plenty of fiſh. It is delineated in one of our charts.

As we were now becalmed, the ſchooner rowed till we caſt anchor in the entrance or mouth, the water being 20 fathoms, and the bottom ſoft mud. At this time we were not more than two muſquet ſhots from the land, and wiſhed to lay down the interior parts, but were not able to effect this for want of wind. We now experienced a pleaſant temperature, which probably aroſe from ſome large volcanoes, the light of which we perceived during the night, though at a conſiderable diſtance. This unexpected warmth totally reſtored the health of our crew [s].

As we thus lay at anchor, and ſo much to our ſatisfaction, our Captain gave me orders (being himſelf indiſpoſed) that I ſhould land with ſome of our crew, and with the ſame precautions as at *Los Remedios*. He alſo directed me to take poſſeſſion for his Majeſty of this part of the coaſt, and name it Bucarelly [t]. I accordingly obeyed his inſtructions in all particulars, without ſeeing a ſingle Indian, though there were the following proofs of the country's being inhabited; viz. a hut, ſome paths, and a wooden outhouſe [u]. On the 24th we went a ſecond time on ſhore, and provided ourſelves with as much wood and water as we wanted.

[r] It is to be ſuppoſed on account of the cold.

[s] It muſt be recollected, that they were now ſheltered from the wind as well as warmed by the Vulcanoes.

[t] Then Viceroy of Mexico.

[u] Corral.

We

We made two obſervations on different days, and found our latitude to be 55. 17. and W. Long. from S. Blas 32. 9.

The mountains near this port or inlet are covered with the ſame trees as thoſe at the other places, where we had landed, but I can ſay nothing with regard to the inhabitants, from what hath been before ſtated.

To the S. we ſaw an iſland of a moderate height, at the diſtance of ſix leagues, which we named S. Carlos, and ſailed on the 29th with a gentle breeze at N. but which fell calm at noon, when we were oppoſite to a bare iſland, which ſcarcely appeared above the ſea; there are many rocks however, both to the E. and W. Here we anchored in 22 fathoms, and about two leagues diſtant from the iſland of S. Carlos.

In this ſituation we obſerved a Cape, which we named St. Auguſtine, at the diſtance of four or five leagues; after which the coaſt trended to the E. ſo much that we loſt ſight of it. We found alſo that there were here ſuch violent currents in oppoſite directions, that we could not ſound. As theſe currents roſe and fell with the tide, it ſhould ſeem that this inlet hath no communication but with the ſea.

This cape S. Auguſtine is nearly in 55 N. Lat. and we having heard that in a former voyage D. Juan Perez had diſcovered an arm of the ſea in this ſame parallel, where there were many currents, we juſtly concluded this muſt be the ſame, though ſeveral ſeamen who were in that voyage, did not recollect either the cape or mountains in the neighbourhood, but this probably aroſe from their not approaching them in the ſame direction.

What we obſerved on this part of the coaſt ſtrongly inclined us to have a more perfect knowledge of it; the wind however (it being new moon) became variable, and fixed at laſt in the S. W.

We

We concluded that it would thus continue till the full[x], which would prevent us from approaching the mouth of this bay, and consequently make it impossible to explore the sides of it. We likewise considered that we were now in such a latitude that we might easily reach 60 degrees if the wind was favourable[y], that moreover we were provided with what we had occasion for, that the health of our crews was re-established, and that for all these reasons it would be better to attempt reaching the highest Latitude we could.

To these arguments it was added, that we should have fewer difficulties in this trial from our knowledge of the coast; and this measure being thus resolved upon, the two ships divided some cloaths[z] (which the schooner had on board, to truck with the Indians at Port Trinity) so that our people seemed now to have forgotten all their sufferings. We accordingly sailed, steering N. W.

On the 28th the wind was variable, obliging us to approach the coast at 55. 50. when it fixed in the evening to the S. W. according to our wishes.

On the 29th and 30th the wind was S. though often veering to the S. W. with occasional squalls and tornadoes, accompanied by high seas, which drove us on the coast in 56 70 from whence we clawed off with the land breeze and tornadoes, in which disagreeable situation we continued till the first of September

During the two preceding days six of our crew were seized with strong symptoms of the scurvy, which not only shewed

[x] The Spaniards, during this voyage, seem to have paid great attention to the moon, as having an effect upon the wind.

[y] A S. W. was so.

[z] This additional cloathing was probably thought necessary, as the ships were now to sail N. whilst the winter was approaching.

itſelf in their gums, but from the great ſwellings on their legs they had loſt the uſe of them. From this calamity we could only muſter two on each guard, one of which ſteered, and the other handled the ſails. We unfortunately caught this terrible diſtemper from the ſeamen of the frigate, with whom we had occaſional communication. In conſequence of this diſtreſs we agreed now to return, making as many obſervations as we could in relation to the lying of the coaſt.

At the beginning of September the wind was variable, but on the 6th it fixed in the S. W. blowing with ſuch force that at midnight we were obliged to take in all our ſails, and turn the ſhip's head to the S. whilſt the wind and ſea increaſed, in ſo much that at two in the morning of the 7th neither veſſel could reſiſt its violence, though we each endeavoured to keep where we were, on account of the coaſt being at ſo ſmall a diſtance.

Whilſt we were thus employed a ſea broke in, which damaged moſt of our ſtores. [The particulars of other damage to parts of the ſhip here follows, but is omitted for reaſons that have been before mentioned.]

On this ſame day (viz. 7th of September), both wind and ſea became more calm; on which we ſteered E. from 6 in the evening till day-break of the next day, when the wind was favourable from the N. W. and we purſued our intentions of falling in again with the coaſt, in Lat. 55. finding ourſelves, ſince the ſtorm, with only one ſeaman who could ſtand to the helm, whilſt the captain or myſelf managed the ſails.

The wind continuing favourable, our captain endeavoured to cheer thoſe who were ſick, but we could only prevail upon two of them who were recovering to aſſiſt us during the day; as for the maſter's mate, we conceived that he would die.

On

On the 11th we ſaw land, at the diſtance of eight or nine leagues, and in Lat. 53. 54. but as we wiſhed not to approach ſo near as not to be able to leave it, on account of our having ſo few hands capable of working, we kept at a proper diſtance, only having a view of it from day to day, and not examining its capes, bays, and ports.

In Lat. 49. however we endeavoured to draw nearer to the land, both becauſe we were perſuaded that the wind would continue favourable, and that ſome of the convaleſcents might now begin to aſſiſt us; ſo that in Lat. 47 3. we were not farther diſtant than a mile, when we attended to all proper particulars*, as before.

On the 20th, at eight in the morning, we were within half a league, preciſely in the ſame ſituation as on the 13th of July; we found however 17 leagues difference with regard to our Longitude.

On the 21ſt, being ſtill nearer the coaſt, the wind blew from the S. & S. W. which, though moderate, obliged us to ſail from the land.

On the 22d the wind was N. W. but as both the captain and myſelf were ill of a fever, the ſhip ſteer'd for the port of Monterey. This our ſickneſs made the reſt of the crew almoſt deſpair; for which reaſon the captain and myſelf ſhewed ourſelves upon the deck as often as we could, in which efforts the Almighty aſſiſted us.

On the 24th, finding ourſelves ſomewhat better, we diſcovered the land in 45. 27. ſailing along the coaſt at about the diſtance of a cannon's ſhot; and as we therefore could diſtinctly ſee every conſiderable object, we lay to during the night,

* That is for laying the coaſt down in their charts.

hoping thus to find the river of Martin Aquilar, and continued this ſearch till we were in Lat. 45. 50. when we diſtinguiſhed a cape exactly reſembling a round table, with ſome red gullies [b], from which the coaſt trends to the S. W. From this part riſe ten ſmall iſlands, and ſome others which are ſcarcely above the ſea; the Latitude of this Cape hath before been mentioned, and its Longitude is 20. 4. W. from S. Blas. As we therefore could ſee nothing of Martin de Aquilar's River in this ſecond trial, we conclude that it is not to be found, for we muſt have diſcovered it, if any ſuch river was on this part of the coaſt.

It is ſaid indeed that Aquilar obſerved the mouth of this river in 43 [c], but the inſtruments of thoſe times [d] were very imperfect. Allowing the error however to have been in making the latitude too high, and that therefore we might have found it in 42 or lower; yet this we can ſcarcely conceive to be the truth, as we examined all that part of the coaſt, except about fifty minutes of Latitude.

After this laſt return to the coaſt, we endeavoured to make for the port of S. Franciſco, which having diſcovered in 38. 18. we entered a bay which is ſufficiently ſheltered from the N. and S. W. We ſoon afterwards diſtinguiſhed the mouth of a conſiderable river, and ſome way up a large port exactly reſembling a dock [e]; we therefore concluded this to be the harbour of S. Franciſco (which we were in ſearch of), as the Hiſtory of California places it in 38. 4.

[b] Barancas.

[c] This is ſtated before, when the river was looked out for in that latitude.

[d] Viz. in 1603.

[e] Digue.

We

We wiſhed, on this account, to enter this port, which we ſhould have eaſily accompliſhed, if the ſea had not run very high.* We began however to doubt whether this was really the harbour of S. Franciſco, becauſe we did not ſee any inhabitants, nor the ſmall iſlands which are ſaid to be oppoſite. In this ſtate of ſuſpenſe we caſt anchor near one of the points which we called *de Arenas*, in ſix fathoms and a clay bottom.

A vaſt number of Indians now preſented themſelves on both points [f], who paſſed from one to the other in ſmall canoes made of *Fule* [g], where they talked loudly for two hours or more, till at laſt two of them came along ſide of the ſhip, and moſt liberally preſented us with plumes of feathers, roſaries of bone, garments of feathers, as alſo garlands of the ſame materials, which they wore round their head, and a caniſter of ſeeds, which taſted much like walnuts. Our captain gave them in return bugles, looking glaſſes [h], and peices of cloth.

Theſe Indians are large and ſtrong, their colour being the ſame as that of the whole territory [i]; their diſpoſition is moſt liberal, as they ſeemed to expect no recompenſe for what they had furniſhed us with: a circumſtance which we had not experienced in thoſe to the Northward.

We were not able to ſound the interior parts of this port, on account of our ſick, who were to be as ſoon as poſſible landed in a place of ſafety, in order that they might have the better chance of recovering.

[f] Sc. Thoſe juſt now named by the journaliſt *de Arenas*.

[g] Some ſort of wood, and probably well known in the province of Mexico.

[h] In the former intercourſe with the more Northern Indians the Spaniards never produced this article of barter, which ſeems to have been ill-judged œconomy. They were now returning however, and muſt have thrown away theſe trifles at S. Blas.

[i] It is not very clear whether the Journaliſt means by this of Mexico, or the whole N. Weſtern continent of America.

Whilst we were in this port (which we did not conceive to be that of S. Francisco) we had no further intercourse with the inhabitants, and we prepared to clear the point *de las Avenas*, in order that, with a N. W. wind, the next day we might, with less difficulty, leave this part of the coast. Having effected this, we cast anchor in six fathoms, the bottom being a clay.

This port, which we named de *la Bodega*[i], is situated in 38. 18 N. Lat. and 18. 4 W. Long. from S. Blas.

On the 4th of October, at two in the morning, on the first flow of the tide, in a contrary direction to that of the currents, the sea ran so high that our whole ship was entirely covered by it, at the same time that the boat on the side of her was broken into shivers.

There is not sufficient depth of anchorage at the mouth of this port, for a vessel to resist this violence of surge, when it is occasioned by the causes before-mentioned.

If we had been apprized of this circumstance, we should have either continued where we were first at anchor, or otherwise sailed further from the mouth of the harbour.

In all parts of this port, which we had an opportunity of sounding, the bottom is nearly of the same depth[k]. The entrance is very easy with the prevailing wind of N. W. but in leaving it, if the wind blows from the same quarter, it is necessary to get further out to sea from the *Points*[l]. If the wind blows from the S. W. E. or S. it is not necessary to take this precaution[m].

[i] The Captain of the Schooner. The Latitude of this harbour coincides nearly with that discovered by Sir *Francis* Drake; but the Spaniards would scarcely insert this brave heretic in their Calendar.

[k] A draft was made of this harbour.

[l] Sc de las Arenas.

[m] Because then the wind and currents do not oppose each other.

We observed, that the tides in this Latitude are regular, as in Europe, it being high water at noon, when the moon is new.

The mountains near this port are entirely naked in every part of them[n]; but we observed that those more inland were covered with trees.

The plains near the sea-coast had a good verdure, and seemed to invite cultivation.

About eight in the morning of the 4th of October the sea became more calm, on which the Indians came round us as before, in their canoes, offering us the same presents, which had the same return.

At nine we set sail, and having doubled the point *del Cordon*[o] we steered S. S. W. the wind being moderate, and at W. in order to reach a Cape, which appeared to the S. at the distance of about five leagues.

On the fifth we sailed near those small islands which the charts and history of California place at the entrance of the harbour of S. Francisco; but as we were very clear that the harbour which we had just left, was not that thus called, we continued to steer N. E. (and between some of these islands) in order to reach the Cape before mentioned, when we intended to approach the coast, and look out for the port of S. Francisco.

At noon on this same day we had an observation, and found these islands to be in 37. 55. N. Lat. lying to the S. W. of the Cape at the distance of three leagues.

As soon as we reached the Cape we ran along the coast which lay to the E. and N. E. about the distance of a cannon's shot; and by six in the evening we were not above two miles distant

[n] This probably arises from their being exposed to the N. W. which is the prevailing wind.

[o] This point undoubtedly is marked in the Spanish Chart.

from

from the mouth of the harbour of St. Francis; but having no boat[p], or other convenience for this purpose, we resolved to stand for Monterey, and double another Cape, which projected still further from the coast[q].

At ten at night it fell calm; which continued till the 6th at noon, when the wind was moderate at W. and we steered S. S. W.

By eight at night the wind freshened from the N. W. with squalls and mists.

On the 7th, at eight in the morning, we conceived ourselves to be in the latitude of Monterey, which we endeavoured therefore to keep in, though the weather was so misty, that we could not see half a league.

At three in the evening we discovered the coast to the S. W. at the distance of a mile; and finding that we now entered a bay, we soon afterwards discovered the S. Carlos at anchor, and therefore knew that we were now in the port of Monterey. On this we fired some cannon, and boats immediately came out to us, by whose assistance we anchored in three fathoms, the bottom being a sand.

This port is situated in 36 44. N. Lat. & 17 W. of S. Blas.

On the 8th we landed our sick, and amongst the rest our captain and myself, who had suffered more from the scurvy than any of them. Not one of the whole crew indeed was free from this complaint.

We immediately experienced the kind offices of the Fathers established at this mission, who procured for us all the refreshments they were able, with the most perfect charity. In truth,

[p] It having been demolished by a heavy sea not long before.
[q] That is, than the before-mentioned Cape.

we

we could not possibly have so soon recovered from our distressed situation, but by their unparalleled attentions to our infirmities, which they removed by reducing themselves to a most pitiful allowance.

Don Fernando de Rivuera, who commanded at this port, was equally kind, in supplying our wants, so that in about a month we were pronounced to be so much better in point of health, that we determined to return to S. Blas.

We sailed therefore from Monterey on the 1st of November, and D. Bruno Heceta supplied us with some hands from the Frigate, the crew of which had not suffered so much from the scurvy as that of the schooner. At the distance however of two leagues it fell calm so that we continued in sight of the port till the 4th, the wind being at S. & S. W.

On the 4th at noon the wind was favourable from the N. W. aud we continued steering S. till the 13th when we approached the coast of California in 24. 15. N. Lat. and kept along it till Cape St. Lucas, which we left at six in the evening on the 16th.

We suppose this Cape to be in N. Lat. 22. 49. & W. Long. from S. Blas 5. 0.

On the 16th we saw the Islands of Maria, and on the 20th in the evening we cast anchor in the port of S. Blas.

Thus ended our voyage of discovery; and I trust that the fatigues and distresses which we suffered will redound to the advantage and honour of our *invincible* Sovereign, whom may God always keep under his holy protection!

FRANCISCO ANTONIO MAURELLE.

Obser-

Obſervations of the Journaliſt D. ANTONIO MAURELLE; ariſing from what happened during the courſe of the voyage, with regard to the beſt method of making Diſcoveries on the W. coaſt of AMERICA, to the Northward of California.

IT may be objected, at the outſet of theſe Obſervations, that the experience ariſing from a ſingle voyage in thoſe ſeas is not ſufficient to form any ſolid advice on this head, which may be thoroughly depended upon. To this I anſwer, that our continuance on this coaſt was for more than eight months, and therefore muſt have afforded us ſufficient grounds on which to build reaſonable preſumptions, though I cannot preſume to offer them to future navigators in any ſtronger light.

There is no occaſion to give any directions about the paſſage from S. Blas to Monterey, ſince this courſe hath been ſo frequently failed after the eſtabliſhment at the latter, and the beſt method of making this navigation is therefore ſo well known.

Suffice it then to ſay, that the ſhort paſſage to windward, as far as the iſlands of Maria, is neceſſary, on account of the currents, which would otherwiſe ſoon carry a ſhip in ſight of Cape St. Lucas, where probably the voyage would be retarded by calms.

Some are of opinion, that you ſhould not ſail Northward till you are conſiderably to the Windward of theſe iſlands; but I do not ſee the uſe of this loſs of time, and think that it is ſufficient juſt to get to the W. of them, and then ſteer Northerly on the very day you reach the parallel of the Marias.

In order to effect ſuch voyage of diſcovery, it is neceſſary to gain as much W. Longitude as the winds will permit, which

blow

blow from the N. W. to the N. as far as 15 degrees W[a]. and which only permit a course to the W. N. W. E. or E. S. E. whilst often such trade wind extends still further to the W. Notwithstanding this circumstance the ship should never lie to, much less steer Eastward, as thus the voyage would be much retarded.

From these 15 degrees of Westing, to 30 in the same direction, the wind is generally from N. E. to N. which will permit a N. W. course. It may perhaps be advisable even to get a Westing as far as 35 degrees, if the object of the voyage is to reach 55. 60. or even 65[b] of Northern Latitude, because the greater the Westing, the greater is the certainty of S. & S. W. winds, which will be so favourable to such a destination.

If when this Westing hath been gained, the winds should prove variable, I should still advise a N. E. course[c]. Under the supposition that the discoverer wants to fall in with the coast of America, in 55 N. Lat. he should keep between 35 & 37 W. Long. till he reaches that Latitude. If, on the contrary, he wants to explore the same coast in N. Lat. 60. I should then advise a N. W. course to be pursued till he hath gained a Westing of 39 degrees. If the navigator wishes to make discoveries even so high as 65 N. Lat. I conceive that he should then have a westing of 45 degrees, when he hath gained this parallel.

With these precautions I imagine that the persevering navigator would accomplish the height of his wishes.

[a] i. e. probably from S. Blas.

[b] It appears by the Journal, that they were instructed to proceed thus far N. if possible, which idea was probably taken from Ellis's Preface to the N. W. Passage, many extracts from which are made by Venegas, in his History of California, and particularly what relates to this supposed Latitude of 65.

[c] *en el primer quadrante*, as I conceive the Spaniards make the N. E. the first quarter; the S. E. the second; the S. W. the third, and the N. W. the fourth.

As accidents however will happen in all voyages, which may drive the ſhip upon the coaſt in a lower latitude, I would then by all means adviſe to gain a Weſting, as far as 200 leagues from the land. But it muſt be remembered that at perhaps 150 leagues W. the wind may be variable, though I am confident it cannot be depended upon, as favourable for any time, and would ſoon veer to the N. W. For theſe reaſons I hold it to be abſolutely neceſſary, that a weſting of at leaſt 200 leagues ſhould be procured, till N. Lat. 50 is reached.

If the ſhip is blown upon the coaſt in lower latitudes, the crew not only ſuffers commonly from fatigue and ſickneſs, but ſo much time is loſt, that winter comes on before the great object of ſuch a voyage can be compleated. I would therefore adviſe ſailing from S. Blas at the end of January, or at lateſt the beginning of February; and for this additional reaſon, that the crew would not ſuffer ſo much from change of temperature in the different climates, if without ſtopping in any lower latitude, they at once come upon the coaſt of America in 55. Here they might reſt a little from their fatigues, procure water, recover by that fine air [d] if indiſpoſed; beſides, that in this latitude there would be no occaſion to loſe time in procuring a further Weſting, as here the winds are very variable.

It need be ſcarcely ſaid, that the knowing the weather, which commonly prevails in theſe ſeas, is of much importance to navigators; and it is ſtill leſs neceſſary to adviſe, that particular attention ſhould be paid to the appearances in the horizon which

[d] The port of *los Remedios* is here alluded to, which is in 57. 18. and where the crew recovered very faſt from the warmth of the air, attributed to Vulcanoes in the neighbourhood. S. Blas, being in N. Lat. 22. is conſequently more cool in January than perhaps any month of the year, whilſt they would be in 55 perhaps at Midſummer.

threaten

threaten a ſtorm. Theſe however are not much to be apprehended till N. Lat. 40. as between S. Blas and that parallel, ſuch lowering clouds either diſperſe themſelves very ſoon, or fall in rain, which lulls the ſea.

From 40 to 50 degrees N. (ſuppoſing the ſhip to have gained a Weſting of 200 leagues from the American coaſt,) theſe appearances are more to be watched, as in theſe latitudes the S. wind blows freſh, though pretty conſtant.

It is to be obſerved alſo, that the S. W. in theſe parallels is ſometimes ſtronger than the S. for which reaſon I would adviſe not to carry much ſail.

This laſt precaution is ſtill more neceſſary in higher latitudes than 50, ſince the S. W. often blows ſo violently that it is prudent to lie to, as theſe ſqualls do not laſt for any time.

I alſo particularly adviſe the navigator to guard againſt the effects of winds from the E. which ſometimes are violent in theſe latitudes; not but that ſometimes W. winds are equally bluſtering, yet they are not ſo common, nor laſt ſo long. It ſhould alſo be noticed, that the higher the latitude, the more ſuch weather is to be apprehended.

When the coaſt of America *is very near*, there is no regular wind but the N. W. and this holds to the Southward from 54 N. Lat. it ſometimes blows indeed freſh from this quarter, but there is no objection to this, when the ſhip is on its return [e].

The ſea from S. Blas to 40 degrees N. Lat. runs commonly high, when the wind is at N. W. or N. but as it does not often blow with violence from this quarter, theſe ſeas are generally

[e] It muſt be remembered, that for this reaſon the Journaliſt adviſes the navigator who wants to reach a high N. Latitude, to gain ſo large a Weſting from the coaſt of America.

navigable. From Lat. 40 to 50 (when near the coaſt) the ſea often runs ſtill higher, meeting the tide from the ſhoar, but I do not mean to raiſe too great apprehenſions on this account.

At the diſtance however of 100 leagues from the coaſt the ſeas are often ſtill heavier; ſo that I would adviſe lying to, if the wind is not favourable.

From 50 degrees upwards the ſeas riſe proportionably with the winds, particularly if they blow from the S. or S. W. but ſoon become calm when the weather clears.

[Here follow ſome obſervations, with regard to the effect of the moon upon the weather, which I ſhall not tranſlate, as the influence of this planet in ſuch reſpect ſeems now to be much exploded.]

As approaches to the coaſt ought always to put the navigator on his guard, he may depend upon the following ſigns for its not being far diſtant.

When the coaſt is about 80 or 90 leagues to the E. thoſe ſea-plants appear which I have before called *Orange heads*; but I muſt now add, that from the ſtate of them, as they float, one may ſometimes infer, that the land is not ſo far diſtant.

Its figure much reſembles the fiſtular ſtalk of garlick[e]; and from the top of its head hang ſome long leaves, by which the plant is fixed to the rocks. Now if theſe leaves are tolerably perfect, they afford a ſtrong preſumption, that they have not floated far from the coaſt. On the contrary, thoſe which have been waſted to a conſiderable diſtance, have generally loſt this head, and the ſtalk becomes more rough, when you may ſuppoſe that you are 50 leagues from the land.

[e] The appearance of this plant on the coaſt of California, is noticed in Lord Anſon's Voyage.

6 At

At the same distance the sea begins to indicate, by its colour, that you are in soundings, but this circumstance requires some attention and habit; when you are not more than 30 or 40 leagues from the coast, this appearance is much more distinguishable, though if you was to cast anchor you would not find any bottom. In this same situation you will likewise perceive birds, sea-wolves [f], otters, and whales, together with the plant Zacate del Mar before-mentioned, which hath long and narrow leaves. When these circumstances are observed, you may depend upon seeing land the same day, or that following.

At the same time you will perceive, that the sea is of an iron colour, and looks as if it had small boats, with sails upon the surface [g], whilst birds resembling lories, with a red head, bill, and legs, fly around; their body is black.

As concealed shoals are often so dangerous to the navigator, I think I may pronounce you may sail in perfect safety at the distance of a league from the most suspicious parts of this whole coast.

If the discoverer should first put into port in N. L. 55. 17. he will find an inlet [h], which hath good soundings in all parts of it towards the N. and perhaps the best point [i] of the whole coast, if the ship keeps at the distance of three leagues from it.

[f] Lobos Marinos, perhaps Seals.

[g] Unas aguas malas de color morado, que parecen unos barquichuelos con belas latinas.

[h] Una entrada.

[i] The Journalist does not any farther explain why [illegible]

1775. Day of the month	Latitude by reckoning	Latitude by observation	W. Long. from San Blas	Variation of the Needle	Dist. from the coast of America
March 1					
4					
5					
6					
7					
8					
9					
10					
11					
12					
13					
14					
15					
16		21 25			
17					2
18					1
19					2
20		21 34		4 30*	2
21		21 39		*	2
22		21 43		*	1
23		21 47			2
24		21 14			3
25	21 36	21 34	1 20		38
26	20 15	20 10	1 59		48
27	19 51	19 49	3 2	5	73
28	19 25	19 17	4 10		79
29	19 23	19 4	5 1		86
30	18 56	18 42	5 37		100
31	18 42	18 33	5 37		104

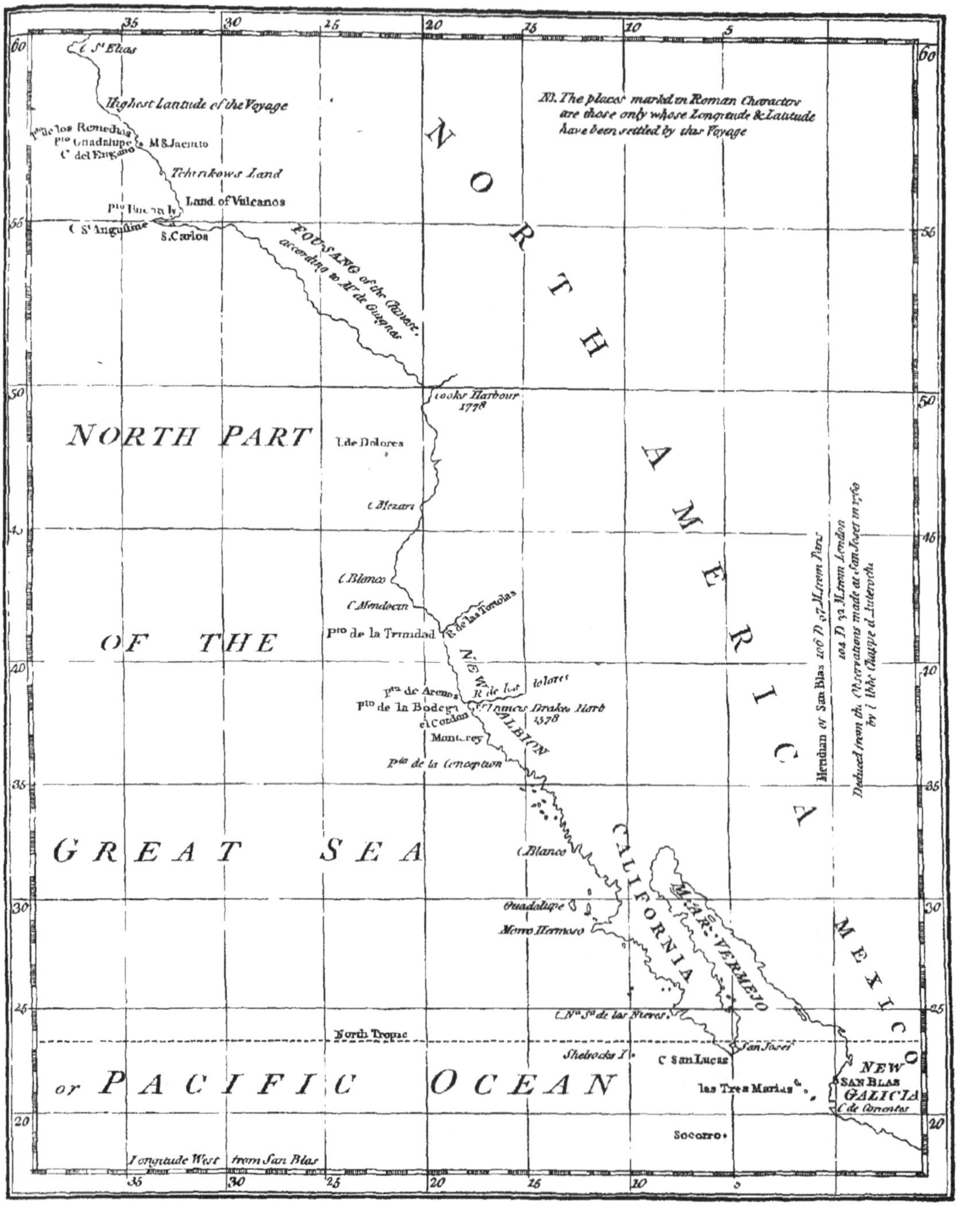

NB. The places marked in Roman Characters are those only whose Longitude & Latitude have been settled by this Voyage

NORTH AMERICA

NORTH PART OF THE GREAT SEA or PACIFIC OCEAN

C. St. Elias

Highest Latitude of the Voyage

Pto. de los Remedios

Pto. Guadalupe

C. del Engano

M. S. Jacinto

Tchirikows Land

Land of Vulcanos

C. St. Augustine

S. Carlos

FOU-SANG of the Chinese, according to Mr. de Guignes

Cooks Harbour 1778

I. de Dolores

C. Mezari

C. Blanco

C. Mendocin

Pto. de la Trinidad

R. de las Tortolas

NEW ALBION

Pta. de Arenas

Pto. de la Bodega

el Cordon

Sir Francis Drakes Harb. 1578

Monterey

Pta. de la Concepcion

C. Blanco

CALIFORNIA

MAR VERMEJO

Guadalupe I.

Morro Hermoso

MEXICO

C. N.ra S.ra de las Nieves

North Tropic

Shelvocks I.

C. San Lucas

San Josef

las Tres Marias

NEW GALICIA

SAN BLAS

C. de Corrientes

Socorro

Meridian of San Blas 106 D. 7 M. from Paris

104 D. 52 M. from London

Deduced from the Observations made at San Josef in 1769 by l'Abbe Chappe d'Auteroche

Longitude West from San Blas

35 30 25 20 15 10 5

60 55 50 45 40 35 30 25 20

1775. Day of the Month	Latitude by reckoning	Latitude by observation	W. Long. from San Blas	Variation of the Needle	Dist. from the coast of America.
April 1	18 36	18 33	5 37	5	104
2	18 35	18 33	5 48	5 13*	107
3	18 56	18 48	5 27	*	102
4	18 36	18 30	6 8		108
5	18 25	18 15	6 37		117
6	18 2	17 48	7 31½		132
7	17 48	17 43	8 36		140
8	17 42	17 42	9 28		148
9	17 43	17 45	10 22½		155
10	17 42	17 35	11 8		165
11	17 47	17 48	12 42	6	166
12	17 54	17 44	12 22½		176
13	17 49	17 44	13 54		181
14	17 55	17 47	14 39		186
15	18 28	18 20	15 35		186
16	19 6		16 24½		190
17	19 51	19 50	17 25½		201
18	20 33	20 19	18 16½		206
19	20 42	20 37	18 50½		209
20	20 53		19 14		210
21	21 8		20 47		211
22	21 16	21 4	21 34½		222
23	21 24	21 21	22 15		232
24	21 55	21 47	23 13		248
25	23 31	22 32	23 8		259
26	23 20	23 22	24 13		277
27	24 8	24 14	24 58		284
28	24 48	24 50	25 32		294
29	25 25	25 17	25 30		300
30	26 3	25 57	26 22	7	

1775. Day of the Month	Latitude by reckoning	Latitude by obfervation	W. Long. from San Blas	Variation of the Needle	Dift. from the coaft of America
May 1	26 29	26 31	27 07	7	302
2	26 45	26 44	27 19		303
3	26 55	26 50	27 31		303
4	27 39	27 30	28 18		304
5	28 39	28 37	28 12	8	295
6	29 30		29 15		281
7	30 9		30 14		284
8	30 19		30 54		284
9	30 36	30 45	31 41		291
10	31 18		32 15		297
11	32 12	32 10	32 50		294
12	33 13	33 15	32 45		280
13	33 57	34 3	31 56		261
14	34 29	34 35	30 50		239
15	34 26	34 30	30 12		231
16	34 46	34 54	31 6		238
17	34 50	34 50	31 82		240
18	34 49	34 49	31 17		240
19	35 46	35 45	30 20		220
20	36 42	36 45	28 42	9	184
21	37 6	37 1	27 46		167
22	37 42	37 46	28 41		178
23	38 9	38 8	29 33		185
24	37 48	37 46	29 10		183
25	37 29	37 26	29 3		184
26	37 14	37 11	28 51		179
27	37 6		29 12		186
28	37 10		29 3		185
29	37 48	37 25	28 15½		174
30	37 47	37 45	27 21		156
31	37 59		26 35	10	145

1775. Day of the month	Latitude by reckoning	Latitude by obfervation	W. Long. from San Blas	Variation of the Needle	Dift. from the coaft of America
June 1	38 21	38 14	26 12	10	128
2	39 3		25 26	12	122
3	39 46	39 51	24 38		107
4	40 13		23 55	13 30	89
5	41 11	41 22	22 58		70
6	41 41	41 37	21 15		42
7	41 49	41 30	20 19	14	33
8	49 59	41 14	13 13	14 30	
9	41 25		19 4		
10					
11					
12					
13					
14					
15		41 17			
16					
17		41 7			
18		41 7	19 4		
19		40 59	19 21		
20		40 53	19 41	14	12
21	40 59	40 7	20 56		31
22	40 25	40	21 41		48
23	40 2		23 1		67
24	39 45	39 23	24 7		85
25	39 24	39 20	25 40	13	106
26	39 21	39 21	26 40		121
27	39 22		26 30		113
28	39 51		26 45		118
29	33 43		26 25		107
30	40 26	40 16	26		

1775. Day of the Month	Latitude by reckoning		Latitude by obfervation		W Long. from San Blas		Variation of the Needle	Dift. from the coaft of America
July 1	41	2	41	1	26	14	13	100
2	47	17	42	15	26	49	14	90
3	43	25	43	24	26	50		70
4	44	21			26	30½		57
5	44	27			26	10	15	47
6	44	24			25	47		32
7	46	10			26	6	16	26
8	46	59	47	3	25	47		12
9	47	44	47	37	24	20		
10	47	45	47	35	23	28½	17	
11	48	32	48	26	22	17		10
12	48	1	47	39	21	53		6
13	47	41	47	28	21	34		2
14	47	24	47	20	21	19		
15	47	23	47	7	21	40	17 30	9
16	47	20	47	13	22	3		17
17	47	17	47	9	22	22	17	18
18	47	3	46	32	23	32	16*	35
19	46	34	46	26	24	28		50
20	46	18	46	17	25	29		61
21	46	6	45	57	27	5	15	82
22	45	50	45	44	28	18		100
23	45	44	45	41	29	24		115
24	45	51	45	52	30	32		124
25	46	4	46	9	29	59		120
26	46	34	46	32	29	52		199
27	47	6	47	5	29	19	16*	117
28	47	45	47	40	29	41		103
29	48	10	47	50	28	44		92
30	47	21	47	21	29	32		102
31	46	55			30	9		117

1775. Day of the Month	Latitude by reckoning	Latitude by observation	W. Long. from San Blas	Variation of the Needle	Dist. from the coast of America
Aug. 1	46 34		30 56	16	131
2	46 45	46 40	31 52		141
3	46 40	46 35	32 46		157
4	46 29	46 16	33 39		157
5	46 47	46 47	34 5		171
6	47 49	47 50	34 6		164
7	48 26	48 24	34 12		159
8	48 39		34 7	17*	156
9	49 11	49 9	34 7		154
10	50 18		34 54	18	160
11	51 24	51 34	34 58		159
12	52 18	52 27	35	19	158
13	53 39	53 54	35 26		161
14	54 58	55 4	36 7		166
15	55 53	56 8	35 47		154
16	56 43	56 44	35 15		4
17	56 54	57 2	35 27		1/3
18	57 21		35 27		
19					
20					
21					1/3
22	57 55	57 57	38 2	20	
23	57 10	57 8	35 50	22*	2
24	56 1		33 46	24*	1
25	55 17	55 17	33 24		
26	56 6	55 6	33 22	24	
27					
28	55 36		34 39	23*	2
29	55 55	55 55	34 32		1/3
30	56 21		35		1/3
31	56 41	56 47	35 32		1/2

1775. Day of the Month	Latitude by reckoning	Latitude by observation	W. Long. from San Blas	Variation of the Needle	Dist from the coast of America
Sept. 1	56 31		16 10	23	10
2	56 5	56 3	36 22	23 30	17
3	55 45	55 47	36 39	23	21
4	55 28		36 33		22
5	55 8	55 7	37 5		26
6	54 40	54 42	36 27	22	20
7	54 53		36 56	23	26
8	55 4		36 56		26
9	54 39	54 32	35 22	21	7
10	54 4	54 6	34 6		6
11	53 54	53 52	32 19	20	8
12	52 58		31 5		8
13	52 11	52 9	30		9
14	51 14	51 16	29 35		9
15	50 4	50 12	27 2		9
16	49 23	49 21	25 38		9
17	48 51	48 53	24 35		7
18	48 37	48 33	23 40	19	6
19	47 50	47 49	23 10		½
20	47 11	47 12	22 33		½
21	46 21		21 58		11
22	46 20		22 42		10
23	45 38		22 35		⅓
24	44 47	44 47	21 12		⅓
25	44 17	44 19	21 2	18	½
26	43 15	43 16	21 20	17	10
27	42 37		21 41		12
28	42 37		21 41		10
29	41 1	40 54	21 41		½
30	39 38	39 42	21 11	16	½

1775. Day of the Month	Latitude by reckoning	Latitude by obſervation	W. Long. from San Blas	Variation of the Needle	Diſt. from the coaſt of America
Oct. 1	39 17	39 15	20 26	16	½
2	38 49	38 49	19 5	16	½
3	38 16	38 16	19 2	16	
4	38 16	38 16	19 22	16	
5	37 54	37 53	19 24	15	3
6	37 45	37 43	19 4	15	1
7	36 43	36 42	18 47	14	
8	36 46		17 17	14	

1775. Day of the Month	Latitude by reckoning	Latitude by observation	W. Long. from San Blas	Variation of the Needle	Dist. from the coast of America
Nov. 2	36 44	36 42	17 5	14	7
3	36 28		17 27	13	8
4	36 6	36 11	17 42	12	8
5	34 41	34 36	17 25	11	23
6	32 50	32 48	16 58	10	45
7	30 56	30 57	16 2	9	48
8	29 32		15 18	8	46
9	28 52		14 45	7	45
10	28 21	27 52	14 13	7	42
11	27 16	27 8	13 26	7	35
12	26 16	26 12	12 13	7	24
13	25 18	25 16	10 46	6	38
14	24 53	24 37	8 58	6	6
15	24 15	24 1	6 56	6	10
16	23 2	23	5 25	5	1½
17	22 20	22 22	4 3	5	40
18	21 54	21 53	2 38		10
19	21 45	21 44	0 46	5	3
20	21 36	21 34	0 2	5	

A D-

Lightning Source UK Ltd.
Milton Keynes UK
UKOW06f2200051214

242735UK00004B/59/P

9 781170 596937